...AND THEN I MET
THE GETTY KOUROS

...AND THEN I MET THE GETTY KOUROS

An Engineer's Odyssey from the Streets of Tehran to the Hills of Malibu

JACK NJDEH YAGHOUBIAN

QUANTECH
P R E S S
SHERMAN OAKS, CALIFORNIA

PRODUCTION MANAGER AND EDITOR
Monica Faulkner, Faulkner Editorial Services, Los Angeles CA

DESIGN AND LAYOUT
Glenn Wong, GW Graphic Works, Los Angeles CA

PROOFREADING
Tammy Ditmore, eDitmore Editorial Services, Newbury Park CA

INDEXING
WordCo Indexing Services Inc., Norwich CT

FIRST PRINTING, PRINTED AND BOUND IN THE UNITED STATES OF AMERICA BY:
Edwards Brothers Malloy, Ann Arbor MI

5 4 3 2 1

ISBN 978-0-9960561-0-6

For information or to order:

Quantech Press
PO Box 55684-0684
Sherman Oaks, CA 91413

www.quantechsystems.com

DEDICATION

This book is dedicated to my father and mother,
Hagob Hagobian (Yaghoubian) and
Arashalous Harutunian Hagobian (Yaghoubian).

Their tragic childhood as orphans of the
1915 Armenian genocide inspired them with one
unwavering objective—that I, their son,
would enjoy a better life than they had known.

I am grateful that they made it possible for me
to uphold the legacy of my ancestors, and that
they lived long enough to see their dreams fulfilled.

Without them, I would never have become the man I am.

CONTENTS

AUTHOR'S PREFACE

WE ALL HAVE SOMETHING TO OFFER THE WORLD. In my case, it has been through engineering. I was born to be an engineer, and the main reason I've written this book is to pass on the joy of thinking innovatively to future generations. My hope is that readers will experience the same excitement and love of their work that I have always known.

Apparently, I was born with the knack for thinking "outside the box," and America, my adopted country and the birthplace of so many innovations, has allowed me to continue exploring how to do new things.

Sometimes people ask me, "How did you do what you've done?"

Whenever they do, I have to stop and think. For one thing, I was fortunate enough to have dared to think otherwise. In fact, although no one I worked with over the years ever said so to my face, I know that people sometimes referred to me behind my back as a "nonconformist."

Often, the biggest problem I faced was not finding solutions to the engineering projects I tackled but convincing other people that those solutions would work.

For example, in the mid-1960s, just few years out of college, I was instrumental in convincing the project team for design and construction of the landmark California Bank headquarters in San Francisco to utilize the first slurry trench system in the United States.

Then, in the 1980s, when I began working with the John Paul Getty Museum, the antiquities conservation establishment was jolted by my unconventional methodologies for both restoring the Getty Kouros and protecting it from earthquake shaking. The systems I devised for the Getty are now being utilized by art museums worldwide.

Throughout my career, my mantra has been "I can do it—I know it's going to work." And so I somehow always had it in me to approach even the most challenging projects—the ones that had other project members biting their fingernails—with innate confidence.

"Don't worry," I always said. "I can engineer this thing. I know it's going to work." And it always did.

THIS MEMOIR TOUCHES ON MANY PERSONAL as well as professional subjects—growing up in the Armenian minority in Iran during the 1950s, the challenges of adapting to life in America, the ways in which careers are shaped, the excitement of having played a role in innovative engineering and US environmental initiatives, the American system of jurisprudence, and what it means to be an informed citizen of one's adopted country, to name just a few.

However, my lifelong goal has been to make a difference in the world by the work I've done and described in this book. That is why my biggest reward would be to learn that my story has inspired readers to go beyond existing boundaries and to imagine possibilities not yet known.

Throughout my career, no matter how challenging a project was, the intellectual and emotional involvement I experienced was always bigger than the project itself.

It is that kind of involvement that created the career I have found so rewarding, and I hope that my story will inspire readers to take that attitude into their own lives.

Jack Njdeh Yaghoubian
Los Angeles, California

PART ONE

FROM TEHRAN TO AMERICA
(1956–1961)

Chapter 1

THE NEW WORLD

THROUGH THE TINY PORTHOLE window of our SAS plane, I watched the clouds disperse over the Southern California coast to reveal the land and vast city below. The late-afternoon sun still glinting off steel, rows and rows of parked cars, the ballet of huge eagle-like planes taxiing along the runways, the blur of buses speeding from one terminal to the next...

It was Los Angeles International Airport on Tuesday, May 29, 1956—the day I arrived in America.

As our plane touched down on the runway with a bounce followed by the squeal of rubber tires on asphalt, I marveled at the scene, and the fatigue of the almost forty-eight-hour flight from Tehran to Los Angeles fell away. My classmate and friend Andre Minassian and I followed the other passengers to the half-finished airport's makeshift passport control area where the two of us, along with a few other passengers, were separated from the rest of the group and ushered into a small room with plywood floors, rows of benches, and an official behind a window.

As we took our places on the benches, another airport official told us to wait until our last names were called and then to present our travel documents to the official at the window.

Andre and I were the last two passengers to be called. The official seemed to be having difficulty pronouncing a name, and after several attempts he came over to us and asked me what my name was. I stood up and pronounced it in Farsi.

He shook his head. "Spell your first and last name."

"N-j-d-e-h," I responded. "Y-a-g-h-o-u-b-i-a-n."

The official looked at his list and nodded. Apparently it was my name that had been giving him such a hard time. "What kind of name is that?" he asked.

"It's an Armenian name," I proudly answered. "'Yaghoub' in English is 'Jacob.'"

3

The official smiled and, with a wave of his pen, said, "So, why don't I just call you 'Jack'?" As I nodded my agreement, he added, "Okay, Jack, follow me, please." That was how I was christened with my American first name. From then on, I was Jack Yaghoubian, and the process of bettering my English had already begun.

Clutching my carry-on bag, raincoat, my stamped travel documents, and the wool blanket I had brought with me from my parents' home in Tehran, I entered the customs inspection area. My big suitcase was already waiting on the counter. I placed the rest of my belongings next to it.

After a moment, the inspector standing behind the counter gestured at my carry-on and asked, "Salami inside?"

At that point in my life, my English was rather marginal. So, thinking that he was greeting me in Farsi, I held out my hand, gave him a big smile and replied, "*Salam! Salam, salam!*"

Of course, he left my hand hanging in mid-air and just looked at me poker-faced. "What's in the carry-on bag?" he asked.

Stung by his unfriendly attitude, I replied, "I don't know."

He unzipped the bag and then exclaimed, "What the hell have you got in there?"

The other inspector, who was investigating Andre's bag, leaned over and whispered something in my inspector's ear. I started wondering whether I had done something wrong, but he simply zipped up the bag and gave it back to me. Apparently noticing my disappointment at his unfriendly behavior, he said curtly, "Welcome to the United States." Those words were such beautiful music to my ears that they made my eyes tear up even though I later learned that all passengers arriving from abroad were greeted the same way.

Dragging my suitcase and other belongings, I entered the arrival hall and saw Andre talking with a young man our age and an older man. Andre introduced me to them as Soorik Hadjian and his rancher uncle, Misak, who had come to pick us up and drive us to our hotel. Soorik was a friend of Andre's from Tehran who had come to the US a year earlier to attend Los Angeles City College (LACC). They had come to greet us because Andre had written to Soorik telling him when we would arrive and giving him the address of the hotel where we were to spend our first night. The next morning, our first task would be to find our way to Pepperdine College, a two-year college where we would enroll in summer courses before beginning pre-engineering courses, including physics, chemistry, drafting, etc., in the fall.

As Soorik and his uncle were driving us to the hotel with Andre and me in the backseat of his uncle's Buick, I basked in the glory that was "America."

Although the May sun was shining brightly, the heat was nothing like the stifling temperatures in the Middle East, and the surroundings were colorful, from the storefronts hung with multicolored banners and awnings to the lush green palm trees that lined the roads and the bright, flashy clothing of the pedestrians strolling along the sidewalks.

I was also impressed by the interior of the car, so I asked Misak how much a car like theirs cost.

"Twelve hundred dollars," he explained.

I felt bewildered because I knew the term "twelve thousand" but had never heard of "twelve hundred." Soorik, sensing my puzzlement, explained that "twelve hundred" was the same as "one thousand two hundred."

It was getting dark when we arrived at the Cecil Hotel, on South Main Street in LA's downtown. Fourteen stories high, it was the tallest structure I had ever laid eyes on. Soorik handed Andre some coins and said, "Just in case you need some change." We registered and were given a room on the tenth floor. A burly black man took our suitcases and led us to a small chamber in the wall. After we entered, he pulled at a retractable metal gate, which shut with a loud squeal. Then two sliding doors closed in front of us and, with a jolt, I felt the whole chamber moving upward. Startled, I grabbed the railing on the wall and looked over at the man. He was smiling, his white teeth gleaming in his dark face.

Seeing our apprehension, he asked, "Where are you boys from?"

"Iran," Andre answered sheepishly.

"And where's that?"

Andre not having an immediate answer, I volunteered, "Persia."

"Oh! Camels!" the man exclaimed as the chamber stopped moving. The sliding doors parted, and he slid the grate aside so we could exit the chamber.

We followed him along a narrow corridor lined with numbered doors on each side. He stopped in front of one room, unlocked the door, and set our suitcases inside the door. Then he extended his palm, which was very pink in contrast to his face, in an internationally recognizable gesture.

Andre reached into his pocket, took out all the change that Soorik had given him, and held the coins out on his own open palm. The man smiled and took two similar-sized coins. He glanced down, muttered, "Nickels!," and left, closing the door behind him.

The room contained two beds, an armchair, and a nightstand between the beds that held a black telephone and a small brown radio with a narrow slot on the top.

The drapes were drawn, and when I opened them I freaked out at the sight of the street so far below, with its toy-sized cars and streetcars moving around. My head began spinning and, feeling an overwhelming vertigo, I sat down on the edge of the bed.

"This is not our place," I told Andre, who was busily unpacking. "I'm going back to Iran right now."

"Are you crazy?" he replied. Then he went to the window as I had.

"Oh, my God!" he whispered as he stared down, as shocked as I was. He jerked the drapes closed and sat down next to me. "How the hell did we get so high up?"

But he recovered a lot faster than I did, and he tried to cheer me up by turning on the radio. Next to the slot, the word "Nickels" was inscribed on a metal plate. He must not have paid any attention to the porter's remark about the coins, so he asked me, "What is 'nickels'?"

"That's what the black man said when he took your change."

With that, he picked out a nickel from his pile of change and dropped it into the slot. Nothing happened. He began to play with the dials. Still nothing. He then picked up the radio, turned it upside down, and began shaking it violently, cursing in Farsi, calling the hotel all sorts of names, and swearing that he would break the damn thing to get his coin back.

His determination reminded me of apes in Tarzan movies trying to crack open coconuts, and this gave me a fit of giggles that turned into such uncontrollable laughter that I could hardly catch my breath. Eventually Andre started laughing, too. He continued cussing heaven and hell, but he did put down the radio.

Our laughter brought me back to my senses and reminded me that we were in America to stay and that we might as well get used to this crazy new world.

By this time we had not slept for more than forty-eight hours and were very tired, so we put on our pajamas and went to bed. We both fell asleep immediately, but at some point I dreamed that someone was banging on our door trying to break into our room. I awoke to see Andre standing by my bed shaking my shoulder.

"There's someone at the door," he said.

At first we ignored the knocking, but when it did not stop I got up and cracked open the door. Two Armenian women were standing there. The older woman smiled at me and said in Armenian, "We are here to pick up the packages that your mother asked you to carry for us."

Andre, hearing Armenian being spoken, turned on the light and I asked them to come in. Neither of us had the slightest idea what packages they were talking about until the older woman pointed to our carry-on bags, which were sitting side by side on the floor, and said, "Oh, I can smell the heavenly aroma of *shanbelileh*!"

She introduced herself as Mrs. Anoush and told us that her companion was her daughter, Audrey Gregor, who was married to Vaughn Gregor. "As a favor to Mr. Gregor for his help in arranging for your college admittance," she explained, "your mothers were asked to have you bring us some *shanbelileh* because it is not available in the US." This special spice, called fenugreek in English, is an important ingredient in Persia's national dish, *ghormeh sabzi*, a savory stew of meat, lemons, beans, and herbs.

She told us that Mr. Gregor had reserved our room for the night as well as transportation to the Pepperdine campus the next morning.

Before the women left, they told us that Audrey's brother, Alfred Babakhanian, an old friend of ours from Tehran, would pick us up at ten o'clock the next morning and take us to the campus, which was located on Vermont Avenue in an area known as Watts. I was ecstatic at the prospect of seeing him again because he had been one of the 350 Boy Scouts in the troop that I had headed up in Tehran before coming to the United States. I had not seen him since he had left Iran three years earlier. He was now attending school and working for Mr. Gregor.

WHEN WE AWOKE in the morning, we both thought that we might have dreamed about our visitors until we saw that our carry-on bags, still smelling faintly of *shanbelileh*, were now empty.

We dressed, gathered our belongings, and left our room wondering how we would get down to the street. Luckily, another guest was waiting in front of the sliding doors. We saw a glowing round button next to the doors and a sign above them that read "Elevator."

Soon the doors opened, and the porter from the night before greeted us with a cordial "Good morning, boys!" As the carriage descended, it stopped at several other levels to pick up more guests. I was amazed to see that everyone did the same thing—they would walk in, turn around, face the door, and remain absolutely silent and motionless, only to step back and make room each time the elevator stopped and more guests entered.

By the time we reached the street level, we were as tightly packed as sardines in a can. It was a relief to shuffle out of the elevator and through the lobby to the street, where we could breathe the fresh morning air and take in our new surroundings in daylight. The streets were filled with cars and large, noisy streetcars that looked like gigantic Matchbox toys. As we looked around to find something to eat, we spotted a shop that looked exactly like a delicatessen in Tehran. We walked in and saw an assortment of cold cuts and sausages inside a glass-fronted cooler.

Andre pointed to the sausages and said, "Two."

The man behind the counter asked, "Two hot dogs?"

Andre turned to me and said, "These sausages are made of dog meat."

Like a smart aleck, I retorted, "In Iran, we ate cow, sheep, and goat organs, and here they also eat dog meat."

Andre eyed the revolving "dog" sausages. "So, we should go ahead and eat them?"

"Well, as my uncle always used to say, 'When hungry, man should eat anything softer than a rock.'"

So we devoured the hot dogs, washed down with Pepsi, and then took a walk around the block.

Whenever I think back to our second day in America, I cannot believe how events unfolded. It was as if an angel of good luck was watching over us that whole day because we met so many people we knew who were able to help us as soon as we arrived.

At ten o'clock sharp, a large two-door car stopped at the curb and Alfred jumped out and began walking toward us. We ran toward him eager to give him a hug and a kiss, as we would in Iran, but he sensed what we were about to do. He stopped in his tracks, put out his hands in a "Don't come closer!" gesture, and exclaimed in Armenian, "Don't you dare come too close! People will think we're queers!" So instead we all shook hands. As we got into the car, I thought what a strange place this country was.

Alfred, who told us that his new American name was "Fred," began telling us about driving in America and how vehicles had to stay between the two white lines and stop at red lights and stop signs as well as for pedestrians and animals crossing the street. This left us speechless because no such regulations were ever observed in Iran.

When we arrived at the Pepperdine campus, Andre and I were both impressed with its beautiful, manicured landscaping, palm trees, and lush green shrubbery. Fred drove us to the boys' dormitory section, wished us good luck, and drove off.

Not knowing any better, we dragged our suitcases into the first empty room we found. We knew it was unoccupied because the two beds had mattresses but no sheets or pillows. We had no idea where we were, and there was no one around to greet us or tell us what to do next. However, we were impressed with our parents' foresight in insisting that we bring along our Persian wool blankets and pajamas because otherwise we would not have had any bedding and would have died of cold.

As Andre and I were debating whether we should unpack, another student who apparently overheard us speaking Farsi tapped on our open door—and I was flabbergasted to see Cyrus Poorarian, a classmate of mine from Firuz Bahram High School in Tehran. We hugged and kissed cheeks and could not stop talking about how ironic it was to meet again in this crazy new world.

Cyrus had already attended one semester of classes and knew his way around the campus, so compared to us he was already a veteran.

When we asked him what we were supposed to do and why there were no students around, he replied, "First, shave off your mustaches so people won't take you for Mexicans." Then he went on to say that it was Memorial Day, a national holiday, so the college was closed and only international students living in the dorms were on the campus.

He then showed us the bathrooms and the closets stacked with pillows and sheets ready for the summer semester. He also advised us not to unpack until the next day, when we would be assigned to our own rooms.

After he left, I decided to take a shower and to shave my mustache, although I did wonder what was wrong with looking like a Mexican. When I opened the door to the shower room, I saw that it was one big, open space with no partitions for privacy whatsoever. I decided that the only way I was going to take a shower was to lock the door so no one else could enter while I was there. Because nudity was completely taboo in Iran, I had never taken a shower with anyone else.

I locked the door, then went to the far end of the room and turned on the shower. Moments later, I heard someone banging on the door and yelling, "Open the fucking door! Who the hell d'you think you are?"

At first, I decided to ignore the guy, but he got louder and more obnoxious by the minute, so I finally took the bar of soap, lathered myself with thick foam head to toe, went to the door, and opened it. Standing there was a naked little Chinese guy half my size. The moment he saw me, he freaked out as if he had just seen a huge white Bigfoot. He stumbled back a couple of steps repeating: "Oh, my God! Oh, my God—" and took off running, leaving his clothes and towel behind. I locked the door again and finished my shower and shave. But how was I going to take my showers while living at the dorm?

Thanks to the hot shower and to having met some familiar faces, I was gradually getting my can-do self-confidence back, although I was also feeling the fatigue of two sleepless nights and the emotional aftereffects of having left my family behind.

By mid-afternoon, though, I was ready to explore my surroundings. Andre and I took a long walk around the campus. The streets bordering the campus were deserted. As we were ambling past the main entrance and admiring the administration building, a souped-up blue Oldsmobile pulled up in front of us. While gunning the engine, the driver gestured for us to come over to his side window. We looked around to see if he really meant us. Then, not seeing anyone else around, we walked over to him. He had a scarred and deformed face.

He asked in Armenian, "Are you Armenians?"

When we replied yes, he said, "Jump in!" in English. Not understanding what that meant, I asked in Armenian what he wanted. He got out and introduced himself as Herand Gevorgian, an Armenian-Iranian Pepperdine student, and asked if we would like to have some tea at a nearby coffee shop. We agreed and got into his car.

After some small talk about when we had arrived, what we were going to study, and what part of Tehran we were from, he pulled into an almost-deserted parking lot outside a small coffee shop next to a movie theater on Vermont Avenue within walking distance of the campus. As he turned off the engine and got out of the car, I reminded him that he had not removed the ignition key, or the windshield blades and the hubcaps, all of which was customary in Iran, or else everything would have disappeared in a matter of minutes!

Herand shrugged. "That's Iran. Such things don't happen in America. In this country, we don't even lock our front doors."

Inside the coffee shop, Herand sat at the counter and gestured for us to sit as well. The waitress brought three cups, three small, square paper packets, and three small, steaming-hot metal pitchers with lids. As I was studying my packet, Andre opened his and pulled out a tiny cardboard tab. A string attached to it was attached to a small paper-mesh bag. Without hesitation, he ripped open the bag, saw that it contained tea leaves, and dumped them into his empty cup. He then poured steaming water from the pitcher into the cup and began stirring it with a spoon. However, the tea leaves would not sink and kept floating on the water's surface. I was about to follow his example when Herand stopped me and showed us how to dunk the whole tea bag into the water so it gradually sank to the bottom of the cup with no need to open the tea bag. It was a novel experience for us, to say the least—but the tea was nothing like home.

Before long, I realized that neither Andre nor I could stop rubbing our eyes. I thought we were just suffering from lack of sleep, but when Herand noticed our discomfort, he told us that we were being affected by "smog." He explained that "smog" was a combination of the words "smoke" and "fog" and that the air was so polluted that the San Gabriel Mountains north and east of the city were often hidden by the haze. He also assured us that we would soon get used to it.

We soon found out that Herand was a few years older than we were and that his deformity had been caused by an accident when he was a teenager. One day while he was riding his bicycle in Tehran, an American military jeep had rear-ended him. The impact had sent him flying onto the hood, but he had then slid off and hit the concrete edge of a *joob*, one of the deep, trash-filled storm drains that line many of Tehran's streets. He had landed right on his face, and his injuries had required four hours of reconstructive surgery on his skull. However, during the operation the tip of the surgical scissors broke and could not be removed because of their critical position to nerves that controlled his facial movements.

Herand turned out to be a sincere and likable guy who gave us much useful advice. He recommended that we look for room and board in a private home near the campus rather than staying in the dorm and that we take some time the next day to check out a house owned by an elderly lady who lived within walking distance of the campus and rented out rooms to students. He also offered to go with us to open checking accounts at a nearby bank. We also learned that he worked as the manager of the Congress Theater next to the coffee shop. He invited us to see the current film, a Hitchcock feature, that night but we were too tired.

Before he drove us back to the campus, he stopped to buy gas at the Flying A station across from the café. It had two red pumps and offered S&H Green Stamps as well as household items to attract repeat customers. Back then, in the late 1950s, a gallon of gas cost twenty cents, and this included full service—checking the engine oil and the pressure of all four tires as well as washing the front and rear windshields.

By the time we returned to the dorm room, it was late. As I was falling asleep, I realized that I had been learning and absorbing something new every minute of the day. We had no sheets or pillowcases for the dorm bed and the pillow, which were stained and smelly, but the sweet, comforting smell of home from my wool blanket sent me off to sleep in minutes.

At Pepperdine College 1956: (from left) me, Vaughn Gregor, Andre Minassian

Chapter 2

SUMMER SCHOOL DAYS IN LA

THE NEXT MORNING, VAUGHN GREGOR himself paid us a quick visit to make sure that we were all right, and a short time later, we met Herand. He took us to a nearby Bank of America, where we each opened an account, and then to the house he had mentioned.

It was a typical two-bedroom California bungalow right across from the campus. The woman who owned it was a widow. When we arrived, the front door was open and breakfast smells were wafting through the screen door. Inside, we could see the owner, a heavyset woman in her seventies wearing a muumuu, in the small living room. She and the Persian cat on her lap were watching television.

She led the three of us to the second bedroom, which had two beds and a small bathroom, and told us that it was available with or without three meals a day.

While I was looking around the bathroom, I reached up to open a small cabinet above the toilet and knocked a washcloth into the toilet bowl. Instinctively, I reached down to grab it. She turned around, saw me holding the dripping cloth, and with a stunned expression said, "Oh dear, dear! No, no! We don't wash our hands and face in there." She then pointed to the sink and added, "Here, here!"

I was so taken aback by her cultural misunderstanding that I was speechless and had no idea how to respond. What could I say? All I could do was hand her the washcloth. Nevertheless, we moved into "Mom's" house that afternoon and unpacked.

THE FOLLOWING MONDAY, we both enrolled in the summer session and signed up for mathematics, history, and English classes, which were scheduled to start in the middle of June. This gave us two more weeks to get acclimatized and start finding our way in this new world.

While we were registering, we heard from another Iranian student that the college maintenance department had some part-time job openings during the summer session. Any paying job offered a unique opportunity to students like us, who received financial assistance every three months from the Iranian government. The assistance program allowed students' parents to provide for their education by buying US dollars at just fifty percent of the free market rate. However, once in the US, the students would find work and send dollars back home that the parents would then sell in free markets for twice the amount they would receive in the "official" market. This arrangement was a great help to both parents and students.

Andre and I immediately applied for jobs and were hired part-time for the rest of the summer at minimum wage—seventy-five cents an hour. I was assigned to tend the grounds of the president's residence, an old mansion. The grounds were dotted with a large number of old pine trees, and my main task was to rake up the needles every day. Andre was assigned to the dorms, where he cleaned, moved furniture, and carried out other tasks.

A tall, bald, retired man named Joe headed the maintenance department. His assistant looked just like him and so was known as "Little Joe," and under him was a black man who was also named Joe. To keep track of all these Joes, Andre and I nicknamed the black Joe as "Mook Joe" because *mook* means "dark" in Armenian.

Mook Joe looked just like Parviz, a classmate of mine from elementary school, and he was one of the kindest people I ever met. He would show us how to do physical work without getting hurt. Nor have I ever forgotten the day he asked us if we were eating fruit every day. We told him we did not because Mom did not include it on the daily menu. The next day after work, he took us to a Ralphs supermarket near the campus and led us around to a steel bin behind the store. He crawled into the bin and brought out several large apples, oranges, and peaches. He showed us that they all had small blemishes and bruises and told us, "These are free because customers don't want to buy them, so the supermarket discards them."

In Iran, the fresh produce we saw always had blemishes because everything was grown without pesticides. We had never seen fruit as big and beautiful as what Mook Joe showed us, so all summer we enjoyed fruits from that Ralphs bin.

WE WERE KEPT SO BUSY BY our jobs and our ongoing discoveries of the secrets of life in America that the two weeks before classes started passed quickly, and soon the first day of classes arrived.

We found ourselves in the algebra class waiting for the instructor to arrive and listening to a male student who was wearing shorts and beach sandals and playing a tune on his guitar. When the instructor—a middle-aged woman—walked into the classroom, Andre and I immediately stood up, as was the custom in Iran. But the other students remained seated and the fellow with the guitar kept on strumming. The teacher stood silently at the front of the room until he caught on and stopped, but we were shocked to hear her tell him, "It's all right, you can go ahead and finish the song you're playing"—which he proceeded to do! Andre and I were shocked because none of our teachers in Tehran would have permitted such behavior.

To me, Pepperdine felt like a continuation of Mehr, my elementary school because it was a Christian school, with morning prayers and hymns in the auditorium before classes started each day. This was all very familiar to me. The only difference was that everything was in English.

The history class was much harder than the English. We filled the margins of almost every page of our textbooks, which were in English, with scribbled translations that we looked up in our Farsi and Armenian dictionaries. Mathematics, on the other hand, was a breeze. We both earned the only "A" grades in our classes, and that was essential if we were to be given scholarships for the fall semester.

DURING THE SUMMER, A SLOW transformation also took place in our appearance and behavior. We began wearing blue jeans and penny loafers and sporting crew cuts. Our English improved so much that we all but stopped using our dictionaries, and we were able to find our way around the city. I signed up at a nearby Vic Tanny's gym to continue my lifelong interest in bodybuilding. But every day I checked my campus mailbox hoping for mail from home.

Because 1956 was an election year, I keenly followed the presidential campaign, in which President Dwight Eisenhower and Vice President Richard Nixon were running against Adlai Stevenson and Estes Kefauver on the Democratic ticket.

I was not fluent enough in English to understand the political and ideological differences between the two parties. This was not too important because I was not a citizen and so could not vote, but I had always liked General Eisenhower, and I found the comments about the hole in Stevenson's shoe puzzling because to us that indicated poverty. I did not realize that Americans saw this as an indication that even though he came from a wealthy background, he was also thrifty. Still, following the campaign made me aware that Americans' knowledge about the Middle East was limited to nonexistent. This was both disappointing and humorous.

Checking for mail from home

For example, local YMCAs and churches often invited students from the Middle East to show-and-tell dinner gatherings where we were invited to speak about our countries and our cultures. We attended these gatherings because they were a chance to get a decent meal—a change from our constant diet of hot dogs and hamburgers. The people at these meetings were polite and genuinely kind, and they made special efforts to show their concern for our well-being. Typically, before dessert we would be asked to say a few words about where we had come from and to answer questions.

However, the kinds of questions we were asked made it clear that our listeners did not understand our heavily accented English. For instance, I would be sure to mention that Iran had a rich history and a fairly modern standard of living—only to be asked immediately afterward how it felt to put on a pair of shoes for the first time, or whether everyone in Iran had camels tied to their front doors for daily transportation. Some listeners, having never seen a live camel, actually believed it when I would jokingly reply that we had "Hydra-Matic camels" back home.

A NUMBER OF ANDRE'S AND my friends and former classmates from Iran were attending LACC, several miles north of Pepperdine on Vermont Avenue, and the ones who had cars would drive down and join us to see free movies at the Congress Theater. My high-school friend Henry Gabrielian, who was attending the Northrop Institute of Technology, would drop by and buy us dinner because he had a car and a dishwashing job in a local café. Our favorite food was the whole rotisserie chicken that we would pick up at a market in Hollywood and eat in Henry's 1947 Plymouth, where he kept small salt and pepper shakers in the glove compartment.

Soorik Hadjian, who had picked us up at the airport and given us change for our hotel porter that night, was also studying at LACC. He owned a green 1950 Cadillac and used to drive Andre and me to the beach and on general outings. Cars with air conditioning were a rarity then. Only movie stars and the "rich and famous" could afford them. That summer, we spent many hours in the Cadillac during the unbearably hot and smoggy days cruising up and down Hollywood Boulevard with the windows shut so Soorik could impress other drivers by pretending he had an air-conditioned car. Elvis Presley and his gyrating hips were the rage of the day. The other biggest recording stars included Pat Boone and Connie Francis and groups such as the Platters. They were the soundtrack to our lives as we drove around in Soorik's Cadillac.

As our excursions began to extend beyond Pepperdine and farther afield, our expenses quickly ate up our limited funds. Our Rolex watches seemed to be just the ticket. Selling them would alleviate our financial shortfall at least temporarily, if not longer. However, a few days after we started searching for the best place to sell our timepieces, my Rolex stopped working, so we started seeking out a watchmaker who could fix it.

We learned of an Armenian watch repairer in downtown LA who was known to repair exotic pocket watches. When he examined it, he said he would be unable to fix it if he could not open the back. Waterproof Rolexes had special finely threaded backs that could only be opened with a special tool. The watchmaker said he did not have that tool and that the only way he could open the back of the watch would be by cutting two notches so he could grip it and twist it open.

We agreed and left my watch with him. But when I went to pick it up a week later, the back was severely mutilated. It was working again but had lost much of its value. Soon after, Andre's Rolex also stopped working and ended up suffering the same fate as mine—functioning but valueless.

Even if we had been able to sell the Rolexes, which we did not, we knew that we would still have a struggle making ends meet. At one point, we spent several nights going to bed with empty stomachs before Herand, who knew about our money problems, got his boss at the theater to let him hire us for one afternoon to scrape all the old stuck-on chewing gum from the cement floor, which sloped downward to the screen and the stage below it.

He offered us each a dollar an hour and told us that the job needed to be finished within five hours, before the theater opened.

Equipped with two metal scrapers, we turned on the hose at the entrance and got busy scraping the hardened, black, gooey old gum from the cement floor by using a lot of free-flowing water. After about three hours of hard work, Herand came to check on our progress. He was admiring the top few rows of spotless concrete when he suddenly screamed: "What the hell are you guys doing!? Look at this pool of water! How the hell am I going to open the theater?"

Sure enough, the water had accumulated at the "deep end" of the floor in front of the stage. It did look like a swimming pool. We had no time to get the water pump out, so we had to cordon off more than half of the seats in the theater because they were drenched. Needless to say, we did not get paid for our backbreaking work.

Nevertheless, Herand and Andre soon came up with another scheme to make money. The following night was Keno night, and Herand was responsible for running it. Resplendent in a suit and bowtie, he would conduct the game from the stage, which held a board with hanging numbered red cards that hid cash prizes—all one-dollar bills except for one ten-dollar bill. And as manager, Herand knew the location of the ten-dollar prize.

The numbered spinning wheel that was projected onto the movie screen would stop on a succession of numbers, and when a patron matched those numbers on the free Keno card that they had received along with their movie ticket, he or she would shout "Keno" and go to the stage. Herand would diligently check the numbers on the winning card and, if they matched, would ask the winner to select one of the numbered cards. Herand would then lift the card and give the winner the prize.

I was too tired to go to the theater that night, so Andre went alone to carry out the scheme that he and Herand had concocted. About halfway into the game, Andre shouted "Keno!," went to the stage, and handed his card to Herand, who examined it and asked him to choose one of the hanging cards. Andre mumbled a number. Herand stated the number that Andre had supposedly chosen and then lifted the corresponding card—which of course uncovered the ten-dollar bill. He handed it to Andre, who walked back to his seat as the audience applauded politely.

That money bought us several days' worth of food, but it was hard for us to manage on the hundred dollars that we each received from home every month. Even with our scholarships, there was always "too much month left at the end of our money" after we paid for our books, rent, food, and sundry expenses. Before long, we learned only too well what the English phrase "tightening your belt" meant. It meant "empty pockets"—except that our parents, anticipating such an eventuality, had, without telling us beforehand, tucked a number of small Iranian handicraft items in our luggage that we could sell if we had to.

And one of those small items led to a series of events that would later shape the rest of my life, both personally and professionally, in ways that I could never have imagined.

One late-summer day, as we were searching for items to sell, Andre came upon a small silver pillbox. We had totally forgotten about it, but it reminded us that we needed to fulfill a vital obligation to the benefactor who had made it possible for us to come to the United States in the first place.

The Iranian government required that families who wanted to send their children to school in the United States had to put up collateral, which would guarantee that the students would return to Iran after finishing their studies, before passports would be issued. The only acceptable form of collateral was real estate. At that time, however, few Iranian-Armenians even owned their homes, much less other real estate. So Andre's and my parents had to look for a benefactor who would be willing to help them. One of Andre's relatives connected us with a Mr. Aghassi, who was kind enough to fill that role for us. In return, he had given Andre the pillbox and asked us to locate Aris Bassentzian, a friend of his who had recently immigrated to the United States and was living in Burbank, and give it to him.

Our parents had been thrilled by Mr. Aghassi's request because they knew that we would do as he asked. Also, our meeting Mr. Bassentzian reassured them that we would know at least one Armenian man in California who could help us in that faraway land if we ever needed it.

WHEN ANDRE ASKED HERAND HOW far away Burbank was and whether he should mail the pillbox instead of delivering it in person, Herand replied that Burbank was about thirty minutes from campus and that he would drive us there that Saturday.

That weekend was sunny and warm, and there was little traffic on the 101 Freeway. When we pulled up at the Burbank address, a two-story apartment building, Herand and I stayed in the car while Andre went to deliver the pillbox.

He went up to the apartment and knocked several times, but no one answered. When he came back to the car, we decided that since we had come all that way, we would wait for a while and then try knocking door again. Herand parked in the shade of a large tree next to a small park a few hundred feet from the building and turned on the radio.

Andre was in the front seat, and I lounged in the backseat with my feet propped up on the edge of the open window. About fifteen minutes later, I heard Andre whistle. I looked out and saw a very pretty girl about fifteen years old walking past us. She was wearing a white tennis outfit and was carrying a tennis racquet on her shoulder. When she heard him, she hastened her pace to escape his rude behavior and disappeared behind the trimmed hedges.

About ten minutes later, Andre said, "I'm going to try one more time to deliver the pillbox, and if no one answers this time, we'll go back." He went back to the building and returned several minutes later, his face red with embarrassment. "The girl I whistled at opened the door. She's Aris's daughter!" he told us. "She said that he should be home shortly and invited us to come in and wait for him."

We went up a steep staircase to a second-floor apartment. The door was ajar, and Andre announced our arrival by knocking gently. When the girl, who was now in street clothes, came to greet us and saw me, she exclaimed, "Oh, my God! It's Njdeh!"

This surprised me because I did not remember ever having met her, but she was strikingly beautiful and I was sure that if I had met her before, I would definitely have remembered her.

She told us her name was Lilit and invited us to sit down on the couch. Awkwardly, the three of us lined up and sandwiched ourselves between its armrests. The apartment faced west, and the day was so hot that the three of us sweated as if we were sitting in a sauna.

As we were chatting, Lilit noticed my puzzled expression and explained, "My brother, Aram, and I were your Scouts until we immigrated to America." A few minutes later, a fourteen-year-old boy walked in. He was as surprised to see me as I was to see him, but I immediately recognized him as a rambunctious lad whom I had selected to lead the taking of the Scouting oath a year before I left Iran because his Armenian pronunciation was perfect.

Lilit's and Aram's parents returned home a short time later. They were pleasantly surprised and glad to see us in their home and told us that they remembered their children's Scouting events and my leading the activities with great fondness.

While Mrs. Bassentzian got busy in the kitchen, Lilit served Armenian coffee and Aris told us something about their family's history.

He had been born in Leninakan (Gumry), Armenia, and was an expert in leather fabrics with a degree in chemical engineering from the then Soviet Union. After graduating, he had immigrated to Iran to escape the Communist rule.

His wife, Zabel Khanjian, had been born in Constantinople and had moved to France at a very young age with her parents and siblings to escape the Turkish genocide carried out against Christian Armenians that began in April 1915. She received her education in France and was an accomplished musician, while her brothers became involved in international export-import commerce. Because French was the preferred language for international trade in Iran, the brothers decided to move the family to Iran and to continue their activities from Tehran, which had been undergoing modernization under Reza

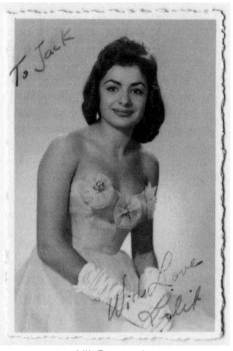

Lilit Bassentzian

Shah. Aris and Zabel met in Tehran, married, and moved to the city of Hamadan, where Aris was appointed manager of a large leather factory. Lilit and Aram were born in Hamadan in 1941 and 1942 respectively.

Several years later, Aris and Zabel, concerned about their children's education, moved back to Tehran. Lilit attended a French school for girls, Aram attended the Armenian Davitian School, and they both joined the Ararat Scouting division that I headed up. Finally, again concerned about their children's future education, Aris and Zabel moved to the United States and settled in Burbank, where both Lilit and Aram entered Burbank High School.

The smell of Armenian food, which we had not enjoyed since arriving in California, was filling the warm air as Andre finally gave the pillbox to Aris. But when Herand reluctantly said, "Okay, guys, time to leave," Lilit's mother protested, "No, you're not going anywhere! Dinner will be ready soon."

This was music to our ears. However, Middle Eastern etiquette dictates that it is rude to accept an invitation when it is first offered. Accordingly, all three of us said, "No, no, we can't stay," when in actuality our stomachs were rumbling in anticipation of the feast that lay ahead.

The dinner was absolutely out of this world. The company was great, and the conversation very interesting. We learned that both Lilit and Aram were having a hard time in their new surroundings because they did not know the language. They missed their friends in Tehran and had not yet made new friends. Also, their father did not have a job and their mother was taking in sewing. When Aris saw how much they were enjoying spending time with us, he invited us to visit them more often. And we did.

In the months that followed, it became clear that Lilit and Andre were interested in each other, and before long their relationship blossomed into a love affair. The two of them would talk on the phone for hours, after which Herand, Andre, and I would drive to Burbank and Herand and I would talk with Aris while Lilit and Andre would exchange starry-eyed glances and talk about all the things they had not gotten around to saying during their last long telephone conversation less than an hour earlier.

On weekends, Soorik would join us and we would all go to the beach together. Lilit offered to introduce me to some of her girlfriends, but I was not interested. I was not about to betray my girlfriend, Aida Astvatsaturian. Although we had never gotten formally engaged, she was waiting for me back in Tehran.

AFTER THE SUMMER TERM ENDED, Herand, Andre, and I rented a furnished house on 78th Street across from the campus. We were fast becoming fairly proficient in English. We had learned many new American customs and now knew our way around the town. I decided it was time to get my driver's license. This taught me an important lesson in cultural differences between America and Iran.

I drove Herand's souped-up Olds to the Department of Motor Vehicles and parked on the street while I went in to take the written test. After I passed, the examiner and I went outside for the driving test.

A new dark-green Studebaker was parked right in front of the Olds. We got in and I turned on the engine. Then, to show how skillful a driver I was, I turned the front wheels to the left until they locked and then floored the gas pedal. But the engine was so powerful that with a roar, the front end literally lifted off the ground and landed on the Studebaker's trunk! As I backed it off, I could hear the clunk of the Studebaker's rear bumper falling off.

I turned to the examiner and asked, "Should we continue?"

He stared at me in disbelief, then opened the car door and got out. "No, we don't continue! You get your butt out and leave a note on the windshield of that car with your address and phone number!" He then marked my application "FAILED" in large red letters, handed it to me, slammed the car door shut, and marched back into the building in disgust.

THAT NIGHT, WE HEARD A knock at the door. When Herand opened it, a middle-aged couple were standing there, and behind them at the curb was the Studebaker. So we all knew why they were there. I was peeking through the drawn curtains, which gave me a view of the porch, and was all ready to join the fistfight that normally followed car accidents in Tehran. But I observed none of that. Instead, after a few minutes of conversation, Herand and the man exchanged some papers and shook hands, and the couple left.

When Herand came back inside, I impatiently asked, "Now what?"

"Now my insurance company will pay for the damage you caused to both of our cars," he replied.

I was staggered that everything had been resolved so simply—and without a single black eye or bloodied nose. It was another reminder that things were quite different here, and that we still had much to learn about America and its customs.

WHEN OUR SCHOOL YEAR ENDED in May 1957, neither Andre nor I had yet decided which engineering school to attend. Our choices were the California Institute of Technology (Caltech) and the University of Southern California (USC). Both were private institutions that offered four-year and advanced degrees in civil engineering. Our other option was the University of California at Los Angeles (UCLA), a state institution, which was more affordable but offered a general engineering curriculum.

Most of our friends were attending or planning to attend USC. Tuition there was forty dollars per unit, so a full course load of twelve units would come to more than five hundred dollars a semester—well beyond our reach. Caltech cost much less, but, because of the fierce and growing competition between the United States and the Soviet Union to conquer space, it was devoting most of its attention to aerospace. This had undermined its reputation in civil engineering. Still, I was inclined to attend Caltech because it would cost less than USC.

ONE DAY, LILIT CALLED and invited us for lunch to meet Professor Smbat Abian, a mathematics professor and longtime friend of her father who was visiting from the University of Pennsylvania.

Andre and I arrived just as Lilit's mother was putting the main course of a fairly elaborate lunch on the table. During our lunch Smbat asked me what I was studying. I answered that Andre and I had completed our first year of pre-engineering and wanted to study civil engineering.

When I added that we were considering USC and Caltech, Smbat put down his fork and told us, "There's only one school in the United

States that any serious student who's considering civil engineering should attend—the University of Illinois at Urbana-Champaign. It's ranked number one in the nation. Also, Dr. Narbey Khachaturian, a professor in that department, is a friend of mine, and I'd be happy to write to him and ask him to send applications to you."

He went on to tell us that because U of I was a public university, the tuition was very reasonable compared to private institutions.

Everything he said was music to my ears, and I told Andre that if I were accepted, I would go there. Within two weeks, our applications arrived. We filled them out and sent them back, and in August 1957 we were notified that we had been admitted to the U of I college of engineering starting in the fall semester.

The acceptance letter also contained a note from Professor Khachaturian telling us that U of I had its own airport and offered commuter flights to and from Chicago, about 150 miles away. He also offered to pick us up when we arrived at the university airport and to help us find lodgings.

I was ecstatic and could not wait, but the news depressed Andre because he could not bear the thought of being separated from Lilit. Although U of I made a lot of sense both economically and academically, to Lilit and Andre, who was just twenty, it felt like halfway around the world.

By now, it was a foregone conclusion that they were destined to marry each other. Lilit's parents had accepted that eventuality, but they also realized how important it would be for their future son-in-law to have a good education. After consulting with Andre's family in Tehran, everyone decided that it would be best for Andre and Lilit to get officially engaged before we left for Illinois.

Just a few days before we were due to leave, Andre received a package from his mother. It contained a beautiful white engagement dress for Lilit and a bar of soap. In a separate letter, his mother informed him that the engagement ring was hidden inside the soap. Lilit and Andre celebrated their engagement at a small party attended by friends and family. In accordance with Armenian tradition, I witnessed the event as their best man.

In front of the Bassentzians' apartment building: (from left) me; Professor Smbat Abian; Lilit's mother, Zabel; Lilit; Lilit's father, Aris

Andre's and Lilit's engagement ceremony. I am standing just behind Andre, and Lilit's mother, Zabel, is standing behind her.

Chapter 3

UNIVERSITY OF ILLINOIS
College Life in the American Heartland

ON A HOT SUMMER NIGHT TWO WEEKS LATER, Andre and I said good-bye to Lilit, her family, and a few friends. Then Herand drove us to the Burbank Airport, where we boarded an American Airlines red-eye flight to Chicago. I spent much of the flight trying to cheer up Andre, who was sorely missing Lilit.

We landed in Chicago at daybreak, found the Ozark Air ticket counter, and soon were airborne again, this time in a small half-empty commuter plane that landed at U of I's Willard Airport, 150 miles away, in the late morning.

As we made our way outside the surprisingly substantial U of I terminal, we spotted a man with Armenian features who was holding the hands of two young boys aged about four and six. As we approached, he smiled and said, "You must be Njdeh and Andre. I'm Narbey Khachaturian. Welcome to U of I! These are my sons, John and Gregory."

We piled our suitcases into the trunk of his blue-green Plymouth, and off we headed toward the campus. Urbana-Champaign looked nothing like Los Angeles. The cloudy, humid air gave the area a gloomy and oppressive feeling. Due to the heat and humidity, the old red-brick buildings on the campus were covered with moss. To the two of us, arriving as we just had from sunny California, the whole scene was very depressing.

Soon we were driving through residential areas lined with large trees and old two-story houses with porches and attics. We looked at some vacancies, but none were to our liking. Our final stop was an old three-story building on West Oregon Street. The rooms we looked at were in a remodeled attic with steep sloping ceilings—three rooms, each furnished identically with two twin beds, chairs, tables, and old lamps with discolored shades marked up with scribblings from previous student occupants. Each room also included makeshift open closets and one scratched-up, dark-brown wooden chest of drawers. Unappealing, to say the least.

However, by the time we got back to the car and told Dr. Khachaturian that we had rejected these lodgings as well, the children had gotten tired and bored and were nagging him to go home. He was visibly agitated and took out his frustration on us, saying in a not-too-friendly tone, "You know, guys, in a few hours, the trains from Chicago are going to arrive with thousands of students looking for rooms. My wife is waiting for us and I have to get the children back home, so you'd better take whatever room you just saw."

With that, he opened the trunk, took out our suitcases, set them on the street and drove away. Moments later, a handsome, well-dressed man came out of the house, smiled at us, and said, "Hi, guys. Looking for a room?" He held out his hand. "I'm Dick, the owner. Let me show you the room."

We told him that we had already seen the room, but we were in such a panic at being left in a strange place that we decided to take it on the spot. The rent was one dollar a day per person—a bargain compared to Los Angeles.

As we lugged our suitcases up the three flights of stairs and past the pay phones at each landing and sullenly emptied the contents of our suitcases into the drawers, I felt as if we were reliving our first gloomy day at the Pepperdine dorm all over again.

Still, when I looked out the window to the streets below, I could see them filling with students. They were arriving in large numbers, as Dr. Khachaturian had warned us, and before nightfall the other two rooms on our attic floor were filled.

Before long our building was echoing with laughter and jokes, and we got to meet our housemates, many of whom were freshmen from small towns in Illinois who began running around in their underwear and horsing around in the narrow corridors. None of them had any idea where Iran was. When we noticed that the first thing they all did was to unpack framed pictures of their girlfriends and place them on their desks, Andre took out Lilit's large framed picture and placed it on his desk, and I placed Aida's on mine.

We were relieved when the guys on our floor invited us to get a bite to eat because we had no idea where to go. We all walked to the student union, a beautiful building on the main quadrangle that had cafeterias on the lower floors. From that day on, it was our favorite place to hang out, study, shoot pool, and have our meals.

The next day, we were scheduled to meet with the dean of foreign students in the administration building. At Pepperdine, we were known as "international students," which we thought sounded a little more dignified than "foreign students." While we were waiting to be called into his office, two Iranian students who were passing by stopped by to say hello. We had not met them before, but they introduced themselves as Bijan Mohraz and Kiavash and invited us to visit them at their house, where mostly Iranian students lived. We later did so and over the years spent many hours there.

When we went into the dean's office, he nodded for us to take a seat and then began to review our files. To me he seemed as gloomy as the weather outside. "I see," he commented, "that you've answered no to the question 'Do you know how to swim?'"

This seemed like an odd thing to focus on until he informed us that swimming was a required course and that we had to sign up. I was embarrassed that although I had been a head Scoutmaster in Iran, I had never learned to swim. Also, we were puzzled that in Los Angeles, right on the Pacific coast, no one had ever asked us about swimming—but that here in the landlocked Midwest, we needed to learn.

The dean also told us that before we could enroll in classes, we had to take an English placement exam to measure our language skills. Based on those results, we would be enrolled in further English classes as well as our regular courses during our first year. The exam was scheduled for the next day. Clearly, the pace of things here was noticeably faster and more formal than in California.

THE FOLLOWING MORNING, Andre and I arrived at the examination hall early and seated ourselves in the front row. Before long, the several hundred seats were packed with students from all over the world speaking different languages. It looked like the United Nations.

When the examination proctors—four young women—walked in carrying stacks of paper, the noise level quieted in moments from talking to whispers to silence. One of the women, who seemed to be the leader of the group, was tall and strikingly beautiful, with thick reddish hair. Her tight gray skirt and white shirt, with its rolled-up sleeves and with the two top buttons undone, accentuated her perfect body. As she proceeded to write the proctors' names on the blackboard, they raised their hands so we could identify them. Finally she added her own name, "Miss Carol Gurolnick," and began reading us the test instructions, enunciating them in clear, precise, slow English.

The proctors then walked along the rows of seats handing out the test sheets. As it happened, it was Miss Gurolnick who handed my test to me. As she did, she asked if she could borrow my Rolex to time the test. After I gave it to her and she moved away, Andre commented in Armenian, "She liked you."

I answered, "Yeah, right. I hope I get it back!"

The two-hour test was soon over, and I was relieved to get my watch back from Miss Gurolnick.

SEVERAL DAYS LATER, WE received the results of our placement exam and were told which level of English class we needed to take. There were so many foreign students at U of I that we could have signed up for any of several classes.

Enrollment was held in the Armory, a large hangar-like structure on the edge of the campus. When we arrived, it was jammed with students rushing to line up in one long queue after another under makeshift signs that listed the course names and numbers.

The hustle and bustle reminded me of Tehran's Great Bazaar just before our Iranian New Year, but Andre and I were overwhelmed and a bit frightened by the students' panicky efforts to get into their courses. We were wondering what to do and where to go when suddenly a familiar voice greeted us in Farsi.

"*Salam*, guys, how are you doing?" It was Bijan Mohraz, the student we had met outside the dean's office.

His knowledge of undergraduate courses and related classes and schedules was nothing short of amazing and helped us not only that day but throughout our entire four years at U of I. Andre and I signed up for English, swimming, physics, and basic structural analysis. Although we had intended to take as many classes as possible together, with the exception of swimming we ended up in different classes of the same course.

When we registered for each course, we were handed a list of the books and other items we would need. The list for the swimming class had only one item, "swim cap." But, thinking that swim trunks were obviously necessary for swimming although they had been left off the list, we also bought trunks.

The next morning, we arrived at the gymnasium for our first class on the first day of the semester—swimming, at 8 a.m.

When we walked into the locker room with our swim gear, I was pleasantly surprised to see so many young American students there who did not know how to swim either. However, the surprise soon turned into a terrifying reality for Andre and me when we saw that they were grabbing towels but walking naked, with only their swim caps on, as they made their way talking and laughing into the pool area.

The shower room incident at Pepperdine flashed in front of my eyes, but this time I had no soap to use to cover my nakedness. I asked Andre, "Now what?"

"Uh...I guess we have to do what the others did."

So he proceeded very slowly and hesitantly to put his cap on first and then take off his clothes. Just as slowly and hesitantly, I did the same. Meanwhile, we heard the swim instructor calling out our names several times as he took roll call.

I wrapped a towel around my waist and walked out to the pool near the deep end. The moment the other students, who were sprawling naked on bleachers at the shallow end of the pool, saw me with my towel, they began whistling. Panicked, I tossed the towel away, jumped into the deep end of the pool, and began flapping my hands and arms every which way.

The instructor grabbed a long bar that was mounted on hooks fixed to the wall and held one end of it out to me. I grabbed it and he pulled me to the shallow end. As I got out, there were no laughs or whistles. Later, Andre told me that as I was getting out of the pool, kids were asking him if I was a weight lifter.

Within a few days, I realized that I was way ahead of the other students because I was able to swim to the deep end, while the instructor had to keep coaxing them because they were afraid. Several weeks into the semester, he told me that the reason I had no fear of the deep end was not due to my athletic abilities. Rather, unlike the other beginners, I had jumped into the deep end on the first day and that had erased my fear of the deeper water. So some good had come from my modesty about being seen naked!

I soon got used to wearing only my swim cap, and I was thrilled about being able to swim. All my life I have been grateful to U of I for making swimming a requirement because I cannot imagine life without being able to swim.

As I SETTLED IN AT U OF I, I SOON BEGAN noticing sharp contrasts between student life there compared with Los Angeles. In that sprawling metropolis, with its many universities, entertainment centers, movie studios, and miles and miles of beaches, being a student was just an extension of life in the big city. It was very different at U of I, where most of the students around us, though vibrant and energetic, seemed to be there to pursue the "Three Ls" of student life: "Learn, Love, and Laugh."

Chartered in 1867 as a land grant agricultural college and surrounded by vast cornfields as far as the eye could see, U of I had grown into one of the largest educational and research and development centers in the US. It developed the Illiac, the first mainframe computing system and a forerunner of the modern computer.

From an academic standpoint, U of I fulfilled all of the dreams I had had about American universities after reading stories in popular pictorial magazines like *Life* and *The Saturday Evening Post*. I was absorbing and learning about the mechanics of structural systems and the behavior of materials from academic giants in the field who had developed advanced structural design theories and participated in the design and construction of landmark structures such as the Golden Gate Bridge, the Empire State Building, and Mexico City's Latin-American Tower, to name a few.

In addition, the campus offered plenty of opportunities for recreational activities such as football and basketball games, and visiting nearby historic sites. The Chanute Air Force base, located near the campus, offered not only a collection of vintage and active aircraft but also a cinema that showed recent movies. And on hot summer days, the manmade Lake of the Woods was a popular place to swim, and the parkland around it was a popular picnicking site for local families.

THE FOUR YEARS THAT ANDRE and I spent at U of I were fruitful and rewarding. We received both our civil engineering education and an ongoing

Posing with my alma mater

education in American customs. We remained roommates throughout our time there. Andre spent his summers in Los Angeles while I took summer courses at U of I to accelerate my graduation to return to Tehran.

Every semester of the next four years, we took classes in physics, strength of materials, and civil engineering. This was considered a full load, especially for foreign students. The engineering classes themselves were unremarkable—a lot of reading, analysis, and hands-on laboratory work that left little time for fun and recreation. I had hoped to join ROTC (the Reserve Officer Training Corps) as a continuation of my beloved Scouting, but I could not because I was not a US citizen.

In essence, our daily life during the semester stayed substantially the same for all four years. After dinner, Andre and I would return to our room. He still kept the oversized framed photograph of Lilit on his small desk. It gave him the strength and patience to bear their separation, and each night he would embark on writing his daily—and lengthy—letter to her while I would do my homework. By the time he finished, I would be fast asleep. I often asked him what there was to write about every night when nothing different had happened from the day before. His answer? "You'd never understand." (Meanwhile, Aida and I continued to exchange letters every month.)

For me the only exception to this monotonous routine was my English class because it ignited a forbidden romantic affair that began the day I first walked into that class and lasted almost to the end of my four years at U of I.

DURING THE FIRST WEEK OF CLASS, I got lost on the campus and arrived late to the first session of my English class, which was to meet on Mondays, Wednesdays, and Fridays. When I opened the classroom door, I immediately recognized that the instructor, who was writing on the blackboard, was Carol Gurolnick, the attractive proctor who had borrowed my watch during the English proficiency exam.

The class was almost full, and she was busy teaching the correct pronunciation of English words that included "th" letters, such as "father," "brother," etc. My arrival distracted the students, and she turned, saw me standing in the doorway, and said, "You're late. Take a seat and see me after class." With that, she continued teaching.

I took the only empty seat, which was in the front row, where I could see and follow every move that she made. She was focusing on intonation, so there was no need to take notes. Instead, I could focus on her. She looked even more attractive than I remembered.

When the bell sounded, she put down her chalk and dismissed the class.

A couple of female Asian students approached her desk and began asking her questions, while I stood behind them silently waiting for my turn. Noticing a pair of earrings on the desk, I leaned over to take a closer look because they were a very different design from the ones my mother wore. Curious because they apparently attached to the ear with small screws rather than with the thin wires I was used to seeing, I picked one up to examine it more closely. But as I was playing with it, I dropped it on the floor. It landed right next to the instructor's shoe, and as I reached down to pick it up, and I could not resist looking at her shapely legs, which were right in front of my eyes. I also noticed a slight sag in her stockings.

But as I stood up, and before I could even place the earring back on the desk, I saw Miss Gurolnick glaring at me. "Put that back!" she snapped. I hurriedly put it back and went on waiting for my turn to see her.

After the other students had left and I was the only one remaining, she studied her roster and asked my name. When I told her, she checked it off and told me, "If you're late one more time, you won't be able to continue in my class. You understand?" She began to collect her papers. Clearly I was being dismissed.

"Okay," I replied nonchalantly. Then—for reasons that I don't understand to this day except that maybe I wanted to be helpful because I thought she might be embarrassed if she realized that her stockings were drooping—I added, "Please pull up your nylons," turned away, and started walking to the door. As I left, I heard her mumble some angry words that I could not understand.

I made sure to arrive on time for the next class, but, hoping to escape her wrath about our first encounter by avoiding meeting her glance and looking down every time she looked at or walked to the back of the classroom, I sat in the last row.

The following week, I was having coffee at lunchtime at a café on the same street as my house. It was crowded, so I was sitting at a long counter fixed to the wall with a large window looking out to the street. Suddenly, the guys sitting next to me began whistling and exclaiming, "Look at that piece of honey!" and "The lucky bastard who gets to..." and similar comments.

Naturally, I looked out to get a glimpse of the subject of all that attention—and saw Carol Gurolnick walking along on the opposite sidewalk carrying books and a purse. She stopped at a gray two-story house with what looked like an attic tucked under the eaves, walked up the stairs to the porch, and went inside through the open front door. A few minutes later, I saw a light go on in the attic window. I concluded that Carol lived up there and had turned on the light.

A FEW WEEKS LATER, I arrived for class but saw that she had not arrived by the time the class was due to start. The door opened, and a large-framed black man came in and announced that she was down with a bad cold and that he would be her substitute while she recovered.

She was absent for a couple of weeks and, every day as I passed by her house, I saw the attic light on and the open front door. One day, I became concerned about whether anyone was helping her by bringing her food or other necessities. Remembering that in Iran people with colds were fed soup and toasted sweet bread, I went to the grocery store nearby and bought a couple of cans of chicken soup and a package of toasted sweet bread.

As I walked to her building, my heart began to pound and I wondered whether what I was about to do was proper in America. I was about to find myself standing at her door. What was I going to say?

When I reached her house, I summoned up all my courage and went inside. The entryway was a narrow corridor with a staircase on the left side that led to the second floor. I walked up to the second floor and saw another narrower, darker staircase that took me to the attic level.

There was only one door, so I gave it a gentle knock and waited. I felt relieved when no one answered, and I was about to turn around and leave when I heard the click of the lock.

The door opened and I was face to face with my teacher. She was wearing a white bathrobe. I felt so panicky that I could not speak. All I could do was hold out the shopping bag. She smiled and said, "Mr. Yaghoubian, what are you doing here?"

Her smile reassured me that she was not going to scold. All I could reply was, "I brought you some soup."

At that, she giggled and said, "Come on in, come on in."

I followed her into a small room with a slanting ceiling and all the walls covered with pink flower-patterned wallpaper. To my left was the small window that looked out onto the street. In front of the window was a desk with a lit lamp—the light I had seen—standing on it. A small TV set with a black telephone resting on top of it stood at the foot of a dark-brown sofa, while a bookshelf on the opposite wall held books and also a menorah.

She went into a tiny kitchen, and I saw that her nylons were drying on a sagging rope that stretched from one wall to the other. She set the bag on the small kitchen table, took out the two cans of soup and the bag of bread, and eyed the bread curiously. "What's this?"

I told her that in Iran people with colds would eat only sweet toasted bread, to which she replied, "You're too much! Thank you!"

"You're welcome," I responded, and I started to walk to the door.

"No, no," she said. "Please sit down."

She gestured at the sofa, and I sat down as I was told without saying a word. She took a seat at the other end and began asking me about myself. I was very conscious that she was a teacher and answered her questions about when I had arrived in the US, how I liked California, what my major was going to be, my family, and so forth, without daring to ask her anything in return. She listened attentively and asked more questions.

After a while, I started feeling a little more relaxed, so I walked over to the little window and looked out. From there, I could clearly see the café and the telephone booth on the street next to it.

I stayed much longer than I had expected to, and it was dark outside by the time I left. Finally, I said, "I must go. My roommate will be worried about me. I hope you feel better soon and come back to class. And please let me know if you need anything."

She walked with me to the door and said, "Thank you again. And you don't have to come all the way up and get exposed to my cold—you can call me." She wrote her number on a piece of paper and gave it to me.

She locked the door behind me, and I made my way down the dim staircases feeling confused but glad that I could be of help to her.

CAROL STAYED HOME FOR THE NEXT TWO WEEKS. I called her every day from the phone booth to ask how she was doing and whether she needed anything. Each day our calls grew longer, from a couple of short sentences to long conversations. On the third or fourth day, she began coming to her window when we chatted. It was as if we were in the same room sitting across from each other. I made her laugh as we talked and talked about everything and nothing for an hour or two at a time.

By the time she started feeling better, the days were growing noticeably shorter and colder. During my whole time in Illinois, I always felt as if fall bypassed us entirely and summer turned winter overnight. By the end of September, gone were the long hot and humid days. The foliage turned quickly, and winds began to blow the leaves from tall trees that just a few days earlier had provided lush surroundings and shade. The streets became carpeted with dry leaves, and the trees turned into stark skeletal structures.

The sudden change of seasons caught me off guard. In California, we had never needed topcoats or heavy jackets. My lined raincoat, which I had brought from Iran and never used in California, soon proved no match for the cold and damp. The campus clothing stores were featuring parkas—a good indication of what winter in Illinois was going to be like.

I had enough money to buy a hooded parka with a fur lining and oblong wooden buttons that hooked to leather loops (mostly for looks because it also had an inside zipper). Now I felt like an Illinois native—or at least that I had a fighting chance against the climate I was facing.

BY THE TIME CAROL RETURNED TO the classroom, I felt as if we were old friends. I still sat in the back row, but things were very different from two weeks earlier when I did not dare look at her. Now there was something special when our glances met. However, I was not sure if she had the same feelings as I did—and I was unsure what my own feelings were.

In class, I was very circumspect so it would not be obvious to other students that something was going on between Carol and me. I would purposely enter and leave the classroom with the other students, but I still arranged to be in the first group to arrive and in the last to leave so I could be in her presence as much as I could.

As I was reluctantly leaving after class on the Friday of the week she returned, Carol called out, "Mr. Yaghoubian, can I see you for a moment?"

I stopped and turned toward her. "Sure." My heart started pounding uncontrollably. I had last talked to her a week earlier from the phone booth while she had been at her attic window, and now I was standing close to her and in the exact location where I had picked up her earring.

With a special smile, she said, "Jack, I want to return your kindness while I wasn't feeling well. Would you like to join me for dinner tonight?"

Without hesitation, I answered, "I don't want to trouble you..."

"It's no trouble," she replied. "I'll see you at seven."

THAT EVENING, THE TEMPERATURE PLUMMETED and the weather grew windy and tumultuous, with dark thunder clouds spitting lightning. At five minutes to seven, as I was slinging on my parka, one of the wooden buttons caught one of the knobs of our dresser and ripped off. But I had no time to deal with it, so I tucked the button in one of my pockets and left for Carol's.

Three minutes later I was knocking on her door. She opened it with a smile and invited me to come in and make myself comfortable while she finished cooking dinner.

Her place was warm and smelled like heaven from the aromas of the meal that she was preparing. The TV was on, and the news was predicting the arrival of a wet cold front in our area. After watching for a few minutes, I went into the kitchen and we started to talk as she was cooking. The table was set for two with sliced French bread and cheese as hors-d'oeuvres.

As we went on chatting, I found out that she was five months older than I and had just received her masters degree in English literature at U of I. They had offered her a teaching position while she was waiting to begin her doctoral studies in the same field, but at the University of Chicago.

That hit me really hard. Here I was, almost exactly her age—twenty-two—and only a sophomore. I got very quiet because I felt so far behind her. Perhaps sensing my discomfort, she began asking me about my family and about life in Iran.

I told her about my parents and about Andre, and about my impressions of America. When the dinner was finally ready and we sat down to eat, the atmosphere was very pleasant but not as comfortable as our easy exchanges and our continuous laughter during my calls to her from the phone booth. There were uncomfortable moments of silence broken only by the commercial jingles coming from the TV. One thing struck me as a little odd—in class she would look at me, but now she seemed to be avoiding meeting my gaze.

The food, a stew of meat and mushrooms, was great. It had been a long time since I had had a home-cooked meal. We went on just making small talk while I helped her clean off the table, wash the dishes, and tidy up the kitchen. I started feeling antsy and wanted to leave because I felt that she had paid me back and that it was time to close the chapter on this whole awkward teacher-student situation.

After we finished in the kitchen, I fetched my parka and started putting it on while thanking her for the great dinner. As she was replying, I did not know whether to shake her hand or to just say good-bye when without even thinking about it I reached into my pocket and felt the button. I took it out and looked at it because I had forgotten all about it. Carol looked at it and said, "Good thing you have it. Let me sew it back on for you." I simply took off the parka and gave it to her.

She sat down on the sofa and reached into a small basket on the floor next to her. It was a sewing box. She took out a needle and bundles of sewing thread, and we sat in dead silence as she sewed the button back on. After she finished, she handed the parka back to me, but as I put it on she proceeded to reach for the zipper and to pull it all the way up to my neck. Then she buttoned it and pressed down the collar with both hands.

Her face was only inches from mine.

I do not know what gave me the courage to put my arms around her waist and embrace her. I felt her breasts pressing against my chest when our lips met. Instead of pushing me away, she closed her eyes, gently put her arms behind my head, and pushed her fingers into my hair. Suddenly, a streak of lightning flashed outside, followed by a loud thunderclap. We

Carol Gurolnick

stood embracing with our lips pressed together, and I felt her body trembling as she clung to my neck. I took one step and carried her to the sofa where we continued passionately kissing—I with my parka on and zipped and buttoned—well into the night.

During that entire time, neither of us uttered a word. Finally, I let her out of my embrace, stood up, walked to her door, and went down the stairs and into the street. Freezing rain was pouring down, but I was scarcely aware of it. I felt as if I was walking on clouds. When I got back to my room, Andre was sound asleep and snoring.

BY MORNING, THE STORM HAD PASSED and the weather had turned bright and sunny. As one of my weekend chores, I filled my laundry bag, balanced it on the handlebars of my bike, and began riding to the coin laundry nearby. As I neared Carol's house, I saw her standing at her front door talking to an older woman. I decided to pretend not to notice them and just pedaled past them when she called out to me. As I looked back at her, she smiled and gestured for me to come over to them.

I stopped in front of them and stayed on my bike while keeping my balance by resting my foot on her front step.

"Jack," she said, "I'd like you to meet my mother. She arrived from Chicago this morning."

Her mother then told me that ever since she had arrived, all Carol had done was tell her about me. I was so embarrassed that I could not say a word as I extended my hand to shake hers. Eventually I managed to say that it was nice to meet her.

Carol looked very happy and kept looking at me with a devilish smile. Finally she asked if I would like to come up for a cup of coffee. I thanked her but excused myself, telling her that I needed to do my laundry.

For almost two years, Carol and I had a very special relationship. I would often have dinner at her place and stay all night. (I guess her mother approved.)

IN THE SPRING OF 1959, AT THE END of my junior year, Carol told me that she had decided to finish her doctorate at the University of Chicago. She moved a few weeks later, and that summer I visited her once and stayed at her parents' home. She also came back to U of I occasionally to visit.

Besides her friendship, which I cherished immensely, she also gave me two gifts that I treasure and that remain inseparably part of me—my U of I class ring, which she gave me for my graduation a year after she had gone back to Chicago, and a sterling cross and chain from Marshall Field's in Chicago.

During our time together, my relationship with her underwent subtle changes due to my distant connections with Aida, my "official" girlfriend, and with Lili Nanajanian, whom I had met in 1952 after I became a Scout. She was the leader of the Ararat Girl Scouts, and I had developed a huge crush on her that developed into a serious romance.

Letters were the only way I could keep in touch with them because phone calls were too expensive, so I wrote to Aida in Tehran, where she was working, and to Lili in Italy, where she was studying at a music conservatory. Aida later went to Italy as well, and in the summer after my junior year, she surprised me by calling me and asking me to join her in Rome. I had to say no because I could not afford to go, but this created an irreparable breach between us. She broke off communicating with me, thus ending our long-distance relationship, and I never heard from her again.

Chapter 4

CIVIL ENGINEER IN TRAINING

On October 4, 1957, the Soviet Union launched the first Sputnik satellite. It was just weeks after we had arrived at U of I, and like American universities nationwide, our school began placing an urgent new emphasis on engineering and the sciences to catch up with the Soviets.

Programs and professors became more demanding. Undergraduate courses were upgraded to include graduate-level content, the grading of exams became more rigorous, and "A" grades were more difficult to come by. The U of I civil engineering department came under even more pressure to excel in order to maintain its glorious ranking as the number one program in the nation. And we students were challenged to keep up with the new pressures.

My friendship with Carol substantially reduced my anxiety regarding school social activities such as dating and partying, so I was able to concentrate not only on my coursework but also on ongoing research and development in structural engineering and construction materials at the Theoretical and Applied Mechanics Laboratory (TAMS), also known as the Talbot Laboratory. My classes in the design of reinforced concrete structures and highway engineering were held there, as were most of the advanced civil engineering classes.

With the enactment of the Federal Highway Act of 1956, the US Department of Transportation (DOT) began funding research and development for the design and construction of the planned national interstate highway network. U of I was the recipient of a large number of DOT R&D grants on the design of bridges that would be subjected to cyclic stress from heavy vehicular traffic. The proposed structures were to be constructed of steel, reinforced concrete, or a combination of the two.

The lab housed full-size bridge elements such as beams, slabs, and columns that had been fabricated for testing. Heavily instrumented concrete slabs were subjected to fatigue or cyclic stresses that simulated repetitive traffic loads, and the behavior of the slabs was monitored around the clock. Large numbers of cyclic loads resulted in the appearance of hairline cracks at different locations with different patterns. The measurements gathered by the instruments were compiled and analyzed as backup to be taken into consideration in the final design recommendations. This also provided useful data for predicting the safe life of highway elements.

In my laboratory classes on the strength of materials, I had observed that stress/strain measurements of 28-day-old concrete cylinders made from the same concrete batch varied greatly because the ingredients in fresh concrete—coarse aggregates of different sizes, shapes, and compositions, and mixed with sand, Portland cement, and water—were randomly distributed throughout each sample. This resulted in a nonuniform paste with its various ingredients distributed randomly throughout each specimen that hardened into a heterogeneous, brittle conglomerate.

In addition, concrete shrinks when it hardens, which results in microcracks. Under constant long-term loads, concrete becomes susceptible to creep, and in the absence of ductile reinforcing steel, it cannot withstand tensile stresses.

Every chance I had, I would go up to Talbot Lab's upper-floor balcony, which offered a bird's-eye view of the entire floor below, and observe the full-scale testing of reinforced concrete structural elements. It became clear to me that the different fracture patterns and locations that were being recorded were caused by the heterogeneous composition of the concrete, which prevented the creation of a uniform bond with the reinforcing steel.

I was very keen to discuss my observations with Professor Henry Maulton, who taught the course on the design of reinforced concrete fundamentals, and I finally had an opportunity to do so one day when the subject was conventional formulas for calculating bonds between concrete and steel. After he completed his lecture, I raised my hand and offered my observations and interpretations of what I had seen in Talbot Lab. When I then summed up by stating, "The applied safety factor in the formula on the board does not adequately address the issue," I could feel the uneasiness that I had created. Moments later, the professor showed me the door and asked me to refrain from attending his class in the future because as "top dog" I was taking up other students' time.

I was upset at being called a "top dog" because in Iran there is no worse insult than to be called a "dog." So I went out to the balcony and watched the activities on the lab floor below as I waited for the class to end. I wanted to ask the professor what I had done that he should call me a "dog."

When he emerged from the classroom, I followed him to his office,

Main entrance to the U of I Civil Engineering Department

where to my amazement he acknowledged that I had a good point and that he was impressed with my argument. However, he did not think that his class was an appropriate forum for discussing topics that undermined the textbooks and would cause confusion in the students' minds. He added that I did not have to attend his class any longer and that I could take the final exam only if I wanted to because my final grade would be an "A" regardless. He also told me the meaning of "top dog" in English, which reassured me.

Thanks to Dr. Maulton, I was given two part-time jobs at the lab. One had to do with preparing a footing model that rested on confined, compacted soil to measure the model's response to impact loads. The other was a very boring task of reducing raw data produced by the full-scale testing to develop design factors.

Being an extremely curious undergraduate, I was not satisfied with just trying to find out all I could about the projects being carried out in Talbot Lab. I also put together binders of articles regarding recent developments in the design and construction of roads, bridges, runways, and petroleum and petrochemical complexes that I clipped from civil engineering trade journals discarded by the library.

I kept wondering why the results of compressive strength tests were being used as the critical design parameter when the test specimens would actually fail in tension. I was not satisfied with the logic that applying safety factors compensated for the observed anomalies.

I HAVE NEVER FORGOTTEN THE WORDS of my last structural engineering professor: "One of the most important things you've learned during the past four years is where to look for the information you require to discharge your duties as a professional engineer—and what to look for."

I thought this odd because I expected that by the time I graduated, I would have all the knowledge and skills I needed to design buildings, bridges, and anything else that civil engineers design. My professor was absolutely correct, however. Graduating was just the first baby step toward becoming a practicing engineer.

Ultimately, the events and life experiences that follow engineering school are more important than the degree itself. And that all begins with one's first job, which most often determines the course of one's future career. This certainly held true in my own case.

After I graduated, I kept in touch with a number of U of I faculty members, including Dr. Nathan Newmark (Newmark Lab, built in 1967, was named for him) as well as Dr. Narbey Khachaturian, Dr. Moe Amin, and my friend Dr. Bijan Mohraz, as consultants for my major projects. Before his passing in 2009, Dr. Khachaturian nominated me for the U of I Distinguished Alumnus Award.

ONE OF THE REQUIRED CIVIL engineering courses was hands-on surveying techniques, taught at U of I's surveying camp, which was located at Lake Bemidji near Blackduck, Minnesota. I attended the camp in the summer of 1958. We were housed in barracks that had rows of army-style bunk beds, showers and toilet stalls, and we had our meals in a large mess hall.

The training included both day and night surveying using compasses for day surveying and star alignments at night. We were warned that when we were surveying at night, we should use our flashlights as little as possible or wear fine-meshed net bags over our heads and shoulders to avoid the swarms of mosquitoes that infested the area. The marks from their bites could last as long as a year. Still, night-time swimming in the lake was a favorite activity.

With my surveying camp classmates, Lake Bemidji, summer 1958.
I am in the front row, third from right.

We also took part in the traditional prank that heralded the arrival of U of I students—sneaking into the town late at night and covering the huge black duck that stood in the town center with white (washable) paint.

Senior Year

In the summer of 1960, Andre went back to Los Angeles to see Lilit. I stayed at U of I and enrolled in some summer classes so I could lighten my academic load in the fall and enjoy my last semester. In fact, I completed all the courses I needed for my bachelor of science degree in civil engineering by the end of the summer. However, Andre still had a few more courses to take. Also, he had injured his shoulder and would require surgery, which was scheduled for the fall, so I decided to stay and help him while also taking graduate courses in soil mechanics.

On the afternoon of the Fourth of July holiday, I drove to Lake of the Woods to escape the sizzling summer heat. The park was filled with families and children, and as I was looking for a spot to spread my beach towel, I ran into three Iranian students from Arizona who were also taking summer courses at U of I. They invited me to join them, so I spread my towel next to theirs on the grass and began chatting with one of them while the other two went down to the lake.

When they returned, one of them told me while drying his hair that

The ill-fated town duck

they had met three girls on the floating platform in the middle of the lake who had told them that they wanted to meet me. I was too far away to get a good look at the three young women, but I was also curious to know who wanted to meet me, so I swam out to the platform.

When I levered myself up onto it, the girls ignored me and continued chatting. "Hello," I finally said. "I was told that one of you wanted to meet me?" One of them replied icily, "I bet those two creepy guys told you that!"

I decided it was better to leave, so I apologized for having intruded on them and gently slid back into the water so as not to splash them. Then one of the three asked, "Do you mind if I swim back with you?" She was tall, slim, and attractive with a warm, friendly smile, and I replied, "No, not at all."

As we swam back together, I introduced myself and she told me that her name was Lynn and that she had come to U of I to spend the holiday with her friends. After that we seemed to have nothing more to say, and we finished our swim in silence.

We got out of the water and began walking back together but the path, which ran alongside a grassy picnic area, was only wide enough for one person at a time. It meandered through a landscaped area featuring a water wheel that was bordered on both sides with large, smooth boulders. Lynn stepped up onto the boulders and held out her hand to me so I could help her keep her balance and we could walk side by side.

When we reached the end of the path, I let go of her hand and turned to go look for my towel, but she pointed to a large vividly striped blanket nearby and asked me if I would like to sit and chat until her friends returned. We sat down and she told me that her last name was Kreuzberger, that she had completed her sophomore year at U of I in education, and that she would be returning to campus in the fall to start her junior year. She was spending the summer at her parents' home in Lansing, a small town about twenty miles south of Chicago, and working for a Buick dealership. She had driven her friends down in one of the dealership's cars that day.

Lake of the Woods, Illinois, summer 1960

Before I could tell her anything about myself, her friends returned from the lake and Lynn introduced us. I stood up, shook hands with them, and said I had to leave because I had an exam the next day. When I got back to my towel, the students from Arizona were long gone, and I was annoyed that I had missed the chance to tell them off for having made a bad impression on the girls.

THE SUMMER ENDED, ANDRE RETURNED from Los Angeles, and the U of I campus came alive again. A day or two before classes began, an Iranian student friend of mine, Darush Javedan, called to tell me about a party that weekend. He added that his girlfriend had told him to be sure to let me know that a Lynn Kreuzberger would also be there. For a moment, I drew a blank. Then Darush explained that both Lynn and his girlfriend lived in Wescoga House, a women's residence just a block from me, and gave me the number so I could call her there.

I called Lynn the next evening, and we agreed to meet at the mathematics library and then go for a drink. She showed up wearing a skirt and a red sweater and looking quite different than she had at our first meeting at Lake of the Woods.

We walked to a nearby tavern in Champaign. When the waitress arrived to take our order, Lynn asked me, "How about sharing a Coke?" I liked hearing that because I was not a drinker and did not care for people who drank excessively, so we shared a tall glass of Coke that the waitress brought with two straws. It was my turn to tell her about my background and to learn more about hers. The bar was full of loud students—many of them drunk—but by the time we got to the last sip of our Coke the place had quieted down and I realized that we had been talking for more than three hours. In fact, we had to hurry to get Lynn back to Wescoga before the midnight curfew warning, which consisted of turning the porch lights on and off three times. After that, no one was allowed back into the house.

The party that Friday was a noisy affair that included a lot of drinking and yelling that neither of us cared for. Lynn suggested that we call it a night and suggested that we take a day trip the next day to Allerton Park, which was located halfway between Champaign and the city of Decatur. I dropped her off and drove to my house relieved at not having had to spend more time at the noisy party.

The following morning, we drove to Allerton Park. I had never seen a more beautiful place in my life. The manicured landscaping of the 1,500-acre park, which featured graceful sculptures and buildings surrounded by lush vegetation as far as the eye could see, was mesmerizing for both of us. We spent the whole day walking and getting to know each other better, and returned home fairly tired.

From that day on, we met frequently after classes and sometimes were together until almost midnight, when we—along with other dating couples— would park in front of Wescoga House. We would all stay in our cars until the second warning light. Then all the car doors would fly open and the girls would rush up to the porch and into the house a split second before the porch light went off for the last time and the door was locked.

LYNN AND I WERE FAIRLY COMPATIBLE in many aspects except for our political leanings, which we tried to avoid discussing. A few days into the fall semester, Senator John F. Kennedy, the Democratic candidate for president, made a campaign stop at the campus. A large crowd showed up to hear him. I must have been one of the few who did not attend because, although I was not a US citizen and knew nothing about the political differences between the parties, I was still an unwavering supporter of Eisenhower and therefore a Nixon supporter.

That evening, Lynn could not stop talking about Kennedy's inspiring speech—blah, blah, blah. That turned my mood sour and led to our first quarrel. I did not want to hear any more about Kennedy and the Democratic Party, and we agreed never to talk about politics. With that issue settled, she and I enjoyed social activities, among them New Year's Eve in Chicago, when we celebrated the arrival of 1961 on a double date with Andre and Lilit.

However, marriage was not on my radar at all. I knew that I would be returning to Tehran shortly after the fall semester ended in February, and I was preoccupied with finding a job and reestablishing my relationships with friends and family after my almost five-year absence.

ACTUALLY, MY FELLOW STUDENTS from Iran considered my determination to return home unusual and odd because almost every Iranian student who came to study in the US wanted to stay. It was much more common to avoid going back at any cost by seeking opportunities to stay in the US permanently and become a citizen.

A number of legal options made it possible to extend student visas. Students could stretch out their undergraduate studies by carrying only the minimum number of academic units per semester, or they could continue studying for master's and doctoral degrees and then embark on postdoctoral research. Such tactics could stretch a student visa stay by about ten years.

Those who hoped to stay for a longer time (for instance, forever) could try to obtain full-time work with employers who were willing to petition the US government to grant permanent residency status. This could be followed by citizenship after having resided in the country for a specified number of years. However, many students chose to marry US citizens, which guaranteed citizenship in a relatively short period of time.

Whenever I would insist that I planned to return to Iran as soon as I got my bachelor's degree, my friends would remind me of all the advantages and job opportunities in America and would try to convince me that my decision to return to a developing country like Iran was wrong.

I had no doubt that what they were saying was true and that following their path would most likely lead to a brighter future for me and my whole family. But I had never been a follower, and also I felt strongly that this was a matter of honor and integrity. I was determined to keep my commitment by serving the country that had made it possible for me to obtain a university education. I also wanted to return to my family and friends. And there was one more reason: if I did not return, Mr. Aghassi, Andre's and my guarantor, stood to lose his home.

Chapter 5

DEBT OF HONOR
Home to Help My Country

So it was that in mid-February 1961 Lynn and I parted as friends and promised to write to each other after I returned to Iran, and Andre and I drove back to Los Angeles in my 1952 Chevrolet. He was moving back because he needed only a couple of elective courses to complete his civil engineering degree and had decided to take them in Los Angeles so he could be near Lilit.

Meanwhile, with my plans graven in stone, I already had my Los Angeles-Tehran plane ticket and was due to depart on Saturday, March 4, 1961. My parents had sent it to me less than a week after I requested it, and I would have a week or two to visit before leaving.

I drove the entire way because Andre had finally undergone his shoulder surgery and was still recuperating. We took Route 66, passing Burma Shave signs and small rural Midwest farmhouses.

Halfway to LA, we spent the night at the legendary Wigwam Motel in Holbrook, Arizona, where I mailed postcards to friends.

When we got back to LA, Andre stayed with Lilit's family in Burbank, and I stayed in a motel a few blocks away. Lilit was attending UCLA, and for the following two weeks, I drove Andre around during the day so he could look for work while he finished his last few courses.

The motel was a typical Southern California "bungalow court," with the rooms, all of which had striking red doors, lined up on both sides of a long courtyard with a rose garden and other plants. The rooms were starkly finished with a twin bed, a luggage rack, a scratched nightstand with a heavy black telephone squeezed next to a lamp with a crumpled shade, a heavily used copy of the Yellow Pages (and a never-used Bible in the nightstand drawer), and an old black-and-white TV with a rabbit-ear antenna.

The room was most notable for the old brown enamel wall heater on the wall opposite the door because it seemed to also serve the adjoining room. When I turned out my light, I could see the pilot light glowing through a tiny round glass "porthole," which also allowed light from the next room to shine into mine. That opening also made it impossible for me to avoid hearing noises coming from the next room, and throughout my stay I experienced frequent and audible proof that rooms were available for hourly rates. However, the weekly rate was less than ten dollars. I could still barely afford that because I had no job, and also, I wanted to spend what little money I had on souvenirs to take home to my family as well as some hard-to-find toiletry items, such as deodorant and an electric shaving kit for myself.

FRIDAY, MARCH 3, 1961, WAS MY last day in the United States. That evening, I had a farewell dinner with the Bassentzians. After dinner, I bade them farewell and Andre and I walked back to my motel. I stopped at the office and asked the manager to give me a wakeup call at six in the morning. He, no doubt accustomed to avoiding lingering eye contact with the fleeting patrons of his establishment, merely nodded, waved his hand, and continued reading a well-thumbed paperback.

After Andre left, I entered my room and was greeted by the last gasps of lovemaking next door. Soon after, I felt the adjoining wall shake as the door of the next room slammed shut. In a split second, all was quiet.

Feeling both melancholy and excited, I began neatly packing my meager belongings and purchases in the same suitcase and carry-on bag that I had brought with me five years earlier. I felt anticipation about the adventure ahead but sadness at leaving everything else behind. I remembered having felt the same way when I had left Iran, and now here I was, moving on again, from the life that I had forged in America back to my homeland.

My packing finished, all that remained was to get some sleep. But as it turned out, packing had been the easy part. By the time I went to bed, it was past eleven. However, I could not sleep. After tossing and turning in the squeaky motel bed, I turned on the TV. Unfortunately, this led to more stirring because I kept having to get out of bed and struggle unsuccessfully to adjust the reception. Eventually, I gave up, turned out the light, and let sleep overtake me.

Sometime later, I woke up. I did not know the time. The room was not completely dark because light from the next room, which the last guests had failed to turn off when they left, was filling my room with a faint glow that reflected off the wood floor and painted walls. I caught sight of my suitcase and bag. After gazing at them for a few minutes, I began pondering my decision to return to Iran. Was I doing the right thing after all? But I soon realized that I still felt as I had when my fellow students had tried to persuade me to stay... No, it was time to return.

THE NEXT MORNING, ANDRE AND Lilit drove me to LAX in my car, which I had given to him. As I left them and headed for the passport control booth, I turned one last time and saw them holding hands and still waving good-bye to me. (Soon after my return to Tehran, I learned to my surprise that Lilit and Andre had broken off their engagement and ended their relationship later that very day.)

I handed my passport to the immigration agent, who took the obligatory good look at me, compared it with my photo, stamped it with an exit date, and wished me a good trip. I checked that my flight, again on SAS, was on schedule. I had plenty of time to kill, so I began to look around.

Much had changed since my arrival almost five years earlier. The old "small-town"-style terminal was now a futuristic-looking complex of buildings and facilities. Jets, which I had not seen before, were landing and taking off.

When we boarded and I took my window seat, I glimpsed the Theme Building, which looked like a flying saucer standing on four legs. Soon the engines started to roar and our jet, a Boeing 707, rolled forward faster and faster until it became airborne. I had never flown on a jet before—our flight to the US had been on a propeller-driven DC-7—and I was not re-assured by the absence of propellers on the 707. As it gained altitude above the Pacific Ocean and turned east, the land features below shrank, playing hide-and-seek with us as the plane passed through patchy clouds, and I started to relax.

Moments after I sat back and closed my eyes, one of the flight atten-dants offered me some orange juice. I opened my tray table and said, "Yes, please," set the glass on the tray, and smiled, remembering hearing the same words when Andre and I had taken off from Tehran five years earlier. On that flight, I had known so little English that I had reached, without daring to utter a word, for the first glass on the flight attendant's tray when she had held it out to me.

At that moment, I became aware of the transformation I had under-gone. It was not just that I was now five years older. It was also that I had been away from my family and friends for all that time and had become used to student life in America without actually trying to do so. I felt caught up in mixed emotions—sad to be leaving the US for good but excited that in twenty-four hours I would be seeing my family and friends again after so many years.

And as my past rose up in my memory, I wondered, "Exactly who am I? Who is Jack?"

PART TWO

FLASHBACK
Growing Up in Tehran (1934–1956)

Chapter 6

SURVIVORS
My Parents' Story

YES, WHO WAS I? I was Njdeh, the son of an Armenian couple who met as children in an orphanage established by an American Presbyterian church to help Armenian children whose parents had perished in the Turkish genocide of 1915. My parents had named me Njdeh after the well-known Armenian freedom fighter, Garegin Njdeh.

My father, Hagob Hagobian, was born in 1908 into a family of farmers and raisin growers in Khanbabakhan, a suburb of Gardbad in the greater Urmie (Urmia) area of northwest Iran near Kordestan (Kurdistan).

In 1915, the Muslim Kurds, emboldened by their Turkish brethren's plans to annihilate the Christian Armenians in Anatolia, regularly attacked nearby Armenian villages, massacred the farmers and their families, stole their livestock, and set entire villages on fire. That year, my father, then only seven years old, saw his parents murdered in just such an attack. Horrified at the sight of their burning corpses and the flames advancing through the village, he grabbed his brothers' hands and ran. They joined the other panic-stricken villagers, who were scattering in all directions to make it harder for the ferocious sword-wielding Kurdish horsemen to round them up and massacre them. Some of the survivors fled on foot toward the city of Kermanshah. Many stayed there, while others continued on to Baghdad.

In the confusion, my father led his brothers east toward the city of Tabriz, where the Presbyterians found them huddled in a ditch and rescued them.

Those same missionaries also found my mother, Arashalous Harutunian, near the border of Iran and Azerbaijan. She was several years younger than my father, but I never learned from her or from anyone else how she managed to survive.

When my father turned sixteen, he left his brothers at the orphanage and went looking for work so he could support himself. His first job was as a carpet weaver in Tabriz, and at eighteen he became an assistant truck driver.

New Year's Day (1924) at the orphanage in Tabriz.
My father, Hagob Hagobian, is in the top row at the far left.

Nine years later, still a truck driver, he married my mother and they moved to Tehran, where I was born in 1934.

As a long-haul driver, my father was absent from home for long periods, and my mother was the primary family disciplinarian. She managed the household and laid down the rules for me and for my sister, Rima, nine years my junior, based on authoritarian principle that "children should be seen and not heard."

Due in part to the education that my parents had received in the orphanage, my mother became a self-taught poet whose poetry was published in Tehran's Armenian newspapers. She also had a keen interest in literature, music, the arts, and other cultural pursuits. She and my father both desired and unselfishly strove to help us achieve the advantages that they had been deprived of, although they differed in their aspirations for me. My father wanted me to earn degrees in medicine and engineering, while my mother wanted me to excel in literature and music. Also, they both wanted me to be an exemplary Armenian nationalist in Iran, but they lacked the education and childrearing skills to nurture and guide me so I could fulfill their dreams.

Their aspirations for me were also thwarted by my intense curiosity, starting at an early age, about how things work and how objects move and break, and by my eagerness to fix malfunctioning or broken items. However, by giving me my first erector set, a Meccano construction set, when I was six, they saved many clocks from being disassembled and then reassembled only to never to work again.

I also suffered from being left-handed in a society where this was considered only a bad habit that needed to and could be corrected by constantly slapping the left hand and placing the pencil in the right hand. Finally, I was hampered by dyslexia, which of course was not a diagnosable medical condition at the time and was therefore easily mistaken for a lack of intelligence.

My mother, Arashalous Harutunian (left), a few days before her wedding.

Chapter 7

CHILDHOOD IN THE COMPOUND
Days of Peace and War

FOR THE FIRST THIRTEEN YEARS of my life, we lived in a two-story brick house in an old gated compound that had probably been built when the property was still outside Tehran's city walls.

The entrance to the compound, which was off Estakhr Avenue, a main street, stood at the end of a short unpaved segment of an alley that passed three houses and narrowed at a heavy wooden gate and a square passageway so wide that a sedan could be driven through it and into the compound. Thirteen families lived in the compound. Ten were Armenian families who had children, mostly boys and mostly my age. Our house was the only one that had direct access to the outside of the compound, through a main door next to the wooden gate. The gate remained open most of the time, and the ceiling of the passageway was actually the floor of one of the rooms in our house.

The houses in the compound were owned by a wealthy orthodox Muslim merchant who rented the units to Christian families. The residences were connected to each other by freestanding common walls. Each had its own small backyard with a flowerbed, a few fruit trees, and a shallow pond. There was also a common underground reservoir where the compound's nonpotable water was stored. On warm summer evenings, we would dine and sleep in the backyard while listening to our neighbors' radios, which they cranked up for the benefit of those who did not have their own. Because Tehran had only one radio station, all three of the compound's radios would be tuned to it.

THE ALLEY THAT LED TO OUR COMPOUND was our playground where we played hide-and-seek, soccer, and improvised baseball-like games. The tenants in the three houses that lined the alley included an Armenian family, and a pediatrician, Dr. Keshavarz, who was also head of the Tudeh Communist party in Tehran. The house directly adjacent to ours was rented by a well-to-do Jewish family that had escaped to Iran from Poland before the start of World War II.

Each day, vendors of all kinds would arrive leading caravans of donkeys loaded with live chickens, fresh fruits, vegetables, kerosene for cooking, and ice in the summer. They would announce their arrival by calling out loud, melodic jingles to alert the women of the compound.

On hot summer days, we children were always eager to see the iceman because our favorite activity was to cool ourselves down with the chunks of ice that would fly into the air all around us as he used his pick to chop his large blocks of ice into the sizes ordered by his customers.

By the time I was seven or so, I became fascinated by the vendors who offered services such as repairing utensils and household goods, sharpening knives, and making quilts and mattresses out of washed, fluffed-up cotton and wool that they would stuff into large cotton sacks.

And for us children, there was sometimes entertainment. Our favorite was the *shahr-e farang*, a mechanical peepshow. Each month the *shahr-e farangee*, "the man with the peepshow," would arrive carrying a large, four-legged metal box on his back. He would unload it in a corner of the alley and wait while we gathered around and held out the coins doled out to us by our parents.

The top of the box had a small peephole in its center flanked by two small metal towers that each concealed a metal crank attached to a vertical shaft that extended down inside the box. The front of the box had three four-inch-wide peepholes fitted with magnifying lenses, and housed inside the box was a roll of color prints of old paintings and photographs of real and imaginary lakes, castles, kings, queens, wild animals, and centuries-old battle scenes interspersed with classic paintings by Rubens, Rembrandt, and other artists. The roll of images wrapped around the two shafts and were illuminated by four candles, two on each side, inside the box. Pairs of metal flaps just behind the peepholes blocked our view of the magical images until we paid our "admission."

After the *shahr-e farangee* accepted our coins, we would take turns stooping or squatting in front of the peepholes and cupping our hands around them to keep the outside light from interfering with the light from the candles inside the box. Then, in his melodic voice, he would announce, "Now behold the wonders of the world!" and open the flaps that concealed the images.

Positioning himself so he could look down into the box through the peephole on its top, he would begin speaking, weaving the sequence of images passing before our eyes into exciting stories. Occasionally, a concerned

Looking into the *shahr-e farang* (peepshow)

mother would rush over and yank her child away while screaming about the dangers of looking into the filthy, germ-infested peepholes. Within moments, though, another of us would hand over our coins and grab the ejected kid's spot.

By the time we turned twelve or so, we started going to the movies and left the peepshow to the younger children. But my first view of the world outside Iran was shaped by the images I saw through those tiny peepholes and the tales told by the *shahr-e farangee.*

HOWEVER, MY FAVORITE VENDOR of all was the *chin-e band*—the china restorer.

In those days, delicate china from Europe and especially from Germany was the most fashionable tableware in Iran. Because World War II put an end to exports of German china to Iran and elsewhere, china pieces, being hard to get, were treated as valuable antiques to be taken out only on special occasions and handled with the utmost care. But breakage inevitably occurred when pieces were being set out, put back into cabinets, or dropped while being used or washed.

The housewives of the compound would save every precious fragment until the *chin-e band*'s next visit. When they heard his jingle, they would bring out the pieces and ask him whether the china could be repaired and how much it would cost.

These encounters always followed the same pattern. The *chin-e band* would state his price. The housewife would protest, "You must be crazy! I could buy new pieces for a lot less!" He would reply, "Okay, lady, how much do you want to pay?" She would make a ridiculously low counteroffer. He would pretend that he was offended and make as if to leave. This song-and-dance would continue until both sides eventually agreed on a price, whereupon the housewife would hand over the broken pieces.

And at that point I would find a place where I could squat with my chin resting on my knees and, mesmerized, follow the *chin-e band's* every move.

After spreading out a three-foot-square piece of gray cloth on the ground, he would remove his trousers, revealing his pajama-bottom-like underwear, fold the trousers into a pillow, and sit down cross-legged with his legs folded under him.

Then he would reach into his bag and take out a wooden bow with a loose string fastened to each end, and a pencil-sized wooden shaft with a sharp metal pin at one end and a swivelling knob at the other.

I would watch fascinated as he wrapped the loose string with two loops around the middle of the shaft. This assembly was a drill. The sharp pin at the end of the shaft was his drill bit, and the movement of the bow created the sharp spinning movement of the shaft that allowed the pin to bite into the china fragments. He would also set out his other supplies on the cloth in front of him—a coil of thin, flat wire, a small bowl in which he would pour some white powder, a pair of needle-nosed pliers, a miniature hammer, and a small empty bottle. He would hand it to me and order me to fill it with water.

He then began the repairs by spreading out all of the broken pieces and matching them with one another by using the broken edges and the decorative patterns to guide him.

After laying out all of the fragments like the pieces of a big jigsaw puzzle, he would anchor the two largest matched-up pieces between his bare feet, pick up his bow-and-shaft assembly, and, by moving the bow from one end of the stick to the other, proceed to drill two rows of tiny holes along the entire length of the fracture. Each set of holes was directly opposite to the other, and the sets of holes were spaced one centimeter apart along the entire length of the fracture.

His next step was to take the flat wire and use his needle-nosed pliers to bend a centimeter-long piece of wire into u-shaped "staple." He would place the ends of the "staple" into one set of holes and pound it in using the tiny hammer. Singing as he went along, he would fall into a machine-like rhythm of drilling, cutting, and hammering hundreds of staples into the drilled holes, which then lined up like the teeth of a zipper.

After stapling all of the broken pieces together, he would create a grout-like paste by adding water to the white powder and then fill in the hairline gaps between the joined pieces by rubbing the paste into the rows of staples with his index fingers. Setting that piece aside, he would then move on to the next.

His final step was to fill all of the repaired pieces with water to make sure that he had sealed all of the cracks. He prided himself that should one of his repaired pieces ever be dropped again, it would crack along new "fault lines" and never along breaks that he had repaired.

As the *chin-e band* was repairing and stacking up the restored china with dizzying speed, I would barrage him with questions. But the only responses I ever got were either "You ask too many questions, kid!" or "Why don't you go play?" One time, though, toward the end of his work—perhaps he was getting tired—he made my day by asking me to search for a plain, undecorated china fragment in the heap in front of him. When I handed him the missing fragment, his "Well done, kid" emboldened me to keep on pelting him with questions, but he remained as unresponsive as ever.

The skills of the *chin-e band* remained in demand throughout the country many years after the World War II ended. Today, of course, "superglues" that can bond broken porcelain and other objects instantly are available in every supermarket and drugstore. How was I to know that decades later my childhood observations of this *chin-e band*'s skills would provide a foundation for my getting involved in the conservation and protection of rare art objects and antiquities?

Wartime

I was five years old in 1939 when World War II began and eleven when it ended in 1945. Although Iran was not a battle theater, the war cast its dark shadow over our daily lives. When I think back to those days, my memories seem like the silent images I used to see in the *shahr-e farang*, and most of those images are of our life in the compound.

SOME OF MY MOST VIVID MEMORIES are of the "nights when the water would arrive."

Tehran, set against the backdrop of the perpetually snow-capped Alborz mountain range fifty miles to the north, stands on alluvium that washed down from the mountains over millennia, leaving boulders, coarse rocks, and aggregates at the foot of the range and finer soils farther some miles away to the south, and creating arid flatlands and fertile plains.

Even today, snowmelt from the Alborz range remains the main source of nonpotable water for both the city's residents and for the agricultural industry to the south. Until the 1950s, when the present-day network of dams, reservoirs, and distribution systems was completed, an ingenious system of underground tunnels called *qanats* transported groundwater to the city and to the arid southern lowlands.

When the surface water reaches the city, it is channeled into narrow, shallow concrete-lined gutters called *jubs* that line both sides of the streets and separate them from the sidewalks. Rainwater also flows into the *jubs*, which in effect are storm drains although foreign visitors often mistake them for open sewers.

During my childhood, potable water was delivered every other day by the *aabee*, or "water man," who would arrive on a horse-drawn carriage that held a large metal barrel filled with water from springs next to the Shah's palaces and refill the large pottery water jugs brought out by the women. But in those days, the *jubs* were the only way that the city's residents could obtain nonpotable mountain runoff for other household needs.

Every two months at midnight, the city would distribute the runoff to neighborhoods through the network of *jubs*, which divided the city into blocks and were connected to residences by clay pipes. The water would flow into underground storage reservoirs in each home. It was later pumped into cisterns mounted on the rooftops and then fed by gravity into the pipes that supplied the home.

Like all the other kids in our compound, I looked forward eagerly to the nights when the water would arrive. While our parents kept watchful eyes on us as they too waited while socializing with the neighbors, we would play until early morning instead of going to bed at dusk as usual.

At about midnight, our excited shrieks would herald the arrival of the water into the neighbourhood through the *jubs*. As the water flowing through the *jub* reached each house or compound, a wooden gate would be lowered to block the flow, diverting it into the clay pipes that fed each house.

After each house received its allotment, another makeshift wooden gate would be lowered into the jub to block any more water from flowing to it. The continuously flowing water would then rise, spill into the street and back into the *jub*, and flow into the next compound downstream from us.

It was rumored that on water nights, serious fights would sometimes break out between neighbors and that people would even fight to the death over water supplies. These skirmishes came to the attention of the then monarch, Reza Shah Pahlavi.

REZA SHAH WAS A LEGEND—a modern, authoritarian ruler who had succeeded in establishing security in Persia after centuries during which the country had been a patchwork of different tribes and powerful land owners. Judging by the photographs I saw in magazines, he was a larger-than-life figure—a gigantic, dark-complexioned man with a majestic moustache and a forbidding, no-nonsense expression who sported a black cape and full-length black boots.

Late one hot summer water night while we kids were running around playing as usual, the adults' usual loud talk and laughter died in a sudden, ominous silence so frightening that I hid behind my dad and clung to his legs—because standing right in front of him was the towering figure of the Shah. He was wearing the cape and boots of the photographs, and his white teeth, white mustache, and eyebrows glowed eerily in the moonlight.

"Is all well?" he asked my dad, whose tongue-tied, heavily accented "Yes, sir" was barely audible.

As the Shah nodded and slowly walked away, no one moved or uttered a sound. And when I went to bed on that night, I was still so frightened that I hid under a heavy blanket, even though I spent the entire night sweltering.

IN 1941, WHEN I WAS SEVEN, Reza Shah was deposed by Britain and moved to Mauritius. A year later, he was moved again to South Africa, where he died in Johannesburg in 1944.

The days and weeks after his departure were tumultuous, with widespread rumors that mobs were organizing to attack and loot homes and businesses.

Everyone in our compound was so panic-stricken that the men decided to close the wooden gate. However, when it came to security, our house was the weak link. Because our front door opened onto the alley, all it would take would be two men at most pushing their way through our front door to allow the rest of the mob to follow them into our compound.

To reinforce the door against what we all feared might be an imminent attack, the men stacked stores of firewood from several of the residences behind it. Still, although it would now be slightly more difficult to breach the door—perhaps requiring four or six rioters instead of just two—it remained vulnerable.

Stronger tactics were called for, so the small bathroom window above our front door became the strategic front line of defense. Led by my dad, the men of the compound (perhaps influenced by movie sequences in which they had seen fortresses being attacked) decided to set pots of boiling water and oil near the window to pour onto any attackers.

Meanwhile, our Jewish neighbors asked if they could store a large box, which presumably contained their most precious belongings, at our house.

That night, I was excited to see the large pots of water and oil heating up on a battery of kerosene stoves of different sizes and shapes that had been moved into the bathroom while my dad and a number of the neighbors, all in fighting spirit, bustled around planning how they would dump the hot liquids when the mob arrived.

With my usual curiosity, I was dying to ask how they were going to dump anything out of the tiny window since the pots were too big to fit through it, but I assumed that my dad had figured all that out.

By daybreak, however, boredom set in. The mob never materialized, and eventually the defenders of the compound went to bed. By noon, the men began dismantling their weapons, and by the next day my mother had returned the box to our neighbors. Then the wooden gate was unlatched and we kids went back to playing hopscotch in the alley.

EVEN NOW, DECADES LATER, "the balloon saga" is one memory of the compound that still makes me smile every time I think of it.

I was probably six or seven the day that Armik Aghabekian, the oldest kid in our gang of seven, came out of his house carrying a red balloon. At that time, balloons were all imported, and most were of such inferior quality that they popped almost as soon as you touched them. This is exactly what happened when one boy innocently reached out and touched Armik's balloon despite his attempts to keep it out of reach. Armik flew into a screaming rage and began chasing the rest of us, who scattered trying to escape.

The youngest of us, Sevada Megerdichian, who was no older than five, dared to approach Armik and told him that there were a lot of balloons in his house and that if Armik would stop crying, he would bring out one balloon for each of us.

Armik quieted down and Sevada ran home. He returned with a handful of small, square packets that he handed out to all of us. He then tore open his packet, pulled out a soft white circular object, unrolled it, and blew it up. We were thrilled to see that it instantly turned into a two-foot-long white balloon, and soon we were all running around waving our balloons in the air like kites and screaming with joy. These were not the usual inferior balloons. They seemed able to handle all the air we could blow into them.

Shortly before noon, Sevada's dad drove into the compound in his two-door black Ford. But when he saw us waving our balloons, he stopped short and began pounding his hands on the steering wheel. Meanwhile, we ran over and began circling the car—until he flung the car door open, stepped out, and grabbed Sevada by the back of his neck.

"Where did you get those?" he thundered in a voice so stern that we all froze.

Sevada, wincing with pain, replied, "From the drawer next to your nightstand."

At that, his father ordered us to hand over all of our balloons and dragged Sevada into their house.

When we kids all came outside again after our usual noon naps, Sevada was very somber and silent. Since none of our parents had shown any reaction to our tale of his father's rude behavior, we chalked the incident up as another of the unaccountable behaviors that grownups routinely engaged in, and we forgot all about it.

It wasn't until several years later when I was in my teens that I learned what the white "balloons" really were.

MR. MEGERDICHIAN'S CAR WAS ONE of the rare personal vehicles in Tehran. About the only time we would see more than three or four cars going the same direction in the streets was on special occasions such as weddings or funerals. Due to the lack of public transportation, most residents got around the city by hiring horse-drawn carriages.

When not in use, these carriages, called *doroshke*, would be lined up at the major intersections, where the drivers would wait for customers. The end of Estakhr Avenue, near our compound, was a *doroshke* station, and when my parents needed one, I would run to the line of carriages, get on the first one, and ride back to my house so my parents could take it.

There were different types of *doroshkes*. Some were pulled by two horses and featured closed passenger compartments, decorated wheels, and shiny lanterns on either side of the driver's bench. The less attractive ones had only one horse. It was the luck of the draw which kind of *doroshke* would be the first in line.

Some of the older sections of the main streets were paved with cobblestones, and the rhythmic clop-clopping of the horses' shoes on them was magical, especially late at night. However, the cobblestones often caused the horses to slip and fall, which resulted in cuts and sometimes serious injuries to passengers, drivers, and horses alike.

Unfortunately, the wartime food shortages affected not just the people but also the horses. Bread was rationed, and so was feed for the horses. Over time, the two-horse *doroshkes* began to disappear, and the horses that remained in service grew noticeably thinner. As malnutrition took its toll, the horses fell more often, and sometimes after they fell, they could not get up and simply died on the streets.

Chapter 8

MY EDUCATION BEGINS

In 1941, my formal education began on two
fronts—the first of thirteen years of academic studies, and, unfortunately,
seven years of violin lessons.

One day when I was seven, my mother came home with a German-
made violin and informed me that I was to begin taking lessons with Rubik
Grigorian, a famous Armenian-Iranian and violinist. Like many parents,
mine believed that music lessons were proof that a child's parents were
cultured people who were committed to raising cultured children as well.
And, as I would soon learn was also true in school, some students eventually
excelled and came to be considered prodigies.

It was customary for boys to study violin and girls, piano. I was never
asked whether I wanted to play violin, or, later on, whether I liked playing
it, and if I had had my choice, I would have studied piano, not violin.

My mother's decision saddled me with being forced to try to play
an instrument better suited to the right-handed. Still, when I saw my
violin for the first time, I was enthralled by the beauty and intricacy of its
construction—the thin, gracefully curved wood of the body and the four
strings stretched tightly over the bridge.

I spent every day until my first lesson taking it out of its case, polishing
it and tightening and loosening the strings, and I did the same with the
bow. I had seen people play the violin, and I tried to mimic them by holding
mine in my right hand, sliding the bow over the strings, and moving my
fingers on them at random. This of course resulted in many strange and
raucous noises.

My favorite string was the farthest left one, which was the heaviest of
the four and was wrapped with thin silver wire. When plucked, it vibrated
visibly. I also noticed that when I moved my fingers along it or slid the
handle of a knife along it toward the bridge, the vibration became less
visible and the sound rose to a higher pitch. However, sliding the bow

along the same string did not change the pitch. I was equally fascinated by the bow and the shiny screw at its end that tightened and loosened the bundle of white horsehair stretched over it.

ON THE DAY OF MY FIRST LESSON, my mother accompanied me to Grigorian's apartment. One room was dedicated to music lessons. It held a black baby grand piano, and I was struck by the framed sketches of old men who, I was told, were famous composers named "Schubert" and "Mendelssohn" as well as by a plaster mask of Beethoven that hung on the wall and a bust of Mozart on the piano.

The first thing that Grigorian did was take my violin out of its case, inspect it, comment good-naturedly, "Someone's been tampering with this," and move the chin rest from the right side to the left side of the violin. He was right. I had moved the rest from the left to the right. He began tuning the strings, and, once satisfied with the sound, placed the violin in my left hand. This shocked me because at home I had of course held it in my right hand with the bow in my left. He then positioned my chin on the rest and proceeded to bend my head left and right like a photographer looking for the best angle before snapping a picture.

By the time he finished freezing my body, hands, and fingers in a most awkward and contorted position, I was perspiring profusely and sweat was dripping from my fingers onto the fingerboard. Grigorian told my mother that I should spend the time until my next lesson doing nothing but practicing holding the violin in the proper position.

However, she became visibly upset when I fired a barrage of technical questions at him, asking what the bow hair was made of, why I could not hold the bow in my left hand, why the position of the bow did not change the note, at which point she broke in and apologized for my rudeness.

Grigorian responded politely that the bowstrings were made of horsehair and that he did not know why changing the position of the bow did not change the note whereas changing the finger position did. He added, "One does not need to know these things to become a violinist."

On our way home, my mother dragged me along by one of my hands while I tried to hang on to the violin case tucked under my other arm, and berated me for having embarrassed her in front of the eminent teacher. "He must have thought I have an idiot for a son!" she kept reproaching me throughout our entire walk—except when we would pass someone she knew. Then she would smile and greet the acquaintance as if she and I were simply out on a pleasant mother-and-son stroll.

I endured Grigorian's classes, which were torture, for the next five years. He never allowed me to ask any technical questions, and my parents constantly ridiculed me because I never gave solo recitals like the other young "prodigies" they knew. To please them and get them off my back, I did play in the violin sections of a number of orchestras that accompanied choral group performances at Armenian cultural functions because the crudeness of my technique (which was due to my lack of practice) was not noticeable.

Ironically, my lack of interest in the violin was accompanied by my absolutely pitch-perfect ear, which helped me to consistently produce the correct notes. I could whistle classical pieces after hearing them only a couple of times, and one of my favorites was the legendary Jascha Heifetz's recording of Pablo Sarasate's "Zigeunerweisen," which I could reproduce note for note by whistling.

After Rima was born, I started to hope that she would deflect my parents' attention away from me. Also, they would probably buy a piano for her and I would be able to stop playing violin. Hope springing eternal, I did not mind waiting for a few years for that welcome day to arrive.

MEANWHILE, I FARED LITTLE BETTER at school than I did playing violin. My education began at Mehr, a private elementary school that was affiliated with the same American Presbyterian Church that had established the orphanage where my parents had been brought up. The student body was made up predominantly of Muslim and Armenian Christian students along with a handful of Jewish children. It was also coeducational and equally divided between boys and girls.

Our days began with morning worship, which was required (as was participation in the school's Christmas plays) of all students, no matter what their faith. This assembly included the singing of hymns translated into Farsi from English hymn books, a sermon and the reading of Bible verses by the school principal, and finally a loud recitation of the Lord's Prayer.

All of the Muslim students in the student body came from high-ranking Iranian military families who were driven to and from school in large fancy cars and had their lunches delivered to them each noon by uniformed grunts who would arrive carrying stacks of metal pots containing hot Persian dishes that filled the air with wonderful aromas. The soldiers would go to the mess hall, set out china plates and utensils on the long tables, and wait while the children ate their lunches. Afterward, the soldiers would clean up and take everything back.

The Christian students were mainly Armenians and lived within walking distance of the school. Most of the time, we would walk home for lunch. However, on cold and rainy days, we would bring sandwiches and join the Muslim students in the mess hall, where we would munch on our cold sandwiches while eyeing their hot meals with great envy.

One day, though, a Muslim student named Parviz who was one grade behind me offered to trade his dish of steaming rice and its sauce, a stew-like mix of lamb, vegetables and spices for my sandwich. I did not hesitate for a moment. I handed over my sandwich and dug into the heavenly food. The crowded mess hall was noisy, and all the other kids were too busy talking and laughing to notice that the sandwich he was eating contained pork, which was of course forbidden by both Islam and Judaism. From that day on, whenever the weather was rainy or cold, Parviz would ask me for my sandwiches. He even knew the names of different cold cuts and would ask me to bring his favorites to school.

Parviz stood out among the students because he had very dark skin, bright white teeth, pinkish skin on his palms and the soles of his feet, and kinky jet-black hair. I was so intrigued by his hair that after we became friends, I would try to rumple it, but without success. He was tolerant enough to never object. And though I was such a curious kid, for some reason I never wondered why he was so dark when his sister, who also attended Mehr, had light skin and long, straight hair. At the time, I had no idea that black people lived anywhere except in Africa, and I did not realize that I had actually met a black person before until I arrived in the United States.

ALTHOUGH BOYS AND GIRLS ATTENDED classes together until the end of fourth grade, we were taught separately during our final two years.

By the time the girls reached fifth grade, they had already started to mature and looked very different from the younger girls—sophisticated, mysterious, and not particularly friendly. Those qualities only became more apparent once they reached sixth grade. Most remained unapproachable, but one girl named Jaleh stood out because of both her looks and her flirtatious manner, especially with the teachers in the schoolyard during recesses.

Because of Tehran's elevation, snow often fell during the winter. I always found the snowy streets picturesque and quiet. The only noise I could hear as I walked under the rows of barren trees, their boughs sagging under the weight of the snow, was the squeaking of the freshly fallen flakes as they were compressed by my shoes.

Mehr had a tradition of greeting arriving students and teachers by throwing clumps of snow at them. I have indelible memories of the schoolgirls arriving in their shiny black rubber boots and colorful scarves, and of my friends and me gossiping about how much the male teachers liked throwing snowballs at Jaleh. Instead of running away like the other girls, she would stand in the schoolyard and shriek in simulated outrage while shaking the snow from her flowing black hair.

MY DYSLEXIA, COMBINED WITH my uncontrolled curiosity, made me a mediocre student. Because my disability made me a slow reader, I had to read exam questions multiple times before I could grasp them. The result was that I often failed to finish in the time allowed.

Because of my unrecognized learning disabilities, my parents were convinced that not only had I been born with low intelligence, I was also lazy. Unfortunately for me, most of their friends had apparently been blessed with "straight A" children, and those proud parents never failed to show off their progeny's report cards and medals to my parents—and in my presence—on every possible social occasion.

I of course dreaded these situations, but my parents, hoping that the prodigies' achievements would awaken my competitive spirit and spur me to improve my grades, always forced me to attend. Their hopes were never fulfilled because I had no desire to compete with those kids, whom I considered uninteresting.

Instead, trapped at the dining table while boring subjects like schoolwork were being discussed, I would spin saltshakers and other small objects on the table. As they slowed down and spun more and more slowly, they would start to wobble, and I would try to predict if they would fall over or stop in an upright position. Ignored by my parents, who were awestruck by the outstanding grades achieved by their friends' offspring, I would then pour out some of the contents of the containers and try to predict what the effects would be when I set the container in motion again.

Totally absorbed in my experiments, I was oblivious not only to the occasional pitying glances that my parents' friends would give them but also to the recurring barrages of questions from the adults as to why I could not be more like their super-kids.

MY ACADEMIC DEFICIENCIES AND DIFFICULTIES reached a crisis point on my first day of fifth-grade math class.

At Mehr, the "blackboards" were actually unfinished black-painted plywood sheets affixed to the walls, while the chalk consisted of irregularly shaped lumps that made low-pitched scraping sounds whenever the teachers wrote. It would also disintegrate into dust every time the teachers tried to emphasize a point by tapping on the board. In the course of the class, the chalk marks would grow thicker and thicker, the blackboard would turn into a "grayboard," the words would become indistinguishable despite all of the teacher's attempts to wipe down the board with a felt eraser, and the teacher's hands and clothes would end up covered with the white dust. After each class, the board had to be wiped down with a wet cloth.

The teacher of fifth-grade math was Dr. Larudi, a well-dressed man with meticulous manners who was known to have studied child psychology in the United States. (He was also the most enthusiastic thrower of snowballs at Jaleh, which reinforced our envious childish belief that there was something special between the two.)

On our first day of class, Dr. Larudi positioned himself in front of the pristine blackboard and pulled a white cigarette out of his pocket. When he proceeded to write on the board with it, we immediately realized that the "cigarette" was actually a piece of chalk the likes of which we had never seen before. The marks he made were clear, crisp, and uniform in thickness, and there was no dust.

However, some of the marks he made created an excruciating screech. This diverted my attention from what he was explaining because I started to wait for the next screech while wondering what was causing it. I kept listening but could not figure it out. Was it the blackboard or the special chalk? Was it another case of the "violin phenomenon," with the chalk behaving like the strings and the blackboard acting as the sound box? Or was the chalk like the bow that "excited" the board?

When the school bell rang and pulled me out of my speculations, I realized that I had missed everything that Dr. Larudi had said during the class. But I figured that he would be the ideal person to explain the screeching cigarette to me, so I approached him and asked him if he could answer a question.

He leaned over attentively, obviously expecting a question about the subject that he had just covered. But when I asked him about the cause of the screeching, his face turned a furious red and he prodded me painfully in the chest with a stiff index finger.

"Tomorrow morning," he growled, "I want to see your parents at the principal's office." Then he walked away.

I went home terrified.

When I told my mother what had happened and that she needed to meet with Dr. Larudi and the principal, she grabbed me by the ears and almost lifted me off the ground while screaming, "God, what did we do to deserve a child like this?"

THE NEXT MORNING, MY MOTHER, who was so nervous that she could hardly speak, and I waited on a bench outside the principal's office until Dr. Larudi arrived and had us follow him into the office.

Before she could even begin to apologize for my terrible behavior, Dr. Larudi stated quite calmly, "This kid is never going to amount to anything. You should just douse him with kerosene and set him on fire right now."

To my horror, my mother agreed with him and repeated several times that he was absolutely right in his assessment. I was so shocked and terrified that I almost wet my pants, so it came as a huge relief when the principal made a dismissive hand gesture and told me to get lost.

I tore out of the office and straight to my classroom, which was already in session. Being late, I was of course subjected to a lecture by the teacher for having disrupted the class.

Also, these nightmarish events had made me forget that we were to have a soccer match against the sixth graders for the school championship that afternoon. And although the sixth graders were only a year older than we were, they looked ferocious, mean-spirited, and invincible.

As soon as classes were over, the gravel-covered schoolyard was sprayed with water to keep down the dust, and the faculty and other students filled the spectators' chairs just outside the playing area. As the underdogs, we fifth graders entered first, and I saw Dr. Larudi smilingly chatting with the young female teachers and the sixth graders (including Jaleh). We heard muffled cheers from our fifth-grade classmates, some of whom were waving small flower bouquets that they had most probably picked from the gardens of the Presbyterian church next door.

Moments later, our classmates' cheers were drowned out by the roars of the spectators when the sixth graders took the field. Our teams lined up in the center of the field facing each other and were introduced to the crowd one by one. My teammates and I exchanged apprehensive glances because we were all expecting a massacre. But to me this was still a much more palatable option than going home and getting burned alive.

Within the first minute of the first half, Boozarjomehr, the most-feared sixth-grade player, scored the first goal. I was not surprised. However, buoyed by their early score, the sixth graders then became careless and unorganized. They all tried to show off their power and prowess by kicking the ball toward our goal from any distance and any place in the field, but our goalie was able to defend all their shots. And toward the end of the first half, our star player, Caro Vartanian, scored a goal and tied the game.

To us, a tie game at first half was an exciting miracle. The score remained tied at one to one until toward the end of the second half—a

Our victorious fifth-grade Mehr soccer team (I am standing, far right)

fact that visibly upset the sixth graders and made them abandon what little remained of their teamwork in favor of unsuccessful individual efforts. Just seconds before the end of the game, Boozarjomehr, in an effort to drive the ball toward our goal, committed an uncharacteristic foul by touching the ball, which gave us a free kick.

We huddled to discuss our strategy, and my teammates decided that Caro should kick the ball. I disagreed and suggested that we should try to fool our opponents by having him approach the ball as if he was going to kick it but that he should then jump over the ball, with me following behind him and kicking it. Reluctantly, my teammates agreed.

The ball was set and Caro took his proper distance from the ball. As he began running toward it, I followed right behind him. The moment he jumped over it, the defenders instinctively reacted to block the "phantom" ball, which created an opening that allowed me to kick the ball very hard and straight—right into the net.

However, my momentum kept carrying me forward. I lost my balance, crashed onto the ground, and scraped my knees and elbows very badly. As I lay on the gravel doubled up in pain and hugging my bleeding knees, I heard the whistle that ended the game.

My classmates rushed onto the field and began throwing their bouquets at me and attempting to lift me up onto their shoulders, but Dr. Larudi (followed by Jaleh) ran toward me, picked me up, and (still followed by Jaleh) carried me to the principal's office, where I had been sentenced to be burned just a few hours ago.

He took out the first-aid kit out, began picking the gravel out of my wounds, and then poured iodine on them, which made me scream at the top of my lungs.

"I know it hurts," he murmured, and kept me from moving until the bleeding stopped. I thought he might still be mad at me from the previous day because he said nothing about my winning kick. And despite all the pain, I felt thoroughly embarrassed by the presence of Jaleh, who was treating me like a helpless child (which of course I actually was).

As I limped home clutching a drooping bouquet of flowers for my mother, I envisioned her greeting me with a tin of kerosene in one hand and a box of matches in the other. But when I knocked on our door and she opened it and saw the blood and iodine stains on my legs and arms, she grabbed me in a frantic hug and began to cry.

Sympathy hugs from my mother were such rare occurrences that I did not mind her crushing the bouquet as she hugged me. I told her about the game and my winning goal and that Dr. Larudi had tended to my cuts and bruises, but she did not react. Instead, she kept thanking God that I was still alive, and she promised to sacrifice a sheep and light some candles at the church.

Needless to say, I was thrilled by how that day turned out. But neither my victory on the soccer field nor my healing wounds ended my problems at school or at home.

THE ONLY BRIGHT SPOTS IN MY less-than-perfect childhood and elementary school years were the summers. Not only was there no school—there were no violin lessons either because Grigorian always took take his family to Tabriz during Tehran's hottest summer months.

However, despite the apparent inadequacies I suffered from that so disappointed my parents, I was popular among my friends, who looked up to me because I always displayed self-confidence and leadership. Also, I was physically bigger than most of them, and this enhanced my standing because I always stood up for the weak and the underdog.

In fact, looking back, I realize that most of my character and personality traits, as well as my capabilities, which were established during my formative years and continued through my adult life, were shaped by my being painstakingly observant and paying attention to minute details about subjects that interested me. Material things never interested me, but I was a good listener, keenly interested in people's life stories and empathetic toward their life situations. Anything else seemed too unimportant to bother with.

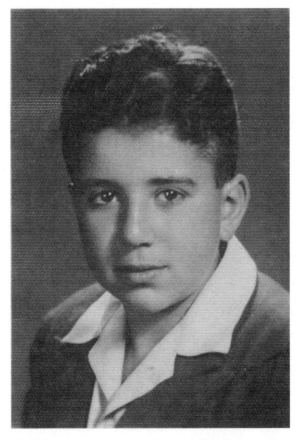

My Mehr sixth-grade graduation photo (1946), age twelve

Chapter 9

FIROOZ BAHRAM HIGH SCHOOL

In 1945, the war ended and the United States and Britain warned the Soviet Union to remove its forces from Iran's Azerbaijan Province within forty-eight hours or face the fate of Hiroshima and Nagasaki. At that time, the US was ahead of the Soviet Union in developing, testing, and deploying its atomic arsenal.

The end of the war also resulted in the collapse of my father's business—and the breaking of his spirit—due to events beyond his control. Stalin ordered the retreating forces from Azerbaijan to confiscate every vehicle on wheels that could be towed. This included my father's truck, which was our family's only source of livelihood. The loss hit him very hard, and his hatred of the Bolsheviks, which he had harbored since his days in the orphanage, intensified to such an extent that he broke off ties with my mother's side of our extended family because most of them were Communist sympathizers.

Also, later that year, when the Allied forces left Iran, the contents of many of their military bases were auctioned off to the locals. My father bought the contents of a British camp and salvaged items that he could sell or recycle. Those that he did not succeed in selling were stored in our backyard. Among them were a number of dartboards and sets of cross-country skis.

Although his venture into a non-trucking business was ultimately unsuccessful, we had fun taking the skis out on snowy days even though we had no idea of how to use them. The dartboards were also fun (for as long as the darts lasted).

In the summer of 1947, soon after I graduated from Mehr, we moved out of the compound and into a more modern and convenient apartment nearby, at the corner of Estakhr and Jaamee streets.

I was thirteen, and the move coincided with my starting high school, which was my first step along the path that would eventually see me on my way to the United States.

The two most prominent boys' high schools in Tehran at the time were Alborz High School, on the northern fringes of the city, and Firooz Bahram High School, a more centrally located school that had been founded by the Zoroastrian community in 1895. My parents chose Firooz Bahram because it was within walking distance of our home.

Iran's six-year high school curriculum was modeled on that of France. From seventh through eleventh grades, the courses provided students with enough general knowledge that those who did not want to enter a specialized profession would become useful and productive members of society, while those students who wished to pursue higher education gained a solid base for future studies. The sixth and final year was a college preparatory year for students who had desire and the financial means to pursue higher education.

Courses were classified into natural sciences, mathematics, economics, and literature. Although Firooz Bahram did not offer college preparatory math studies, that was not an important factor for me when my parents decided to send me there because at the time I was neither interested in nor inclined to any future profession. However, the two most popular choices for male students were engineering or medicine.

To me, five years was a lifetime away, and choosing my future profession was anything but a pressing matter. My new school meant new friends and newfound freedoms that became my private universe to explore and learn from. Everything around me was new and exciting.

Firooz Bahram was light-years from the protected environment of Mehr with its morning prayer assemblies, Bible verses, and exhortations to be kind to one another and conscious of social justice.

On my first day, I found myself surrounded by a much larger, older, and rowdier student body than anything I was used to and who came from every area and social class in the city. Before the end of that day, both my wristwatch and the Parker fountain pen that my parents had given me for my sixth-grade graduation had been stolen while I was trying to navigate the chaos in the corridors crammed with frenzied students hurrying to find their assigned classrooms. And during recess, I witnessed clashes among the older students that sometimes escalated into violent fistfights and outright knife and screwdriver attacks. Within the first few hours, I realized if I were to survive, I would need to grow up fast and keep my wits about me at all times.

Also gone were the days of conversations with soft-spoken girl students and caring teachers in small classrooms with well-maintained furniture. I now found myself in large classrooms full of desks and benches carved with profanities or arrow-pierced hearts.

And unlike the first days of the year at Mehr, when our familiar teachers would ask us to recount how we had spent our summers, my inaugural day at Firooz Bahram started with physics, where the loud student chatter was suddenly interrupted by a furious, booming shout of "Shut up!" from our instructor, Dr. Sheykh.

We students, who customarily would stand up to honor the instructor and remain standing until told to take our seats, were so startled that we all remained standing. Dr. Sheykh, a tall, imposing man, positioned himself at the desk in front of the blackboard, pulled a six-inch switchblade out of his pocket, and stabbed it deep into the top of the desk. While it was still quivering, he warned us in effect that he was a tough guy who would not tolerate street behavior or bad language in his class.

The room went so quiet that for several moments the only noise I could hear was the buzzing of a fly circling around our heads. Then, in the same furious voice, Dr. Sheykh roared, "Sit down!"

After we had all sunk into our seats, he pulled the knife out of the desk, replaced it in his pocket, and proceeded to describe the subjects to be covered during that academic year.

Some minutes into his lecture, a student asked sarcastically, "What is the purpose of learning physics?"

Dr. Sheykh calmly told him to open the classroom door, walk to the blackboard, and stand between him and the open door. He then explained to us that one of the laws of physics defines the behavior of a large object colliding with a smaller object, and asked the student if he knew that law.

When the student replied no, Dr. Sheykh ordered him to face the door. "I will now demonstrate this law by example," he told us, and as soon as the student turned around, he kicked the student's butt so hard that he became airborne, flew right through the door, and crashed onto the corridor floor.

Dr. Sheykh surveyed the rest of us and then inquired, "Now, does anyone else have any questions?"

The classroom was so silent that I could hear my heart pounding. Needless to say, there were never any disruptive incidents in his classroom— or in his presence anywhere else in the school.

That day I also attended my first classes in several subjects that I had never been exposed to, including English, Arabic, and Islam. The latter immediately became my favorite subject when the instructor's first announcement was that Christian students were excused from attending. As we filed out of the room, I could see the envy on the faces of those who had to stay!

ONCE I SETTLED IN AT FIROOZ BAHRAM, I paid a visit to the athletic director to see if I could join the soccer team. He invited me to attend a practice, but I realized immediately that I had no chance of competing with the team. Most of the boys were much older and more experienced than I. And although most were mediocre students and some had even failed and repeated the same grades several times, the school kept them on so they could compete against the other schools in the city.

In addition to sports, politics, though almost totally foreign to me, was an important focus and frequent topic of discussion. The students who were interested in politics were either pro-monarchists or anti-monarchists. The latter were Communist sympathizers and would openly hand out pamphlets and try to recruit students to their political gatherings.

I decided to avoid both and to spend my extracurricular time on music instead. During my first two years, I joined the school orchestra and played violin at cultural events. These musical performances consisted of light and popular classical pieces. However, we orchestra members enjoyed one benefit that made us the envy of many of our classmates—every so often we were invited to play at Anooshiravan-e Dadgar, Firooz Bahram's girls-only sister high school. Our nonmusician classmates would listen mesmerized to our accounts of being mobbed like rock stars by hundreds of screaming girls when we arrived at their school for concerts. And the stories were all true.

UNFORTUNATELY, FROM AN ACADEMIC standpoint, one thing that did not change from primary school to high school was the fact that our grades depended solely on how well we could memorize and regurgitate the material in our textbooks word for word. And again, because this parroting was considered proof that we had gained a thorough understanding and grasp of the subject, bookworms were usually the top students, and the "best of the best" could not only recite exact texts but also reproduce the sketches and graphs in the books, complete with titles and footnotes.

Although the theoretical discussions of the subjects we studied were obviously more technical and complex, we had no laboratories where we could see demonstrations and carry out hands-on experiments.

For instance, our chemistry textbooks offered detailed descriptions of how to determine the pH of water. However, these were presented like cookbook recipes, with lengthy paragraphs explaining how to add a reagent to a sample of water in a test tube held in the left hand "while the reagent, after being extracted from a bottle resting on a table with a pipette held in the right hand, is added to the water sample at a given rate of drops per unit of time," and so on. The more closely we could recite the exact text, the higher our grade.

Totally bypassed was the fact that we had been given no experience in the practical realities of holding a pipette or test tube (in either hand). As a result, students could graduate from high school with excellent grades and be admitted to college to study chemical engineering without ever having set eyes on a test tube, let alone having handled one.

Still, every so often a few of the teachers would bring their own supplies or experimental equipment to class and offer show-and-tell demonstrations of the phenomena that we were studying. This did not always work out as well as they had hoped, however.

For example, one of my teachers brought in a working folding camera one day so he could show us the lenses and how images get transferred to film. After his demonstration, he passed the camera among the students so they could examine it more closely. Unfortunately, by the time he got it back, every removable part had disappeared and only the camera shell was left. Naturally, he was furious and shouted at us that he had obviously mistaken a gang of thieves and idiots for students seeking an education. None of us received passing grades in that class.

And, unfortunately, my never-diagnosed learning disabilities continued for the most part to keep me from doing well.

Two Libraries on Naderi Street

Firooz Bahram was located at the northwest corner of the very busy intersection of Naderi Street, which ran east and west, and Ghavam Saltaneh Avenue, which angled north-south and dead-ended at the gates of the Soviet Embassy. Naderi was home to many trendy, upscale stores that were crowded with pedestrians all day and late into the evenings. But for teen boys at Firooz Bahram, Naderi was where they could spend recesses watching girls.

Typically, when the bell for recess rang, a music store near our campus named Swedish Merchandise would start broadcasting romantic western melodies out onto the street through a loudspeaker. This created a romantically charged atmosphere that made the exchanges of glances between the watchers and the watched even more mysterious and alluring. The ritual would reach its peak each school day at around 12:15 p.m., when large groups of students from Noor Bakhsh, the girls' high school a few blocks away, would pass our school on their way home for lunch.

THE CLOSEST POINT OF INTEREST to our school was the Soviet Embassy, only a block away. We were intrigued because its ornate wrought-iron green gates were always closed, and we would speculate about whether brigades of armed Soviet troops were stationed inside ready to take over Tehran if the Kremlin ordered it.

The only time I remember the gates ever being opened was in March 1953 after Stalin died. For the first time, the populace was able to enter to pay their respects by signing a heavy leather-bound registry on a table draped with the Soviet flag and decked with a huge portrait of Stalin.

The line was so long that people had to wait for hours to get inside the embassy, and my friends and I spotted many of our leftist classmates, with tear-filled eyes and somber expressions, in the crowds. We were there as well because we were so curious to see what lay behind the embassy walls that we were willing to put up with the wait. However, we ultimately decided it had been a waste of time because we saw nothing to substantiate our speculations about the presence of secret Soviet forces there.

NORTH OF NADERI ON GHAVAM-SALTANEH Avenue stood the large Armenian Church and the Armenian school. During Christmas and Easter, large crowds of Armenian families would cause traffic jams. Although Firooz Bahram did not close for Christian holidays, that fact did not prevent Christian and non-Christian students alike from mixing with the churchgoers and taking part in the Armenian Easter ritual of egg fighting. For all practical purposes, our school was unofficially closed on those days. Across from the church was the Armenian-owned Mikaelian meat factory, the only cold-cut company in the country. It catered to the Russian community, to Soviet Embassy employees, and to Muslims who chose to bypass Islamic dietary laws.

A few blocks away, at the intersection of Ghavam-Saltaneh and Naderi, was the Soviet Information Service, known informally as the "Russian Library." Its glass display windows were filled with large sun-bleached posters of heavyset Russian women smiling broadly and showing their gold-capped teeth while they happily milked cows, and others of smoke-belching factories surrounded by manufactured goods ready to be shipped to the various USSR republics.

The United States Information Service office, widely known as the "American Library," was also on Naderi, a few blocks away, and during the Cold War years, the Americans' and Soviets' efforts to capture the hearts and minds of Iranians with competing and contrasting propaganda were fascinating.

The American Library was large and bright, furnished with polished cherry-wood furniture and a small black-and-white portrait of the current US president mounted on the wall. Rows and rows of matching bookshelves held reference books and a variety of popular magazines such as *Life, Time, The Saturday Evening Post,* and *Look.* We students particularly enjoyed the color photographs of America in general and of college life in particular. The librarians, all of them well-dressed bilingual women, were eager to assist us and answer questions. During my visits there, many tiny seeds of curiosity were planted, and I started to think about someday visiting America and continuing my education in the colorful land depicted in the books and publications.

The Soviet Library, on the other hand, was small, dreary, and crammed with unorganized gray-covered books and never-changing magazines with worn pages. The huge posters of Soviet Central Committee members and the ubiquitous images of Lenin and Stalin with large Red Stars and hammer-and-sickle images superimposed on them contributed to a spooky, suspicious atmosphere. There were no visible librarians or staff to assist or answer any questions. During my years at Firooz Bahram, I set foot there only once. However, unlike the American Library, which had no materials in Farsi, the Russian Library offered Marxist and Communist materials in translation.

I WAS A REGULAR VISITOR TO THE American Library, and I vividly remember the day I saw the head librarian come in carrying a large flat parcel. A maintenance man with a ladder followed her in. They stopped in front of the portrait of President Harry S. Truman. The maintenance man climbed up and took down the portrait while the librarian unwrapped the parcel, which proved to be another large portrait, and handed it to him. He climbed back up and hung a portrait of a middle-aged man in a business suit. I recognized the man as General Dwight D. Eisenhower because I had seen his image many times before, only he was usually wearing his military uniform.

I immediately concluded that Eisenhower must have overthrown Truman in a coup, as happened so often in the Middle East, so I asked the librarian when the coup had taken place.

"There are no coups in America," she replied offhandedly. "People elect the president, and Eisenhower has been elected as the new president."

I had a hard time believing her but, coup or no coup, I was happy to see Eisenhower's portrait on the wall. I had always admired him for his honesty, and especially for the letter he had written on the eve of D-Day in which he accepted total responsibility should the invasion result in a defeat for the Allies. To me, Eisenhower was the embodiment of America and all things American. (And after I became a naturalized US citizen, I registered as a Republican because of him.)

I often visited the American Library with my friend Henry Gabrielian, an Armenian classmate whom I had met in ninth grade. Henry was a quiet, shy, and private person. His English was superb, as he had taken private English lessons for years. He and I shared a fascination with mechanical and oscillating systems that contributed to our lifelong close friendship. Whenever we went to the library, he would translate the magazine photo captions for me. Also, the reference books helped both of us to better understand the workings of the systems outlined in our textbooks and proved instrumental in our choosing engineering for our future studies.

IN THE FALL OF 1954, after our five years at Firooz Bahram, Henry and I, along with many of our other Armenian classmates, transferred to Hadaf High School for our twelfth-grade studies in mathematics. Hadaf was highly regarded for its respected and well-known faculty, many of whom were also teaching at the prestigious Tehran University.

That year was magical for me. I liked and excelled in all of the technical and mathematical subjects, and, for the first time in my academic life, I finished my last year at the top of the class!

Chapter 10

ARARAT AND SCOUTING
Coming Into My Own

THROUGHOUT MY HIGH SCHOOL YEARS, my life was divided into two main areas—my studies at Firooz Bahram and my deep involvement with the Armenian Youth Cultural Organization (AYCO), which later became known as Ararat and which I joined when I was twelve. And although Firooz Bahram gave me an adequate foundation for my higher education, it was Ararat that shaped my soul and my outlook on whatever lay in store for me in terms of my future relationships with my family, my friends, and my profession.

Discovering Ararat

It all started one summer day in 1946 when my mother took me to a two-story building on Ghavam Saltaneh Avenue, a block away from Mehr. The bottom floor was a Persian bread bakery. We went up a narrow stairway to the second floor, which had a small entrance hall to the two offices that comprised AYCO's headquarters. The aroma of freshly baked bread wafted up into the offices, where a young woman named Hilda Arzangoolian was busying herself behind a small wooden desk. My mother announced that she had read about the organization in *Alik*, the Armenian daily newspaper, and wanted to enroll me.

Hilda explained that two years earlier a group of young Armenians had established AYCO to create opportunities for Armenian young people to make friends and enjoy after-school activities such as literature, performing arts, and sports. She told us that AYCO had just started a section for preteen kids that had about a dozen members at that point, and that she would register me in it. When she started to ask me about my interests and favorite school subjects and learned that I played the violin, she recommended that I meet with the head of the music section about taking part in their musical events.

The idea of having yet other occasions when I would have to play the

The first headquarters of the Armenian Youth Cultural Organization (AYCO)

violin did not thrill me at all. I didn't think much of AYCO's facilities, nor could I envision what I would do there. But my mother wanted me to register and it would have been useless to object. Still, my studies at Firooz Bahram left me little time for Ararat, and for the next three years, my activities were limited to rehearsals and playing in concerts.

The summer after I joined, AYCO moved to an ornate two-story masonry building on a sprawling park-like property landscaped with mature pine trees, shrubs, and flowerbeds. As visitors entered through its large wooden gate, they were greeted by a majestic oval pond with white water lilies floating in it.

Because the new AYCO quarters were across from the exclusive Park Hotel, which housed foreign guests and dignitaries, AYCO's informal address soon became "across the street from the Park Hotel."

The move had been prompted by AYCO's rapidly expanding membership of young people, both girls and boys, in their preteens to late twenties. Although most of the members were high school or college students, a number of other young working people, including cab drivers, mechanics, and shopkeepers, also belonged. Among the college student members, most were studying engineering, medicine, or architecture, with very few attending law school at the University of Tehran, Iran's only university.

More broadly, though, AYCO consisted entirely of Armenian families from every social class from wealthy to poor and from all walks of life.

Amazingly, once inside the club, all those factors melted away, and friendships and associations grew entirely out of our personalities. What ultimately resulted were genuine and long-lasting friendships based on congeniality, honesty, sociability, and leadership.

As an organization dedicated to bringing people together, Ararat was a huge success. Although at first I had felt that it was not a place where I felt I would ever belong, I soon realized that it was a welcoming and nurturing environment where I could meet, talk, and socialize with a wide variety of other young people my age.

At the end of the school day, students would arrive with their books and other supplies and would take part in music, literature, sports, and other activities. Some would simply socialize, gathering in small groups to engage in casual conversation about what had happened in school that day and other topics. Before long, the building and grounds would come alive with laughter, conversation, and the sounds of musicians and performers rehearsing. At the end of the workday, the members who were working would arrive.

Over time, the wide range of sports-related activities that AYCO offered—weightlifting, boxing, gymnastics, mountaineering, swimming, and cycling—resulted in the organization becoming recognized as one of the premier sports organizations in Iran. As such, and because most sports organizations were identified by one-word names rather than acronyms, in 1950 the decision was made to change AYCO's name to "Ararat."

FOR MY FIRST SIX YEARS IN ARARAT, my activities focused on camaraderie and fellowship. There was a lot of socializing and sharing of knowledge and information among the members. Ararat provided a private, protected, safe, wholesome (and fun) environment where Tehran's Armenian girls and boys could spend time together after school—for which parents were both grateful and supportive.

Starting in the afternoons and extending well into the evenings, the club would be abuzz with the sounds of classical and occasionally popular music that acted as accompaniments to members' discussions and laughter. Occasionally the sounds would be punctuated by the clanging of dumbbells coming from the basement, where bodybuilding and weightlifting were offered.

In the course of an evening, lively discussions about a wide range of subjects, from the most recent international news and the daily political pulse of the city to recent sports news, would inevitably arise.

The three Kurkchian brothers attracted the largest and liveliest groups for discussions by far. The two older boys were weightlifting champions who drove taxis by day and trained in the evenings, while the youngest was an outstanding engineering student at the University of Tehran. All three would take turns discussing local and international sports, the performing arts, philosophy, information about local politics that they picked up from their fares, events and life at the university, and other topics. I and many others were fascinated by them and what they had to say.

Other Ararat members would bring copies of American publications such as *Life*, with its articles and full-page photographs of memorable events such as Joe Walcott's fight with the Italian-American boxing champion Rocky Marciano and Sir Edmund Hillary's and Sherpa Tenzing Norgay's ascent of Mount Everest. In the political area, photos of the Korean War and articles on East-West relationships led to interesting discussions about Iranian politics, which were of special interest to Armenians my age.

One incident recounted by an honors student in his final year of college engineering studies left a lasting impression on me because it reinforced my belief that memorizing textbooks did not give us command of its subject matter, especially when it came to technical fields.

Specifically, he explained that he had been taken on in an entry-level summer position at a German communications firm in Tehran. He and his supervisor had been in the storage facilities, which were stocked with large quantities of spare parts. The supervisor stepped out and while he was gone, a worker arrived with a written request from a project superintendent for a flywheel. The student, confident that he knew what a flywheel looked like, marched to the metal racks at the back of the storage room and began looking into the boxes stacked there.

Several minutes later, he heard the storage room gates screech open, followed by loud machinery noises. He hurried back and saw that the supervisor had returned and was overseeing the loading of a very large, heavy wheel, more than six feet in diameter, onto a low-bed truck. When he asked the supervisor where flywheels were being stored, the supervisor pointed to the wheel being loaded onto the truck. Naturally, the student felt embarrassed that he had been looking for the kind of small object he had seen in his textbooks and had had no idea of the actual weight and dimensions of a flywheel.

I of course had no desire to live out any similar embarrassing scenarios, so I made it my business to go from group to group and to pay careful attention to the subjects of their conversations.

Firooz Bahram, with its basic classrooms and archaic teaching methods, offered no opportunities for meaningful exchanges with our teachers, who were revered as both judge and jury in all matters and ruled according to the premise of guilty until proven innocent. I don't remember our teachers ever telling us about new developments in science or literature.

However, everything that was lacking in my home and at school was available at Ararat. This was where I learned and developed. Furthermore, the presence of young women put drastic limits on the teen boys' normally rambunctious behavior and less-than-appropriate language. Also, the older boys understood, without being told, that they were role models for the younger ones and behaved accordingly.

My Life in Scouting Begins

Because I was physically bigger than most of the boys my age, I looked older and associated with friends several years my senior. Among them was Leonidas Ohanian, affectionately nicknamed "Lolo." One day early in 1951, he told me that he was envisioning establishing an Armenian Scouting organization at Ararat because of his experience of having been a Scout as a young boy.

Although my parents had a childhood photograph of me with an Armenian relative who was wearing a US Scout uniform, I had no memories of Scouting and no knowledge of the earlier Scouting movement in Iran, nor had I ever come across any Scouts or Scouting groups.

From Lolo, I learned about how Lord Robert Baden-Powell, a British Army officer, had founded the Scouting movement in the early 1900s. He told me that the Armenian version of the Scout oath was "Being faithful to God, *nation*, and fatherland," and that "fatherland" referred to Armenia, whereas the Iranian version required faithfulness to "God, *king*, and country." He described the Scout uniform, accessories, and equipment—the bandana, whistle, and hunting knife, as well as the special Armenian belt buckle, which was inscribed "*Bardzratseer/Bardzratsour*" and referred to the spirit of Scouting as being "to strive to excel, and to help others to do likewise."

I was fascinated because what he was telling me was much in tune with my beliefs and interests, although I was less interested than he was in the more militaristic and disciplinary aspects of Scouting, such as organized marches and similar activities.

I later learned that Scouting in Iran began in 1928 when an Iranian national Scouting group, Sazeman-e Pishahange-e Iran, was formed as a division of the ministry of education. It was headed by the then crown prince, Mohammad Reza Pahlavi. In 1941, after Reza Shah was deposed by the Soviet Union and England and Reza Pahlavi was installed as shah, the Scouting organization was abruptly suspended and its facilities, consisting mainly of the Manzanirye campgrounds in the north of Tehran,

My first "encounter" with Scouting at age three in Kermanshah, Iran

were transferred to Sazeman-e Badane-e, the national physical education organization, which also happened to oversee Ararat's sports activities.

A FEW MONTHS LATER, LOLO WAS able to form a Scouting organization and recruit many Ararat members. He assigned different ranks and positions to the older members, who led the patrols, and in short order, the new Scouts were wearing uniforms that displayed patches inscribed "Hy Aree," which meant "Armenian Boy Scouts," as well as other Scouting paraphernalia. Most of the activities were ceremonial in nature and consisted of marches and parades before audiences of admiring parents and relatives who considered the Scouts as the Armenian army in diaspora.

Lolo was disappointed that I did not join his Scout group at the outset, but although I was keenly interested in learning more about Scouting, I was not drawn to the narrow range of activities that his group offered. I tried to search out information about Scouting but failed to find any in either Persian or Armenian.

However, during one trip to the American Library that year, I came across a magazine that had a pictorial feature article about the Boy Scouts of America (BSA). The images of Scouts canoeing, hiking, and building camping structures such as bridges and towers intrigued me, and my friend Henry Gabrielian, seeing my enthusiasm, told me that there might be some books about Scouting in the reference section. The librarian noticed me searching through the books and directed me to the manuals section, which contained dozens of books and magazines on outdoor activities such as fishing and hiking as well as on the BSA.

She also told me that because the library updated their collection with the latest editions of the manuals every two years, she would give me one of the outdated ones. She disappeared for several minutes and returned with a copy of the *Scout Field Book*. I thought I was dreaming and hurried out of the library before she could change her mind and take it back!

I found a shady spot and sat down with the well-thumbed book, which was full of pictures and easy-to-understand illustrations, even with my beginner's proficiency in English. One thing I noticed was that there were no pictures of parades or marches. Rather, the book focused on wilderness outings, camping and survival skills, and outdoor sports, and on values such as physical and mental fitness in the service of both survival and having fun outdoors.

Using the guide as a kind of textbook, I mastered tying several kinds of knots and also used string and sticks to build models of camping and outdoor structures like those shown in the book. I became so caught up in the photographs that I felt I was actually living the illustrations and photographs, not just looking at them. And, unlike at school, I was putting my learning into practice!

After three or four months of intense study, I knew the book backward and forward and could locate any topic in a split second. I could also tie knots with my eyes closed. Although I had never been interested in memorizing the contents of my school textbooks, I could not get enough of the Scouting book. Its messages and themes reinforced my spiritual leanings and my basic sense of goodwill toward fellow humans. I also benefited from the wonderfully fulfilling feelings that I always experienced whenever I would extend a helping hand, without expecting anything in return, to my friends or to anyone else who could use assistance. The Scout field book imbued me with a self-confidence I had never felt before, and I came to believe that there was nothing I could not do if I put my mind to it and persevered.

WHILE I WAS TEACHING MYSELF to tie knots, Lolo was organizing the first Scouting oath-taking ceremony. Because George Mardikian, an Armenian-American dignitary who was a member of the United Nations Department of Humanitarian Affairs involved with worldwide food distribution, was visiting Tehran at the time, he agreed to be the obligatory "witness" for the ceremony.

For weeks before the ceremony, the Scouts would gather at Ararat to rehearse by marching around the pond to practice their music, how to salute the Witness, and how to take the oath. The ceremony, which took place on May 27, 1951, went off without a hitch in front of a large crowd of Armenian-Iranian dignitaries and the Scouts' parents, who could not hide their tears of joy when they saw their sons in uniform. I was in the audience that day, but afterward I deeply regretted not having joined that first group of Scouts so I could have been part of the historic occasion.

In the days that followed, huge numbers of Ararat members, and nonmembers as well, applied to join the Scouts. Hordes of parents holding their children's hands would walk into Ararat to register them. But there were simply not enough leaders in the existing organization to handle so many new Scouts. In addition, parents were also making a strong push to set up Scouting activities for girls and for children under twelve.

The organization also needed to register with the Iranian government. Sevak Saginian, an attorney who had been one of the founding members of the Ararat sports club, was assigned this task. Unlike the former Iranian Scouting organization, which had been a division of the education ministry, the Armenian organization was annexed to the Iranian Physical Education Organization, which was renamed the Iranian Physical Education and Scouting Organization. The Ararat division was its sole Scouting entity in Iran, and the Iranian government made no demands that the group adopt any of the old, abandoned Iranian Scouting practices.

Meanwhile, in response to the demand that the Scouting organization add Girl Scouts and Cub Scouts, Lolo held a meeting to recruit prospective male and female Scouting leaders. I was among them, and I joined in 1952. I soon moved up the ranks and headed up the Ararat Scouts from 1955 to 1956, when I left Iran to attend college in the United States.

A recent photo of Ararat Stadium, in the Vanak area of northern Tehran

Chapter 11

FACTIONALISM IN THE STREETS
—and in the Scouting Movement

In general, most Ararat members in Tehran
were fierce anticommunists and identified with the Dashnak party. This
was a contradiction because Dashnak's political philosophy embraced socialist
principles, but neither the Dashnak sympathizers in Ararat nor Ararat's
management tried to proselytize in favor of any political system or philosophy—except, of course, loyalty to the Armenian heritage, which included
the fatherland of Armenia, the Christian faith, and the Armenian language.

Most Armenian-Iranians I met detested the Soviet Union's imposition
of Communism on Armenia. It undermined Armenia's cultural and Christian heritage, which dated back to the third century AD, when Armenia
became the first nation in the world to adopt Christianity as its national
religion. Nevertheless, some Armenian-Iranians were Soviet sympathizers
and card-carrying members of the Tudeh Communist Party. As open anti-
monarchists, they were antagonistic to the Shah and engaged in subversive
activities aimed at overthrowing the regime. It goes without saying that
none of them belonged to Ararat.

However, those of us whose parents, grandparents, and other relatives
had been victims of the twentieth century's first genocide were grateful to
our host country Iran and to its monarch for giving us the opportunity
to live, thrive, and prosper as a Christian minority in a Muslim country
without experiencing any discrimination or any restrictions on practicing
our religion or speaking Armenian. This acceptance was due in part to the
Iranian government's recognition of Armenian-Iranians' continuing contributions that began during the reign of Safavi King Shah Abbas the Great,
who ruled from 1588 to 1629.

For these reasons, Ararat members resented the ungrateful and
unpatriotic behavior of Tudeh's Armenian members, and this resulted in
constant skirmishes—some fairly serious—between the two groups.

In July 1953, an incident occurred that could have escalated into an armed conflict between Ararat and Tudeh. At the time, Tudeh's members were at the peak of their openly subversive anti-monarchy activities. One sultry day, almost 30,000 Tudeh members, emboldened by the rift between Iran and the British-Russian coalition related to the nationalization of oil, were allowed by the then prime minister, Mohammed Mosadegh, to march peacefully through the streets of the capital.

Carrying banners and flags fastened to sticks, the demonstrators smashed the windows of anti-Tudeh businesses, defaced establishments with Communist slogans, and attacked any bystanders who dared to heckle them with sticks and makeshift clubs.

At a certain point, the Tudeh demonstrators arrived at Naderi Avenue, a short distance from the Ararat complex. Earlier that morning, however, an anonymous informant had warned Ararat that Tudeh was planning to have a designated group of demonstrators split off from the group, force their way into Ararat, and set it on fire. The police had also been told of the threat and had promised to send out armed personnel that afternoon.

But before the police arrived, a small group of Dashnak party members, headed up by a man named Gevork Marzbetuny, showed up at Ararat laden with several crates of German Mausers and ammunition. These were distributed among us, and we took up positions at the windows and on the roof. When the Tudeh group arrived, we would be ready and waiting to strike first, and to shoot to kill if necessary.

A small team of police officers arrived early in the afternoon, but when they got close to the building and saw us on the ramparts, they announced, "They've got more arms than we do! They don't need us!" And with that, they left.

The news that we were armed must have reached the demonstrators, because no one showed up. We remained at Ararat all night and by daybreak the next morning we felt almost disappointed at not having gotten our chance to battle the Communists. So, reluctantly, we left our positions and went home.

IN 1953, A YEAR AFTER I JOINED the Scouts, I felt deeply grateful to my field manual because it helped me to avoid a serious embarrassment when I and several hundred Ararat members were invited to meet the Shah and his queen, Soraya Esfandiary, at one of the royal palaces.

The invitation was in recognition of Ararat's participation in the August 1953 uprising when the Shah, assisted by the US Central Intelligence Agency, was returned to his throne.

The Shah of Iran and Queen Soraya's reception for Scouts (1953).
I am standing next to the uniformed officer.

The first cadre of Ararat Scouting leaders, 1952: (standing, left to right) David Davidian,
Odet Garone, Seza Tamrazian, me, Irene Nanajanian, Rubik Voskanian; (seated, left
to right) Ardashes Yerganian, Emil Markarian, Valod Hovanessian, Sevak Saginian,
Lolo Ohanian, Lili Nanajanian, Vachik Khachaturian

We waited, chatting and laughing in a large reception hall, for the royal couple to arrive. When a court official opened a large double door and announced their entrance, we all froze. To this day, I have no idea how I managed to give the order for the Scouts to stand at attention and salute the royal couple.

As the Shah and his queen drew near us, he stopped in front of me. "Who was the founder of the Scouting movement?" he asked. "And where are you getting the instructions you use for training?"

Without hesitation, I replied in mixed Farsi and English, "Your Majesty, Lord Baden-Powell, and the field manual of the Boy Scouts of America."

He nodded, murmured, "Very good," and walked away. For a long time afterward, the thought of what I would have done if I had not known about the manual made me break out in a cold sweat.

Iranian and Armenian Scouts—Rivalry and Comradeship

I first met Ebrahim Sadri, a Persian, during a weeklong camping trip at Manzariye in the summer of 1952, soon after I had joined the Scouts. Early one morning while we were having breakfast, a fully-outfitted Scout sporting a Baden-Powell hat, Bermuda shorts, and a backpack appeared seemingly out of nowhere at the entrance to our camp area. Standing at attention and offering the Scouting salute, he announced in loud Farsi: "Iranian Scout Ebrahim Sadri is requesting to join the camp."

I had not seen him arrive because I was sitting with my back to him, so I was as startled by his bold announcement as my Scouts, who stared at me and seemed to be asking, "Who is this character, and what are you going to do about it?"

I swallowed the last bite of my cold hard-boiled egg, turned around, and saw him still standing at attention. I went over to him and returned his salute, saying, "Welcome to Ararat Scouting Camp." Then I led him to the breakfast table, where I introduced him to the rest of the campers. However, his badges and insignias were unfamiliar to me, so I had no clue as to what he was thinking or whether he had gotten lost while looking for some other group.

As Persian etiquette demanded, I asked him to join us for breakfast.

"No, thank you," he replied. "I will make my own breakfast. Please show me where I should pitch my tent."

I told him to pitch his tent next to mine. However, he did not appear to even be carrying a tent because the only ones we knew about were large, heavy canvas ones that took several people to carry and set up.

Ebrahim Sadri at entrance to our Manzariye campsite, summer 1952

Ebrahim Sadri (left) and me, our first meeting at Manzariye, 1952

I and all the Scouts were therefore amazed when Ebrahim put down his backpack and pulled out a smaller green fabric pack. He proceeded to unfold it, pull out some short white rods and a thin cloth with straps dangling from its sides and, in just under two minutes, pitch the first pup tent I had ever seen. After that, he reached into his magic bag, brought out a tiny single-burner stove, a pan, one egg, and a Swiss Army knife. As he began frying his egg, we all looked at each other in astonishment. Who was this guy?

Ebrahim took his fried egg to a large rock nearby and sat on it to have his breakfast. Dying of curiosity, I approached him and asked him if he would like bread and hot tea. He set down his breakfast and went to his backpack while I eyed his knife. I had never seen one with so many tools, but there was not enough time for me to examine it before he returned with a tin cup and said, "Some hot tea would be nice."

WE SOON BECAME FRIENDS, and the Scouts gave him the Armenian nickname "Setrak," which sounded like his last name, "Sadri," and made us feel that he was one of us. I learned that he had just returned from England, where he had attended an International Boy Scout Jamboree and also bought all of his camping gear. I also learned that he was the only Iranian Scout in Iran and was very keen to resurrect the abandoned Pishahange-e Iran Scouting organization.

However, the authorities never took him seriously as a candidate for that job. Instead, in mid-1954, Dr. Hossein Banaee, who had a PhD from the US, was given that responsibility—along with substantial financial assistance from the Iranian government. Except for a few older Iranians like Ebrahim who had a keen interest in Scouting as individuals, the entire leadership of the new organization was recruited from high-school teachers who lacked any background in Scouting. Their only training consisted of occasional participation in the Ararat Scouts' camping trips and my teaching them some of the wilderness survival activities that I had learned from the BSA field book.

We Ararat Scouts resented the extensive government support of Pishahange-e Iran when our expenses were entirely funded by parents and private Armenian sources. However, that lack of support also allowed us to remain independent and free of the government's cumbersome rules and regulations. It also gave us the freedom to continue developing as an innovative and competitive organization, and this was greatly enhanced by our three-year head start.

During our joint activities, we would even pull Scouting pranks to embarrass the much older and slower Iranian Scout leaders.

For example, on one occasion in the late summer of 1954, shortly after the reestablishment of Pishahange-e Iran and just before Sevak assigned me to establish the Ararat Explorer Scout division for older Scouts, I took the Ararat Scouts on a last trip to Manzariye to take part in joint camping activities with the Iranian Scouts.

The Shah was to be present to officially declare the reestablishment of the Iranian Scouting movement and to witness both groups' wilderness skills. In preparation for the ceremony, the Iranian Army leveled a large circular area and erected a tall flagpole with tent pads arranged around its base for the Scout leaders from each group.

On the eve of the Shah's visit, there was a traditional bonfire, after which the Scouts retired to their tents—but not before my Scouts approached me and asked for my permission to teach the green Persian Scouts a lesson they would never forget.

When the bugle sounded before dawn the next morning, we Ararat Scouts quickly donned our uniforms, hurried out of our tents, and formed a half-circle around the flagpole. I positioned myself next to Dr. Banaee, and we waited for the Persian Scout leaders to join us so we could proceed with the raising of the Iranian flag.

It was a different story in the Iranian Scouts' tents. I and my Scouts could barely stifle our laughter at the sight of the canvas walls bulging and wobbling and shaking as the frantically confused Scouts inside tried to get dressed.

Dr. Banaee, furious, shouted at them to come out of their tents immediately. They complied, but ran out half naked and shivering in their underwear. Their uniforms were nowhere to be seen.

Only then did Dr. Banaee look up and see that all of their uniforms were dangling from the top of the flagpole. He turned to me and in a low voice, said, "I told those idiots to be on the lookout for pranks by the Armenians! So much for 'be prepared!'"

I suppressed a smirk and asked one of my Scouts to lower the uniforms, which he did as slowly as he could. The resulting commotion as the Iranian Scouts tried to find and put on their uniforms was hilarious.

The Shah arrived at mid-morning with a large entourage consisting of his brothers and cabinet ministers. As I stood to attention on our "parade ground" and saluted, he responded with a smile and a nod that I interpreted as meaning that he remembered me from the awards ceremony the previous year.

I followed behind as Dr. Banaee led the Shah and his party on a tour of the campsite and showed off the communication towers, the camp benches and tables, and a footbridge. All of these had been assembled by Ararat Scouts, a fact that Dr. Banaee did not mention. Nor did he correct the Shah's comment that Pishahange-e Iran had "acquired good skills in a short period of time." All Dr. Banaee responded was, "Yes, sir."

After the Shah left, my Scouts asked me if Dr. Banaee had told him that it had been our group that had assembled the structures. When I told them no, they were furious and wanted to take their revenge by concocting another prank that would make that morning's seem like child's play.

I told them that it was not important because we were all Scouts and should share the credit equally, but that did not sit well with them. Their spirits plummeted after all the excitement of the Shah's visit.

What was worse, their disappointment turned to grief when a messenger arrived a short time later with the devastating and tragic news that Felix Menatsakanian, our 24-year-old leader and a close friend of mine, had been killed while climbing one of Iran's most treacherous mountain peaks in foul weather.

That night there was no bonfire and no singing. The dead silence was broken only by the whisper of autumn leaves falling from the tall trees that surrounded the campground. I visited every tent and in every one found the same solemn scene—my Scouts lying on their beds fully clothed, staring up at the tent ceilings with their hands clenched at their chests and with silent tears rolling down their young faces.

I could find no words to console them because I had never faced such a close and personal tragedy before. It seemed as if the silence was the only way we could try to collect our own thoughts. There was nothing to discuss because we had no other details about Felix's death.

The silence persisted the next morning as we got up at the crack of dawn and began packing. The only sound was the dripping of condensed dew falling from the leaves of the trees onto the roofs of our tents—dull, muted sounds that reminded me of an inexperienced drummer who was somehow unable to get into rhythm. Although we had not been scheduled to leave until afternoon, the campground was cleaned and the tents folded and moved to the warehouse by mid-morning. We picked up our camping gear and started our descent to Manzariye's entrance gate in silence except for the sound of gravel crunching under our shoes.

Our palpable grief over Felix's death lingered for weeks and remained a sad chapter in an otherwise very happy period of our youth.

IN THE MONTHS THAT FOLLOWED, the Ararat Scouts pretty much let go of their resentment about not having received credit for their Scouting skills during the Shah's visit to Manzariye. But then another opportunity arose for the truth to prevail.

Every year on the fourth day of Aban (the eighth month of the Persian calendar, which spans thirty days in October and November), the Shah's birthday was celebrated with parades, exhibition games, and fireworks at Tehran's Amjadieh stadium (known today as Shahid Shiroudi Stadium). Sporting clubs would line up in alphabetical order with their flags and banners and would march with military precision along the tracks that circled the soccer field. The flag bearers would lower their flags as the groups approached the stand where the Shah and his guests, including numerous dignitaries, were observing the festivities.

Because the Ararat Scouts were the first group alphabetically, we were always the first to enter the field. Every year, I would walk a few yards ahead of the flag bearer with my right fist straight up. As I approached the stand, I would lower my arm to signify the start of the parade, whereupon the Iranian Army band would begin to play and the Shah and his guests would stand up to view the marchers.

The 1954 celebration was to include a joint demonstration by the Ararat and the Persian Scouts of their skills, so Dr. Banaee decided that each Scouting organization should assemble and erect a communication tower. One Scout from each group would then climb to the top of the tower and use semaphore flags to spell out "Happy Birthday." However, we were not notified of his plan until just two weeks before the Shah's birthday, while it was rumored that the Persian Scouts had begun practicing months earlier.

While the parade was still going on, both Scout groups bustled around lining up and organizing the precut logs and elements of their towers on the grassy edge of the soccer field near the reviewing stand. After my Scouts organized their logs, I told them that this was their chance to correct Dr. Banaee's misrepresentation at Manzariye by showing what they were really made of. However, deep down I was concerned because most of the Persian Scouts were older and had been given such a long head start.

In any case, we both completed our preliminary preparations at about the same time. Then, as a courtesy, I went over to the Iranians to give them a Scout handshake and wish them well. We all then took our assigned positions, with the Ararat Scouts to the Shah's right and the Persians to his left, and waited for the parade to end.

However, when I had been greeting the Iranians, I had noticed several bundles of brand-new white cotton rope among their supplies. I knew that this could spell trouble because new ropes could stretch, but I said nothing. Meanwhile, my Scouts, per my instructions, had brought bundles of used precut cotton rope to tie the joints of the logs together.

After the parade ended, Dr. Banaee's booming voice blared over the loudspeakers and announced that "in the spirit of friendly competition" the Ararat and Persian Scouts would compete to demonstrate their Scouting skills. At his call of "Ready? Go!," both groups started assembling their logs.

While directing my Scouts' activities, I kept an eye on the Iranians and saw that, as I had expected, the unwrapping, untangling, and cutting of the new ropes was taking so much time that we quickly pulled ahead. Before long, the base of our tower was assembled and ready to be raised to its upright position so the upper sections, which would support the platform, could be erected next. During this whole time, the Shah used his binoculars to watch both groups' progress.

Just as our flagman was about to climb up onto our tower, Dr. Banaee ordered us to wait because our rivals were not yet ready. They kept working furiously and were just about to have their flagman climb up when thunder and lightning broke out and the skies opened up. Our flagman was already safely atop the tower, but as his counterpart began his climb, the ropes on the Iranian tower got wet and stretched, and the joints began to come loose. Moments later, the tower started tipping to one side. By then, visibility had dropped to just a few feet and bystanders were running for cover from the downpour.

When the thunderstorm stopped about ten minutes later, the Ararat tower was still triumphantly standing, but the Persians' tower had collapsed into a pile of logs. I could not tell whether the Shah had seen our Scout at the top of our tower before the storm broke, but the Ararat team ended the day soaked yet happy that we had beaten our rivals by a wide margin.

For the rest of that month, movie theaters all across the country showed clips of the birthday celebration, which began with footage of me raising my arm to begin the parade. I found seeing my larger-than-life image on the screen somewhat embarrassing, but the films were a pleasant reminder of our victory over our Persian rivals.

Heading up the Shah's 1953 birthday parade (the year before the
1954 competition between the Ararat and Iranian Scouts)

Chapter 12

SCOUTING TAKES HOLD IN IRAN

AFTER FELIX'S SUDDEN DEATH, my boyhood friend from the compound whose burst red balloon had precipitated the "balloon saga," was appointed interim head of the Ararat Scouts pending his departure from Iran to attend music school in Italy.

At the time, I was organizing the Ararat Explorer Scout division and had selected four trustworthy ranking Scouts to draw up organizational plans and procedures for accepting male and female members from a long list of interested Ararat members who were too old to join the regular Scouts. We chose army green with white gaiters and belts for the uniforms.

After Armik left for Italy, I took over Ararat's entire Scouting organization, which became unique because of our large numbers of Girl Scouts (unlike the Iranian organization, which had no Girl Scout groups).

Our activities sometimes included day-long joint camping activities where Boy Scouts and Girl Scouts practiced wilderness survival skills. Although the boys sometimes complained that all-boy trips were "boring," the joint camping trips were fun and magical. The boys would carry out the heavy tasks enthusiastically with sparkling eyes, ear-to-ear grins, and constant attention to their appearance. (Their leader was not immune to this typical male behavior. It was during one of these excursions that I developed my crush on Lili Nanajanian, the leader of the Ararat Girl Scouts.)

IN ADDITION TO REGULAR CAMPING ACTIVITIES, we sometimes took Scouts on visits to other Iranian cities that had large Armenian communities. On one especially memorable trip, I took eighteen of our Girl Scouts (accompanied of course by two adult women chaperones) to Esfahan, a city of great historical significance for Armenian-Iranians, for a week.

In 1590, Shah Abbas the Great established the city of Julfa for Christian-Armenians, who for the following three centuries lived separated from the Muslim population of Esfahan by the Zayandeh-Rood River, with its famous masonry bridges. Also famous is Julfa's historical complex, the site of the magnificent Vank cathedral and of a museum where Iran's first printing press, built by Armenians, is on display.

On the Sunday of our visit, the cathedral, whose ceiling and walls are decorated with frescos depicting the life and times of Jesus Christ, was packed with worshippers who had heard that Armenian Scouts were in town and had turned out to honor them. The girls were cheered and welcomed to the city by hundreds of families eager to invite them into their homes for dinner. Because we did not have enough days in our schedule for our entire group to attend all the dinners, invitations to breakfasts and lunches were also added.

Even so, some families remained disappointed, so the only way to fulfill the residents' eagerness to host the Scouts was to divide our group into smaller and smaller groups, and sometimes to even allot only one Scout to a family.

The community was very grateful for our visit, and as the word spread, Armenian families in other cities with large Armenian communities also wanted to welcome the Scouts to their communities and homes. And when these families' children saw the uniforms and Scouting rituals, they became eager to have Ararat branches in their cities as well.

SEVERAL MONTHS AFTER OUR VISIT to Esfahan, Sevak Saginian, the attorney who had been one of the founding members of the Ararat sports club, asked me to meet with him. He was one of two elected minority representatives in the Majles (the Iranian House of Commons) that represented all Armenians in Iran, and he was the only channel through which Iran's Armenian communities could contact the Iranian government to register grievances or regarding other matters.

"Have you ever been to Tabriz?" he asked.

"No," I replied, "but I've heard that they're all Communists."

Sevak said, "Good," and continued, "It's a nice city with a large Armenian population, and not all of them are Communists. They need our urgent help."

He told me that a group of Armenians, encouraged by the success of Tehran's Ararat, had organized their own local Scouting organization, the "Tabriz branch of Tehran Ararat." However, because the local government in Tabriz was unwilling to recognize the group, Sevak had been asked to help.

He then informed me that the Tabriz group had asked the Ararat Scouts to help them officially introduce their Scouting organization to the provincial government and to organize the group's first oath-taking ceremony. I realized immediately that, given the political realities in Tabriz at the time, we were about to step into uncharted territory.

Tabriz, the capital of Azerbaijan province and within a day's drive of Yerevan, the Armenian capital, was another major Iranian city with a large Armenian population. In fact, there was fierce competition between Esfahan and Tabriz regarding their respective beauty and importance, with Esfahanis bragging that "Esfahan is half of the world," to which the Tabrizis would retort, "Only if Tabriz did not exist."

Although the Esfahani Armenians were by and large apolitical, many Tabrizi Armenians openly held leftist leanings, were much involved in the politics of neighboring Armenia (at that time a USSR republic), and were hostile to Tehran's Ararat and what it stood for.

In fact, most of the leaders of Tudeh, Iran's Communist party, were from Tabriz. In the late 1940s, the city was a pro-Soviet hotbed, and in the 1950s, the Tudeh fomented a full-blown revolt against the Iranian government in an attempt to separate Azerbaijan from Iran and annex it to the Soviet Union. Soviet armed forces entered Azerbaijan and were welcomed by cheering crowds throwing flowers. However, the United States and Great Britain eventually forced the Soviets to end the unprovoked occupation.

After that, Iran's central government kept a watchful eye on the province by installing governors with military backgrounds who could respond quickly to any potential unrest. Nevertheless, the situation in Tabriz remained dicey, with daily reports of Communist agitation and unrest among the region's minorities, which included Kurds, Turks, and Communist Armenians.

Sevak told me that he wanted to send me to Tabriz to introduce the Tabriz Scout organization to the province's governor and to organize an oath-taking ceremony that would be attended by the local government's top brass. "Be sure to mention during the ceremony," he added casually, "that the Tabriz organization is on the same political axis as Tehran Ararat. And you had better get going right away."

I immediately called together my inner circle of Explorer Scouts—Ashod Serafian, Jorjik Sourenian, Amour Mouradian, and Vigen Mouradian—and gave them their marching orders. Within a week, our camping gear was packed and we were ready to set out. Deep down, though, I had doubts about whether I would succeed in accomplishing my mission. Although I had total faith in my four dedicated assistants' ability to plan and carry out a successful oath-taking ceremony, the diplomatic aspects of bringing together the most influential political figures in the province under one roof in less than a week was entirely my responsibility.

I went on wrestling with my doubts during the entire nineteen-hour bus trip to Tabriz. As our driver inched along the treacherous hairpin turns that rose higher and higher into the Shibli mountains, I kept wondering whether my mission would prove impossible.

On the one hand, my innate drive to accept apparently impossible challenges and my can-do attitude were giving me an emotional high, and I had a burning desire to reach Tabriz as quickly as possible so I could get on with whatever it was that I had to do. On the other hand, the sight of the treacherous gorge beneath us growing deeper with every turn made me ponder that the slightest hasty decision or mistake on our driver's part could send us all careening into the rocky abyss.

I could not help applying this metaphor to what I was about to face, but I soon decided to reassure myself by expanding the metaphor. I told myself that, just as the driver had to see the terrain ahead of him before he could decide how to negotiate the turns, I would cross my bridges when I came to them.

And with that, I wedged myself comfortably into the corner of my seat, yawned hugely, closed my eyes, and turned my mind to more enjoyable subjects like girls. It is amazing how thoughts of girlfriends can make all other worries disappear when one is nineteen.

WHEN WE ARRIVED IN TABRIZ that evening, a local member of the Ararat organization took us to the home of our host, a pharmacist who operated one of the city's main drugstores.

As had happened in Esfahan, the news of our arrival spread like wildfire. The next morning, people were already lined up at our host's door to invite us to their homes.

We stayed at our host's house, an old brick edifice with flower gardens and vegetable patches, for the next several days. We slept on wool mattresses on the dining room floor, which was covered with Persian carpets. Each morning we got up before the rest of the household, folded our mattresses, blankets, and pillows in neat piles, and stacked them in a corner. Then we would set the dining table and chairs back in their usual places and go out to the garden for our daily calisthenics.

At our first breakfast, I told our host that someone other than the Explorers would have to be in charge of our social agenda because we had to deal with the first part of our mission, which was to see the governor that day. After thinking for a while, he made a phone call to the Armenian archdiocese. A short time later, a middle-aged man wearing a dark suit arrived at the house to help us.

When we were introduced, however, he appeared to be so struck by my uniform, the number of stars I wore that indicated how long I had been a Scout, my badges, my medals and ribbons, and the large hunting knife at my belt, that he failed to respond to the questions I asked him about arranging the social agenda. (My decoration that day included my "uprising" medal, which I and four other Ararat members had been awarded for bravery during the August 1953 uprising and restoration of the Shah to his throne.)

And when I asked him the governor's name and the location of his office, he appeared shocked and murmured sarcastically, "You certainly have come prepared." He then told me that the governor's name was Golshaian, that he was an army general, and that his office was in the main government building downtown, a short walk from the house.

When we set out for the government building, people stopped and stared at us. Apparently they were not sure whether we were police, or gendarmes wearing new uniforms. They found our hunting knives, green uniforms, white gaiters, and Armenian-language badges even more baffling. We maintained silent, serious demeanors throughout the walk because we had no idea what we were going to face next.

The guards stopped us at the gate to the governor's office, but when they saw that we had more medals and stars on our uniforms than they did, they saluted and told us to enter. As we walked through the extensive grounds and mounted the steps of the building, another officer approached us. Seeing my uprising medal, he too saluted and asked us who we were there to see. The governor, I told him. He asked us to wait for a moment, went into his office, returned a few minutes later, and told us that the governor would see us immediately.

My Explorers stared in disbelief, but I was not surprised. I had learned that the uprising medal gave me open entrée to every governmental or private entity. Also, because I could not wear it with street clothes, I made several copies of the letter conveying the medal to me that I carried with me everywhere, and these too worked like magic. I never had to wait in line for anything, not even to buy theater tickets. The only surprise I experienced that morning was that my medal was being treated with respect in such a bastion of anti-monarchy as Tabriz.

We were ushered into a large room decorated with Persian carpets, Iranian flags, and a color portrait of the Shah. A distinguished gray-haired man wearing civilian clothing and rimless glasses greeted us cordially and invited us in flowery Farsi to seat ourselves around a large coffee table. Tea was brought in, and after we all spent some time engaged in small

Planning our first day in Tabriz: (from left) Vigen Mouradian,
Ashod Serafian, me, and Amour Mouradian

Meeting with Governor Golshaian: (standing, from left) Jorgic Sourenian,
general's staffer, Ashod, me, Amour, and Vigen

talk, he asked me: "What, may I ask, has provided us with this delightful opportunity to meet you?"

I explained that the purpose of our visit was to officially recognize our sister Ararat organization in Tabriz at a gala gathering to be held in the gardens of the local Armenian Diocese. He nodded thoughtfully and responded that he and his staff would be honored to attend. Then he asked if we could all be photographed for posterity.

As we were leaving, he warned us that local "left-leaning" elements might want to harm us and asked if we would like police protection during our stay. I thanked him but assured him that we could defend ourselves. I later wondered whether, when he saw our determination—and our large hunting knives—he realized that I had not been exaggerating.

As it turned out, a band of young Communists did corner us in a blind alley one evening. However, we had no need to resort to our knives because, due to the strict national laws that forbade civilians to own or carry firearms, they were unarmed.

Needless to say, I was pleased that we had been able to accomplish our mission without encountering any red tape. And when I told our host that we had met the governor and that the oath ceremony would take place two days later, he was astounded.

When the Tabriz Scouts heard the good news, they were so excited that they carried me to a nearby swing set and pushed me higher and higher into the air. I found this much scarier than meeting the Commies in the alley because there was a shallow pond very near the swing, and they could very easily have dumped me into it.

Flying high after our successful mission in Tabriz

THANKS TO THE ALMOST AROUND-THE-CLOCK efforts of the Tabriz Scouts and their parents and to the planning and direction of my four assistants, the ceremony did take place on the grounds of the Armenian Diocese two days later.

That afternoon, the narrow streets leading to the compound became a sea of black sedans bearing government license plates. The ceremony went perfectly. The governor announced that the Tabriz Ararat Scouting Organization was officially recognized and expressed his delight at being able to witness sunshine again after the dark clouds of pre-uprising events, when the country had been in imminent danger of losing its glorious 2,500 years of monarchy.

The night of the ceremonies, Tabriz. Top row: Governor Golshaian (center, in suit), flanked by his generals. I am standing on the far left next to Reverend Karapet, head of the Armenian archdiocese.

OUR FINAL DAYS IN TABRIZ WERE filled with the same outpourings of kindness and hospitality that we had experienced in Esfahan.

As I was saying good-bye to our new friends the morning of our departure, I was told for the first time of a long-lost centuries-old Armenian cathedral and monastery complex rumored to be located in a remote, mountainous region of the province. When I learned that Tabriz's Armenian community leaders were organizing an exploratory trip to search for the "Ghara Kilisa" ("Black Church" in Turkish), and that much of the trip would involve hiking through rough terrain, I decided that this would be an ideal and exciting culmination of our achievements in Tabriz. So, without alerting my Explorers because I wanted to surprise them, I called Sevak Saginian and told him that we were extending our trip by a week.

However, when I actually met the trip organizer, I learned that the rumors about the church's location were only rumors after all. Over the centuries, people had lost track of its location, and it was said that a group of local Muslim Turkish peasants had turned it into a cattle corral. There was no doubt that the church was an Armenian one because so many Armenian archaeological sites were scattered throughout the region, but the ancient archives in the Armenian Diocese of Tabriz made no mention of any church by that name.

I soon realized that my enthusiasm had been premature. We had no reliable information that would have allowed us to plan and organize an expedition through such an unfamiliar region, and none of the military maps of the province showed a church named Ghara Kilisa. Disappointed, I reinstated our original schedule and we returned to Tehran.

To my even greater disappointment, I was not a member of the joint group of Armenians from Tehran and Tabriz who actually did locate the Ghara Kilisa the following year. It turned out that the church was actually one of Armenia's holiest shrines. It had been built of black volcanic stones 1,700 years earlier and had been known as Saint Thaddeus Cathedral. After its rediscovery, the complex was renovated, and today thousands of tourists and pilgrims from all over the world visit the sacred grounds, which are lined with rows of large white tents to accommodate the visitors.

Needless to say, I regretted not having been able to be among the first Armenians to step into the Saint Thaddeus Cathedral after it had been lost and almost forgotten for more than a millennium.

Chapter 13

PLANNING FOR THE DREAM
College in the States

THE TABRIZ TRIP WAS MY LAST major Scouting activity. I was now twenty, and it was time to decide what I was going to do with my life as an adult. It seemed that everything was coming together perfectly for whatever I chose to do. I just needed to make up my mind.

In the spring of 1955, shortly after my twenty-first birthday, I graduated from Hadaf at the top of my class. This made my parents proud of me and eradicated the stigma, brought about by my unrecognized learning disabilities, that I was dense and lazy. I was liked and respected as a trustworthy and responsible person by my friends and acquaintances, and was in love with a beautiful girl, Aida Astvatsaturian, who complemented my personality and was an ideal future spouse.

I loved Iran, its people, and its culture, and I was eager to be of service to the country that had sheltered and protected the Armenians after the Turkish genocide. Iran's monarchs had been kind and generous to their Christian subjects and forgiving to those who became involved in subversive activities, so I felt I owed the country a great debt.

Ultimately, I had no difficulty choosing my path. My experience as an Ararat Scout leader had anchored me in my Christian faith and instilled in me a strong moral compass based on honesty, responsibility, and a readiness to help the less fortunate. Added to that, the values I had learned from my parents about the importance of education and the immorality of greed and excess made it clear to me that my next goal in life had to be to continue my education. But because I found Iran's academic system lacking, I set my sights on attending college abroad.

SINCE I HAD GRADUATED FROM HADAF after completing my year of college preparatory mathematical and technical studies, my only option was to study engineering. The most popular specializations within that field were mechanical, electrical, or civil engineering. I chose civil engineering because it would give me the opportunity to help Iran as a developing country. At the time, the Iranian government was providing financial assistance to students who wanted to pursue higher education abroad. Although Europe was a favored destination because of its proximity to Iran, the United States was also very popular. In addition, a number of American colleges and universities were also offering scholarships to high-achieving students from abroad.

I began researching American colleges and universities and, after seeing photos of the University of North Carolina at Chapel Hill in a magazine at the American Library, I decided that was where I wanted to go. However, a few days after I told my parents about my choice, my mother told me that under no circumstances would she let me go there. She refused to listen to my glowing description of UNC, and her final words were, "Absolutely not!"

When I insisted that she tell me why, I learned that she had searched an English-to-Armenian dictionary for information about UNC. She found nothing about the school but had come across information about the "Carolinas" and their menacing mosquitoes. So there was no way that she would allow her only son to live in such a dangerous place. She preferred that I go to school in California because one of my uncles lived in San Francisco.

THE TWO MAJOR PREREQUISITES FOR attending US colleges or universities were to pass a US-mandated English proficiency exam and to obtain an I-20 acceptance certificate from an accredited college or university. I gave up most of my responsibilities at Ararat and began exploring the options available that would prepare me for the language exam. These choices ranged from individual tutors to institutes that offered formal classes and certificates.

In general, students who wanted to study in the United States preferred to work with individual tutors who offered package deals that included not only language tutoring but also a guarantee that students would receive an I-20 at the end of their studies. These tutors also had contacts in the United States who could expedite the processing of the documents necessary to obtain the I-20.

I soon found out that we had an English tutor living right next door to us. George Piroomian assured me and my parents that that he could get me an I-20 from Pepperdine College in Los Angeles through a friend of his, Vaughn Gregor (whom I would later meet after I arrived in Los Angeles). Meanwhile, Andre Minassian, a friend of mine from Ararat who also wanted to study in the States, began studying with Mr. Piroomian as well.

Obtaining the I-20 required that a certified translation into English of a student's academic records be submitted to the chosen college, which would evaluate them and then accept the applicant as a full-time student.

Mr. Piroomian was true to his word. About six months after Andre and I each began working with him, we received our acceptances from Pepperdine. He then pronounced us ready to take the English exam. We both passed the written test and soon afterward received governmental notification that we had been approved for financial assistance.

We were on our way and getting excited about what lay ahead.

OUR FIRST STEPS WERE TO OBTAIN our Iranian passports and our student visas from the US Embassy in Tehran. When Mr. Aghassi stepped forward and put up his house as collateral for us, those issues were quickly resolved.

Next, we had to buy our airline tickets and shop for shoes, shirts, suits, pajamas, wool-lined raincoats, and other clothing. We also included Persian wool blankets, the heaviest English-to-Farsi and English-to-Armenian dictionaries we could find, anything else that our parents deemed as either unavailable in the United States or very expensive if available, and, last but not least, enough US dollars to get us through our first couple of months in America.

Each of these tasks could only be accomplished through a series of other tasks that involved monumental effort on the part of our parents. For instance, before we bought shoes, our parents would ask the parents of students already in the United States about the most suitable manufacturers and types of shoes for the US setting. Those parents would then write to their children in America and ask them about which shoes we should buy. All of which could take weeks.

Departure Day Finally Arrives

Before we knew it, our departure date—Monday, May 28, 1956—was upon us. Our final days in Tehran were consumed with the frantic last-minute activities of obtaining documents, visas, shopping, and packing. But we did accomplish everything, and our last act in Iran was to say our good-byes to our families and friends the night before we left.

That evening, our house filled with relatives and friends waiting to wish me well. The atmosphere was festive, with singing and the reciting of poetry by young and old alike, and tape recorders available so everyone could record their good wishes and farewell messages. I was in a daze, feeling both melancholy about leaving and excited about boarding an airplane for the first time and flying halfway around the world to a land known to me only through movies and magazines.

The partying lasted into early hours of the morning, until my dad approached me and gestured at his watch with tears in his eyes. "Son," he said, "it's time to go." We all boarded the waiting buses that he had hired to take us to Mehrabad Airport, where a large contingent of my Ararat Scouts and friends waiting to see me off showered me with tearful kisses and long hugs.

As we approached the chain-link fence beyond which only passengers could go, I gave my mother, father, and sister one last farewell kiss. Aida was not with them, but I knew that her father, a customs official, had arranged for us to say our last good-byes privately.

Then Andre and I, each carrying a raincoat, a thick wool blanket, and a foul-smelling carry-on bag whose contents we only learned about later, walked into a building where customs officials were inspecting our suitcases to make sure that we were not carrying rare Persian antiquities out of the country.

Aida was waiting for me inside. As I held her in a last embrace, the reality of our parting hit me. Still, I was confident that our separation would be temporary and that I would return.

Finally, Andre and I crossed the tarmac where our propeller-driven SAS DC-7 was waiting. I climbed the stairs, stopped, and turned to wave at

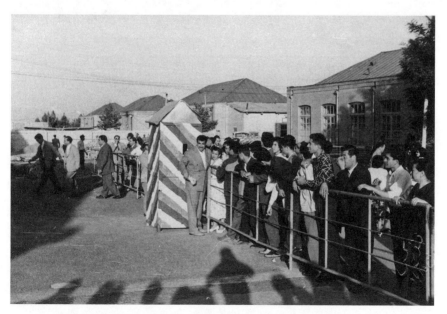

Saying good-bye to my mother at Mehrabad Airport

my well-wishers for the last time. I have never forgotten the sight of my dad continuing to wave his white handkerchief even after our plane began taxiing to the end of the runway.

Minutes later we were airborne. The mud-hut villages of southern Tehran and the connecting dots of the water qanats originating in the mountains north of the city became miniatures below us. We were on our way, and the novelty of blonde stewardesses in their beautiful uniforms with their Scandinavian accents took away our sadness at leaving our loved ones behind.

I sank back in my reclining seat feeling as if the heady events of the past days had been like a restless night's sleep in which it was difficult to sort out dreams from reality.

Our twenty-four-hour flight made a short stop at Copenhagen to refuel before we reached our final destination in Los Angeles.

I am halfway up the stairs of our SAS DC-7 waving (inset), with
Andre still on the tarmac looking around for me (center).

PART THREE

RETURN TO TEHRAN
My Early Career (1961–1967)

Chapter 14

MY FIRST JOB AS AN ENGINEER

I SPENT MUCH OF THE LONG FLIGHT back to Tehran revisiting the path that my life had taken so far and wondering what would come next. As the plane began to descend and my ears started popping, I looked out the window and saw the small white lights of Tehran shimmering on the distant horizon. In less than an hour I would be back with my family and friends, whom I had not seen for over four years.

We landed at Tehran's Mehrabad International Airport and when I disembarked and was walking toward the terminal, I saw three of my friends, Ardashes Yerganian, Amour Mouradian, and Vram Gorjian waving vigorously. It was as if I had never left. After a lot of hugging and kissing, we made for the baggage claim area, where I saw my parents and other relatives waiting behind a heavy glass door holding bouquets of flowers. I went over to the door and kissed my mom, dad, and sister through the glass. The joy on everyone's faces was such a contrast to the day I had left.

My bags were returned to me without being inspected, and the airport staff welcomed me as if I had been one of their own long-lost relatives. My friends fought to carry my bags and vied for my attention as if I were a celebrity. I was finally back among my own people, and it felt great.

We drove home in a caravan of cars and taxis. A big dinner party had been prepared, and there were a lot of questions about America and lots of welcome-home speeches. My dad kept calling me "my engineer son," and my mother announced that she had promised the Armenian Church that when I returned home safely, she would sacrifice a sheep in gratitude. Being among all the smells and sounds again was so familiar, and yet somehow like a dream.

The reality of being home became unmistakable when I finally crawled under my quilt and smelled the fresh sheets and the large pillow. Because of jet lag, I woke up well before dawn and looked around my room. Nothing had changed. My large cross was still hanging above my bed. The shadows

My arrival back in Tehran, March 1961: (from left) me,
Amour Mouradian, Ardashes Yerganian, Vram Gorjian

created by the streetlight shining through the branches of the big tree outside took me back to the days when I would fall sleep gazing at the shadows
and thinking about going to America. But as I recalled the speeches that
my dad and my friends had made during the dinner party, I realized that a
lot was going to be expected of me now that I had returned as an educated
person and an engineer. Suddenly a string of thoughts and questions began
racing through my mind. What am I going to do first? Where will I go
to look for a job? Who will I call? But soon I fell asleep again, and in my
dreams I was driving my 1952 Chevrolet in Champaign-Urbana...

The conversations of the previous night continued the next morning
at the breakfast table. I learned that a lot of my older friends and acquaintances who graduated from Tehran University had established their own
engineering firms in Iran. Most were contractors, and a few had consulting
offices in Tehran. That news was comforting because it gave me some leads
to follow in my search for a job.

Later that day, I decided to visit Ararat, where I had spent so many happy
years. As I made my way there, I was surprised to realize that everything
seemed to have shrunk from what I remembered. The streets were very
narrow, and the buildings that had seemed so tall to me then were only
three or four stories high. Because there were no marked traffic lanes, cars

would change course at will, and taxis would stop in the middle of the street to pick up passengers, forcing the vehicles behind them to come to screeching stops. Somehow it all seemed normal, but it was also totally unorganized and chaotic compared to life in the US. The thought of crossing the street was more than I could face.

On my way, I passed a newspaper vendor who was hawking *Etelaat* (*Information*), Iran's most prominent newspaper, at the top of his lungs while pushing copies of it into the faces of the passersby. I saw that the paper bore a huge headline: "PRIME MINISTER DR. ALI AMINI ASKS FOR BELT-TIGHTENING," followed by a smaller line that read: "Due to the nation's dire economic situation, all expatriates have been ordered to return home."

This news sent a shockwave through me, and I could not help thinking, "This was a heck of a time to return home."

When I got to Ararat, the hustle and bustle that I had left behind were the same as I remembered them, but no one recognized me. A young boy approached me and asked to see my membership card. I told him that I was no longer a member and asked if any of the officers were around. He could not tell me, but he said I could go upstairs and look for myself. I decided not to because Ararat, my former "home away from home," now looked so strange and unfamiliar. The Ararat era was definitely over for me, and the newspaper headlines had shattered my exuberance of the night before.

ON MY WAY HOME, I MET A FRIEND who had heard that I would be coming back but had not known when. He told me that his older brother, who had returned from attending university in the US, was also looking for work but that he first had to get his diploma approved by the education ministry. This was crucial news for me because I was unaware of that requirement.

In my rush to return home, I had obtained a short note from U of I that certified that I had graduated from the civil engineering curriculum. However, when I presented this at the ministry, the official I was speaking with merely gave it a cursory glance front and back, said, "We need your diploma, decorated with flowers and birds and bearing the university seal," and tossed it down on the table in front of me.

I wrote to U of I and received my official diploma. When I went back to the ministry and to the same official, he recognized me. As he had with the certificate, he studied both sides of it—then shook his head and informed me that all diplomas obtained by Iranian students from abroad required verification by the Iranian ambassador in that country that the school was an accredited institution.

Fortunately, the Iranian ambassador to the US, Ardeshir Zahedi, the Shah's son-in-law, happened to be in Tehran on a short visit at that time. I got his home phone number from the US Embassy, called, and was surprised that he answered it himself. When I told him of my problem, he said that he was returning to Washington DC the next day and that my only chance of getting the diploma signed would be to bring it to him early in the morning.

The next morning, I arrived at the ambassador's gate at daybreak and was ushered into his living room. A few minutes later, he came in still in his pajamas. He apologized for all the red tape and signed the back of the diploma. I went directly from his home to the ministry, submitted it, and was told that the document I needed would be ready the next day. But I went back every day for the next two weeks only to be told that I had to return the following day. This went on for fifteen days until I finally was given the official translation of my degree.

MEANWHILE, THE NOVELTY OF being back home was wearing thin and I was learning that the employment situation was discouraging, to say the least. Even so, one of my friends advised me not to be in a hurry because with my degree from U of I, employers would be knocking at my door.

In the middle of all this, my mother informed me that we needed to go to the big bazaar in the southern part of the city to buy the promised sacrificial sheep. When I asked her why I needed to go with her, she said that tradition required that I walk among the flock of sheep and place my hand on the one that I want to be sacrificed. It had never paid to argue with her before I left Iran, and I soon learned that it did not pay to argue with her now that I was back.

She and I took a taxi to the bazaar and asked where the sheep were sold. We walked quite a distance through the bazaar to reach the livestock area and a herd of sheep and goats of all sizes and colors. As we made our way among them, I accidentally brushed a fairly large sheep with my hand. My mother noticed this, told the herder with great joy that she would take that one, and spent the next thirty minutes using her bargaining skills to reduce the price. After she and the herder finally came to terms, she ordered me to grab the rope tied around the sheep's neck and pull it through the hordes of shoppers and laborers who kept yelling "Watch out! Watch out!" at me. As I was trying to pull the unwilling and uncooperative animal through the crowd, the only thought that went through my mind was, "How stupid of me to have left America!"

Eventually we got out of the bazaar and found a taxi driver who was willing to take both the beast and us, provided I held the sheep on my lap. My mother thought I should sit in front with the sheep because tufts of wool were flying every which way and landing on her dark-colored outfit. Had it not been for my years of weight training, there was no way I would have been able to keep the struggling sheep under control. By the time we got home, I was soaking wet and covered in sheep droppings.

Waiting for us in front of our apartment building was the man who would slaughter the sheep. A tall ladder with ropes hanging from it was propped up against the wall near him. He would tie the sheep's legs to the ladder to anchor it while he dismembered it. With lightning speed, he grabbed the sheep, wrestled it down, and with a huge knife proceeded to cut the sheep's throat. I was so nauseated that I was about to run up to my room, but my mother told me that I had to witness the sacrifice and be sprayed by sheep's blood. I started to protest but then felt a warm liquid running down the back of my neck. That did it. I could not take any more. I began cursing using some choice English gutter language and left the grotesque scene.

Later that day, the sheep's meat was distributed to the poor, who prayed that God would accept my mother's sacrifice and make her wishes come true.

UNFORTUNATELY, IF ONE OF MY mother's wishes had been for me to get a good job, it did not happen. No employers came knocking at our door, and the ones that I visited were not interested in a newly graduated engineer from the US because of the economic problems that the country was facing.

After several frustrating weeks of job hunting, I decided in desperation to apply to Kampsax, a Danish firm with a thirty-year history of working on projects in Iran. Rumor had it that the head of the firm had close ties to the Shah and had been awarded a number of lucrative highway construction contracts as part of the nation's Second Seven-Year Plan.

The First Seven-Year Plan, put in place between 1949 and 1955, had fallen apart in the wake of the 1953 oil nationalization crisis. The Second Seven-Year Plan (1955-1962) included the design and construction of highways to connect the nation's major cities and feeder roads to connect smaller communities, as well as dams, water supply systems, airports, and other infrastructure projects.

The body that administered the plan was called the Plan Organization and acted as a pseudo-ministry. Starting in the 1950s, almost all development contracts in Iran were awarded to European firms and a handful of US firms, with Iranian companies carrying out the actual construction. For example, Mowlem, a large UK construction firm, was awarded a contract to set up and manage a large laboratory, which turned out to be the largest of its kind in the Middle East, for the testing of construction materials and to provide quality control services. The laboratory, known as the Plan Lab, was located in Tehran and managed by Europeans. By the end of the 1950s, however, several American engineering firms, for example Ammann & Whitney, had also managed to secure some contracts.

Before the announcement that foreigners were being expelled, a large expatriate community resided in Iran. Most lived in Tehran's exclusive northern suburbs in mansions with gardens and ornate wrought iron gates and staffed with servants, groundskeepers, chauffeurs, nannies, and cooks. A European supermarket stocked expensive European and American foods that the expatriates, who were paid astronomical salaries compared to local engineers, could easily afford.

By 1960, due to the loss of revenue in the wake of the nationalization of the oil industry, the costs of the proposed infrastructure projects had exceeded the resources available. Gradually, the Iranian Oil Operating Companies (IOOC, known informally as the "Consortium"), which was made up mostly of US oil companies but also included a few European firms, replaced British Petroleum (BP) in exploring and marketing Iran's oil and gas resources.

So I SET MY SIGHTS ON applying to Kampsax. When I entered the building, I was impressed by the large halls crowded with drafting tables and draftsmen busy at work. I recognized one of the draftsmen, approached him, and learned that most of the draftsmen were actually graduate engineers supervised by foreign designers. He also told me that to make more money, most engineers had taken construction-related jobs outside Tehran.

When I asked if Kampsax was hiring any new engineers, he said that the firm had actually begun laying off employees several months earlier. This confirmed the newspaper headlines regarding belt-tightening. As I was leaving, I met an older engineer friend of mine who greeted me cordially and suggested that I approach the Plan Lab because there was always a need for inspectors at jobsites outside Tehran. That was a ray of hope although the prospect was not attractive to me.

The Plan Lab

The next day, I called the Plan Lab and was told to see a Mr. Robinson who headed Mowlem in Iran and worked from a separate office. I decided that I wanted to see the Plan Lab before meeting with him. After all, what if he were to offer me a position that I did not want?

The lab, a four-story building, was a forty-five-minute walk from my parents' home. When I arrived, the gate was open, and a dark-blue Bentley was parked in the courtyard. I followed an arrow to the reception desk, which was staffed by a young, well-dressed Iranian man who greeted me by standing up, smiling, and extending his hand. He introduced himself as Shahreis and asked, "Didn't you call yesterday to ask if we had any openings?"

"How could you remember?" I responded.

I was surprised to hear him reply, "Your Farsi is mixed with a little English accent." He then offered me a seat in a nearby chair and pushed a button next to his desk. A few minutes later, a man wearing a blue smock knocked on the door and came in. Mr. Shahreis asked him to bring us two teas. Then, apparently noticing my class ring and my crew cut, he began asking me friendly questions about when I had arrived, where I had gone to college, what I had studied, and so forth. It was the first pleasant meeting I had had since my return.

During our conversation, two clients arrived, one with two sacks of material to be tested and another with a worker carrying two concrete cylinders. After asking both clients to set their samples on the floor, Mr. Shahreis filled out two receipts on which he checked the types of tests to be carried out and the cost. He then asked the clients to pay the cashier and bring the receipts back to him. After that, he marked the samples and pressed the bell again to summon another blue-smocked attendant who came in and took the samples away. All during this, he and I continued chatting. And among other things, I learned that of the dozens of foreign experts who had been project managers at the lab, all but three had been let go due to budget cuts.

Eventually, Mr. Shahreis asked me if I would like to see the lab, and I said that of course I would. On our way to the lower floor, a blue-eyed man with blond hair came out of the building and went over to the Bentley, whereupon an Iranian driver opened the back door for him before driving him away. Mr. Shahreis told me that the man was Simon Van der Wal, a Dutchman who was the director of the Plan Lab.

A number of Iranian technicians and engineers wearing knee-length white lab coats were working on the lower floor. One of the first rooms we entered housed large British-made testing machines, soil-testing equipment, and monitoring gauges that reminded me of U of I's Talbot Lab.

Mr. Shahreis introduced me to the department head, Mr. Yaghmai, a short man with dark complexion who was overseeing the testing of concrete, asphalt, steel, and all types of masonry as well as the strengths of structural cables and their connectors. The upper floors also housed a petrography and mineralogical studies department; a chemical and metallurgical department headed by a woman engineer, Mrs. Lucik Mouradian; the drafting department; accounting, which was headed up by an Englishman; the archival department; and a library that contained complete British, French, German, and US ASTM (American Society for Testing and Materials, now known as ASTM International) standards. It was headed by a German named Mr. Schteinberg, who had an artificial right hand.

Parked in the courtyard near the Bentley was a large trailer truck equipped with built-in hydraulic pumps and jacks for performing plate-bearing tests and that carried large concrete cubes as counterweights. Both sides of the truck had retractable awnings to protect the technicians from the sun and wind while they were performing tests. This area also contained stacks of simple auger-type portable drilling equipment, two Dutch cone penetrometers, and other testing devices suitable for site investigations, as well as several Land Rovers and an assortment of larger equipment too big to be stored indoors.

The tour took us about an hour because the Iranian workers were eager to talk about their departments and the types of projects they were working on. Apparently my knowledge of the equipment and the test procedures impressed Mr. Yaghmai, who told me, "We really need someone like you here because we're getting tired of these foreign idiots who, thank God, have been ordered to leave."

I was so invigorated by the tour and by what I had seen that I would have paid them to let me work there. It was right up my alley in terms of my passion for problem solving. Before I left, Mr. Shahreis gave me Mr. Robinson's phone number and office address.

When I called, his secretary set up an appointment for the next day. That night I had trouble sleeping because I could not stop thinking about what I had seen at the lab.

I ARRIVED PROMPTLY AT MR. ROBINSON's office the next day. The place looked disorganized and half empty, with only a handful of Filipinos outnumbered by the empty desks all around them. Soon a tall, thin Englishman with a graying goatee and wearing thick glasses, khaki pants, and a yellow shirt ushered me into his equally disorganized office.

"So, Mr. Yaghoubian," he said in his British drawl, "you're looking for employment in our laboratory?"

"Yes, sir."

"I understand that you visited the laboratory yesterday," he went on.

Surprised that he knew of my visit, I replied, "Yes, sir. I did. Very impressive."

After studying my diploma, he said, "I'm going to be very honest with you. Due to budget cuts, we've had to send a lot of brilliant foreign engineers back to their home countries, and we do need to hire locals like yourself." Reaching for his pipe, he continued, "I'm sure you'd like to know about the salary."

I replied, "Yes, thank you."

"Well, I'm afraid that we could pay you only 7,000 rials a month. But of course we also provide free medical care and a monthly ration of cooking oil, rice, and soap."

I slumped in my seat. "That's only a hundred US dollars a month. Is that what the foreign engineers were paid?"

With a smirk, he said, "If you had blond hair and blue eyes and your name was Johnson, your monthly salary would be about five thousand US dollars, plus living expenses and transportation. But since you're an Iranian..."

I felt torn. On the one hand, I was ecstatic to be offered a job at the lab. But I was also offended by his demeaning comments and by being offered only 100 dollars a month. Seeing my disappointment, he said, "Think about it and let me know as soon as you can. We do have other applicants."

As I left his office, I muttered glumly to myself, "Welcome home, Mr. Engineer!"

When I told my parents that night that I had decided to take the job, my father was visibly upset. "You could make ten times as much if you took construction management jobs outside Tehran like many engineers are doing," he told me.

The only way I would be able to survive on that salary was by continuing to live with my parents and sister. After five years of being on my own in the US, it felt like an unwelcome step backward. Fortunately, I had no expensive tastes, and money had never been my primary concern. So it seemed as if my "starving student" lifestyle was going to continue.

When I started work the next day, the staff members I had already met were happy to see me again. I also met Mr. Van der Wal in his large office. He welcomed me and told me to let him know if I had any problems. He also said that I would be reporting to a Mr. Sevaldson and sharing an office with him.

Mr. Sevaldson, a well-known Norwegian soil engineer, was a polite but hopelessly humorless man. The only furnishings in his barren, bare-walled office were our two desks and chairs and a large freestanding wooden closet. There was one telephone, and it was on his desk. Since it was my first day and I had no assignments to carry out, I asked him if there was anything that I could do for him.

"Yes, there is," he replied, "if you know how to design concrete mixes."

I said, "Yes, but isn't mixed concrete delivered to the job sites in cement trucks?"

Very seriously, he replied, "Not in Iran. We provide the mix design based on the materials available."

I realized immediately that I was in a sink-or-swim situation because these people were not interested in training locals, so I said, "Sure. Do you have any information on aggregates?"

He grabbed a file folder from the stack on his desk, came over, set it politely in front of me, and without a word went back to his desk and back to work.

The file contained a work order and the results of grading analysis on two samples of aggregates. The order stated that a sack of cement had also been delivered along with the samples. The mix was for concrete culverts and required the standard twenty-eight-day strength of 700,000 kg/m². Because I had completely forgotten the metric system, the first thing I needed to do was convert the measurements to pounds per square inch (psi).

I went over to the library and asked Mr. Schteinberg for conversion tables and for references on concrete mix design. He was very helpful, so I returned to my desk armed with the needed references and was able to generate the mix parameters in a few hours.

I then asked Mr. Sevaldson if he wanted to look at my calculation, but without glancing up from his work he said, "Go down to the first floor and see Mr. Vanbrumlen," whom I had not met. His tone was so peremptory that I felt as if I were being treated like one of the blue-smocked helpers who brought tea and did other menial tasks. Except that I was not wearing a blue smock.

As I neared Mr. Vanbrumlen's office, I heard several people shouting in broken, Farsi-accented English, "It won't work! It won't work!" and saw a tall, thin European man standing with his hands on his hips over two Iranian technicians who were using shovels to mix aggregates submerged in a large pan of water on the floor.

"Keep mixing!" he ordered them.

When the technicians saw me, one of them dropped his shovel and said in Farsi, "He keeps ordering us to mix this crap, but there's just too much water in the mix. The guy's an idiot!"

I asked the tall man in English if he was Mr. Vanbrumlen.

"Yes," he replied in a European accent. "And who are you?"

"I'm the new engineer, and Mr. Sevaldson asked me to see you."

"Good! Now you can tell these imbeciles what to do in the language that you all speak!"

"What is the problem?"

"This is a concrete mix that needs to be mixed well."

"What water-to-cement ratio are you using?"

"Five."

Puzzled, I asked, "You mean 0.5?"

"No, five!" he snapped, and stormed away.

The technicians told me that he was the concrete inspector, responsible for inspecting all concrete work at all the sites throughout the country, and that he had been transferred to the lab because of staff reductions.

I could not believe what I was hearing. When I checked the job number, I realized that it was the same job for which I had just designed the mix. Mr. Yaghmai came out of his room and told me, "Can you believe this? In Holland the guy was a butcher, and they hired him as an expert in concrete! You haven't seen anything yet!"

I decided to go directly to Mr. Van der Wal. When I knocked on his door, entered his office, and told him what I had just seen downstairs, he asked me to remain where I was and he left the room. A short while later, he returned looking pale and upset.

"Go ahead and design the mix," he told me. "Vanbrumlen is on his way back to Holland. His contract is not going to be renewed."

Because some of the cement was still left, I asked that the aggregates be washed and dried and another grading analysis be carried out. I was surprised that the grading of the washed and dried aggregates was very close to the original grading in the file. None of the finer particles had been lost, which proved how meticulously the aggregates had been washed and dried, and I told the technicians how impressed I was with the care they had taken.

The news of this incident quickly spread throughout the lab, and I was told that my standing up for the technicians had been a breath of fresh air because no one was ever allowed to second-guess the expatriates. Their word was law.

ABOUT A MONTH LATER, MR. SEVALDSON also returned to Norway, leaving Mr. Van der Wal and the head of the accounting department as the only two foreigners left in the lab. Mr. Van der Wal tended to administrative tasks and took part in the Plan Organization's weekly meetings.

I now had Mr. Van der Wal's full confidence and an office to myself. He knew that I could handle all the technical matters that came up. I was settled in a problem-solving job that I loved, and I had the respect of my colleagues. The mood in the lab grew upbeat and patriotic because we locals were no longer being discriminated against in our own country.

One day, I decided to examine the contents of the wooden closet in my office because I had noticed that no one had opened it since I had started working there. I found it stacked with three-ring binders, each full of hundreds of pages of meticulously handwritten notes in English. In fact, the handwriting was uncannily uniform throughout the thousands of pages. Perhaps I found this fascinating because my own handwriting changed so much from word to word that by the end of a page it was all but illegible.

The subject matter seemed to be a daily log of labor utilization. Each line described the activities of given workers at fifteen-minute intervals, for example: "9:15 a.m., Ali went to bathroom; returned 9:20; carried out density test until 10:20; went to bathroom until 10:30." My first thought was to wonder who would sit day after day keeping records of workers' activities. More importantly, I wondered what the value was of such information, although I was familiar with how closely the British had monitored their workers' activities in their colonies.

I eventually learned that a staff member named Shahen Askari had begun keeping the logs years earlier just after the lab had been established. Little did I know at the time that I would soon meet him, or that he would become not only a colleague but also my best friend and confidant throughout my engineering career. He told me that keeping the records was what he had been paid for, but he never knew whether much use was made of them.

AT THE START OF MY SECOND MONTH at the lab, my father surprised me by buying me a 1959 Simca Vedette automobile. Things were going my way, and I was so busy that I had no time to worry about my hundred-dollar monthly salary.

Every day, I looked forward to going to work. My practical knowledge was growing by leaps and bounds, and I was absolutely convinced that having good ideas was the key to a successful career in any field. I had already carried out foundation investigations throughout Iran and had made design and construction recommendations for bridges, tunnels, pipelines, dams, harbors, hangars, and other projects in widely varied geological conditions, from desert sand dunes to rugged, mountainous regions to soft, recent marine deposits (in geological terms) in the Persian Gulf area to the south and the Caspian Sea in the north.

Also, as I spent time in the lab watching crushing-strength tests being done on thousands of concrete samples made with different standards, I came to believe even more strongly that the theories about reinforced concrete and steel that I had been taught in college were inadequate.

The Plan Lab's recommendations had to be in compliance with differing building standards that varied depending on the nationality of the particular consulting firm managing the project in Iran. I was amazed to see how drastically the standards for testing and design varied from country to country. For instance, German firms carried out the grading used to determine the sizes of aggregates using sieves with round openings, whereas US firms used square ones. Also, many European design criteria for reinforced concrete structures were based on the crushing strength of various-sized cubes rather than of cylinders. Similarly, procedures for extracting soil samples for testing also varied widely from country to country.

It was fascinating to hear engineers from different countries defend their own methodology for determining the physical and chemical properties of materials—and amazing to see that they all made sense and arrived at about the same design parameters. Our recommendations had to be in different formats that were acceptable to each client. In addition, design philosophies were also very different. Some companies from some countries were more conservative and depended on calculated theoretical values, while others, especially those from the US, were more pragmatic and based their judgments more on experience.

Within a couple of months, I was being given more and more challenging assignments, such as forensic investigations in general and research into why construction materials failed in particular, that the lab had previously always turned down.

On September 1, 1962, the devastating magnitude 7.4 Boin-Zahra (Boinzahra) Earthquake struck near the city of Ghazvin, about 160 kilometers northwest of Tehran. It killed an estimated 12,000 people, caused widespread destruction in the region—and provided needed momentum for expanding the Plan Lab's activities in forensic investigations.

Most of the fatalities were caused by the catastrophic collapse of mud huts during the first few seconds of shaking that caught the inhabitants by surprise and prevented them from escaping.

However, I was puzzled to learn that in some villages, none of the huts were left standing, but in others, scattered dwellings remained intact when apparently identical huts all around them collapsed. The villagers attributed this to divine providence, but this phenomenon made an indelible impression on me that would, after I experienced the 1971 San Fernando Earthquake, shape my perceptions regarding ground shaking and the response of structures to earthquakes.

After the quake, the Shah issued a decree that simple, inexpensive systems be developed to reduce casualties in future earthquakes. On behalf of the Plan Lab, I developed a system of simple tubular frames that supported chain-link fencing, which could withstand the weight of the collapsed heavy mud roofs and walls and allow the residents to escape. The system could be installed in existing huts as well as integrated into newly built ones.

I also found the response of reinforced concrete structures to the strong shaking very interesting because I had never observed the aftermath of a large earthquake. For example, I saw partially collapsed buildings whose concrete beams had completely disintegrated, leaving their steel reinforcement bars hanging like cut wires dangling from electric poles. After the quake, there was much speculation that the heavy damage was due to shoddy work, the use of substandard materials, especially cement, all of which was imported, and corruption.

The damage to partially completed buildings led to many disputes between owners and contractors, with the owners alleging mismanagement, stealing, and cheating by the contractors and therefore refusing to pay them. As a result, the Plan Lab was inundated with samples of broken concrete to be tested for both their cement content and for the generic properties of their aggregates. In addition, the more sophisticated engineering firms ordered strength tests on core samples taken from their damaged structures.

This situation offered me, as a new college graduate, unheard-of opportunities to advance my knowledge and experience. With every successful project, I grew more confident in my ability to think beyond the conventional boundaries of solving problems. The tools available in the lab made it possible for me to verify the accuracy of my assumptions and theoretical calculations as well as the viability of the solutions I was developing.

Outside the lab, my social life was limited to dating Lili, my Ararat Scout "crush," who had returned from Italy, and to visiting Ardashes and his wife, Clara. They made working in Iran bearable. I also kept in touch with Lynn, who had graduated from U of I and was now working in Chicago. In her frequent letters, she often expressed a desire to visit Tehran, but I did not take that notion seriously and tried to discourage her.

Meanwhile, my mother's friends and acquaintances, all in full match-making mode, kept bringing their unmarried, dolled-up daughters to our home to "visit" her. After each visit, my mother would tell me that she couldn't approve of my marrying any of the daughters. To me it was all hilarious because marriage was the farthest thing from my mind at that point.

The Abadan Airport Project

In spring 1962, toward the end of my first year at the Plan Lab, Mr. Van der Wal informed me that his contract was due to expire in three months, that it was not going to be renewed, and that the lab was looking for a new director. He told me that he had recommended me for the post but that I had been rejected for being an Armenian and because I lacked a PhD. He added that he had therefore nominated me for a Dutch government fellowship that would involve a one-year postgraduate program based in Rotterdam.

By that time, I had become the "face" of the Plan Lab in Iran. Most consulting engineers and, more importantly, the National Iranian Oil Company (NIOC) and the Consortium knew of me. I had earned their respect and they were confident that I could carry out complex assignments.

Two months before Mr. Van der Wal's departure, the International Federal Aviation Administration (FAA) and the International Civil Aviation Organization (ICAO) had ordered an evaluation of the newly revamped Abadan Airport on the Persian Gulf to see whether it could accommodate the heavy wheel assemblies of Boeing 707 aircraft and be classified as an international airport.

It was no secret that the Shah was very interested in having Abadan classified as a second international airport, in addition to Mehrabad, so the Consortium could have direct overseas flights in and out of the hub of Iran's oil industry.

Since none of the foreign consulting firms in Iran were capable of carrying out the evaluation, the Plan Organization announced—arbitrarily and without consulting us first—that the Plan Lab would carry it out. Never before had we undertaken an assignment that would be scrutinized by international authorities. In addition, naming a government agency to evaluate a government facility created the immediate appearance of a conflict of interest, to say the least.

The load classification number (LCN) method of runway evaluation was among the accepted evaluation methods, and I vaguely remembered having either heard or read about how to evaluate pavement by determining its LCN, but I could not pinpoint where I had come across it. I only knew that it had not been at the Plan Lab's library.

That night, I searched through the binders of trade-magazine clippings that I had compiled at U of I and was elated to find an article that included a brief discussion of the procedure for determining the LCN of a pavement. Even more helpful, it included examples that plotted the field data.

After the lab received the authorization to start, I had the plate-bearing trailer moved to Abadan and sent a team there with a list of the tests and procedures that they were to carry out.

Because the testing and its possible results were so sensitive, the technicians were ordered not to discuss the project with anyone, not that anybody would have understood the meaning of the raw test data in any case. I flew to Abadan on the last day of the testing to observe the final tests and review the raw results. I noticed that in several locations on the runway, the pavement had failed and that even the first application of loads on small plates had created permanent half-inch depressions in the blacktop.

This was not a good sign because there should not have been any permanent depressions on pavement that deep. Also, any deflections should have rebounded as soon as the load was removed. I ordered the testing halted and called Mr. Van der Wal with the bad news. He in turn told me that he had received several anxious calls from the office of the contractor, a very wealthy and influential man named Khoram, inquiring about the test results.

I sent the crews back to Tehran and checked into Abadan International Hotel planning to fly home the next day. That night, as I was reviewing the test results, I heard a loud knock at my door.

When I opened it, I saw three large-framed men standing there. One of them held out a bulging white envelope and said, "Courtesy of Mr. Khoram."

I was so stunned that I could barely speak, but I replied, "Please give my regards to Mr. Khoram, but I cannot accept this. I really haven't had a chance to analyze the results and won't be able to until I get back to the lab."

He took back the envelope but stated, "Mr. Engineer, this is just a down payment for your efforts."

I replied, "No, no... thank you very, very much..." and tried to close the door, but he stuck out his foot so I could not close it and said, "Be warned that if the results aren't good, you'll never return to Abadan because your family will find your dead body floating in the Gulf." He then moved his foot away and the three of them left.

The next day, I flew back to Tehran with the firm intention of never returning to Abadan.

The test results and analysis were no surprise. I included them in my report along with a short cover letter stating that the load-bearing capacity of the Abadan runway could not handle the weight of jumbo jet landing gear assemblies. Both Mr. Van der Wal and I signed the letter and the report, which were then hand-carried to the Plan Organization.

I later heard that the Shah was upset about the shoddy work that had been carried out on the runway and disappointed when Abadan's application to be classified as an international airport was rejected.

IN THE FALL OF 1962, Mr. Van der Wal left Iran and I was appointed interim deputy director of the Plan Lab. Two weeks after he left, I received a letter notifying me that I had been granted a Dutch Government fellowship to study in Holland beginning that spring. With that letter in my pocket, I could not have cared less who the new Plan Lab director was going to be.

Three months later, I was informed that an Iranian engineer with a PhD in soil mechanics from the Massachusetts Institute of Technology (MIT) had been named to the post. I was also asked to show him the utmost cooperation.

At my first meeting with the new director, Dr. Erfan, he told me that he had heard quite a bit about me and he wanted to assure me that he was only interested in carrying out research. He added that I could continue running the lab as before.

When I asked him about the nature of his research, he replied, "I'd like to drop a particle of clay in a bucket of water and watch what happens."

I thought he was pulling my leg or trying to be funny because if, after receiving a doctorate from MIT in soil mechanics, he still did not know what happens to a clay particle immersed in water, there was no way he was competent to take over the Plan Lab.

However, at his request, I gave him a guided tour of the lab and introduced him to the staff. During the tour, he did not ask any questions about the equipment or about what the different departments were doing. Two weeks after he was settled in his office, I took my two-week annual vacation.

Chapter 15

WORK AND MARRIAGE

A LOT HAPPENED DURING THOSE TWO WEEKS. First of all, I sold my car and gave my dad the proceeds because I could not afford to keep it while studying in Holland. I also applied for a new passport since I could not renew my expired student passport.

I also received a letter from Lynn in which she informed me that she had accepted a teaching offer from Thailand. Her plane ticket included a stop in Tehran, and she enclosed her flight schedule in her letter.

My main concern was that I could not afford to pay for a hotel room for her three-day stay, but I found a room for her at a fairly affordable small hotel, which had been converted from a house, across from the US Embassy.

The Beginnings of the Ahwaz Airport Project

Meanwhile, a friend of mine told me that he had heard from the director of the consulting engineering firm of Ali Adibi & Associates, where he was a draftsman, that in the wake of the Abadan airport fiasco, the IOOC had decided to build a new airport in Ahwaz so larger aircraft could land there—and that his boss was interested in submitting a proposal for the design.

Out of curiosity, I called an acquaintance who had a fairly high position at the Consortium's engineering office. He confirmed the news about the Ahwaz airfield and added, "Given Abadan, we've decided to retain the Plan Lab for the services we will require." He then asked me if I was excited because the lab would be working on the project.

When I told him about my fellowship and that I was going to leave the lab, he exclaimed, "You can't do that!" and offered to set up a meeting the next day with Dr. Mashayekh, the head of the Consortium's engineering department, and Clark Beckett, the managing director of IMG, a UK management company. But as I hung up from the call, I thought to myself,

"Like heck I can't leave the lab!"

At the meeting, I was asked if I could postpone my studies for one year so I could direct the design and construction of the Ahwaz runway. I replied that the new Plan Lab director was in place and that the lab should be able to handle their needs.

"It isn't the lab that we're interested in—it's you," Dr. Mashuekh stated. "We want you to direct all the phases of the project. And if you want to leave the lab and join another company, the project will go there."

I was flattered, but I was not overjoyed at the prospect of giving up my fellowship. Then Mr. Beckett said, "There are several prominent Dutch firms doing work for the IOOC that could easily get you a one-year extension."

That night I rationalized that because I planned to return to Iran after going to Holland, I needed to remain on good terms with clients like the Consortium. I also decided that under no circumstances would I remain at the lab.

The next day, I called Adibi & Associates and asked to speak to the head of human resources. To my surprise, Dr. Adibi himself got on the line and without asking anything about me or my background, invited me to meet with him at my earliest convenience.

The Adibi & Associates offices were in a high-rise building next to the Consortium's offices. Dr. Adibi was a city planner who held several UK degrees and was providing consulting engineering services to the Plan Organization. He was also trying to obtain projects from the Consortium, and he revealed that during a marketing meeting with them a few days earlier, he had been told that the Ahwaz airport project would go to the entity where I worked, which at that time was the Plan Lab. He then said that he really wanted me working at his company and bluntly told me that whatever my salary was at the lab, he would pay me ten times as much.

When I told him that I would be available for only one year, he replied, "Then we will have to work as fast as we can to get the job done in one year."

THINGS WERE MOVING REALLY FAST. Almost too fast. Lynn was due to arrive two days later, but I could not pick her up or show her around the city because I no longer had a car. I also had to resign from the Plan Lab, arrange for my studies in Holland to be postponed by one year, and—worst of all—inform Lili of Lynn's arrival. The only bright spot was the enticement of that thousand-dollar-a-month salary at Adibi & Associates.

Lynn's flight was scheduled to arrive late on Friday night, so I thought that since the lab was closed for the Iranian weekend, which ran from Thursday at noon until Saturday morning, I could use one of the Land

Rovers. Then I learned that they were all out at various sites. The only vehicle available was a red stake-bed garbage truck. I took it and began driving it home.

While I was stopped at a light, I spotted Jerry, a friend of mine who was a US graduate in electronics, in his German Opel waiting at the same light. I honked to get his attention, and he shouted, "What the hell are you doing in that garbage truck?"

I indicated that I wanted to talk with him, and when the light changed, we drove through the intersection and pulled over. I told him that I needed to pick up my American friend from the airport later that night, and he said I was out of my mind to show up driving a garbage truck. He then offered to go with me, so I drove the truck back to the lab and we agreed that he would pick me up and take me to the airport to meet Lynn.

She arrived at one in the morning wearing a white coat and high heels, and I was thankful that I had bumped into Jerry because if not for him, her coat would have had to be dry-cleaned to remove the stains and odor of trash from the truck. When she came out of customs with her suitcase, we hugged and kissed and then drove to the hotel.

I saw that she was exhausted, so I told her to rest and that I would see her next day. But as Jerry was driving me back to my house, he told me, "You'd be stupid to let her go." I explained that there was nothing I could do because she had to continue her trip to Thailand.

When I told my parents at breakfast the next morning that she had arrived, my dad, who had seen her picture and the small calendars marked with kisses and so forth, advised me, "Son, that girl loves you, and if she stays at our house, you'll have to marry her."

I said, "She's going to Thailand and she's staying at a hotel, and the only reason she's coming here this afternoon is to visit and meet you."

When I went back to the hotel late the next morning, I found her sitting in the lobby with her suitcase and looking very unhappy. I asked her if the hotel was uncomfortable. She replied that she was disappointed that I had not taken her to my parents' home. I was surprised and told her that because her stay was to be so short, I had thought that the hotel, with its European-style bathroom and shower, would be more suitable for her.

I then almost fell over when she announced, "I only have a one-way ticket from Chicago to here, and I'm going to stay in Tehran."

"To do what?" I stammered.

"To get a job and be with you."

My world was caving in all around me. I could not think straight, and for the first time I had no solution for the problem at hand. From that moment

Lynn Kreuzberger

on, it was as if I was on autopilot and no longer in charge of my faculties. But in the midst of all my confusion and disarray, she actually had a calming effect on me. Every time I looked into her blue eyes, a reassuring voice inside me kept telling me, "Everything's going to be all right."

We took a taxi to my parents' home. My dad, who unlike my mother spoke no English at all, greeted Lynn in Armenian and told her that she was welcome. My mother, who knew a little English, was reserved, and I could see her unease at having this strange thing in our apartment. When she saw Lynn's suitcase, she asked her to put it in their bedroom. We had tea and sweets, and I then announced that we were going to visit Ardashes and Clara.

I never needed to let them know beforehand that I was going to visit them, and I was not about to do that just because Lynn was with me. We arrived and went straight up to their living room. I noticed that the kitchen door was open as usual but thought nothing of it, and moments after I introduced Lynn to them, it was as if they had all known one another forever.

But as we were chatting, Ardashes kept jerking his head toward the kitchen. I could not figure out what he was trying to communicate to me, so I went into the kitchen—and saw Lili hiding behind their refrigerator. I grabbed her hand and led her into the hallway, where I announced, "Am I glad to see you here! Come and meet my guest from America!" and led her into the living room.

"Lynn," I said, "look who's come to meet you!"

At U of I, Lynn had heard about Lili. And Lili about Lynn.

Lynn stood and extended her hand to shake Lili's. I could see that it was limp and that she was still trying to recover from the shock. Before long, though, all three girls began chatting, so I dragged Ardashes to the kitchen and asked why Lili had been hiding behind the refrigerator. He explained that she had been visiting and that they had seen us come in through the gate below. Lili could not leave without bumping into us on the staircase, so she had decided to go into the kitchen and leave through the back door. But she had not been able to leave without being seen because the kitchen door was open.

LYNN STAYED AT OUR HOUSE for the next several weeks. My fellowship was postponed for a year, and I started my work on the Ahwaz airport from Adibi's office.

At home, things gradually settled down to a normalcy that nonetheless remained rather forced due mostly to my mother's unhappiness with the unfathomable prospect of her son marrying a woman who was not Armenian.

Lynn quickly found a teaching job at the American School, and with our two salaries, we rented a nice furnished apartment. Lynn was relieved to move into it, and the Armenian landlords were very kind to her. They helped her to shop and taught her to cook Armenian dishes. I had dinner with her every night but slept at home to keep my father happy.

One way or the other, the awkward situation had to be resolved. We decided to get married, which meant that we had to get a marriage certificate not only from the government but also from our Armenian church. However, although I knew many of the members of the Tehran diocese, we were refused because Lynn was not of Armenian descent.

We finally decided to marry at the American Presbyterian church that had established Mehr, my primary school. Dr. Elder, the church primate, had married my parents in Kermanshah more than twenty-five years earlier and was happy to issue the certificate.

The ceremony took place on May 14, 1963. Ardashes was my best man, and my sister, Rima, was Lynn's maid of honor. My parents attended the church ceremonies but not the reception at our apartment, where Lynn and I, Rima, and several of my friends partied all night.

The Birth of N.F. Yaghoubian & Associates

The Ahwaz project was progressing without a hitch. I signed a contract with the Plan Lab to provide the technicians and a site laboratory for quality control, and Dr. Erfan assigned Shahen Askari as the lab's liaison with me. However, Shahen was more than that. He was also my eyes and ears at the site.

The asphalt mix for the pavement would have to withstand daily temperatures as high as 140°F without either oozing or deforming under the weight of aircraft wheel assemblies. Maintaining the uniformity of the mix was a great challenge. The asphalt produced by the plant that been built next to the construction site had to be held to the highest degree of uniformity, which required that every batch be sampled and tested. Also, at night, natural gas that remained in a depleted oil well about five kilometers from one end of the runway was set alight. This created a huge flare that made it easy

Lynn's and my wedding day, the American Church in Tehran, May 14, 1963:
(from left) the Zorabians; my sister, Rima; my mother and father;
Lynn and myself; Clara Yerganian; the Ohanian family

Our wedding ceremony, with Rima as maid of honor

for us to see any shadows cast by uneven areas in the pavement. Any flaws observed were marked and fixed the next day.

After the airport was completed, it was used mainly for flights having to do with the Consortium, and to some extent with NIOC. Starting in 1980 with the outbreak of the Iran-Iraq war (1980-1988), the government's civil aviation agency took it over. During that period, the runway not only remained operational but was used by the Iranian Air Force in its sorties against the Iraqi forces.

The Kharg-to-Khargu Islands Pipeline Project

By the time the Ahvaz project was wrapping up in the fall of 1963, Lynn and I were planning our move to the Netherlands. We were also expecting the birth of our first child in early March, at about the same time that my program was to begin.

The Consortium was happy with the Ahvaz project and made it clear that they planned for me to be involved in all of their projects. However, they were also aware of my impending departure. One night Mr. Beckett called me at home to tell me about a submarine pipeline project between Kharg and Khargu islands in the Persian Gulf. A US firm, Tellepsen, had won the contract, but the exterior concrete liner that would keep the pipeline weighed down on the sea floor remained the Consortium's responsibility. Beckett suggested that I form my own company to design the specifications of the mix for the concrete and also set up a field laboratory to test concrete samples.

I told him that I would get back to him the next day. Lynn and I then talked and concluded that although my studies in Holland would be fully financed by the fellowship, we had no savings and the baby would mean other expenses. However, if I did create the company, it would be a year old and considered established and fully operational by the time we returned to Iran. I came up with a rough budget to cover the needed equipment and monthly operating expenses and estimated five thousand US dollars for startup costs and a monthly salary of twelve hundred dollars for a technician. I doubled that figure to cover miscellaneous expenses and added two thousand dollars a month to be sent to me in Holland.

Luckily I learned about a concrete technician named Albert Azarian who was fluent in English and had worked for the US Army Corps of Engineers in Iran for several years. He had applied to emigrate to the United States with his family and, anticipating a quick resolution to the process, had already resigned from the Corps. However, problems with his papers and documents had resulted in his immigration status being delayed indefinitely.

I was pleased when Albert agreed to take on the technician assignment for one year. The Consortium approved both my plans and my budget estimates, after which I established N.F. Yaghoubian & Associates, my first consulting firm. Shahen willingly agreed to manage our operations from Tehran until I returned from Holland.

Meanwhile, Lynn packed her one suitcase and left for Holland to find us a place to live. I moved back to my parents' apartment and planned to follow her a few weeks later.

During my remaining time in Tehran, I prepared the concrete specifications, which included the use of special imported salt-resistant cement, nonreactive aggregates, and the thickness required for the liner to resist uplift from the seabed.

Shortly after my departure, Shahen arranged to borrow portable concrete strength-testing equipment and forwarded it to the site.

N.F. Yaghoubian & Associates was in business.

Postgraduate Studies in Holland

I landed at Amsterdam's Schiphol Airport around mid-morning on a crisp autumn day in 1963. Lynn welcomed me with her usual easygoing smile. She had a new hairdo, was wearing boots, and looked a little more pregnant than when we had parted but also very relaxed.

We took a train to the busy port city of Rotterdam and made our way to our temporary home, a room that Lynn had rented on the second floor of an old house on Westersingel Street. Construction activity was going on everywhere, but the absence of sun compared to Tehran made for a gloomy atmosphere.

The next day, I reported to the Bouwcentrum, an affiliate of the National Council for Industrial Research. There I met my advisor, Dr. Van Santee, who briefed me on the curriculum administered by Delft University, Holland's largest and oldest public technical university, located in The Hague. The main subjects of my studies were courses in geomechanics, concrete design, highway design, underground construction, and environmental studies, and I was allocated time and money to attend related workshops and international seminars in other European countries.

These included visits to the French Concrete Institute in Paris and to Britain's Road Research Laboratory (now known as the Transport Research Laboratory or TRL) in Crowthorne, Berkshire. In fact, the Road Research Laboratory served as a model for the Plan Organization's Soils and Materials

Laboratory. The entire curriculum I was following was oriented toward merging the theoretical facets of civil engineering with experiencing hands-on practical applications.

Although the focus in France and the UK was on "deterministic" behavior of construction material in general and the creep characteristics of concrete in particular (creep is the deformation of a material to constant load over time), the emphasis in Holland was primarily on the practical uses of construction materials in large projects.

One example of the above was the design and construction of underground motorways in busy urban areas of Rotterdam that were intended to minimize traffic bottlenecks while also taking environmental concerns into account. One important construction procedure known as "slurry trench walls" was used extensively in building the walls of tunnels. These walls then supported the concrete slabs when they were poured, and this allowed traffic to continue using the surface roads while the soil under the slabs was excavated to create space for the underground roadways.

Naderhorst, a long-established firm, was carrying out one such project, and I was fortunate enough to secure an apprentice assignment on it. Aside from the technical aspects of the assignment, I also became good friends with young Eric Naderhorst, who was being groomed to take over the family firm.

The firm had plans to expand operations in the Middle East, so they took a special interest in me as a potential contact in Iran as well as other nations in the Middle East. Eric therefore made sure that I learned about Naderhorst's different projects throughout Holland. That opportunity alone increased my exposure to mega-projects exponentially.

Naderhorst had also established close ties with a newly founded geotechnical firm, Fugro. In this instance, I was able to return Naderhorst's flow-of-information favors by assisting with the expansion of the Fugro laboratory from its original location in a small old building to larger quarters.

There is a saying that "God created the world, but the Dutch created Holland," and that is not far from the truth, given that about 27 percent of its land lies below sea level and has been reclaimed from the sea. Because the only way to accommodate the nation's projected population growth is by creating more habitable land, the Dutch experience has been carefully watched by international organizations with an eye to global population growth, which reached an estimated 7 billion in 2011.[1]

During my studies, I learned a great deal about the relationships between

1. http://geography.about.com/od/obtainpopulationdata/a/worldpopulation.htm

environmental planning and earth, atmospheric, and social sciences. The Dutch have used environmental planning to develop reclaimed lands for use as population centers for centuries, and the planning and construction of Holland's polders—tracts of low-lying land reclaimed from the surrounding bodies of water—were a demonstration of the practical applications of the environmental sciences.

Historically, polders have been built in northern Holland in areas adjacent to the North Sea. The first lines of containment are massive earth dikes that separate the North Sea from the Zuiderzee, a shallow bay that is exposed to large, powerful northern storms. After secondary dikes are constructed to subdivide the protected areas, windmills are used to pump water out of these subdivided areas until the sea bottom, several feet lower than the surrounding water, is fully exposed and can be developed for mixed residential and industrial use.

The draining of the polders often uncovered sunken ships and artifacts that provided information about the lives of the people who lived there in past eras. For decades, teams of archeologists have been mapping the locations of these discoveries, cataloguing them, and archiving and conserving them for research. Significant objects have been housed in the local museums for future generations to wonder at and study.

Many environmental factors, including needed infrastructure, city planning, social services, and projected demographics for optimum living and business conditions, were taken into account in long-term development plans and implemented in the construction of polders. And because Holland is so densely populated, the nation has in place numerous regulations intended to foster a high living standard for its citizens. In fact, the Dutch often joke that the government decides the cradle-to-grave destiny of each and every citizen.

The knowledge of environmental science studies that I gained was fascinating and made a lot of sense for Holland, but at the time I could not see how such studies could possibly be applied in vast countries such as Iran or the United States. Still, what I learned made a deep impression and actually transformed my perspective about the engineering profession itself. I eventually realized that I could no longer look solely at technical engineering solutions without also considering their environmental implications. Not only that, I was able to take these considerations into account in specific projects later in my career.

By the time my studies in Holland ended, I had seen and added so much to my engineering background that I could not wait to get an opportunity to return to Iran and apply what I had learned.

Family Life

The Christmas season in Holland, although frigid, was very special. Lynn was now in the sixth month of her pregnancy. By that time, we had found a larger apartment on Makaver Straat near Rotterdam Harbor. It was one of two units in a narrow four-story building that was laid out in a peculiar alternating-floor design. The first unit's living room and the kitchen were on the ground floor, but the bedroom and shower were on the third floor. Our living room and kitchen, on the other hand, were on the second floor, and our bedroom and shower were on the fourth floor. A long, narrow spiral stairway that (fortunately) bypassed the ground unit's bedroom led to our bedroom. It was unheated, and our only source of heat, an electric fireplace, was in the living room.

The combination of the lack of heat and the difficulties that Lynn was having negotiating the narrow stairway up to our room made it necessary for us to change our sleeping arrangement. This involved moving our double mattress down to the living room. In Holland, multistory buildings have pulleys installed on their roofs so furniture and other large objects can be hosted up and brought inside through the windows. (Obviously, the reverse process is used when residents move out.)

The obvious solution to moving the mattress was by using the pulley, but to save money I decided to maneuver the mattress down the stairway myself.

It was too stiff to be rolled or folded down to a manageable size, but I did my best to fold it in half and shoved it into the stairwell—only to see it instantly spring open like a butterfly spreading its wings. It got wedged against the walls of the spiral stairway and there was no room to get around it. The only way I could try to move it was from above and, for the first time, my two hundred-plus pounds came in handy because I ended up literally forcing the mattress down the stairs by jumping on it repeatedly. Each jump shoved it down a couple more inches as it twisted along the spiral staircase at an infinitesimal pace. At times it was wedged so tightly that I thought the only way I would ever get to the living room floor again myself would be by being hoisted down there on the pulley!

Three hours later, the mattress popped into the living room, and this adventure has always remained one of my fondest memories of life in a typical Dutch dwelling.

Once we moved into the living room, we enjoyed listening to the radio that was installed in one of the walls. It had only two stations, and we listened mostly to the classical music one, which also carried brief local news broadcasts in Dutch every hour. Many Dutch words are similar to English, but with slightly different pronunciations. In fact, there was no need for us to speak Dutch because everyone we met was eager to converse in English. It never failed that when I asked a passerby for directions or gave a taxi driver an address, I was always answered in perfect English.

LYNN AND I HAD HEARD MUCH ABOUT the Belgian city of Bruges, which was only two hours away by train, and on Saturday, November 23, 1963, we planned to spend the day there.

While Lynn was in the bathroom getting ready, I turned on the radio to listen to music, but instead of music, the Dutch announcer was saying something about "President Kennedy," "Dallas, Texas," and President Johnson. At first I thought that the announcer had mistakenly said "President Johnson" instead of "Vice-President Johnson," but when I turned up the volume, I realized that the announcer was saying that Kennedy was dead.

Knowing how much Lynn admired him, I knocked on the bathroom door and told her that there seemed to be bad news from the US. Her first question was whether it had something to do with the Vietnam War, but when she came out and heard the news, she collapsed into a chair and kept repeating, "I can't believe it!"

We had to leave right away to catch the train to Bruges. Since it was a Saturday, the tram to Rotterdam's main railroad station was fairly empty. When the conductor came by to check our tickets, I saw tears in his eyes as he asked us in English if we had heard the news about President Kennedy's assassination. We were speechless.

The same grief was everywhere at the train station, and I saw some women sobbing. The *International Herald Tribune* had the full story about Kennedy's death and the famous photograph of Johnson taking the presidential oath of office standing next to Jacqueline Kennedy on board the plane that was carrying Kennedy's body back to Washington DC.

When we reached the town center in Bruges, we saw tourists walking around looking dazed and in shock. In sidewalk cafes, everyone was reading newspapers with huge headlines about the tragic event. Indeed, like many people, I have never forgotten where I was when I heard the tragic news.

OUR DAUGHTER CHRISTINA LYNN was born in Rotterdam on March 8, 1964. Needless to say, having a Dutch-born daughter has always left me with a soft spot in my heart toward Holland and the Dutch people.

I have always been grateful, and always will be, that I was able to carry out my postgraduate studies in such a truly unique and delightful country and among such special people. The reactions of the Dutch to President Kennedy's assassination were indicative of their compassionate, kind, and generous spirit, even though they had barely begun to return to normal life after the agonies of World War II.

Lynn suggested that we travel to Lansing after my program ended and before we returned to Iran so her family could meet Christina. This was no problem financially because I had enough money from my business that we could afford the trip. So we packed up and flew to the US with our tiny bundle of joy.

We planned to spend three days with Ardashes and his family, who were now settled in New York, before continuing on to Chicago and to see Lynn's family. Then we would return to Iran.

Chapter 16

BACK TO AMERICA
and a Pioneering Project for Dames & Moore

AFTER OUR NEW YORK STAY, we flew to Chicago and took the train to Lansing, Illinois, to visit Lynn's father, James, and her sister, Sara. Lynn's mother had died after I had returned to Iran.

James, a veteran of World War I, was growing frail and was now housebound. Because he was no longer able to drive his 1961 Chevrolet Impala, Lynn suggested that we should buy it and drive out to California. She had never been there and thought we could travel around and sell the car before we returned to Tehran. Since I had friends in California, her plan was fine with me.

One day while she was visiting her family and friends, I drove to U of I, which was less than two hours away, to catch up with my friends Bijan and Moe, who were teaching there. I was very happy to return to my alma mater and spend time with them. Out of curiosity, I stopped by the university placement office and asked a placement officer about salaries for geotechnical engineers in the US because I was curious to know what engineers in Iran should be getting paid. When he learned about our plan to visit California, he suggested that I contact a friend of his who was a placement officer at the University of California at Berkeley.

Two days later, we headed west to northern California via Salt Lake City and Lake Tahoe to San Francisco for our California sightseeing trip. We planned to visit Los Angeles last and to fly back to Iran from there. The three-day trip along the interstate highway system was wonderful. Christina, though only six weeks old, was an easy baby, and we arrived in Berkeley without any problems. I found a small motel on the University Avenue, but with the baby it was not suitable for more than a night or two, so we decided to look for a furnished apartment that we could rent for a month while we were touring California.

Dames & Moore

The next day, while Lynn was poring over apartment ads in the local papers, I went to the Berkeley placement office to ask about the job market and about salaries for geotechnical engineers. The officer pointed to a notice board covered with postings of openings by Bay Area geotechnical firms seeking candidates. I was disappointed that none of them listed the salary information that I was looking for, but as I was about to leave, the officer pointed out a card from Dames & Moore (D&M). He described it as the premier geotechnical firm in the world and said they were recruiting geotechnical engineers.

I noted down their Market Street address in San Francisco, went back to the motel, and told Lynn that I had not been able to get the salary information that I was looking for, so we decided that I would go to D&M. For her part, she excitedly informed me that she had found a furnished two-bedroom apartment in the San Francisco suburb of Mill Valley and was scheduled to see it the following afternoon.

The next morning, I drove to D&M without making an appointment and told the receptionist that I was interested in finding out about salaries for geotechnical engineers. She handed me an employment application, told me to fill it out and mail it back, and went back to her typing. I told her that I was not looking for employment but only wanted to talk with someone about salaries. She called the office administrative manager, whose name was Dorothy.

Dorothy came out to reception area and when I explained what I was seeking, she shook her head and said that all of their technical people were very busy and that I really needed to make an appointment. However, when I told her that I was going to be in the area for only a short time before leaving the country, she asked me to follow her into an open hall so crowded with desks and busy workers that it was hard to maneuver through the room. Individual offices were lined up along the perimeter of the chaotic, disorganized "bullpen." Dorothy sat me down outside one of the offices and told me to wait until the chief engineer, Mr. Horton, called me.

While I waited, I could hear him on the phone. His conversations were aggressive and sometimes ended with him slamming down the receiver. I was seriously thinking of leaving when the door whipped open and revealed a man with a blond Marine-style crew cut who briskly asked me to step into his office. As I took my seat, his phone rang again and he started shouting at the person on the other end.

As I glanced around the office, I noticed a large greenish steel box attached to the wall a few inches above the floor with a sheet of paper taped to it that read "Please do not kick telephone equipment." I dared not smile, but it seemed clear that on occasion the excitable Mr. Horton must have kicked the box and knocked out the phone system for the whole floor.

As his phone call went on, I began to understand that it concerned some large boulders that had been dumped into San Francisco Bay but were sinking under the ocean floor. I gave the telephone box another look and shook my head thinking about his apparent abuse of it. At that moment, he said into the phone, "Hold on, Jim. I think this guy's trying to tell me something. Call me back." Visibly grinding his teeth, he slammed down the receiver and asked, "What are you shaking your head about?"

"I'm sorry," I said hesitantly and in a low voice, "but I thought that your conversation was related to trying to construct a levy or something like that by dumping rock in water with soft sedimentation and—"

"So?" he interrupted gruffly.

I apologized again and told him that I did not know the exact circumstances he had been discussing. Then I began describing the methodology of constructing levees and dikes in Holland.

He leaned back in his chair apparently totally relaxed, picked up the phone, and asked Dorothy to hold his calls. Then, in a very calm voice, he asked the purpose of my visit. When I explained and added that I was returning to Iran shortly, he asked me if I had worked in the US and whether I was a licensed engineer.

I responded that I had not and was not, and he informed me, "The annual salary of a new graduate like you is seven thousand dollars a year. But I'm willing to pay you ten thousand in addition to three months' salary as a bonus," and he then described all the other benefits, such as health insurance and vacations. He ended by handing me his business card.

I thanked him for his kind offer but told him that I had a business in Iran and had to return there.

"Just think about it," he replied, "and call me if you'd like to work for us."

I was more interested in seeing the apartment that Lynn had found than in entertaining this out-of-the-blue job offer—after all, our plans called for us finish our vacation and return to Iran, not to put down roots in America.

That afternoon we drove across the Bay Bridge and the majestic Golden Gate to Mill Valley. The apartment was in a small development set among woods. A young couple about our age, also with a young child, were the current tenants. The husband, Jay O'Shea, was a civil engineer who worked for the State of California. They were going to spend a month with their child's grandparents, who lived in Colorado, and wanted to sublet their apartment while they were away.

It was clean and furnished with pared-down Danish-style furniture— just right for us. When Jay learned that I was also a civil engineer, he wanted to know more about my career and was curious about why we wanted to rent for just a few weeks. I explained our plans and told him about my experience at D&M.

He knew about D&M and spoke very highly of the firm. He also expressed disbelief at the offer I had received and that I had turned it down!

Perhaps that gave Lynn the ammunition she needed to make the case against our returning to Tehran with an infant, but all of a sudden she began persistently pontificating about the virtues of having had work experience in America for my future as an engineer in Iran. She tried to persuade me to at least give D&M a try because we could always return to Iran later. Also, the Persian Gulf pipeline project was nearing completion, and that would spell an end to my monthly income from my consulting business.

So it seemed that the twist of fate that had started in the Berkeley placement office might be worth pursuing after all. A week later, I called Mr. Horton and asked to see him again. He was pleased and joked that "wives always prevail." He also made a point of telling me that our discussion about containment levees, which was for a land reclamation project known as Redwood City, had been very helpful.

My First D&M Project: The San Francisco Airport Runway

At our second meeting, he wanted to know more about my experience. He also expressed a special interest in the Abadan International Airport runway evaluation, but I was still surprised when I was told that my first assignment would be to evaluate one of the runways at San Francisco International Airport because I had expected to be assigned to the Redwood City project.

Before leaving D&M that day, I asked Dorothy where my office would be and whether I could see the firm's laboratory. With a smile, she advised me to arrive as early as possible and to grab an empty desk because all the offices were doubled up.

After that, a very talkative lady named Julie Schwartz, who worked in the lab, took me for a tour. She informed me that the San Francisco laboratory was the largest and had the most testing equipment of all D&M's offices. As I followed her into the lab, my jaw dropped.

"Is this it?" I exclaimed in horror.

"Oh no!" she said. "The rest is in the basement, where compaction tests are performed." She proceeded to show me around some soil-testing machines manufactured by D&M that were resting on a long table.

I was so used to the Plan Organization's well-financed and top-of-the-line laboratory that I started to feel I was trapped in a bad dream. Before I left, Julie advised me, "Go get yourself some work clothes and pair of working boots from the Emporium."

Early next morning, I arrived (wearing the new work clothes and boots that I had bought at that landmark San Francisco department store) only to find that all the desks had already been commandeered by other engineers who knew the routine better than I did. I finally spotted a small open extension of the larger hall that contained a few rows of desks, all with stacks of files on them. However, one smaller desk was empty, so I found an empty chair and positioned myself there.

A few minutes later, a shapely blonde woman walked in followed by Julie. The workers in the bullpen greeted them warmly, calling out, "Good morning, Shirley!" and "Good morning, Julie!" But when the two of them saw me at the empty desk, Julie informed me that I was sitting in the accounting section. I jumped up to leave when she added, "That's Joan's desk, but she won't be in for the rest of the week because one of her children is sick." I nodded as she continued, "Come to the lab and let me smear your shiny new boots with some mud so you'll look experienced in the field."

I felt awkward sitting behind my empty desk without anything to do and suddenly missed the Plan Lab attendants who used to bring me hot tea when I arrived every morning.

A short time later, Mr. Horton walked in and asked me to go to his office. I replied with a formal "Yes, Mr. Horton" and followed him, but when we arrived, he told me, "Call me Mal. We don't call each other by last names here." Then he picked up his phone, called a man named Jim—apparently the same Jim with whom he had been speaking during my first visit—and told him to come to his office as well. When he arrived, Mal introduced him as Jim Click and told him to give me the files for the San Francisco Airport job.

Jim shook my hand, said, "Welcome aboard," and wished me good luck. He went away to dig out the folder and soon brought it to me at my once-empty desk.

As he was turning away, I asked innocently, "Where would I find D&M's plate load test vehicle and equipment?"

Without a word, Jim went away and returned with a thick Yellow Pages telephone directory that he plopped on my desk. "Find it. It's all there," he said, and walked away.

I was seconds away from storming into Mal's office and telling him to take his job and shove it when Julie appeared and asked, "How are you doing, kiddo?"

As honestly and politely as I could, I replied, "I'm quitting. This is ridiculous. They want me to do pavement evaluation without a plate load test vehicle." Then, unable to contain myself, I muttered under my breath, "'Premier geotechnical firm,' my foot!"

Julie told me to stay put, walked away, and came back moments later with a short, round-faced man named James Angameer. Another "Jim."

This second Jim told me that he had done many projects overseas and understood my frustration. He pulled up a chair and asked me to tell him what equipment I would need for the plate load test.

As I started rattling off the list, he made notes, opened the Yellow Pages, and said, "Okay, we'll need a low-bed truck with a bulldozer on it as additional load." He flipped to the page for truck rentals and wrote down several phone numbers.

"Are you serious?" I asked.

"I am," he replied. "Find all the items on your list, then call the rental places, ask for their prices and availability, and reserve everything for delivery to the site."

"And under what heading do I find bearing plates?" I responded sarcastically.

"The plates are in the basement," he replied calmly, then added, "Now, go and get the job done."

As he walked away, I wondered if everyone who worked there was named "Jim."

Of course, this was a challenge like no other that I had ever faced before, and I was not about to throw in the towel just yet. I opened the first Jim's folder and reviewed the proposal and scope of work to be performed. Then I shrugged off my shock and began the next task, which was to find and order the needed equipment from the Yellow Pages.

It was not as bad as I had feared it might be, mainly because in my previous work experiences in Iran I had never dealt with well-organized, helpful, and trusting suppliers who went out of their way to be accommodating and to make useful suggestions.

But that is exactly what happened. I was flabbergasted when the truck rental company asked me if I also needed to rent hydraulic jacks as well as dial gauges to measure deflection. I could not believe that I was being invited to rent expensive items without the endless bargaining, guarantees, and prepayments that I was used to in Iran.

My biggest problem turned out to be locating the bearing plates and dial gauges in D&M's basement. Everything was buried under heavy sacks of sand, soil samples, old equipment, and boxes of files. I finally located the plates under some stacks of materials and rented a pickup truck for the next day.

Two days later, all the equipment and supplies were delivered to the airport. Incoming flights on that runway were rerouted, and within eighteen hours, the plate load test had been completed and I had submitted the draft of my report.

DURING THE NEXT SEVERAL WEEKS, I learned the lay of the land at D&M. Each day I took the bus from Mill Valley to the San Francisco Ferry Building, which was only a few blocks from the office. Our month at the apartment was coming to an end, and my resolve to return to Iran was weakening because each day I found myself enjoying working for D&M more and more.

When Lynn told me that an unfurnished unit in the same development was available and that she had already begun negotiating for a month-to-month rental, she did not have to persuade me. We got busy shopping for furniture on the weekends, and the memory of Iran began fading away. America was becoming our new home.

D&M's partners and employees more than compensated for the company's disorganization and gaps when it came to supplies and equipment. Like all companies, it had a hierarchy and its own formalities and customs, but never in my life had I met and had the joy of working with such a group of smart, kind, honest, and gentle professionals. There was no doubt in my mind that the role model who had set the genial tone of the office was the firm's cofounder, William Moore, an unassuming giant in the field of geotechnical engineering.

I met partners and senior employees who had their own private wood-paneled offices and were known as "associates" or "consultants." The consultants were charged with marketing D&M's geotechnical services to prospective clients. There were also "project managers" who shared four-person offices and reported to the consultants. They all held licenses from the California state board hanging on the walls above their desks. The rest of us, who were known as "field engineers," were relegated to the bullpen and the daily search for a vacant desk.

Of course the office had unwritten formalities and customs that everyone was soon made aware of. For example, the doors of the consultants' offices always remained closed, and one had to knock for permission to enter. At lunch, the consultants would go out separately, and the project managers would eat in their glass-walled offices while they played bridge. We in the bullpen were known as the "Brown-Baggers" and we ate with the secretaries and the accounting staff. This gave us opportunities to learn the office gossip.

D&M added staff whenever the office workload increased, as it did several-fold for mega-projects such as the Bay Area Rapid Transit (BART) and the Redwood City/Foster City development. New hires, who arrived almost daily, added to the already difficult congestion in the office.

I WAS SURPRISED WHEN ONE AFTERNOON Dorothy asked all of the new employees to stay behind at the end of the day. After the "old-timers" left, Dorothy announced that we were going to take an IQ test. She passed out a booklet to each of us, told us not to open them until she said to, set a timer, and ordered us to begin. Twenty minutes later, she asked us to stop, put our names on our booklets, and hand them in to her.

A few days later, I heard—through the grapevine when Dorothy happened to be absent—that Trent Dames, the firm's other founding partner, kept the tests in a locked drawer in D&M's executive offices (known as "the EO") in Los Angeles. Rumor had it that the IQ test results played a crucial role in determining which D&M employees would be invited to become partners. However, this was meaningless to new employees like me.

I soon realized that to advance to any level beyond field engineer, I would have to obtain my California professional engineer's license. I already had my Professional Engineer-in-Training license from the state of Illinois, which made me eligible to take the California exam. Since it required studying subjects related to general civil engineering disciplines, I wrote home and asked to have my engineering books sent to me. As it turned out, however, D&M ended up sending me back to Iran a few months later and I did not get my California license until years later.

D&M was a leader in the development of new testing equipment and techniques that were ultimately adopted worldwide. Professionalism was the code and standard of behavior for every D&M partner and employee, and nothing less was acceptable. I totally subscribed to their philosophy and business model. Despite my earlier reservations, I no longer had any doubt that D&M was indeed the premier geotechnical organization in the world.

For example, although many geotechnical firms were structured according to an "assembly line" model, D&M's services were always tailored and customized to meet each client's needs. Also, innovative thinking was expected of all employees, regardless of their position in the firm, and ample opportunities to be creative were provided. In many ways, exploring alternative and better solutions to problems was not new to me because that had been my modus operandi at the Plan Lab.

The Bank of California Project

About three months after I started at D&M, Robert Darragh, an associate, called me into his office to discuss a new project—an addition to the historic Bank of California headquarters at 400 California Street in the heart of San Francisco's financial district. It was now owned by Union Bank. The plan called for a twenty-two-story addition, including multilevel underground parking, to the two original landmark buildings, which were completed in 1907 as the headquarters of the Bank of California.

Bob told me that the team of engineers for the project, which included structural engineer Henry Degenkolb, founder of Degenkolb Engineering, Professor Ben C. Gerwick Jr. of UC Berkeley, Bill Moore, and himself, were considering the feasibility of a shoring system that Degenkolb had suggested. This proposed shoring solution would consist of building a cofferdam system to support the excavation walls and keep the groundwater out. However, a geotechnical investigation was necessary before the Degenkolb proposal could be decided upon, and I had been chosen to carry it out.

The John N. Pitcher Company, of Daly City, was the drilling contractor for the site investigation. The soils encountered in the borings were typical of downtown San Francisco, i.e., unconsolidated marine deposits with high groundwater very near street level.

During one of John's visits to the site, I asked if he knew how the walls of the excavation and of the surrounding buildings would be supported during construction. He shrugged and replied, "Probably the way it's always done—shoring with internal lagging and bracing. Which is better than the system that Degenkolb has concocted."

I expressed my concern that, given the high groundwater levels at the site, any removal of water down to seventy feet below street level would cause the adjacent buildings and streets to settle drastically. I described the "slurry trench wall" system used in similar situations in Holland and made a rough sketch for him on the back of a boring-log form.

This approach uses bentonite, a powdery mineral that expands into a viscous mud ("slurry") when it absorbs water. Because it is used to drill test borings in clayey formations with high groundwater, I was surprised when John told me that slurry trench wall technology had never been used in the United States. However, he immediately grasped the basic concept, was intrigued by it, and said he wanted to find out more about it.

Photograph courtesy of Degenkolb Engineering

Rendering of the proposed Bank of California headquarters complex.
The dotted line shows the addition, adjacent to and partially
cantilevering over the original 1907 bank building.

The slurry trench wall would serve two main purposes. First, it would create a cutoff wall that would keep groundwater behind the wall and out of the construction site. Second, it would act as an inner liner for the basement wall of the underground parking that would be constructed later. Structural steel frames would provide lateral support as the excavation proceeded.

The next day, I showed John the catalogues from the various foundation firms with which I had been in contact while studying in Holland. He liked one design, a half-clamshell bucket that ran up and down steel "H" soldier piles, and said he wanted to think about it. The next time we met, he showed me how he had adapted the half-clamshell device by sketching a double clamshell that hung from a crane and could excavate between the "H" piles and haul the removed soil to street level. He and I modified the design to simplify its manufacture. We also created a simpler system for carrying out the excavation that would allow us to construct a circle of panels to create the cutoff wall around the perimeter of the addition.

The first step would be to anchor a series of "H" piles in the ground. These would be set apart from each other by a distance equal to the width of the opened clamshell. To do this, seventy-foot-deep holes would be drilled and simultaneously filled with bentonite slurry to keep the holes from collapsing. Then, eighty-five-foot-long "H" piles would be lowered into the holes and pounded an additional fifteen feet into the soil until the piles were level with the site surface. Following this, a sand-cement mixture as dense as the site clay would be injected down into the hole. The mixture would displace the lighter bentonite and stabilize each "H" pile.

The next step would be to excavate the area between two "H" piles using the double clamshell. When fully opened, the clamshell's jaws would slide down the sides of the piles under their own weight while the teeth pulverized and removed the sand-cement and clay between the piles. As these materials were removed, the excavation would immediately be filled with bentonite slurry, again to keep the walls from collapsing. After the space between the "H" piles was excavated to seventy feet down, a reinforced-steel cage the size and shape of the excavation would be lowered into the bentonite-filled cavity.

The final step would be to pour concrete using tremie technology. A seventy-foot-long funnel-shaped tremie pipe would be lowered to the bottom of the bentonite-filled excavation. Concrete would then be poured down the pipe, and this would displace the bentonite from the bottom up. The concrete, reinforced by the steel cage, would then harden into a panel held in place by the "H" piles. The panels would be constructed in an alternating sequence until the entire perimeter of the site was encircled by a cutoff wall of seventy-foot-deep reinforced concrete panels.

The "Slurry Trench Wall" Method involves drilling a series of holes into which "H" piles are placed at widths that precisely match the opened clamshell excavator. The soils between "H" piles are excavated and filled with reinforced concrete. This creates a wall that separates and protects adjacent soils and structures from collapsing while the excavation continues.

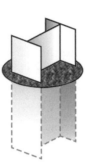

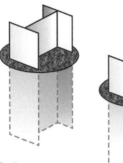

▲
"H" piles are placed in drilled holes and fixed into place with a sand-cement mixture.

The soil between "H" piles is then ▶ excavated with the clamshell and immediately replaced with bentonite to prevent the excavation from collapsing.

BENTONITE

SOIL

▼ A prefabricated steel cage, 70 feet long and the width of the "H" piles is lowered into the bentonite-filled excavation.

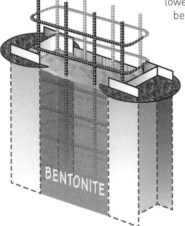

BENTONITE

The bentonite is then displaced with concrete ▶ from the bottom of the excavation up, using a funnel-shaped tremie pipe. A basketball "plug" aids in pushing the bentonite out of the pipe as the concrete is poured.

BENTONITE

CONCRETE

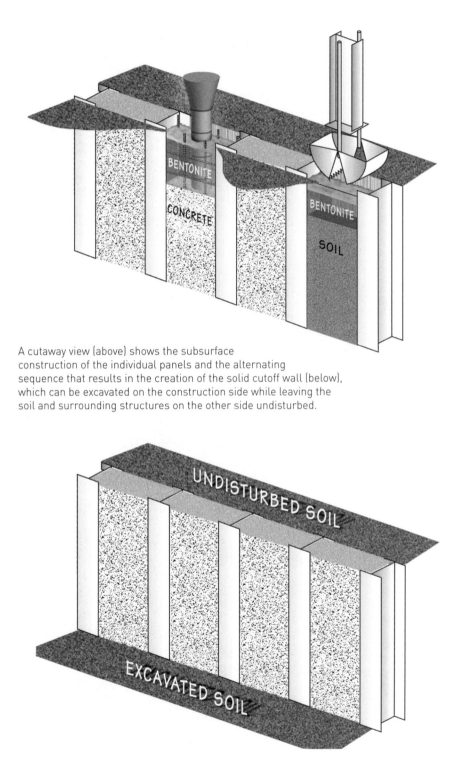

A cutaway view (above) shows the subsurface
construction of the individual panels and the alternating
sequence that results in the creation of the solid cutoff wall (below),
which can be excavated on the construction side while leaving the
soil and surrounding structures on the other side undisturbed.

Steel "H" piles are lowered into the 70-foot-deep holes, which have been filled with a slurry mix.

Photograph courtesy of Degenkolb Engineering

Drilling contractor John Pitcher (second from left) inspects the clamshell excavator.

Photograph courtesy of Degenkolb Engineering

The actual 70-foot-long tremie pipe assembly, reinforced with steel bars to keep it from bending when being transported or moved into position.

Photograph courtesy of Degenkolb Engineering

AFTER OUR DISCUSSIONS, JOHN DECIDED TO present our method to Ben Gerwick, the contractor for the foundation of the building. Ben had misgivings about Henry Degenkolb's cofferdam scheme and eagerly accepted our adaptation of the slurry trench wall method. Bob Darragh, who had heard of the method before, also went along with it.

Both of the original side-by-side structures had been built on timber piles. The building to the north had already been demolished, leaving the tops of the original timber piles exposed, and these had to be removed before the slurry wall could be built.

A large crane with a boom more than seventy feet long was moved into the large pit that had been created when the northern bank building was demolished. By the time I arrived at the site, the workers had already extracted some of the timber piles. I was astonished to see that they were placing a chokehold cable around the top of each pile and then yanking it straight out in one sudden movement—which caused the vacant space to collapse due to developed suction forces and pore pressure surge. Continuing this procedure would have undermined the sides of the existing excavation

Workers jeopardizing the site by using chokehold cables to yank out the timber piles on which the original two 1907 bank buildings were constructed.

Photograph courtesy of Degenkolb Engineering

Photograph courtesy of Degenkolb Engineering

After calling a halt to the chokehold cable approach, I (in dark jacket)
and the crew leader discuss how to remove the piles safely.

and endangered the adjacent buildings including the remaining original
bank building.

I ran toward the site superintendent yelling, "Stop! Stop!"

He looked me up and down and then asked, "Who the hell are you?
And are you going to pay for the downtime?"

I told him I wanted the piles extracted very slowly and gradually, starting at the center of the pit, and that I wanted the holes filled immediately
with fine sand. He pulled off his gloves and walked over to the nearby
coffee shop to call his boss.

Within an hour, all of the parties involved in the project, including
Bill Moore, gathered at the site. Bill listened to the superintendent's com-
plaint and then took me aside and asked me why I had ordered the con-
tractor to stop. After I explained, we walked back over to the group and
Bill very calmly told the superintendent, "I think you have to do what
Jack says!"

I am sure that my recommendations resulted in some monetary adjustments to the contract, but that did not concern me. However, Bill Moore's
handling of the situation showed the magnitude of the respect and admira-
tion that he enjoyed in professional engineering circles and set an example
for me as a young engineer.

After the timber piles were removed, I supervised the initial installation of a section of the slurry wall. The longer time period required to remove the piles allowed me to work with John on necessary adjustments and to solve various operational "kinks" to optimize the installation.

One of the most interesting of these kinks was "the mystery of the missing basketballs." This kept recurring when we were placing the tremie concrete, which was delivered through a funnel whose cone was attached to a pipe the length of the excavation. The hole at the top end of the pipe was plugged with an inflated basketball, and the fresh concrete was then pumped through the funnel. As the concrete gradually displaced the slurry in the tremie pipe, the basketball "plug" would also be pushed downward until it would pop out of the bottom of the pipe, and this allowed the fresh concrete to be deposited at the bottom of the excavation. Because the concrete was heavier than the slurry it displaced, the slurry would "float" up to the top of the excavation, where it was pumped back into the slurry tank to be reused.

We expected that the basketball would float to the surface along with the slurry so we could use it for the next pour, but it seldom did. We dubbed this the "Where did the basketballs go?" phenomenon, and it led to much speculation.

In a letter dated September 8, 1966, John Pitcher wrote to me that BART was interested in using the slurry trench system for the subway's construction

Photograph courtesy of Degenkolb Engineering

"Where did the basketballs go?" As the basketball is about to be dropped into the funnel just before the concrete is poured, I lean over the edge of the excavation (inset) to check and observe the installation of the first-ever slurry trench wall system for a high-rise building in the US.

Excavation revealing the failure of the concrete to reach the bottom of one panel.

Photograph courtesy of Degenkolb Engineering

and asked me to send him some information on modifying our clamshell design. Enclosed with the letter was a photograph he had obtained of the completed concrete wall from the Bank of California project. The wall was dotted with flattened basketballs. Apparently at least some of the basketballs burst under the weight of the concrete and remained embedded in it rather than floating to the top of the slurry.

BART did eventually use the slurry trench system. Also, the same slurry wall technology, down to the identical equipment configuration used in the bank project, was used in the construction of the World Trade Center Twin Towers in the mid- and late 1960s. Because of its shape, the excavated area with its cutoff walls was dubbed "The Bathtub."[1]

1. A photograph of the "Bathtub" is posted at http://en.wikipedia.org/wiki/File:WTC_bathtub_east.jpg

J. N. Pitcher Co.

DRILLING CONTRACTORS

6025 MISSION STREET / DALY CITY, CALIFORNIA / 992-1500

September 8th, 1966

Dear Jack:

I hope this finds you enjoying good health and good business. It must be a great satisfaction go open up an office in your native Country.

The Rapid Transit here is quite interested in the slurry trench type foundations for the subway station and I have been trying to come up with a better method than we used at the Bank of California. Incidently when that site was excavated, the wall looked surprisingly well.

I remember that you showed me a picture of a type of clam shell used by an Italian Company. This used only one half of the clam shell. It was made to go down along side of the steel beam and open away from it. I cannot remember how this was made, so would appreciate it if you could tell me where I may obtain a picture ofthis tool.

If I can solve the problem of making a good clean out tool, I feel that I will have solved all the problems. This clean out tool you showed me a picture of resembled a back hole bucket.

Work here is very slow now and we have about 10 rigs stored.

I hope your office is doing well and will be looking forward to hearing from you.

As Ever

John

John N. Pitcher

John Pitcher's letter

The Mobil Oil Refinery Project

Although I had expected to stay on the project until the Bank of California slurry trench wall had been completed, Mal Horton called me in one day to tell me that he was sending me to D&M's Los Angeles office regarding the projected expansion of a Mobil Oil refinery in Torrance, near LAX.

Sunny Los Angeles was a welcome change from San Francisco's cold and fog. The D&M office was also very different. While the San Francisco office was in a high-rise, the LA office occupied a single-story house on West Third Street in mid-Wilshire, a mixed residential and commercial neighborhood. I stayed at a motel within walking distance of the office.

The individual offices were furnished casually, and the laboratory was uncluttered, clean, and well organized. The partners and the employees were very friendly and welcoming. For example, it was an everyday occurrence for Al Smoots, the senior partner in charge of the office, to ask over the intercom whether anyone wanted to join him and go out to lunch. I really liked the down-to-earth culture there and would gladly have accepted a permanent transfer.

Lou Stern, a consultant at the office, was in charge of the project to which I had been assigned. Like most of the D&M people I met there, he was pleasant and friendly, and he told me that Mal had highly recommended me. He then went on to explain that the project was crucial for D&M not just because of the technical aspects involved but also, I later learned, because it held out the potential for mending fences with an important client.

The fence-mending referred to C.F. Braun & Co., design constructors for oil and gas projects worldwide. The firm was based in Alhambra, a city several miles northeast of downtown LA.

I learned that D&M had formerly been the only geotechnical firm that Braun had used on its projects. However, this special relationship had come to an acrimonious end several years earlier when D&M had miscalculated the lengths of the piles needed for a refinery. D&M's refusal to not only acknowledge its error, much less offer compensation for the damage that resulted, led Carl Braun, the firm's founder and chairman, to issue a directive forbidding any future business with D&M. It appeared that the dispute would never be resolved, especially because Trent Dames had refused to acknowledge any mistake on D&M's part and in fact had informed Mr. Braun during a phone conversation that D&M was no longer interested in providing any further services to his company.

This history was the backdrop to my new assignment, which concerned the construction of new process units at the Mobil Oil refinery in Torrance, near LAX. Unfortunately, Mobil, unaware of the rift between Braun and D&M, had retained Braun for the design and procurement of the proposed expansion.

Because D&M had been performing site investigations for Mobil Oil since 1942, we had already compiled a wealth of technical information about the site, and the proposed expansion would require drilling and sampling only a few borings to update D&M's existing data. This would save Mobil both time and costs.

The problem was that although a great deal of design data had been accumulated, it needed to be compiled so it would be usable. That became my task. I was given an office and a desk stacked high with old reports and recent soils test data. The endless calculations made the assignment a daunting task, and I spent a couple of days just staring at the piles.

Then it occurred to me to find out whether the analysis could be done by computer. I remembered having heard that all of D&M's timesheets from all over the country were processed at the "EO," the executive offices downtown, so I went to see Bill Tenney, the chief engineer, and asked him how they were processed. He explained that timesheets were processed at the EO, and that the raw data were entered into a computer so they could then be sorted according to the various criteria used by the administrative and accounting departments.

The next day, I went to the EO and met with Andrew Reti, a geotechnical engineer who was in charge of the EO's computers. D&M had just leased an IBM Mainframe System/360 to meet the firm's growing demand for accurate cost-accounting purposes.

After I explained the task I was facing, he assured me that the technical data could be handled just the way the accounting data were, and that he would be glad to help me out because it would be the company's first use of the computer for engineering purposes.

During the next several weeks, I organized the raw data and took it to Andy, who had it punched onto IBM cards for processing so I could prepare graphs showing the standard deviations of the raw field data. I was then able to use these to bracket the design values and put them into simple graph forms.

This first computerized engineering analysis was a huge success, and not just technically. It also resulted in D&M and Braun reestablishing their working relationship.

Chapter 17

D&M'S MAN IN TEHRAN

WHILE I WAS IN LOS ANGELES, Don Roberts, a D&M partner there, invited me to accompany him to a meeting with Frank Harvey, a good friend of his and the chief structural engineer at the Fluor Corporation. He added that Frank had just returned from Iran. I looked forward to the visit, especially because I had been spending more than twelve hours a day for several weeks on the Mobil Oil project. It would be nice to get out and to meet a new colleague.

Fluor's offices were located in the City of Commerce, just off the I-5 freeway southeast of downtown LA. Frank Harvey turned out to be a pleasant man who greeted us with a big smile and clapped his hand on Don's shoulder as they warmly shook hands.

When Don introduced me to Frank, he added, "Jack is from Iran," but Frank's response was a perfunctory "Nice to meet you." As I followed them upstairs, and I heard him tell Don, "Man, it's so good to be back home! I got sicker than a dog in that damn country."

At the top of the stairs, we entered a large room with rows of drafting tables. I followed Don and Frank to the farthest desk in the corner of the room. Blueprints were spread on the desk, and a man who looked Middle Eastern was busy turning the pages. I saw that it was a refinery site plan, with "100,000 BBL/day Refinery, Ray Iran" in the title block.

Frank introduced the man as a Dr. Honary, who was the National Iranian Oil Company (NIOC) liaison with Fluor.

Frank explained, "It's a pile job, Don. I flew over the site. There were brick factories as far as the eye could see, which told me that the site is clay and that the units should be supported on piles."

Without hesitation, I stated, "I don't think piles are needed."

Frank frowned at Don and asked, "Who is this guy?"

"He's from Iran," Don replied, "and he's the former head of the Plan Organization's laboratory in Tehran."

Frank appeared unimpressed and went on, "Don, we need 2,000 psf (pounds per square foot) bearing capacity. The soils are clay."

I shrugged and said, "The clays are desiccated, and the bearing capacity of those soils is well over 2,000 psf."

I noticed that Dr. Honary appeared clearly uneasy because I was contradicting Frank. In Farsi, he asked me directly if I knew what I was talking about. I assured him that indeed I did. He then turned to Frank and said, "We're talking about millions of dollars in savings if piles are not needed."

Suddenly, the friendly atmosphere changed and everything became businesslike. It appeared that with that amount of money on the table, the information I was offering had to be taken seriously.

Frank thought for a second and then said, "Well, we have to talk to Dick Lee, the project manager, and to Tim Rogers, the manager of Fluor Iran." He then turned to me and asked, "What did you say your name was?"

"Jack Yaghoubian."

Since Frank still was not sure who I was, he was naturally not certain he was getting accurate information. However, he told Don, "I'll be in touch after I sort out how to proceed."

On the drive back, Don expressed his displeasure with how I had handled my first encounter with Frank and kept repeating that Frank had been "a friend of D&M." However, I was just trying to help, and I was confident that my suggestions would be exceptionally helpful to their project.

Time would tell. My immediate concern was to finish my Mobil Oil report and to get home so I could continue supervising the installation of the Bank of California slurry wall—not a project in Iran.

The Ray Refinery Project

When I got back to San Francisco the following week, Mal told me that he had received positive comments about the Mobil Oil project but that I had apparently overstepped the bounds at Fluor. I shrugged and merely responded that I was really tired and needed to be with my family.

Christina was now two and had grown even more while I was away, and I was happy to be with her and to catch up on lost time. A couple of days later, Mal told me that I was being sent back to LA to prepare a proposal for the Ray Refinery, near Tehran. NIOC had decided that the site of the proposed refinery should be investigated because the cost difference between piles and conventional shallow footings was so substantial.

I had hoped to bring Lynn and Christina with me to LA, but my time there turned out to be very short. I drafted the proposal for NIOC, Don

Artist's rendering of the Ray Refinery

and I signed it, and we took it to Frank at Fluor. Without even looking at it, he asked me when I was leaving for Iran because NIOC had decided that I should investigate the site. I was disappointed that the proposal had been approved so quickly and that I would not have a chance to take the family sightseeing in LA, but I accepted the assignment, expecting that I would be in Tehran only for a short time.

I made a quick trip back to Mill Valley to pack and also immediately got in touch with my friend and colleague Shahen Askari to tell him about the project and when I would arrive.

Almost overnight, I found myself traveling back to Iran alone. All during the long flight, I pondered the fact that I had not anticipated this return. Nor had I ever thought I would find myself leaving my wife and child behind in the US.

When we landed at Mehrabad Airport, Shahen met me and drove me straight to the Hilton hotel north of the city at the foot of the Alborz Mountains. As I was checking in, the receptionist told me that they had had to move an American engineer to another hotel to accommodate me.

As soon as I was settled, Shahen and I sat in the lobby and discussed the project until morning. He informed me that he had already arranged with the Plan Lab to supply everything needed to start drilling and sampling at the site. He had also mobilized the plate load trailer and all of the equipment that needed to be moved to the site.

The following day, despite my jet lag, I went to Fluor's office to meet Tim Rogers. During our meeting, Bruno Laan, the visiting senior structural engineer whom Frank Harvey had assigned to the refinery, walked in accompanied by Arnold Luft, a structural engineer from LA assigned to Fluor's Tehran office for the refinery project.

He asked where I was staying in Tehran and, when I told him the Hilton, he exclaimed, "So you're the guy they kicked me out of my room for last night!"

I thought, "Great! First I make Frank Harvey mad, and now the guy I'll be reporting to is mad at me, too."

While Bruno was asking me about my plans and when the site investigation would start, I noticed that Arnold seemed restless and kept leaving the room.

I replied that I was planning to start the next day, but Bruno said, "Not so fast. There are problems at the site and you can't just start drilling. There are two *qanats* crisscrossing the site, and they can't be disturbed because they're legally protected."

Although I had known since I was a child about *qanats* and how they supplied Tehran with water, I had a much different understanding of them now that I was an engineer. The principal components of *qanats* are vertical shafts and horizontal tunnels.

The genius of *qanat* design from an engineering standpoint is that it can maintain the overall gradient of the horizontal tunnel so water will flow at a minimal rate throughout the length of the *qanat* without causing erosion, which would compromise the water quality at its terminus.

Bruno immediately called to an Iranian engineer, Javad Shokrolahi, and asked him to come to our meeting and provide me with vital information regarding the *qanat* situation. He then informed me gruffly, "I'm catching a flight to LA tonight. From here on, you're reporting to Arnold." And with that, he left.

When Javad and I were alone, I asked him why Arnold kept leaving the meeting. Javad confided that Arnold had arrived from LA about a week earlier and, like all foreigners visiting Tehran, was suffering from a serious case of diarrhea. However, the office workers disliked him because he was very rude, so they had told him to drink *doogh*, a mixture of yogurt and carbonated water that exacerbated diarrhea rather than helping to stop it.

As I was saying good-bye to Arnold, he complained that he had been spending more time in the bathroom than behind his desk and that all the *doogh* that he had been drinking had done no good. I suggested that he should stop the *doogh* and eat only rice and plain yogurt. Two days later, his misery was over, and he and I had become the best of friends.

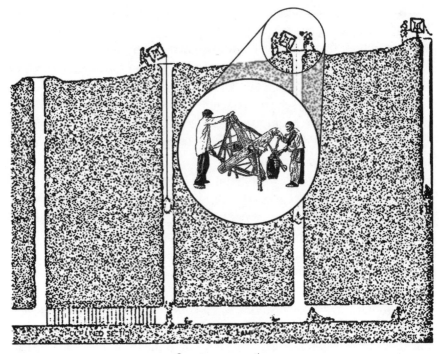

Qanat cross-section

The wooden winch used to lift and dispose of
excavated soil has not changed in more than 3,000 years.

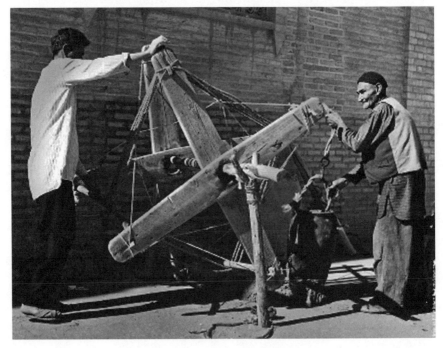

MARCH 21, 1966, WAS THE SPRING EQUINOX and thus, as always, was the Iranian New Year. Because the entire country slows to a standstill, I took full advantage of the holiday to see many of my relatives and friends. On the Saturday after the weeklong holiday, Shahen and I drove to the site, about ten kilometers south of Tehran, for the first time so I could get my bearings and a sense of what I would be dealing with.

When we arrived at the site, the Plan Lab technicians were eagerly waiting for me. As is customary in Iran, I hugged and kissed each of them and wished them Happy New Year. Then Shahen and I got busy marking the borehole locations and excavation pits.

The purpose of excavating the pits to different depths was to determine whether there were any collapsible or expansive soils at the site. The plate load equipment was set up over each of the pits and loaded to 5,000 psf, after which the pit was filled with water and left to soak overnight. No significant deflection was measured, and when the plate load was removed, the soils rebounded over 95 percent from the deformation that had been measured under the load.

It was nice to see the Plan Lab's fully equipped plate-bearing trailer there all ready to go. I could not help but remember what a hassle it had been to assemble plate-bearing equipment for the San Francisco International Airport runway project just a few months earlier.

The load test results were a great relief because they supported my opinion that no piles would be needed to support the heavy process units. This was good news all around.

Plan Lab's 27-ton plate bearing trailer

Because Ray was south of Tehran, the climate there was much warmer, and by April the daytime temperature was almost as hot as a mild summer day. The field investigation was in high gear. The flat site looked like desert, with the brick factories visible in the distance. Several tents pitched at the site served as storage rooms for samples, and we used one as an office so we could work in the shade.

WITH SHAHEN IN THE FIELD, I did not have to stay at the site all day, so I took the opportunity to explore the business climate in Iran and see what had changed since I had left for Holland in 1963.

I learned that many more American firms, like Fluor, had set up offices in Tehran. Most were related to petroleum and petrochemicals. Tidewater Oil, which had plans to drill exploratory wells in the Persian Gulf, was among the prospective D&M clients I contacted, so I arranged to meet with John P. McCabe, Tidewater's managing director in Iran.

When I came into his office, I saw a tall, handsome man with his cowboy boots propped up on his desk. He gestured for me to come in and take a chair, then asked me what had brought me to his office. As I started to tell him about D&M, he said, "Well, Jack, you're too late!"

With that he got up, went over to a small table that had drawings on it, pointed to a circle on the map of the Persian Gulf and said, "This is where the Brits carried out an offshore investigation for our barge-mounted jack-up platform so we could drill exploration wells. The barge is on its way and should arrive in less than a month."

The location was in an area that I had investigated for another installation while I was at the Plan Lab. The relatively shallow sea depth in that area consisted of calcareous deposits, which are calcium carbonates precipitated by marine organisms. They look and feel like quartz sands, but when such deposits are mistaken for marine quartz sands, the results can be grim. Unlike quartz sands, calcareous deposits are formations that are easily crushable. This makes them too weak to support heavy, concentrated loads.

So when I looked at the calculations, the short predetermined length of the platform's supporting legs alarmed me so much that I said, "I'm afraid that your platform's going to end up below sea level."

Clearly not appreciating that comment, he said only, "We shall see!"

I hoped for his sake that I was mistaken, but I knew that wasn't the case. And eventually, so did he. At the time, I had no idea that twenty years later, a meeting with him in Los Angeles, where he was then at Getty Oil, would lead to a conversation about the Getty Villa in Malibu that would ultimately result in my getting involved with the museum.

EVEN IF TIDEWATER WAS NOT interested in having another geotechnical entity in Iran in addition to the Plan Lab, other foreign companies were. And the Consortium actually wanted me to reactivate my engineering consulting firm and set up a joint venture with D&M in Tehran. However, that did not interest me because I did not want to return to Iran on a permanent basis.

In the first week of April, Don Roberts arrived from the LA office to see how the site investigation for his project was progressing. Just before heading out to the site, we met with Tim Rogers and Arnold Luft, and during our discussion, the *qanat* issue came up again.

According to Tim, NIOC was concerned about the *qanats* from a safety standpoint because they offered possible saboteurs uncontrolled access to the site! I assured him that we would investigate the tunnels and work jointly with Fluor to develop a security strategy.

By the time we arrived at the site, it was well past noon and no one was working. The workers were taking their customary afternoon naps. Shahen was in one of the tents checking the labels on the samples against the logs of the completed borings.

Don asked Shahen, "Where are all the workers?"

Shahen answered, "They're sleeping."

Half-joking, Don retorted, "No wonder the country's underdeveloped."

Shahen justified his explanation by replying, "After a heavy lunch, it's hard to work without a little rest," but Don simply shook his head in disbelief.

As he and I walked through the site, I showed him locations of the plate load tests and the alignments of the *qanats* that crisscrossed the site, and we discussed how to investigate the underground tunnels.

By the time we got back to the tents, the drillers and the technicians, refreshed from their afternoon rest, were hard at work again.

Don seemed satisfied with the site investigation activities and understood that the slow progress was due to the archaic drilling equipment. Before we left, I told Shahen to ask his mother-in-law to prepare some Armenian dishes that he could bring to the site for lunch with Don the next day.

The following morning, I took Don to the Plan Lab to show him where I thought some of the samples could be tested. He was impressed with the laboratory's testing equipment and the scope of their services.

Because he was scheduled to leave Tehran twenty-four hours later, we needed to take care of the *qanat* investigation that day. As I had requested, a *qanat* digger and an assistant, both small-framed men, were waiting when we arrived. Fortunately, Don had brought with him two of the innovative disposable cameras that had recently come onto the market. They had built-in flashes, which would prove very handy during our investigation of the dark, cramped *qanats*.

When I asked the digger in Farsi if he had ever seen or used a camera, he answered, "No, sir." I then handed him one of the cameras, placed his index finger on the shutter button, asked him to look through the viewfinder, and had him snap a picture. He quickly got the idea, and I then told him that I wanted him to go down into the vertical shafts and take photographs of the horizontal tunnels.

The digger, holding a plastic bag that contained the camera, was lowered to the bottom of one of the shafts. I called down to him to take a picture of the horizontal tunnel. He took out the camera, held it as instructed, and pressed the button. However, the tunnel was so dark that the automatic flash went off. This scared him so badly that he dropped the camera, lost his balance, fell into the water, and began screaming to be pulled up.

We pulled him out trembling and shaking so much that he could hardly speak except to mumble that it was God's punishment for trying to take the image of the sacred *qanat*. In fact, it had not occurred to any of us to tell him about the flash.

After the digger calmed down, Shahen took him into the tent and showed him that the flash would go off in dim light but not outside. And after we tripled his hourly rate, he went back down and took many pictures of the horizontal tunnels. We later used the photos to design brick liners for the vertical shafts and to install secure covers. Several years later, electronic eyes were installed at the tunnel entrances.

By noon, Shahen had set up a feast in one of the tents. We all sat down on the Persian carpets that covered the floor, leaned against pillows, and dived into the food. Don bravely tasted several different dishes and even took some seconds. Before long, all of us, even Don, found ourselves barely able to keep our eyes open. He finally rolled over onto his side, rested himself on the pillows, and fell fast asleep.

When he woke up two hours later, he sat up and exclaimed, "Man, what hit me? Must've been my jet lag."

I answered, "No, it's the food and the air."

THAT EVENING, DON WANTED to buy some gifts for his family. Having heard that Iranian gold jewelry was renowned, he decided to shop for gold souvenirs. We went to Lalehzar (Tulip Garden) Avenue, a sorry imitation of Paris's Champs-Élysées that had been designed by one of the Qajar kings after his first visit to France and where most of Tehran's jewelers were

Lunch with Don Roberts (right) in the tent at Ray Refinery site

located. We walked into one shop at random, and the shopkeeper, who spoke only Farsi, brought out several velvet-covered trays of rings, bracelets, necklaces, and other jewelry for Don to consider.

Don spent about an hour scrutinizing and selecting several pieces of jewelry, then took out his pocket slide rule and had me ask the shopkeeper to weigh the piece and give him the price in US dollars. With that, the shopkeeper reached under the counter, brought out a large abacus, and converted the Iranian *rials* to US dollars.

Don tallied the weight and the price of each on a piece of paper, turned to me, and said, "I've heard that I'm not supposed to pay this guy's asking price."

"That's right," I replied. "You should offer whatever you think is a fair price."

When Don offered seventy-five percent of the shopkeeper's amount, the shopkeeper put on a show of acting shocked and offended and began replacing the pieces back toward the tray in the little haggling dance that happens all day, every day, in every bazaar in Iran.

After going back and forth and clicking the abacus several times, the shopkeeper reduced the total price by twenty percent, but Don told me that he thought that gold in the US was still less per ounce than the shopkeeper's asking price. By now I was getting tired of the tug-of-war between the two cultures, so I told the shopkeeper that the idiot American had been dragging me all over the city since morning and that he should take pity on me and accept the American's offer.

The shopkeeper replied, "I sympathize with your predicament, but as Allah is my witness, I've given him a bare-bones price. And with your ten percent commission, I'm going to lose a lot of money."

"I don't want any commission," I told him, whereupon he broke into a big grin and said, "Why the hell didn't you tell me that from the beginning?! I'll discount the total by thirty percent!"

When I recounted our exchange to Don, he thought that what I had done was hilarious and asked, "Did you really tell the shopkeeper that I was an 'idiot American'?"

"What difference does it make?" I replied. "You got the price you wanted!"

Exploring Opportunities for D&M in Iran

After completing the site investigation, which took a couple of months, I shipped the samples to D&M's LA office for testing and returned to Mill Valley to be with Lynn and Christina—but only for a short time because I had to complete the refinery report back in LA.

While I was there, Don invited me to a meeting at the EO, but he did not tell me beforehand that he had been asked to make a presentation about business opportunities in Iran for a group that turned out to be an executive committee that included Trent Dames and a number of managing partners.

After listening to Don's and my presentation, Mr. Dames asked me, "What happens if the Shah goes?"

I answered, "If the Shah goes, so does Dames & Moore."

Based on the presentation and our answers to the executive committee's questions, they decided to send James Carter, a managing partner, and me to Iran to explore business opportunities. Less than a month later, I was again back in my homeland. Once we arrived, I arranged for Jim to meet different potential clients. The hub of most business dealings in Tehran was the Hilton, where we all stayed, and the hordes of businessmen arriving, leaving, and hanging around the lobby were a good indication of the business environment. We were definitely in the right place at the right time.

One person I wanted Jim to meet was John McCabe. When I called his office, I was surprised that he answered the call himself, and as soon as I identified myself, he exclaimed, "Dammit, Jack! I'll never do another offshore project without talking to you first! That platform ended up below

Dinner at the Tehran Hilton (from left: Jim Carter, me,
Mrs. Erfan, and Dr. Erfan, Managing Director of the Plan Lab)

water, just as you predicted. We're closing the office, and I'm leaving tonight for the States."

During the days that followed, I arranged a number of meetings with potential D&M clients. As a professional courtesy, we also had dinner with Dr. Erfan of the Plan Lab and his wife. When he learned that D&M was considering opening an office in the city, he told Jim, "Jack knows the Lab better than I do, and he's welcome to utilize any of our resources that he needs."

The Cham Oil Storage Tank Project

Two days before Jim and I were due to return to California after our two-week trip, we met with Tim Rogers at Fluor. Tim was bullish about Fluor's long-term prospects in Iran. He told us that in addition to the Ray Refinery, Fluor had obtained several new projects in the south of Iran and that they were negotiating regarding three more "grassroots" refineries that would be built from scratch, one in Esfahan, Kermanshah, and another in Tabriz. He also mentioned what he called the Cham project in the port city of Mahshahr on the Persian Gulf that was to include the construction of a crude oil depot consisting of a large number of storage tanks.

"At present, though," he said, "our office here in Tehran is a design and coordinating center for our projects in Iran but has no jurisdiction over construction activities in that region. Before we were awarded the Cham project, a British firm had investigated the site and had recommended that the height of the storage tanks be limited to nine feet."

I was not sure I had heard him correctly because the height was so low, and echoed, "Did you say nine feet? I've never heard of such a recommendation." I asked Jim if he had heard of nine-foot-high storage tanks, and he said no. Tim asked us whether we could fly to Mahshahr the next day and take a look at the situation. He informed us that Larry Monroe was the superintendent of the Cham project.

"We're scheduled to leave tomorrow," I demurred. "There's no way we could do that."

Jim then asked Tim to give us a couple of minutes alone, and after he left, Jim put his pipe back in his mouth, gave me a half-smile, and in his Texas drawl calmly told me, "Jack, when a client asks you to do something, the only proper response is 'Yes, sir.'"

I was starting to feel as if I was attached to a rubber band that kept snapping me back to my roots in Iran and was never going to let me return to my family. Nevertheless, when Tim returned, we agreed to go. He arranged for us to fly to Ahvaz and back the next day on the Consortium's private plane, and we pushed back our reservations to LA by one more day.

Jim was obviously concerned because I had dismissed the British firm's recommendation of a nine-foot height limit for the tanks and told me about the failure of a D&M-designed molasses tank in the New York area many years earlier. The incident had resulted in lengthy litigation that remained a blemish on the firm's otherwise flawless reputation because the court had determined that the tank had failed due to D&M's negligence and incompetence. This experience, though jokingly referred to as "the molasses syndrome," had nevertheless instilled D&M's partners with an indelible sense of caution.

We landed in Ahvaz the next day at midmorning. I had never seen the completed airport and was pleased to see the runway's excellent condition. We then took a taxi to Mahshahr, about 100 kilometers east of Abadan.

There was no road, paved or otherwise, on the desert road to Mahshahr. Our taxi had to zigzag constantly to avoid huge potholes filled with fine sand. Also, it was hot and the taxi had no air conditioning. To keep from getting disoriented and lost in the barren terrain, the driver used the series of parallel large-diameter oil trunk lines that ran between Mahshahr and Ahvaz as a guide.

Small shacks, their walls of metal sheets imprinted with tiny images of the Pepsi Cola logo, dotted the landscape. These sheets were typically used to punch out Pepsi bottle caps. We passed barefoot, half-naked children playing on the pipelines who would stop and innocently hold up their little cupped hands to beg for change, but we soon lost sight of them in the dust kicked up by our moving taxi. They were like mirages disappearing into the dunes.

Both the landscape and the children depressed me immensely and, for a moment I thought, "God, how do these people live here?" The stark contrast between the immense poverty and the millions of dollars' worth of oil flowing through those pipes hour after hour outraged me. My anger was directed toward the Western nations who in the name of "technology transfer" were siphoning off Iran's wealth and leaving its people to live off the crumbs that they left behind.

We reached Mahshahr, which was on tidal land, around noon and drove along an almost nonexistent road until we spotted some handmade signs pointing to the Fluor offices. At this point, a rudimentary road that consisted of a thin layer of asphalt on top of the sand made driving easier— except that the asphalt had begun to melt and run in the heat. We could see idle construction equipment and small buildings, but no construction activities were going on, and the only sound that broke the eerie silence was the buzzing of flies around my head in the hot, humid air. I asked the driver to wait and take us back to Ahvaz that evening.

A few minutes later, a tall man wearing green army fatigues, high black combat boots, and a matching baseball cap, with a Havana cigar between his teeth, came out onto the front porch of the one-story Fluor office. "You must be Mr. Carter," he said. "I'm Bob Roberts, Mr. Monroe's assistant. Please come inside."

After the heat and dust of the desert, it was refreshing to be in an air-conditioned building. As we walked through the corridors, I noticed that a few of the workers in the offices were from either India or Pakistan. Bob Roberts led us to a conference room with a table piled with construction drawings and reports.

When Jim asked whether Larry Monroe was in, Bob told us that he was due to arrive from Abadan in about an hour. Jim then asked whether we could look at the site investigation reports while we waited, but Bob responded that he had strict orders not to give us any information about the project. He also disclosed that Mr. Monroe was upset with Tim's having meddled in construction matters. With that, Jim lit his pipe, slumped in his chair, and began to make casual conversation. Between Jim's pipe and Bob's cigar, the air in the room soon became unbearable, and I stepped outside to get some fresh air.

As I stood on the porch taking deep breaths, I had to appreciate the view. Mahshahr is reclaimed land surrounded by periphery levees to keep high tides out of the area, so the area was formed of flat, desolate tidal terrain covered with white salt crystals as far as I could see. In the distance, I glimpsed small red surveying flags sticking out of the ground, and near them the rusted-out hulk of a bus.

Before long, a tanned, bare-chested, pleasant-looking man wearing sandals came out of the bus and headed toward the office. When I walked over to him, he greeted me in Farsi and introduced himself as Houshang All-e Mazkur, the contractor for civil work having to do with the tanks. He was a civil engineering graduate from Boston University, and seeing me fully clothed and wearing street shoes, he immediately asked if I was lost. I told

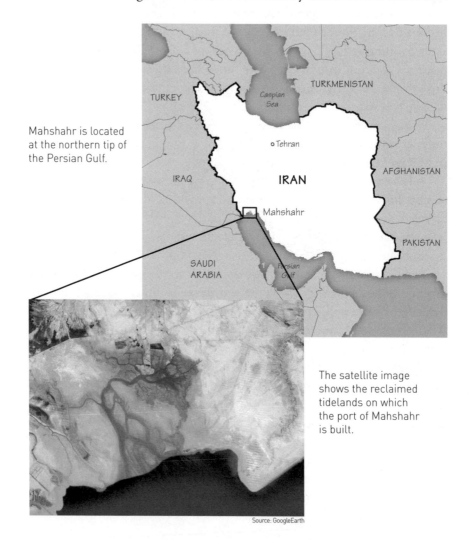

Mahshahr is located at the northern tip of the Persian Gulf.

The satellite image shows the reclaimed tidelands on which the port of Mahshahr is built.

Source: GoogleEarth

him I was there for the project and asked if he had a copy of the site investigation report. He said he did, and we walked back to his makeshift office.

The logs of the borings indicated that the site soils consisted of less than six inches of stiff soils at the surface underlain by unconsolidated soft marine deposits down to the depths that had been explored. The groundwater had been measured at twelve inches below the surface, and the recommendations section stated that the tanks should be supported on piles because the soils could not support fully loaded tanks more than nine feet high. Houshang told me that the design called for two-foot-deep excavations so concrete rings could be built to support each tank shell. The material excavated would be piled up within the ring and compacted.

I absorbed this information, thanked him, and went back to the Fluor office, where Bob and Jim were now out on the front porch but still smoking up a storm.

A few minutes later, a greenish late-model Impala pulled up. The driver hurried around to open the rear door for a very heavyset, double-chinned man wearing a loose white polo shirt and dark glasses who also seemed furious about something.

With a sheepish grin, Bob asked the man if he had had a nice trip but received no answer. Bob then turned to us and announced, "Gentlemen, this is Larry Monroe."

Larry did not bother to greet us but said, "I'm sorry that you've made this trip because there's nothing you can do. We're about to break ground for construction." Then he turned to Bob and ordered him to tell Houshang, who was near a Caterpillar D-9 bulldozer, to start digging.

Bob transmitted the order, and Houshang told a workman wearing an Arab headdress who was sitting on the bulldozer to start. The driver was thrilled that after sitting under the sun since daybreak, he could finally work. When he turned the key, the diesel engine roared to life and dark smoke began billowing from its vertical exhaust pipe. Then he engaged the gear and the big Cat started to move forward with Houshang riding on it.

In a deliberately loud voice that I was sure Larry could not miss hearing, I told Jim, "That guy's not going to be coming back."

Larry glared at me and snapped, "No one asked for your opinion!"

The dozer was moving fast toward the flagged area when its tracks began to break up the thin crust and it started to sink into the soft mud under the crust. The driver and Houshang jumped off and ran toward us as we stood there watching the dozer slowly disappear into the mud.

Larry stood there with both of his double chins trembling and yelled, "What the hell's going on!?" He then turned to me and said, "You're not going *anywhere*."

I said nothing. I just looked at Jim. He shook his head and asked, "What do you want to do, Jack?"

Without hesitation, I repeated what he had told me less than twenty-four hours earlier: "I guess that when a client asks you to do something, the only proper response is 'Yes, sir.'"

However, deep down, the nationalistic feelings that I had experienced with Mr. Vanbrumlen at the Plan Lab in 1961 had resurfaced, and I had a raging desire to show this chubby Neanderthal that he was not dealing with an inferior race of people. Jim pulled me over to one side and said, "Jack, I know you're disappointed and angry. You really don't have to stay if you don't want to."

I replied, "I'll stay. You go ahead. I'll take care of this mess and then fly home later."

After Jim left in the waiting taxi, I asked Bob where I was supposed to stay. Larry, who was still in a daze, replied, "We have guest quarters. You can sleep there."

I STAYED IN MAHSHAHR FOR TWO DAYS. During that time, I went over the report and carried out some rough stability analyses which showed that large-diameter tanks up to thirty-two feet high could be supported on the thin, undisturbed surface crust. However, the Consortium's engineering department had to review my recommendations.

Before I left Mahshahr, Houshang and I visited a dry riverbed with steep banks consisting of a mixture of well-graded gravel, sand, and clay that seemed ideal for the construction of tank pads. I asked him to ship several bags to the Plan Lab for testing.

Meanwhile, I kept my interactions with Larry Monroe to a bare minimum. To me, he was the very embodiment of the main character in *The Ugly American*.[1] The descriptions of expatriate Americans in that best-selling novel were exactly what I was experiencing with him. I was especially reminded of a section in which one native wonders, "For some reason, the people I meet in my country are not the same as the ones I knew in the United States. A mysterious change seems to come over Americans when they go to a foreign land. They isolate themselves socially. They live pretentiously. They are loud and ostentatious."

Of course not all Americans in Iran were "ugly," as Tim Rogers, a true gentleman with whom it was a pleasure to work, proved. He was well aware

1. William J. Lederer and Eugene Burdick, *The Ugly American* (New York: Norton, 1958).

of the construction superintendents' oversized egos, which made them think they were gods. Monroe was no different. The saving grace in my situation was the fact that design changes were outside his jurisdiction and had to be approved first by Tim Rogers and ultimately by the client. Tim informed me by phone that a meeting on my recommendations regarding the tank heights had been scheduled for three days after my return at the Consortium's offices in Tehran and that I had to be there.

When I arrived at the Tehran Hilton, the receptionist handed me several phone messages from some of the clients whom Jim and I had met. They were asking for urgent meetings. The messages included a telex from Jim Carter informing me that the D&M management had decide to open an office in Tehran and was giving me the choice of returning to the US to move my family to Tehran or having the firm make the arrangements for Lynn and Christina to fly there.

ON THE DAY OF THE CONSORTIUM MEETING, Monroe was also in attendance, and not in a good mood. Apparently the changes in the configuration of the proposed storage tanks had caused major problems related to the construction schedules and the resulting cost adjustments.

Dr. Mashayekh, the head of the Consortium's engineering department, presided over the meeting. I had worked with him before going to Holland. Russ McNutt of Gulf Oil, who would become a good friend throughout my assignment in Iran, was also there.

During the meeting, I outlined D&M's recommendation for the storage tanks, which required that the existing soil crust at the site remain undisturbed and on which three-foot-thick compacted structural fill would support the thirty-two-foot-high tanks.

My presentation, followed by further discussions, led to the decision to follow D&M's recommendations. Ultimately, the tanks were constructed and water-tested successfully before being placed in service.

Chapter 18

ESTABLISHING D&M MIDDLE EAST

THE WEEKS AFTER THE CONSORTIUM MEETING were hectic. It was obvious that I could no longer tend to D&M business from my hotel room and that we needed to establish a legal entity as soon as possible. Overnight my priorities shifted to locating a suitable office space, hiring technical and administrative staff, and registering the company with the government so we could do business there.

My first local hire was Shahen, who agreed to leave the Plan Lab and join D&M with my promise that I would do my best to move him and his young family to the US in the not-too-distant future. Dr. Erfan was kind enough to accept Shahen's resignation effective immediately, which helped me a great deal. Shahen's first assignment was to locate office space, no matter how small or temporary, as long as it was furnished and had at least one existing telephone line. Telephone lines, the most essential item for any firm doing business in Tehran, were in critically short supply, and the wait to obtain a new line was twelve months, minimum.

Fortunately, Javad Shokrolahi, the engineer I had met at Fluor during my first visit there, worked out a deal with an architect friend for us to share his small office while I went on looking for a larger space. The office was located above the famous Cabaret Tehran nightclub on Avenue Pahlavi.

Lynn and Christina arrived a few months later and stayed with me at the Hilton while we looked for housing. I was able to rent the ground floor of a two-story house with a small yard located in the Amirabad area. As the adage has it, one thing led to another, and it turned out that our landlord's boss owned a large house—with a telephone—near the US Embassy that he was willing to rent out as an office.

Finding office space was just the first step. Next came setting up D&M's complicated administrative and accounting systems, hiring staff, and purchasing furniture. After Shahen, most of our original hires consisted of Armenians, the majority of whom were my former Scouts. Had we been

D&M's first Tehran office

in the States, we could easily have handled many of these tasks by phone, but in Iran everything was complicated, tedious, and required personal attention. Also, everything was on a cash basis because checks and credit cards were not acceptable.

D&M's head office insisted that their firm-wide auditors, Coopers & Lybrand, set up our accounting system. Similarly, legal matters required that D&M's legal counsel meet with his Tehran counterpart, whose services I had already retained. Because of the language differences, I had to be actively involved in all of these administrative responsibilities.

Language and cultural differences made doing business in Iran a complicated affair. For example, the first round of discussions between D&M's attorney and his Iranian counterpart included a discussion about registering D&M in Iran. The US lawyer asked if the registration could be broad enough to include activities outside geotechnical engineering such as acquiring and holding property. The local attorney replied in English, "Never mind. It's illegal, but we'll do it."

Our attorney's jaw dropped. Then he leaned over to me and whispered, "I can't believe what I'm hearing!"

His disbelief was still in evidence that night at dinner. He kept dwelling on the other attorney's offhand statement, and it took me some time to explain to him that in effect the man had been translating the saying that "there are many ways to skin a cat" while also hinting at his own influence and ability to get things done.

Finding competent and efficient bilingual secretaries was one of the most difficult tasks faced by foreign companies. Expatriate housewives from the US and Europe who were living in Iran because of their husbands' jobs would answer want ads in the local English-language newspaper, but companies really needed bilingual staff.

The twelve-hour time difference between Iran and the States, and the fact that the Iranian weekend begins on Thursday and continues through Friday night, left a window of only three-and-a-half-days for communicating with the home office, so I often had no time to consult with the home office before taking important actions. This boiled down to informing D&M's US management after the fact about decisions that concerned not only the Tehran office but also matters related to other US-based clients with projects in Iraq, Pakistan, Saudi Arabia, Kuwait, the Gulf Emirates, and other Middle Eastern countries.

I WAS SO ENJOYING THE dizzying pace of all the activity I was involved in that I was completely unaware of how my manner and interactions with the staff had changed until the day Shahen came into my office, closed the door, and told me that our staff was at the breaking point due to my less-than-desirable behavior.

Totally taken aback, I asked him, "What are you talking about?"

He proceeded to spell it out for me. In detail. It was hard for me to sit there and be told that I was short-tempered and made unreasonable demands.

Just as Shahen finished, my phone rang. As I reached for it, I told him that I had heard his message and would think about it.

The call was from LA informing me that I had to go to New York for a meeting with the head of Van Houten Associates, a consulting engineering firm that had signed a large contract with the Consortium to build petroleum storage facilities on Kharg Island.

That night I had a long talk with Lynn about what Shahen had told me, and it turned out that she had actually been waiting for such an occasion because she was not happy with my recent behavior either. She gave me an earful of "for instances," none of which sounded so terrible to me.

When I went to the office the next morning as usual, everything looked surrealistically different to me. It was as if I had not taken a good look at my staff for a long time. No one looked up or made an eye contact with me. I slowed my pace, went to my office, and immediately asked Shahen to assemble everyone in my office.

My half-dozen employees came in and stationed themselves near the door wearing somber expressions. I looked around at them and said, "Since when do you remain standing in my office like zombies? What' s going on with you guys? Grab a chair and sit down!" After everyone sat down, I went on, "Shahen told me you guys are unhappy working here." They all avoided my eyes. I then added, "I have to go to New York for a meeting, but after I return I want to meet with each of you individually and hear your side of the story."

After they left, I booked my flight to New York via Tel Aviv so I could be in Jerusalem on Armenian Easter. I had heard a lot about the Armenian Quarter and thought it would be great to be there for the holy day. At that time, passports issued by Middle Eastern countries, including Iran, were automatically invalidated if they showed an Israeli visa. Knowing that, Israel's "interest section" in Tehran issued my visa on a separate piece of paper instead of stamping it in my passport. I reserved a room for two nights at Jerusalem's King David Hotel.

During my flight to Jerusalem, I went back to thinking about what Shahen and Lynn had told me. As I looked back and tried to reconstruct what might have been causing the problems, I began to realize that although in my own mind I was being myself—which I sincerely believed I had always been—I was in an arena where I was being seen and judged in a variety of cultural lights. Each had its own specific sensitivities, idiosyncrasies, and work ethic, and violating those sensitivities would send the wrong signals. To Armenians, I was known as "Njdeh," born and raised in Iran's Armenian community. But Persian Iranians knew me as "Agha-ye Moahndes," an Iranian engineer, while the expatriates I met who lived and worked in Iran knew me as "Jack," an Iranian-American engineer with an American wife.

Naturally, my prime responsibility was to discharge my professional duties to the best of my ability, taking into account the prevailing circumstances there. I had been judging our success on how much D&M's business had increased since the office had opened, so I had been under the impression that everything was fine. However, Shahen had made it clear that not everyone in the office was a happy camper.

By the time I landed in Tel Aviv, I had realized that my staff expected more understanding and compassion from their old friend whom they had been serving so unselfishly. They were right. I was the one who had to turn over a new leaf.

I TOOK A CAB FROM TEL AVIV to Jerusalem, which at that time was a territory of Jordan. The sights and sounds of Jerusalem were like a dream. As we drove past shepherds in white ankle-length robes and biblical headscarves guarding their sheep as they grazed peacefully on the hillside, it seemed as if time had stopped since Christ's birth.

ꞌ   Jerusalem was filled with pilgrims from all over the world. On my first day, I visited the Armenian Quarter and met with the patriarch of the Armenian Church. He invited me to sit and have tea with him on one of the ancient church's several terraces. From there, the whole of Jerusalem was visible. He pointed out a number of sites sacred to all Christians and urged me not to miss the Church of Holy Sepulchre. Before leaving, I followed Armenian tradition and got a small tattoo of an Armenian cross and the year "1966."

As I made my way to the Church of the Holy Sepulchre, a frighteningly calm sensation came over me. It was so powerful that I felt as if I was having an out-of-body experience. I joined the long line waiting to enter the church. It seemed to stretch ahead of me for miles, and I have never been able to remember how long I waited because in the strange state of mind I was in, I felt no fatigue.

Finally it was my turn to enter the small stone chamber, which was filled with burning candles, gold and silver ornamental lanterns, and the pungent smell of burning incense. I walked in and came face-to-face with Christ's tomb. Suddenly my knees buckled and I found myself kneeling with my head touching the cold slab, which had been polished by the touch of millions of believers before me. Perhaps reactions like mine were not uncommon because there were young priests there who gently helped me to stand up and walk out.

I was a new person. Gone were my anger and my anxiety about getting things done. Nothing seemed important. As I walked along the narrow cobblestone passage marked with the twelve "Stations of the Cross" where Jesus had fallen while carrying his heavy wooden cross to Golgotha, I was aware of every breath I was taking.

My visit to Jerusalem changed my outlook—and my behavior toward the people with whom I came in contact. I became a lot calmer and more able to take difficulties and problems in stride.

AFTER THE VAN HOUTEN MEETING, which took place in D&M's office on Church Street just blocks from the World Trade Center, I arrived at an agreement regarding my position with D&M Middle East that included a commitment on my part to remain for either two years or until the new office was fully functional. I then made a quick trip out to LA to meet with the D&M management there before flying back to Tehran.

Several weeks after my return, I had my one-on-one meetings with each staff member, and I became aware that because of the changes in my own behavior, staff morale improved visibly.

The large volume of work at the Tehran office required that we bring in technical personnel from various D&M offices. However, we still lacked a capable bilingual secretary. One secretary was pregnant and could not work full time, so reports were being delayed. Every day the pile to be typed grew higher, and office efficiency overall was also grinding to a halt.

Patricia Farrar's telephone call in response to one of our want ads came not a moment too soon.

When she arrived for her appointment, we were presented with a petite, bubbly, strikingly beautiful blonde wearing a mini-skirt that caused turmoil among the male employees. Shahen walked into my office and announced, "You have to see this applicant! And you have to hire her!"

During the interview, she told me in a British accent that she had arrived from London three weeks earlier and had fallen in love with the city and the people. She wanted to stay in Iran and work. To my astonishment, when I told her that we needed someone who spoke Farsi, she replied in fluent Persian that although she could not type in Farsi, speaking was not a problem.

I tested her by asking her to take down a fairly complicated technical paragraph that I read from an engineering handbook and then to type it out. She went to the secretarial section next to my office, typed at lightning speed for a minute or so, pulled out the paper, placed it on my desk, and announced, "I'm ready to start right away."

She went to the desk where the stacks of reports were waiting, and began to type. She never took a break, and by the end of the day all the reports, flawlessly typed, were piled on my desk so I could review and sign them. I noticed that the mood in the office had shifted totally. The guys were all walking around wearing silly grins, and everything seemed to be moving at a faster pace. Patricia's presence had visibly speeded up the tempo, and her smile and bubbly personality were infectious.

When the day was over, she asked me what the business hours were and told me she would see me the next day. I told her that we had never discussed her salary or the terms of her employment, so she sat down and asked with a giggle what the pay scale was for secretaries. I told her what we were paying our present secretary, and was about to tell her that her salary would be much higher, when she interrupted me. "That'll be fine!" she said. "See you in the morning!"

All night long I kept asking myself, "What's wrong with this picture?" The thought that she might not be there the next day was frightening.

Thank God there was nothing wrong with the picture. When I arrived in the morning, Patricia was already there busily typing. Without looking at me, she gave me a pleasant smile and said, "Good morning, Jack." She already had the office phone on her desk and was answering calls in both Farsi and English.

Before long, we began affectionately calling her "Pafi," for "Patricia A. Farrar," and she soon became not only my indispensable administrative assistant but also the darling of our expatriate clients. Without any doubt, she contributed hugely to the firm's success, and we were well aware that every visitor from D&M's US offices tried to entice her to join them.

One day, Lynn asked me if I recognized a black-and-white photograph in a *Playboy* magazine. I immediately recognized Patricia, in full Playboy bunny costume, serving drinks at the Playboy Club in London near Hyde Park. When I showed her the photo the next day, she confirmed with a big smile that she had worked there before coming to Iran and that her mother was the club seamstress.

BECAUSE OF THE EXPLOSION IN business activities in Iran, the government required that all expatriates who planned to stay and work there for an extended period of time obtain work permits. I asked Shahen to go with Pafi when she applied. They returned empty-handed, and Shahen reported that both the men and the women at the office had stared at her. Also, the official who had taken her paperwork had said that the head of the firm would need to appear with her to answer questions before a work permit could be issued. I planned to go with her the following week, but I failed to mark my calendar and forgot all about it.

The following week, as I was walking through the building to my office, I glimpsed an elderly woman wearing a long floral-print dress and a wide-rimmed purple straw hat sitting nearby. A large straw handbag that matched the hat was resting on the floor next to her, and she was reading a magazine through a pair of reading glasses that rested on the tip of her nose. I figured that she was waiting to see Pafi.

I went into my office and was picking up the phone to call Shahen and ask where Pafi was when in walked the elderly woman.

"Are you ready to go to the permit department?" she asked in Persian.

I recognized her accented Persian immediately and asked in bewilderment, "Is that you, Pafi?"

With her characteristic giggle, she replied, "If you didn't recognize me after all the time I've been working here, then no one at the work permit office is going to recognize me, either!"

When we reached the permit office, which was packed, I asked her to take the last remaining seat on one of the benches while I joined the line in front of the window where a police officer was issuing work permits. When my turn came, the overworked officer asked for my company's name while pushing a piece of paper at me so I could write down the correct spelling. As he was looking for her D&M application, he asked me if the person for whom I needed the permit was present. I turned and pointed to the little elderly woman sitting on the bench clutching her big straw bag on her lap and looking straight at us.

Without another word, the officer stamped the permit, pushed it toward me, and in a loud voice called, "Next!"

Welcoming visitors from D&M's other offices was a big treat, as this gathering with Managing Partner Jim Carter shows: (from left) Shahen Askari; me; Jim Hussey, a transfer from the San Francisco office; managing partner Jim Carter; Patricia Farrar; Avo Gregorian; Eddy Shandi; Rouben Gorjian, Stepan; Norik; Amour Mouradian.

Chapter 19

THREE MAJOR D&M PROJECTS

THE NEXT TWO YEARS saw me supervising a number of D&M Tehran projects throughout the Middle East.

As the price of oil skyrocketed over the next two years, the oil-producing countries of the Middle East, including Iran, embarked on extensive development programs to modernize their production and processing facilities and used some of their oil revenues for infrastructure and other projects. Initially, European, US, and UK firms carried out the design and construction of these projects, but eventually much of this work was taken over by the countries themselves using local companies.

The scarcity of reliable local information about the characteristics of petroleum and petrochemical sites required D&M's involvement in the earliest stages of planning and implementation because many of the sites were in marginal areas. Therefore, most of our projects required complex studies that utilized state-of-the-art technologies and innovative techniques to solve myriad issues relating to constructability, safety, sources of raw material and transportation to processing facilities, and finally the shipping of processed products to global markets.

Some of our assignments, while simple in technical scope, were fascinating in terms of human drama and offered adventurous encounters with local politics, cultures, and religions.

The Riyadh TV Antenna Project

One assignment for a project in Saudi Arabia made me appreciate working in Iran much more than I had before. Apparently the US Army Corps of Engineers, among its military missions, had been given the responsibility of managing the dawn of the television age in Saudi Arabia. The first task was to erect an antenna tower so TV signals could be broadcast in and around Riyadh, the capital. The Parsons Corporation was the general contractor, and D&M was retained to develop the tower's design parameters.

Although there were direct daily flights between Tehran and Riyadh, I had to go to Rome to get a visa. However, having to cool my heels there for a week allowed me to tour the "Eternal City" and its cultural treasures.

Six hours after leaving Rome, we arrived in Riyadh. It was a dreary prospect. From the air, the capital was shrouded in dust as far as the eye could see. Unlike the bustling airport in Rome, the Riyadh terminal was all but deserted.

A tall young Parsons representative named Mike met me and suggested that we go directly to their office in downtown Riyadh. As we left the terminal, I felt the sting of sand grains borne on the hot wind peppering my face. We went over to the taxi queue, where a few idle taxi drivers were sitting on the curb chatting and laughing. Mike approached the first taxi and the driver hurried over, grabbed my small suitcase, and made to put it in the trunk.

Mike exclaimed, "Not so fast! Five riyals to the Parsons office near the water tower!"

The driver smiled. "Yes, yes!"

As we got into the taxi, Mike pointed to a building a short distance from the terminal that bore a "hotel" sign. He told me that I would be staying there because it was the only Western-style hotel in the city.

On the way he gave me a short course on the country's laws and traditions. Alcohol and pork were strictly forbidden. I had to bargain aggressively with taxi drivers about fares, and he warned me to tell them what I would pay before getting in because otherwise they would take advantage of my being a foreigner and overcharge outlandishly.

As we drove along the deserted streets, I saw US-style pedestrian crossing signs featuring the usual images of a walking man. But the heads of these figures had been scratched out or painted over. Mike told me that Arabs believe that only God can make images of humans, so pictures are considered blasphemous and people would erase or paint over the heads on the signs as soon as they were posted.

When I glanced at my watch, I saw that it was set to Italy's time zone, so I asked Mike what the local time was. He replied that the locals in Saudi Arabia did not observe time zones.

"Then why are you wearing a watch?" I asked.

"Expatriates set their watches on official Greenwich Meridian Time plus 3," he explained. "And appointments and meetings with locals are set for a certain number of hours away. You just say you'll meet them a certain number of hours later that day."

On our way to the Parsons office, I heard the Arabic *azan*, the call to prayer, ring out from several directions. Our driver stopped the cab, got out, and knelt to pray on the sidewalk. As we sat perspiring in the cab, Mike told me that Muslims pray five times a day.

Along the way, we saw half-naked children with flies swarming on their faces playing around a large formation of limestone rock. I later learned that it was called "The Camel's Eye" because of the large oval opening in the limestone. The children reminded me of the ones I had seen on my first trip to Mahshahr.

We reached the Parsons office just after noon. It was located next to "the water tower," a huge mushroom-shaped striped structure that was a major landmark visible from most areas of the city. When we arrived, employees were in the mess hall having lunch, and I saw plenty of Pepsi bottles containing alcohol being passed around.

"Where are they getting all their booze?" I asked Mike. He told me that the German contractors had constructed some improvised distilling equipment and were making alcoholic drinks from anything that they could get their hands on.

After lunch, I met the Parsons project manager, who told me that the investigation of the TV tower site was set for the following morning and that several laborers would be there to dig test pits. We agreed that I would be there first thing in the morning.

When I left, I went over to a waiting taxi, got in—and told the driver to go to the airport before remembering that Mike had warned me to always announce what I would pay beforehand. I shrugged and decided to wait until we reached the hotel. When we arrived and the driver had retrieved my suitcase, I asked him, "How much?"

"Riyal," he said, signaling "one" with his index finger. Then, seeing me grin, he asked, "Much?"

I replied, "No, no—it's good, good!" and gave him one riyal and some change. And I walked away thinking that Riyadh's taxi drivers must really love Mike!

WHEN I REACHED THE SITE the next morning, the laborers were already trying, without much success, to dig a test pit and I saw immediately that the limestone formation would be able to support the load of the proposed tower several times over.

The crew boss, who spoke a little English, seemed to be in great hurry to wrap up and leave. When I asked him what the problem was, he explained in broken English, mixed with some Arabic that I recognized from my Farsi, that a lot of "angry" men were on their way to the site. Actually, I was already concluding that there was not much to investigate in the 140-degree desert heat when I heard faint noises coming our away.

For a while I could see nothing, but then, as if in a mirage, a mob of men waving long sticks and shouting in Arabic appeared and headed our way. The crew boss dropped everything and screamed at the workers to run. I was not about to stick around to find out whether the mob had anything to do with the project, so I started racing toward the city as well. Never in my life had I run so fast in such desert heat.

Just as I was almost out of breath, I spotted a car coming toward us. The laborers scattered in different directions, but I was relieved to see that it was a Parsons car that had been sent to drive me back to the office. As I climbed inside and struggled to catch my breath, I felt as it I was in a living nightmare.

When we got back to the office, I learned that the news of the Americans' plans to put images of people into small boxes and spread them throughout the country had enraged the Arabs, who had decided to take matters into their own hands. After I downed several glasses of water and was finally able to breathe normally again, I told the project manager that the location where the tower was to be built was underlain by limestone rock and that there was no need for any further investigation.

As soon as I got back to my hotel, I checked with the male receptionist at the front desk regarding the departure time for my flight to Tehran the next day. He replied nonchalantly, "We have no time in Saudi Arabia. Just go to the airport at sunrise and wait until your flight is announced."

The next morning, I did just that, and shortly after I arrived heard the sweet welcome words telling passengers to go to the gate—which happened to be the only one in the entire terminal.

As our plane approached Tehran several hours later, I found myself thinking that the capital looked much more beautiful and inviting than Rome. Later I realized that two days in the Saudi Arabian desert had completely warped my sense of beauty.

(Regarding the TV tower, a February 2005 PBS *Frontline* production, "House of Saud," examined the relationship between the ruling Al Saud family and the US from the 1930s to the post-9/11 period. It showed that after the antenna was erected, but before it began broadcasting, conservative mobs, this time led by a Saudi prince, attacked it. The antenna survived the attacks and later began broadcasting.)

The Mahshahr LPG Tanks Project

Another very complex project that I was involved with during this period was the planning for the construction of four storage tanks for liquefied petroleum gas (LPG) in Mahshahr. This extraordinary undertaking not only resulted in solutions that far surpassed the existing engineering state of the art but also tested the limits of D&M's clients' trust in its engineers.

In March 1966, Russ McNutt, the Gulf Oil civil engineer whom I had met several months earlier at the pivotal Consortium meeting about the Mahshahr storage tanks (and who had been transferred to the Consortium after leaving Gulf), asked me to a meeting at the Parsons London office. Parsons had been selected to manage the design and construction of Iran's first LPG project, at Mahshahr.

The design shown to us at the meeting included four huge insulated storage tanks 150 feet in diameter and ninety feet high that would store the LPG. Among the exhibits at the meeting was a series of overlays of aerial photographs showing the gas complex located in the tidal flats of Khor-e-Mousa, a large tidal embayment in the Persian Gulf.

Also in the Parsons exhibit was a cross-sectional view of the storage tanks showing them supported, as always, on thick circular concrete slabs supported by closely spaced fifty-foot-long piles.

I recognized the site and its vicinity from the Cham oil depot project that I had visited more than a year earlier. However, this undertaking was much larger and more hazardous because of the dangers posed by LPG.

After the presentation, Russ asked me what I thought about locating the massive tanks in the mudflats.

I replied, "I doubt the feasibility of that configuration at that location," which the Parsons project manager challenged by asking, "Why isn't it feasible?"

I explained that based on my knowledge of the site's geomorphology, I doubted that it contained the thick sand strata at the depths that would be needed to support end-bearing piles. The Parsons team responded that they believed there were sand layers fifty feet down that would support the piles. The discussion then turned to the availability and cost of such piles.

It was agreed that D&M should investigate to locate and measure the depth of sand deposits, if any, at the proposed site. I estimated that the investigation would take about a month, so a follow-up meeting was scheduled for about four weeks later.

We then drilled several borings, extracted soil samples from various depths, and carried out laboratory testing but found no sand layers in borings drilled to fifty feet down. In fact, one boring and several Dutch cone

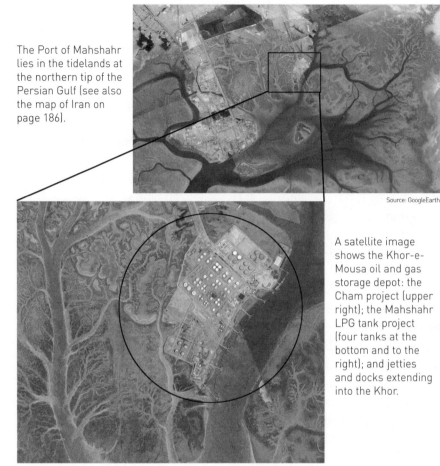

The Port of Mahshahr lies in the tidelands at the northern tip of the Persian Gulf (see also the map of Iran on page 186).

Source: GoogleEarth

A satellite image shows the Khor-e-Mousa oil and gas storage depot: the Cham project (upper right); the Mahshahr LPG tank project (four tanks at the bottom and to the right); and jetties and docks extending into the Khor.

Source: GoogleEarth

penetrometer tests advanced to 100 feet down failed to encounter any sand layers. We relayed our findings to Parsons.

Parsons then consulted by phone with a British geotechnical firm and suggested three different options for getting the project off dead center: first, to increase the number of fifty-foot-long piles; second, to use friction piles 100 feet long; and third, to relocate the site. A meeting to discuss the results of the site investigation and the various options was scheduled in London, and because the decisions to be made were so critical, representatives from the Consortium and from Parsons were also asked to attend.

Evaluating the first two options required that the engineering characteristics of the extracted samples be determined. The test results indicated that the proposed site was underlain by soft, "sensitive" clay deposits, or clays that lose their strength when disturbed. Typically, piles driven into sensitive clays remold the soils, which causes the loss of strength and makes it difficult to calculate the piles' actual load-bearing capacity. That was the case at this site. We could not arrive at reliable calculations of capacity for either adding more fifty-foot piles or using 100-foot friction piles.

Russ had left for London a week before the meeting, and I had not had an opportunity to discuss the test results with him before he left, so I called him in London and informed him that the first two Parsons options did not appear feasible.

He then informed me that the Consortium management was going to reject the idea of relocating the plant. Because that would effectively kill the project entirely, I began questioning whether I should bother to even attend the meeting.

I told Russ that Parsons' insistence on using deep foundation piles had so far ruled out exploring other alternatives.

"Like what?" he asked.

When I said, "Let me think about it," he replied, "Well, you have a week to think. Call me if you come up with a workable alternative."

I immediately had special tests performed on selected samples that we had extracted in the hope of finding technical data related to increasing the strength of site soils by compressing saturated clay particles more closely together. We carried out consolidated drain triaxial tests, which provide parameters for determining changes in the strength of soft clays, and the results were encouraging.

Forty-eight hours before the meeting, I called Russ, told him the results were encouraging, and said it might be possible to construct the LPG tanks at the proposed site without using piles. He immediately asked me to go to London the following day because the meeting had not been cancelled. I warned him that it was only an idea and that I had not yet done a detailed analysis to confirm its feasibility for LPG tanks, but he responded that I would have plenty of time to do the needed analysis during the six-hour flight from Tehran to London.

After we spoke, Russ apparently told Parsons that I had come up with a solution that would eliminate piles and that I would present my recommendation at the meeting. However, his exuberance was obviously exaggerated because I had not yet come up with a workable alternative.

Parsons greeted Russ's news with serious resistance and pointed out, totally correctly, that there was no precedent for supporting large storage tanks containing highly explosive LPG on coastal areas without using piles. In fact, this was such a crucial issue that the existing contract between Parsons and the Consortium included a provision that would hold the firm harmless should any damage to the LPG tanks be caused by ground failure.

The final results of the tests I had requested were delivered to me at Mehrabad Airport just before I boarded my flight to London. On the plane, I did some "back of the envelope" calculations for the LPG tanks and extrapolated the settlement measurements from the adjacent Cham oil tanks to the anticipated dimensions and loads of the LPG tanks.

My preliminary analysis indicated that if the site clays could be consolidated similarly to the way they had been in the tested samples, theoretically they would be able to support the loads exerted by the fully loaded LPG tanks. My extrapolations showed that the loaded tanks would initially settle three feet and would continue to settle over the long term, but at a much slower rate.

When I landed at Heathrow, I directly went to the Parsons offices, where the meeting was already in session in a large conference room. Frank Brennan, the partner in charge of D&M's London office, was present, as were a number of people I had never met.

When Russ saw me, he jumped up, introduced me, and asked if we could be excused for few minutes. Then he, Frank, and I went to a small office, where his first question was "Do you have good news?"

"Yes," I replied, "but it all depends." I added that there were a lot of "things" that had to be undertaken that would require time and a large budget. Before I could elaborate further, Russ said, "Let's get back—we'll talk about the 'things' later." On our way back to the conference room, Frank cautioned me to "go slow."

When we returned to the meeting, I proceeded to briefly explain the theory of increasing the strength of the site's soils by pre-consolidation and added that although my analysis was encouraging, it was preliminary, and much work would be needed to verify that the proposed method was safe.

The Parsons representatives wanted to know more about the behavior of sensitive clays after piles had been driven and did not seem completely satisfied with my explanations. At that point, the meeting broke for lunch. Russ told me that he and the Consortium members would hold further discussions over lunch at a restaurant. Meanwhile, the break gave Frank and me a chance to review my preliminary calculations and our recommendations.

After lunch, the Consortium spokesman said that they fully appreciated the firm's concerns and that the Consortium needed to better understand D&M's concept before making a final decision. He also stated that an alternative site was not feasible and that the feasibility assessment of D&M's proposal would be carried out in Tehran with full participation by Parsons.

OBVIOUSLY, THE MEETING HAD NOT gone as Parsons had anticipated because the firm was now facing the possibility of losing millions of dollars in profits from their cost-plus contract—and a few days after I returned to Tehran, Russ informed me that the Consortium wanted a complete presentation of my recommendations as well as an estimated time frame and budget.

Another meeting was scheduled, and I knew from experience that only a physical model would give the clients a full understanding of my proposed undertaking. I therefore prepared a simple model consisting of a cube of natural sponge that represented the clay soils at the site. I placed it in a shallow rectangular glass baking dish filled with water. When pressure was applied to the saturated sponge, water could be seen to be flowing out of it and it compressed in thickness. As more pressure was applied in increasing increments, the sponge became more resistant to further deflections. This model demonstrated that squeezing water out of the sponge reduced the air space between the sponge's fibers and it became more resistant to pressure.

I therefore concluded that aside from the fact that there was no similarity between a natural sponge and unconsolidated saturated marine clay deposits, the end result was fairly comparable and that "preloading" the proposed LPG tank locations would increase the clays' bearing capacity enough to eliminate the need to use piles.

I realized that everyone present had grasped this proposed methodology when they started asking questions such as: "How do you know that the site clays would behave like the natural sponge?," "The glass dish is transparent and the flow of water is visible, so how would you find out the patterns of water movement underground when the soils are under load?," and "How would you know where and by how much the subsurface soils are going to bulge laterally under the load?"

I explained that an extensive monitoring program utilizing an array of instruments such as piezometers, inclinometers, and settlement markers would be installed at each of the four tank locations and that readings would be rigorously analyzed for each and every preload increment all the way through the water testing of the erected tanks before they would be placed in service.

When the Consortium representatives were told that our estimated costs for this approach were only a fraction of the Parsons proposal, they readily authorized D&M to proceed with a detailed engineering analysis and the design and manufacture of the monitoring equipment we would need.

The critical factor was to calculate as accurately as possible the pore pressure dissipation (how fast the water would drain out of the clay) under incremental loads based on the tests performed on samples from the site. The planned incremental thicknesses of preload and estimated vertical settlement and horizontal deformations were tabulated and plotted in chart form to be used as guidelines for the actual preloading operations.

Over the next several months, D&M US designed and manufactured the necessary monitoring equipment and shipped it to us in Tehran, where the sophisticated analysis and engineering was carried out. I managed the project, James Hussy was the project engineer, and Iraj Noorany, a professor at Shiraz University, acted as a consultant and made valuable contributions in interpreting the complex test results.

After Jim Strom, of D&M's office in Santa Fe Springs, California, surveyed the exact locations of the proposed tanks, the underground measurement devices as well as the monitoring gauges and reading devices were installed and tested. Once the instrumentation was in place, a convoy of dump trucks began transporting soils from the neighboring areas and placing them in designated lift thicknesses on the tank locations. Earth-moving equipment was then used to spread the soils, and as each increment of load was placed, the instruments began registering the response of the subsurface soils.

After each increment of load was placed, pore pressures, vertical deformations, and the lateral spread for each location were measured. The next load increments were added only after the instrument readings were stabilized. All four tank locations were successfully preconsolidated.

Shortly after the surcharges were removed, the pads were constructed and the LPG tanks erected. After successfully undergoing water testing, the tanks were loaded with LPG products and put into service in 1971. Because this was the first time that LPG tanks had been placed on solidified ground instead of piles, the project was the subject of several articles in *The Oil and Gas Journal*, which detailed its unusual nature both before and after the tanks were put into operation.[1]

The Bushehr Nuclear Power Plant Project

By 1967, two other large government entities, the National Iranian Gas Company (NIGC) and the National Iranian Petrochemical Company (NIPC) had been founded in addition to NIOC, which operated as the umbrella organization.

The purpose of above undertakings was to better manage Iran's natural energy resources. D&M Middle East was involved in most of these companies' projects, including refineries, cross-country natural gas trunk lines, pumping stations, petrochemical complexes, steel mills, and power plants.

---

1. "Five units of Iran's first major gas-liquids complex readied," *Oil & Gas Journal*, December 15, 1969.

Aerial view of the surcharge loading configuration for the LPG tanks.
Pore pressures, lateral deformations, and settlements at each location were
measured by piezometers, inclinometers, and settlement markers.

The D&M pressure gauge measuring console and recorder is attached to
piezometer readout stations located at the base of each preload mound.

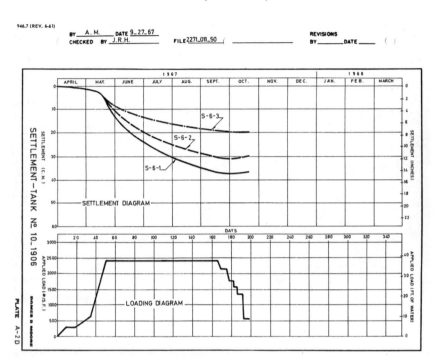

Typical plot of surcharge vs. settlement measured by installed markers

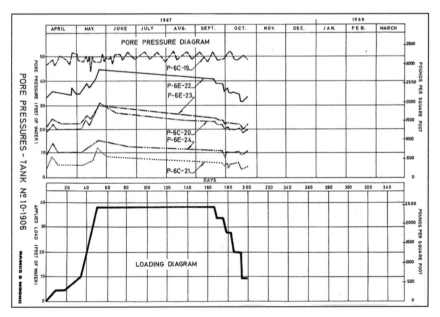

Typical plot of surcharge vs. pore pressure

Earth deformation recorder assembly. The inclinometer is being lowered into the installed 100-foot-long casing.

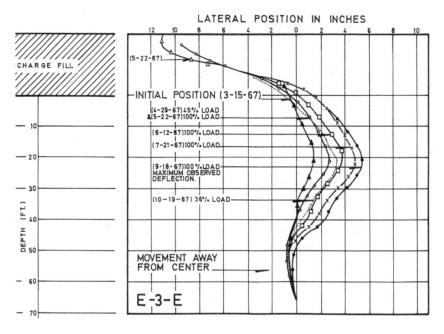

Typical plot of depth vs. lateral deformation of the casing at various depths and incremental surcharge loads.

Source: *Oil & Gas Journal*

The Mahshahr fractionating plant and four LPG tanks,
150 feet in diameter and 90 feet high

Source: GoogleEarth

A satellite image of the four 1970 Mahshahr LPG tanks. In 2000, the Iranian
government attempted to install two more LPG tanks identical with and
adjacent to the existing tanks using D&M's surcharge loading concept.
As shown, however, the attempt failed and the project was abandoned.

During this period, many representatives of foreign companies visited me seeking local input regarding proposals they wanted to make regarding the design and construction of proposed process and energy plants for alternative, more productive, and more profitable utilization of Iran's natural hydrocarbon resources.

In 1966, I also met representatives from US companies including General Electric and Westinghouse, as well as Siemens of Germany, that were quietly creating buzz about the virtues of using nuclear energy rather than Iran's valuable natural hydrocarbon resources to supply the nation with electrical power. This was in contrast to the practice then in place which was for the bulk of natural gas to be flared at the wellheads of vast underground gas fields, while crude oil was processed only for fuel.

In 1967, what turned out to be my last assignment as the managing director of D&M Middle East was related to a request from NIOC that we survey a site earmarked for a combined refinery-petrochemical complex to be designed and constructed by Fluor.

Usually, clients would perform a preliminary site evaluation and then come to us for detailed studies, but NIOC's request was different. We were provided with a small-scale map of southern Iran that was marked with an oblong tracing with its centroid about thirty kilometers southeast of the port city of Bushehr. The tracing extended into the Persian Gulf, which indicated that the proposed complex was to be located in a coastal area for export purposes. The map showed no access roads.

The Fluor representative, whose name was John, had recently been transferred to the Tehran office from Los Angeles. He was a stocky, pleasant man about my age and seemed unfazed by being in a foreign environment. We flew to Bushehr on an Iran Air commuter flight that originated at Shiraz and arrived about noon. The taxi that took us to our hotel was a Russian-made four-door Volga sedan, a car known for being as rugged as a Russian tank. I negotiated a daily rate for our two-day trip with the driver.

The hotel, in the eastern suburbs, had only four rooms. John suggested that we take advantage of what was left of the daylight and drive east along the seashore. I showed the map to the driver and told him to drive as close to the Gulf coastline as possible. He replied that he was not aware of a coastal route, or of any roads in that area at all, and that he would drive on whatever terrain the car could handle.

To my annoyance, John kept asking me to translate my conversations with the driver. After I would translate what the driver had said, John would come back with more questions for me to ask him. After I began greeting his questions with silence, John realized that I was getting annoyed and settled down.

The juddering of the car in response to the rugged Volga's engine rev-ving in low gear on the tidal flats bounced John and me around in the back seat, and we had to clutch the leather loops that hung from above the rear windows to steady ourselves.

After about an hour, we reached an area where the ground was too soft and wet for the heavy Volga, so the driver veered toward higher elevations. From higher up, we could see the vast, desolate vista of the Gulf and its shoreline. I saw no signs of inhabitants, or anything remarkable about the coastline, until I glimpsed a cluster of small white buildings on the coast about a kilometer away. When I asked the driver if he knew the name of the settlement, he called it "Halileh," but I could not find it on our map.

By now it was late afternoon and the sun was beginning its descent to the water, but I asked him if he could drive us to the hamlet. He replied that he would go as far as he could, but only to a point where he would be able to turn around and drive back. Then, with the car still in low gear and one foot on the brake pedal, he began easing the Volga down a gentle slope covered with cattails, bushes, and patches of grass. When we were halfway to the shore, he announced he could not go any farther.

We got out and began walking down toward the white huts. As we got closer, I saw that it was the most beautiful small village I had ever seen, dotted with palm trees and with fishing boats moored on the beach rocking gently on the shallow waves. The low sun reflecting off the whitewashed huts and the silhouettes of the fig trees reminded me of the fishing villages on Greek islands, but on a much smaller scale. As we drew closer, I also spotted a hill above the village with a small shack at its crest. The shack displayed an Iranian flag, which suggested that it might be an Iranian Gov-ernment Gendarmerie post.

As we approached the pristine beach, one of the fishermen, who was pulling his net out of the water, gave us a friendly wave and asked us if we were lost. We pointed to the Volga and assured him that we were not.

He then told us that his family had been there for more than two hun-dred years, and that the fish and shrimp that they netted were for their own consumption only. He said it was rare to see outsiders and asked what had brought us there. We told him that we had been surveying the area for an industrial site but had spotted the village and wanted to get a closer look at the beautiful setting and view. He invited us to have supper with his family, but we had to decline because it was getting dark and we needed to return to Bushehr.

With a worried look, he asked us if the government was going to take the land away from them. I told him I did not think so and we walked back

to the Volga, where the driver was leaning against the hood smoking a cigarette. We decided to drive back the next day to check the Gendarmerie post.

That night I lay awake for hours, partly because of the uncomfortable
wooden bed—the legs of which had been set in pots of water to deter scor-
pions—and partly because I kept visualizing that beautiful little village in
my mind's eye. I tried to push away the image of tall, unsightly refinery
process units belching chemicals into its pure air, but the thought kept me
tossing and turning all night.

EARLY THE NEXT MORNING we drove back to Halileh. The driver was more
confident because he was able to drive in our tire ruts from the day before.
As we approached the hill where the police shack stood, the conformation
of the coast and its setting became clearer. The fishermen who had settled
at Halileh two hundred years earlier had known the patterns of the currents
and conditions of the sea bottom where marine life thrived. This particular
area was well protected from the rough seas and horrific storms that were
prevalent elsewhere along the Gulf.

As we neared the shack, the driver pointed to an army jeep, its long,
thin antenna whipping in the air like a stalk of straw, racing toward the
shack well ahead of us. Our driver veered over to follow in the jeep's tracks.
My shoulders were still so sore from the day before that it was a relief when
we reached the unpaved road that dead-ended at the shack.

The shack was actually a large two-room cabin. An Iranian Gendarme
captain was sitting behind a desk under a shelf that held a two-way army
communication radio which was emitting static-filled fragments of Farsi.

The officer, who spoke only Farsi, stood up, shook hands with us, and
told me that he had been informed of our visit by his superiors. When I
asked him if Halileh was the only village in the area, he took us into the
next room and led us to a large map spread out on a makeshift drafting
table in front of a large window that offered a panoramic view of the entire
coastline stretching for miles. I noticed a pair of military binoculars resting
on the map. The captain pointed to our location on the map and, with a
sweeping hand gesture, said, "As you can see, there's nothing there."

During this, John, who was frustrated at not being able to understand
our conversation, kept pushing me to ask him to give us a copy of the map
and any other information pertaining to the area.

I first asked the captain for permission to use the binoculars, and when
I looked through them, I saw that the coastline a few kilometers south of
Halileh made a relatively sharp bend that was not clearly shown on our
small-scale map.

I then translated John's request, to which the captain responded in Farsi, "Please rest assured that I will have everything ready for you by first thing tomorrow morning." When I translated that to John, he was ecstatic and shook the captain's hand while repeating "Farda, farda" ("Tomorrow, tomorrow") in his broken Farsi.

Before we left, the captain asked me if Halileh was suitable for the plant. I replied, "It would be a shame to disturb the village by putting a plant there. Those people have been there for two hundred years." To this, he replied nonchalantly, "You shouldn't worry about that. Upon His Majesty the Shah's orders, I'll erase that village in no time." His answer sent shivers down my spine.

On the drive back to the hotel, John kept talking how productive the whole day had been and that he could not wait to get his hands on the maps and information that the captain had promised us. He did not believe me when I told him that there would be no information waiting for us when we returned the next day, but I had recognized typical cultural Iranian *taarof* when I saw it. As in some other cultures, saying "no" is considered rude in Iran. So, although the captain had no intention of giving us anything, he told us he would.

Sure enough, the next morning when we drove back, we found a sergeant in the captain's chair. When I told him that we were to be given maps and reports, he gave us a cold look and smirked, "You must have heard wrong. Wednesdays are his days off."

John and I went back down to the village, continued to the bend in the unspoiled shoreline that I had noticed, walked around, and made some notes for our report.

WHEN WE RETURNED TO TEHRAN, I attended a meeting to present my preliminary reconnaissance survey results. I brought maps of the Persian Gulf from my office and referred to them while I explained that the site at the coastal bend south of Halileh was well suited for an industrial complex and one that would not have a detrimental impact on the nearby fishing community. The attendees were interested when I gave them a short description of how the Dutch had handled their coastal developments to preserve significant historical and archeological sites.

However, when I eventually asked whether I should prepare a proposal for preliminary studies to evaluate the viability of the site for a refinery-petrochemical complex, I was surprised to sense a distinct unease spread throughout the room. I noticed some exchanges of glances that I did not understand between the NIOC participants whom I knew and others

I had never met. A few minutes later, the NIOC representative who was chairing the meeting thanked me and said that they needed to discuss what I had told them and that they would get back to me.

On the way out, the attendees whom I had not met made a point of shaking my hand and asking me for my business card. Some years later, I learned that these were the original core personnel of the future Atomic Energy Organization of Iran (AEOI), with whom I maintained regular contact at the time and in years to come after I returned to the States. Later I also learned that AEOI was also interested in building Iran's first nuclear power plant at the site near Halileh, and it did eventually succeed in securing the site for the Bushehr Nuclear Power Plant, Iran's first.

It was gratifying that the plant was built at that location because the village of Halileh not only survived the captain's plan to wipe it out at the Shah's command, but has also been preserved in all its original charm, so typical of Iran's southern coastal fishing region.

Starting in 1972, D&M Middle East performed all the necessary site validation studies and developed the design parameters for the Bushehr Nuclear Power Plant, while Kraftwerk Union of Germany was awarded the contract to build the plant.[2]

By EARLY 1967, BOTH CONDITIONS that I had asked for when I took on setting up D&M Middle East—that I would stay for either two years or until the office was fully functional—coincided, and I was ready to move back to the US. So was Lynn, especially because our son, David, had been born on March 1, 1967.

The lucrative business opportunities available in Iran were luring many Iranian students who had stayed in the US after graduating to return home. Among them was Andre Minassian, my classmate, roommate, and friend at Pepperdine and U of I. He joined us as chief engineer, and his hiring was one of my last activities before my replacement, Robert Newbill, who I knew from D&M in Los Angeles, took over.

My departure in May 1967 was marked by two major occasions. The first was a large reception at the Tehran Hilton that I organized to introduce the new D&M management to our clients. The second was a formal fare-well party, organized by the Tehran office and also held at the Hilton. A few days later, Lynn, I, and the children left for California and my new position D&M's Los Angeles office.

---

2. The above is recounted in US Department of State File P760060-1115 (Subject: The Atomic Energy Organization of Iran), dated April 15, 1976, and declassified on June 25, 2008.

I CONTINUED TRAVELING BACK and forth to Iran frequently until the 1979 revolution. Many of these trips were related to the marketing and management of the Middle East office, and some of my visits were at the request of clients who wanted my input on their projects.

During the revolution, the D&M office, along with other US entities, including the US Embassy, was ransacked by anti-monarchists. Militant students broke into the embassy, took fifty-two Americans working there hostage, and held them in captivity for 444 days.

When the revolution erupted, D&M Middle East was involved in different stages of several major projects, including nuclear power plants in Bushehr and Esfahan as well as other industrial projects throughout the country. These all came to an abrupt halt when the Islamic Republic of Iran invalidated all contracts signed under the Shah's regime and refused to pay outstanding invoices that in D&M's case totaled several million dollars. D&M filed a complaint with the World Court in The Hague for breach of contract and damages, a case that I would become involved with in 1983.

D&M Middle East clients at the Tehran Hilton reception marking my departure

Farewell dinner at the Tehran Hilton with the dedicated employees who contributed so much to the success of D&M Middle East while I was manager

Introducing Robert Newbill (right) to Rose and Russ McNutt

PART FOUR

DAMES & MOORE
Los Angeles (1967–1982)

Chapter 20

RESETTLING IN CALIFORNIA

WHEN I RETURNED TO THE US in May 1967, I
had my choice of positions at three D&M locations: the San Francisco
office; the Los Angeles office, which was now located a few blocks south
of UCLA in Westwood Village; or the Executive Offices (EO) downtown.
Lynn and I wanted to raise Christina, four, and David, just a year old, in
LA's warmer climate and less formal environment, so we decided on the LA
office. Also, it would be an easy commute to the Westside from the small
house that we rented in Sherman Oaks, in the San Fernando Valley.

A week after my return, but before I had informed D&M of my decision, I attended a meeting of D&M principals at the Saddleback Resort in
Phoenix. The focus was on marketing strategies to expand the firm's growth.

To me, "marketing" meant approaching companies about specific projects
that we knew they were involved with and offering them services we knew
they needed along with how much those services would cost. However, I
was surprised to learn that, to D&M, "marketing strategies" were considered
to include such activities as presenting technical papers at conferences of
professional associations such as the American Society of Civil Engineers
(ASCE) and actively seeking out opportunities to serve on committees related
to geotechnical engineering.

Although these seemed like worthwhile ideas, I did not see them as significant avenues for developing future business. None of my college courses
had ever taught students how to "market" our engineering services or "sell" our
technical skills. Rather, we had simply been trained to design and construct
habitats for people. Most graduates were thus content to do the projects that
they were assigned to do competently and with pride. At the Phoenix meeting,
though, I realized that if I wanted to climb to the top of the D&M ladder,
I would have to bring in projects and contribute to the firm's bottom line.

At the meeting, I was asked to do a "show and tell" session on doing
business in Iran. Because I was a newcomer to the group and their concept

Christina, Lynn, me, and David in the backyard
of our rented home in Sherman Oaks, California

of marketing strategies was new to me, I did not feel I could speak to that topic. Instead, I showed slides of the primitive equipment and transportation used in connection with a large gas pumping station at a major river crossing in a remote area. Every item, from drilling equipment to camping gear, had been transported by a caravan of mules and horses from points beyond which four-wheel-drive vehicles could not go. After my presentation, some of the participants commented that my account had brought to mind the 1803-1805 Lewis and Clark expedition, which had opened America's frontiers all the way into the Pacific Northwest. I had no idea what they were talking about, but I smiled nevertheless.

The meeting was a great chance to get acquainted with people from the different offices, but it also made me aware of a certain elitism among the participants from D&M's big-city offices on the East and West coasts, especially those in San Francisco and New York. They discussed their large projects, their sophistication in terms of recent advancements in the geosciences, and their techniques for marketing D&M services. It became clear that the Tehran office, with its antiquated equipment, was perceived as being in the firm's bottom tier and capable of working only on small projects that required basic services in soil mechanics. Apparently, the US offices knew nothing of what was really going on in Tehran, and I saw no point in trying to match wits with the oversized egos present.

During one break, Trent Dames asked me whether I had decided where I wanted to work. When I hesitated, he suggested that I spend a little time in the EO before deciding. Although I already knew that I wanted to be in the Westwood office, I took him up on his offer because a number of issues, such as taxes, currency conversions, and accounting, relating to the Tehran office could only be straightened out from the EO.

I was given the temporary use of one partner's office while he went on vacation. Before he left, he asked me to check his inbox daily and to take any necessary action. He also warned me to always make some response to any correspondence, regardless of its nature. Every day, an avalanche of interoffice memos from different offices and regarding different subjects, all designated "For Information," would pile up in my inbox. Left to myself, I would have decided they did not require responses, but as I had been instructed, I would reply by acknowledging receipt of the memo, adding some comments about the topic (based on the partner's previous responses), and having the secretary type and forward the reply to the sender.

At lunchtime, some of us would go to the California Club or the Jonathan Club near the office, while others would play cards in the executive conference room. However, my overall impression was that the many competent engineers working in the EO were spending their days pushing paper around as I was, and did not look very happy.

I realized almost immediately that I could not fit into that environment for more than a few weeks. Fortunately, I resolved the Tehran office issues within a week and then began counting the days until I could move to the Westwood office.

I HAD MET AL SMOOTS, WHO HEADED UP the LA office, and his two associates in 1965 during my brief LA stay before I had been sent to Iran on the Mobil Oil project. The three of them were responsible for client contacts, marketing, and project management.

On my first day, Al called us all in to discuss my responsibilities as the fourth associate. He said that the office's existing and prospective clients, which included major entertainment companies, engineers and contractors, oil companies, and city and county entities, had been divided among the three of them, and he gave me a list of LA-based architectural firms to contact regarding D&M's services. The list included William Pereira, Charles Luckman, A.C. Martin, and a number of other high-profile firms famed for their roles in designing the city's high-rise structures.

I was happy to be handed my own list of prospective clients so quickly and could not wait to get on with my responsibilities. To my dismay, though, I soon learned that none of these firms wanted anything to do with D&M. They all thought that D&M was expensive, arrogant, and out of tune with the needs of architects. I also learned that LeRoy Crandall, a former D&M partner who had left to establish his own company after a dispute with Trent Dames, was getting a lot of projects relating to LA's boom in high-rise construction in the mid- and late 1960s.

Those first weeks in my new position were a strange period. I felt stymied about how to proceed because, although I knew and had worked with a number of people at the LA offices of Fluor, Bechtel, Parsons, Chevron, Mobil Oil, and other companies, I thought it would be unethical and unprofessional to contact them since they had already been assigned to my colleagues.

Another issue was that although I had been educated in the US and was married to an American, the business culture was alien to me. I soon realized that I had to adapt. So I told myself, "Well, Mr. Yaghoubian, here's your challenge—to learn how to survive businesswise in your adopted country."

It was "The Sixties," and the US was undergoing major changes culturally and politically. The escalation of the Vietnam War was fueling societal discontent as casualties mounted without any resolution in sight. The counterculture, with its drug use, music, and slogan "turn on, tune in, and drop out," was spreading like wildfire among the younger generation. The word "peace" and the symbol for nuclear disarmament were seen everywhere on posters and on jewelry worn by young people of both sexes, while popular music seemed to consist predominantly of antiwar ballads sung at peace rallies and antiwar protests.

The war was shredding the fabric of US society and causing fundamental change. Despite all the turmoil, however, the nation was also making tremendous achievements in science and technology. On July 20, 1969, Neil Armstrong became the first human being to set foot on the moon. Although the "pro-war" members of the population—also known as "the squares"—were extolling the nation's technical achievements and expressing their disdain for Communism, young male "peaceniks" sporting long hair and wearing tie-dyed shirts burned their draft cards to protest the war, while young women showed their support for the women's liberation movement and for the antiwar movement by tossing bras into trashcans and burning them.

Given my conservative values and deeply rooted anti-Communist feelings, I was of course a "square" and believed, along with my D&M colleagues, in the "domino theory," which argued that democracy throughout Southeast Asia would collapse if the Communist regime in Vietnam was not defeated.

Lynn, on the other hand, was a "peacenik," and tears came to her eyes when she saw and heard news accounts of young soldiers being brought back from Vietnam in body bags. Because of her liberal views, my colleagues jokingly called her "Angela Yaghoubian," after the controversial black political activist Angela Davis, at the time a scholar and professor in UCLA's philosophy department.

At lunchtime, UCLA students carrying mock caskets and chanting anti-war slogans would march peacefully in the streets near our office. It appeared that the political climate at UCLA among professors and students alike was toward the liberal end of the spectrum.

Even my own home did not escape the rebelliousness of the younger generation, as I learned one afternoon a few years later when I arrived home from work a little earlier than usual. When I opened the back door and entered the kitchen, I heard guitar music, occasionally interrupted by the sound of voices, coming from the living room.

I also overheard a mild, gentle woman's voice asking David, who was then four and enrolled in kindergarten, why he did not want to go to school. "I just don't want to," he replied in his childish voice, followed by a giggle.

I walked into the living room and found him and Lynn sitting on the floor with a woman who was holding a guitar and wearing the peace symbol on a leather thong hanging from her neck. Lynn introduced her as David's kindergarten teacher. With my arrival, the session—whatever it was—ended, and the teacher left.

When I asked Lynn at dinner what the little musical "conference" had been about, she explained that David had not gone to school for several days because he "didn't want to" and that he had not given her any reason other than that he "didn't want to." She added that his rebellion could be a sign of deeper anger problems that needed to be resolved before they worsened, and that his teacher had agreed that he needed to be gently persuaded to express his anger and to understand why he should keep going to school.

The unspoken rule in our household was that the children should go to their mother first to resolve any problems, and that if the problem could not be resolved, I would have the final word. That night, though, instead of confronting David at dinner, I did not follow up on the subject, which seemed to please him.

After the children went to bed, I told Lynn that David was playing a game and was loving all the attention that he was getting from her and from his teacher. She promptly reminded me that we were living in America and not in Iran where parents and teachers were tyrants, and so forth.

The next morning, as David was watching me pack his lunch before I left for the office, I told him, "Dave, you're going to school!" Without any hesitation, he smiled and replied, "Okay, Dad!"

From that day on, going to school never again became a topic of discussion in our household. I equated his behavior with that of the American young people of the time, who in turn reminded me of the young Tudeh Communists I had encountered in Iran in the early 1950s.

STILL, THE CHALLENGES OF LEARNING about my country of choice during that era were negligible compared to those facing me at D&M. I had never before asked anyone for help in getting things done, and I was not about to ask for guidance about how to meet my responsibilities in terms of being a productive associate, which meant bringing in new business.

My idea of marketing professional services went much farther than the idea of, for example, peddling insurance policies on a commission basis. Whatever I was going to market had to be challenging and give me a feeling of purpose and personal satisfaction beyond the financial rewards involved.

Two important observations shaped my approach. One was my past experience, which had taught me that if one had something interesting to say, people would listen. The second was a slogan that I had seen painted on the sides of ready-mix concrete trucks in San Francisco: "Find the need and fill it." Both of these summed up the challenge that I was facing.

And when I thought about "sense of purpose," I always remembered an anecdote about two medieval stone masons who were both hard at work shaping stone blocks that would be used to build a cathedral. When a passerby approached and asked one of them what he was doing, the mason went on working without looking up and grumbled, "I'm chipping stone." The passerby then approached the second mason, who was singing cheerfully as he worked, and asked him why he was so cheerful. The mason stood up, pointed to the structure in the distance, and replied, "I'm building a cathedral!"

I wanted to be involved in solving clients' problems on an individual basis, not offering robotic, one-size-fits-all solutions. With that in mind, I was constantly looking for ways to improve our involvement with clients' projects so D&M's services would stand out from what was being offered by our competitors, just as I had done in Tehran.

One day a year or so after I had joined the LA office, Al informed us that he wanted us to attend a lunch with an attorney who had been involved in a trial having to do with a lawsuit brought against the City of Los Angeles by a group of homeowners in the upscale community of Pacific Palisades whose homes had been damaged by a landslide during the construction of storm drains in their area.

I was fascinated by what the attorney said about how the definitiveness of the language used in the city engineers' soils and geologic reports for the project had affected the outcome of the case. The homeowners had won because, although the reports were very definite, the engineers had failed to substantiate the reasons for doing what they had done. What the attorney said about the potential liability created by the wording in the reports turned my thinking around because I had always taken for granted that the most important feature of soils and geologic reports was their technical content. However, because the US legal system, like marketing, was not taught in engineering programs, the importance of language had to be learned the hard way, sometimes to the detriment of both engineers and employers.

I was so taken by what I learned that day that I enrolled in the La Salle Extension University in Chicago law curriculum and earned my law degree in 1975. At the time, I was not sure what I would do with my degree, but I thought that a time might come when I would find it useful. In the meantime, I could at least personally avoid, as well as help my clients avoid, some of the pitfalls that I learned about that day at lunch.

The Holiday Inns of America (HIA) Project

Although I read the *Wall Street Journal* every morning, I soon learned that by the time news of a project appeared in print, it was too late to go after it. This was especially true for D&M's services, which were utilized at the front end of proposed projects.

However, I was just in time when in 1969 I spotted a story about plans by Holiday Inns of America (HIA) to build a chain of motels throughout the United States by completing one motel each week.

I promptly called HIA's corporate headquarters in Memphis and asked to speak to the project manager for motel construction. A secretary with a Southern drawl told me that "Eddie" was very busy and that I should either try back at the end of the day or leave a message asking him to return my call. I gave her my contact information and asked her to tell him that I wanted to discuss how HIA could slash their costs on every motel they constructed anywhere in the country.

By the time I got back from lunch, a message from an HIA vice president asking me to call him was waiting. When I called back, he wanted to know how I was going to save HIA "lots of money per motel." I replied that I would like to discuss this in person and would be willing to fly to Memphis at his convenience.

"The sooner the better," he answered. "Just let me know."

When I excitedly informed Al about the phone call and that I planned to fly to Memphis the next day, he became concerned about the extravagant promises I had made. He called Gardner Reynolds, the partner responsible for D&M marketing activities, and informed him of the situation. Gardner then called me, I told him about the conversation, and he said he wanted to go with me to Memphis if I did not mind. I arranged for us to leave the following day and to meet with HIA the day after.

I HAD HEARD ABOUT "SOUTHERN HOSPITALITY" but had never experienced it. As we left the plane, a tall, well-dressed young man met us and directed us to a long black limousine waiting on the tarmac nearby. He invited us to dinner and told us that since Memphis was a "dry" town, he needed to stop and buy wine for dinner.

After dinner we were taken to the company's first US HIA, where we spent the night. The next morning we went to the corporate headquarters, where we were given a tour of a large warehouse where rows of model rooms, mostly distinguishable from each other by different colors and furniture arrangements, were displayed so prospective HIA franchisers could select the decors that suited their taste. After that, we were taken to meet with Kemmons Wilson, the founder of the HIA chain.

After introducing Gardner and thanking Mr. Wilson for HIA's hospitality, I explained that D&M had many offices throughout the US and that for a fixed price we could meet HIA's needs related to developing site-specific data for the design and construction of their two-story structures. Instead of HIA contacting local engineering firms individually to make separate arrangements for each site, which would involve additional time and expenses, HIA could place a single call to me in LA and I would make all the arrangements necessary for the motel sites to be investigated anywhere in the country.

Without a moment's hesitation, Mr. Wilson extended his hand to me and said, "It's a deal!" Apparently, many of their projects were being delayed because of red tape and having to deal with different local entities.

On our flight back, Gardner commented, "That was impressive. I hope you've planned how you're going to do what you promised!"

LIVING UP TO THOSE PROMISES turned out to be simple. HIA would forward me the list of proposed motel sites and the construction schedules. Sites in areas where D&M had offices would receive the plans directly from HIA, make arrangements to investigate the sites, and prepare reports that included design and construction recommendations. The fact that all of the

With D&M partner Gardner Reynolds

motels were two-story structures with identical footprints simplified our task greatly. Also, other D&M offices nationwide were glad to be participating in the HIA construction boom.

While HIA was building motels near airports to serve business travelers, other hospitality corporations such as Sheraton and Hilton hotels began to shift their focus back to building larger and more luxurious establishments. To remain competitive, HIA embarked on a similar program of building more upscale hotels under different names.

The first of these was a twelve-floor, almost 300-room high-rise on Powell Street in Emeryville (it is now the Hilton Garden Inn San Francisco/Oakland Bay Bridge). D&M's San Francisco office handled the project, which required 100-foot-long piles. Within a few years, HIA's signature circular high-rise towers, located near busy intersections and freeway ramps, were visible in dozens of cities. One of these towers, which happened to be D&M's last HIA project and for which I helped to select the site, still stands at the intersection of Sunset Boulevard and the San Diego Freeway north of UCLA. It is now part of the Luxe Worldwide Hotel chain.

The trend to larger and more complex structures required negotiating a new contract with HIA. Although other D&M offices continued to provide services to HIA on a project-by-project basis, it was my nature to tire of repetitive tasks, so after a year I wanted to move on to new ventures.

Marketing Shifts: From Geographical Areas to Multiregional Industries

Besides being a productive business venture, the HIA projects gave D&M an opportunity to explore and develop other marketing strategies for maximizing growth. Although geographical expansion had served the company well up to that point, it had also created a parochial culture in which branch offices had no interest in markets outside their region. The HIA experience served as a model for coordinating and reorienting the firm's services toward specific industries worldwide such as petroleum, natural gas, mining, and so forth.

Implementing this new strategy required a two-pronged approach. In addition to expanding growth in geographical areas, the firm also needed to begin offering a full array of multidisciplinary services—in effect, creating a "one-stop shop" for the different industries being targeted. Each industry was assigned to a marketing director who reported directly to top management, and after I became a D&M partner in 1970, I was assigned to marketing services having to do with natural gas markets worldwide. While taking on that responsibility, I also, of course, continued my involvement with a wide range of other energy-related projects.

I was fortunate in that many of the expatriate engineers whom I had met and worked with in Tehran had returned to their companies' home offices stateside and been promoted to managerial positions. I met routinely with them, which was a huge advantage for me because continuing our working relationships often resulted in new business.

For example, during one visit in early 1974 to Fluor's Southern California headquarters in Irvine, I heard a familiar voice call my name. I spotted a group of people gathered around a drafting table and recognized Tim Rogers, back from Iran. He and a Korean delegation were discussing a proposed fertilizer plant in Yosu (now Yeosu), South Korea, for Namhae Chemical Corporation. Tim introduced me to them as Fluor's international expert and then asked me about using dikes to reclaim land for the project. We spent the next half-hour in a discussion of various alternatives that culminated with the question, "When can D&M begin site characterization studies?"

ASIDE FROM MARKETING D&M SERVICES related to natural gas, I managed numerous large projects, including several 200-foot-diameter deep space tracking dish antennas for the US National Aeronautical and Space Administration (NASA); coal-fired power plants; refineries and petrochemical complexes; offshore oil and gas production platforms; berthing and mooring facilities; and airports located in the US, Algeria, Australia, the South China Sea, England, Greece, Guam, Indonesia, Iraq, Japan, South Korea, Kuwait, the Mediterranean Sea off the coast of Algeria, Mexico, Nigeria, Pakistan, the Persian Gulf, Saudi Arabia, and Spain.

For much of the rest of my career at D&M, I marketed, signed contracts, organized project teams, outlined tasks, oversaw and managed the execution of projects, reviewed the work performed, and reviewed and signed off on reports for projects, with a special focus on environmental studies and seismologic studies.

Moving into Environmental and Seismologic Studies

I had first become interested in earthquake engineering following the 1962 Boin-Zahra Earthquake in Iran, and that interest was reawakened when the magnitude 6.6 San Fernando Earthquake struck the San Fernando Valley north of Los Angeles at 6:01 a.m. on February 9, 1971.

This earthquake turned 1971 into a watershed year for seismology. Although not a "great" earthquake by any means, it nevertheless caused a great deal of unexpected damage and provided a treasure trove of scientific data that changed both scientific theories and previously held beliefs related to earthquake engineering and geosciences. The result was a scientific push to better understand the mechanisms of earthquakes. Efforts to learn more about how damage to structures from future quakes might be minimized or prevented also intensified.

The field of earthquake engineering was already evolving at a steady pace as more information and scientific data from major earthquakes worldwide was becoming available. The phenomenal advances in computer data processing speeds also allowed earthquake engineering to move beyond the "art" of projecting the impact of future earthquakes based on historic seismic events and into the "science" of accurately assessing, with a high degree of confidence, the response of both natural and manmade structures to future earthquakes. However, data processing capabilities were advancing much more quickly than the flow and analysis of data from major seismic events worldwide, and this discrepancy resulted in a wide range of colorful graphic interpretations that were not scientifically accurate.

Ever since the earth was formed more than four billion years ago, tectonic shifts have been the main cause of the constantly changing global landscape. Some of those changes are elastic deformations, while others cause deep rifts or cracks ("faults") in the earth's crust. It is commonly believed that seismic events are caused when two sides of a fault slip and grind against each other. This releases energy in the form of propagating surface and body waves that shake the ground.

However, I believe that until the three-dimensional geometry of areas where high elastic stresses and strains continue to accumulate deep in fractures that cause segments of a given fault to "lock" and be prevented from moving can be measured accurately, earthquake prediction will remain an elusive goal. In short, the times and locations of earthquakes still cannot be predicted with any degree of certainty.

The seismological community has therefore adopted a two-fold approach that uses both probabilistic and deterministic methodologies.

Stated simply, the probabilistic approach consists of calculating the risk of future seismic events occurring in a given area during a specific future period. These calculations are based on data from past earthquakes in the same area and result in predictions like "the probability of a 6.7 magnitude earthquake or larger over the next 30 years striking the greater Los Angeles area is 67 percent and in the San Francisco Bay Area is 63 percent."[1]

The deterministic approach, on the other hand, calculates the strongest possible future earthquakes that could be triggered by one or more active faults that are significant to the site of interest. The parameters taken into account include the length of the fault, the type of active fault or faults, the distance of the fault(s) from the site in question, and the propagation characteristics of waves generated by the relevant faults. In the past half-century, the design and construction of earthquake-resistant structures based on the deterministic approach has advanced greatly, due mainly to the increasing flow of information related to the causes and effects of major earthquakes worldwide.

Although any major earthquake is of great interest to geoscientists, a number of significant global seismic events have resulted in new perspectives on the response of structures to different earthquake-induced ground shaking. Such earthquakes include the Richter magnitude 6.4 Long Beach Earthquake in California in 1933, which prompted the establishment of unified building codes; the 6.9 Imperial Valley Earthquake in El Centro, California, in 1940, where the first time-history of ground shaking was fully recorded; and two 1964 earthquakes, the 9.2 Alaska Earthquake (the second-largest in recorded history) and the 7.5 Niigata Earthquake in Japan, both of which advanced understanding of seismically induced soil liquefaction.

Throughout the 1950s and 1960s, the worldwide consensus among geoscientists and structural engineers in seismology and earthquake engineering was that deterministically the maximum ground acceleration could not exceed 50 percent of the earth's gravity, or 0.5 g. Only Nathan Newmark, of the University of Illinois, was the exception. He believed that ground acceleration could exceed 1g.

---

1. http://digitaljournal.com/article/294234

The San Fernando Earthquake proved him right. A strong-motion station in Sylmar recorded horizontal and vertical accelerations above 1g that had been triggered by an unknown thrust fault. The implications of these findings for the design and construction of critical structures such as nuclear power plants in earthquake-prone regions were huge.

Since 1971, many large earthquakes have contributed immensely to seismologists' understanding of how structures respond not only to earthquake-induced ground shaking but also of how seismic events affect the atmospheric and oceanic elements of the area involved. For example, Japan's Fukushima Daiichi power plant apparently responded satisfactorily to the ground shaking induced by the magnitude 9.0 Tohoku Earthquake in March 2011. However, besides resulting in thousands of deaths, the tsunami triggered by the earthquake swamped the seawalls near the plant and almost caused a nuclear meltdown.

AFTER THE SAN FERNANDO EARTHQUAKE, the California state government approved funds to install a new network of strong-motion stations. Also, instrumentation to measure the response of buildings to earthquake-induced motion at the ground-, mid-, and top-floor levels of designated high-rise structures in the San Fernando Valley was installed.

In terms of my own work, earthquake engineering soon became the most critical discipline for my projects. Seismology had been part and parcel of D&M's core business since its inception and had become a critical factor in the site selection, design, and construction of nuclear power plants.

Following the San Fernando Earthquake, I prepared a presentation and narrative for clients and various industry associations that included a comprehensive set of slides of the damage caused to bridges, highways, buildings, dams, industrial complexes, and other structures. D&M's clients in Iran were especially interested in the presentation because, like California, their country is "earthquake country."

The National Environmental Policy Act (NEPA) and the 1973 Energy Crisis

Throughout the 1970s, numerous events and new federal regulations opened up new business opportunities that enhanced D&M's core business in the geosciences and other disciplines.

One of these was the US National Environmental Policy Act of 1969 (NEPA). NEPA's aim was to create a balance between supporting essential industrial growth and preserving the natural environment. This was to be done through quantitative studies, including environmental impact statements

(EISs) that described the possible environmental impacts of projects and had to be submitted to "lead agencies"—the local, state and federal bodies responsible for reviewing and approving projects and issuing construction permits.

The first step in this process was to gather and develop baseline environmental data—atmospheric, terrestrial, marine, flora, fauna, and socioeconomic—for sites and their vicinities. Second, specifics about the details of construction, operation, emissions, and so forth, had to be superimposed on the environmental baseline that had been developed. Third, the potential environmental impact of projects was to be determined using both objective and subjective analysis. The fourth step was to formulate ways to mitigate environmental impacts. Finally, the studies and recommendations were to be included in highly detailed environmental impact reports (EIRs), which became an integral part of the documents submitted to the various lead agencies.

Most European countries had put environmental protection regulations in place long before 1973. My postgraduate studies in the Netherlands in 1963 and 1964 had included environmental courses and related field trips to large land-reclamation projects where environmental remediation was being implemented. This background facilitated my grasp of NEPA's mandate. However, the US lacked two major elements required to expedite the implementation of NEPA: first, up-to-date published databases in regions of interest; and second, guidelines for carrying out environmental studies now that government agencies were required to evaluate the impact of "major actions" on the environment before approving projects.

D&M was able to offer multiple services in many of these areas.

ANOTHER CASE IN POINT WAS the energy crisis of late 1973, when the price of crude oil began spiking after the decision by the Organization of the Petroleum Exporting Countries (OPEC) to embargo shipments of oil to countries that had supported Israel in the Yom Kippur War of a few weeks earlier.

Before long, US drivers nationwide were spending hours waiting in long lines to buy gas from any stations that had it to sell. Contributing to the supply crisis was the moratorium on offshore drilling that had been put into place after the disastrous oil spill off the coast of Santa Barbara, California, in the winter of 1969. In addition, all proposed energy projects now had to comply with NEPA.

In response to the crisis, many American entities began to advocate developing alternative energy and fuel sources to mitigate the effects of the embargo and to decrease US dependence on foreign oil—and given my wide-ranging management responsibilities, alternative energy was an area I became involved with at D&M in addition to my worldwide marketing activities.

Among the alternatives suggested were coal gasification and extracting oil from Canadian tar-sand and squeezing oil from oil shale deposits. However, both of these were still hydrocarbon-based energy options that involved potentially detrimental environmental consequences such as dealing with the sulfur content of coal as well as processing issues involved with oil extraction technologies.

For example, the coal deposits so abundant in the Southwest contained sulfur, which created acid rain when burned by power plants and also degraded air quality in the national parks in the Four Corners area. This in turn required the installation of expensive scrubber and precipitator units.

The coal industry, in an effort to find a replacement for oil, began searching for ways to remove sulfur from mined coal to create cleaner-burning fuels, and we at D&M learned of many of these ideas. While some seemed reasonable, although untested, others were so outlandish as to be funny.

However, the subject was so important that I did not mind listening to anyone who had any ideas for removing sulfur from coal—so I was intrigued when one day in 1973 I received a call from two nuns who had discovered a species of sulfur-eating bacteria. I knew that there are bacteria on land and in large bodies of water that consume hydrocarbons, so the idea did not seem too far-fetched. I also felt that nuns could be trusted to be telling the truth. The nuns agreed to pay for a sample of their valuable "bugs" to be sent to a research laboratory in Chicago for testing.

The first reports from the laboratory were very exciting because apparently the bacteria did ingest the sulfur when placed in contact with coal and did leave the samples sulfur-free. But our enthusiasm quickly waned after the bugs overdosed on their steady diet of sulfur and stopped eating it altogether. To this day, removing sulfur from coal at a reasonable cost has remained an elusive goal.

At D&M we evaluated non-hydrocarbon sources of energy such as solar power, wind power, geothermal energy, fuel cells, pump storage, power cogeneration (by having industries reuse generated steam-driving plant machinery), biofuels such as corn, and thermal energy conversion (generating energy from ocean waves or using turbines to create energy from the differing temperatures of surface and deep ocean water).

Although these kinds of energy sources were capable of meeting a portion of the US population's consumer energy needs, they could not generate enough BTUs (British thermal units) to meet the country's industrial needs.

Also, the production of electricity by nuclear generating stations was already well underway, but nuclear power generation, although considered environmentally "clean," had its own drawbacks. For one thing, it took a number of years for nuclear plants to be designed, permitted, constructed, and commissioned before they could begin producing. In addition, continuing public concerns about the safety of nuclear power plants resulted in endless public hearings and red tape.

From an engineering standpoint, the planning of such generating stations required detailed site selection and safety analyses, while the permitting process required Preliminary Safety Analysis Reports (PSARs) that included the full range of environmental engineering disciplines but especially related to geosciences.

Nevertheless, the energy crisis created a boom market among engineers and constructors eager to capture a share of the emerging alternative-energy market. Both the federal and state governments encouraged these entrepreneurial efforts by issuing grants to construct pilot plants to explore the feasibility of proposed alternatives. Oil companies were also beneficiaries of such grants.

Many of the technologies being talked about during this period offered the potential for producing non-hydrocarbon-based power, but the economic feasibility of developing these technologies was directly linked to crude oil prices. Studies at the time indicated that alternative energy sources would become economically viable if and when crude oil prices reached $40 to $50 per barrel, and industry leaders and politicians kept predicting that crude oil prices could skyrocket to $100 or more per barrel.

I had long been concerned that the oil companies could artificially manipulate worldwide oil prices and make alternative energies economically unfeasible, thus blocking any progress in that area. For this reason, I also believed that there was too much uncertainty for D&M to consider making heavy investments in alternative energy—a course of action that the firm was considering at that time.

It seemed to me that a more viable option would be for D&M to take part in the exploration of new energy sources by offering its engineering services, especially because the firm was particularly qualified to deal with environmental considerations.

I felt very strongly that D&M should move to participate actively in developing markets. The firm did begin teaming with companies known for their process design capabilities to solicit government grants, with

D&M providing expertise in the environmental sciences and the design parameters for the construction of onshore and offshore energy facilities.

The Glomar Explorer Project

Services related to oceanic disciplines had long been provided by D&M, and in the mid-1970s those services became a formal division based at our LA office. Unbeknown to us at the time, however, one marine services project, though intriguing, turned out to be something totally different than what was presented to us.

The story began in early 1974, when Howard Hughes Global Marine Development Inc. retained D&M to have marine geologists explore the feasibility of mining "manganese nodules" scattered 17,000 feet deep on the Pacific Ocean floor about 2,000 miles from Oahu, Hawaii.

The plan was to locate the small, loose clusters of manganese nodules, vacuum them up, and transport them to a plant where they would be processed into manganese, a prime component of steel used in manufacturing consumer products. This plan received a fair amount of publicity at the outset because it was seen as an attempt by Hughes to corner the manganese market.

Jerry Wilson, a D&M marine geologist, was assigned to manage the field activities for D&M, but after spending a month on board the *Glomar Explorer*, a deep-sea mining vessel, he returned with only a box full of unsightly black lumps of manganese nodules. Nothing more came of the project, and before long the story of Hughes's venture faded away as the global demand for metals fizzled. For some years afterward, I kept some of the nodules on prominent display in a U of I mug in my office, where I enjoyed regaling visitors with the story of their origin.

I did not learn the real story until twenty-five years later. One evening in 1999 while watching a PBS "Nova" special called "Submarines, Secrets and Spies," I almost fell out of my chair when I learned that the entire "manganese nodule" project had been a cover story concocted by the US Central Intelligence Agency, with Hughes's cooperation, to recover the Soviet Union's K-129 submarine, which had sunk near Hawaii in March 1968 while carrying three ballistic missiles aimed at the US.[2]

According to the documentary, the middle of the *Glomar* contained a gigantic room with a retractable floor that opened onto the ocean below. A large, complex frame with claws on either side was lowered to the ocean

---

2. A transcript of the entire program can be found at: www.pbs.org/wgbh/nova/transcripts/2602subsecrets.html

floor, where it grabbed the K-129 and began lifting it. Halfway to the top, however, the submarine began to slip, and one of its nuclear missiles slipped off its silo and sank into the ocean floor. Luckily, it did not explode, and a nuclear catastrophe was avoided. A short time later, the submarine pulled free of the mechanical claws and sank back to the ocean floor. Only one thirty-eight-foot section was recovered and brought to the surface. It contained only some crew members' remains, which were buried at sea.

So it turned out that while the geologists on board the *Glomar* were mapping the area's geology from its top deck, the largest covert US operation since the Manhattan Project had been taking place right under their noses. However, because the ship was as tall as a three- or four-story building, it had been easy to keep the scientists away from what was really going on.

Manganese nodules collected from the *Glomar Explorer*

Chapter 21

ENVIRONMENTAL STUDIES IN CALIFORNIA
The Avila Beach and Point Conception Projects

Avila Beach: California's First Successful Environmental Impact Report

A major opportunity for D&M in the wake of NEPA arose in 1970 when J.T. Powers, of Humble Oil Company of Houston, came to us regarding a planned seventy-mile-long corridor of parallel eighteen-inch oil and wet-gas pipelines between the port of Gaviota, about two hours north of Los Angeles, and Avila Beach, about another hour farther north. When I spoke with him, he already knew that an EIR would be required before a construction permit for the pipeline route could be issued, but he did not know what was involved. He was relieved to learn that in addition to geologic studies, D&M could also carry out the environmental evaluations.

Shortly after Humble Oil authorized D&M to proceed, I realized that our LA office did not have all the experts who would be needed to properly assess the potential impact of the pipeline project. For example, we would require data about the flora and fauna along the proposed corridor, which would traverse thinly populated areas and different climatic zones.

I turned to academia, where I obtained substantial help from a half-dozen experts at what is now California State University Northridge (CSUN). I hired them to go out and look for animal traces so the fauna along the pipeline route could be identified and the project's possible impacts on them be anticipated—for example, whether fish would be affected by dirt getting into the waterways.

Ultimately, I produced the first EIR to be developed in the state of California and approved by both the local and state lead agencies. In fact, D&M's study for this project became a model for future EIR studies and reports (although, due to changes in the energy industry over time, the corridor was never built).

In the years that followed, other large projects contributed to establishing D&M as the premier environmental engineering company in the United

States. Among them were two coal-powered power plants in Arizona, the Navajo Generating Station on the Navajo Indian Reservation near Page (1969-1972) and the Cholla plant near Joseph City (1972-1973), both located in pristine areas close to Grand Canyon National Park.

The LNG Terminal Project at Point Conception

As part of the ongoing effort to reduce US dependence on imported oil following the energy crisis and the enactment of NEPA, gas companies nationwide began promoting liquefied natural gas (LNG) as a viable, clean-burning, and efficient energy source that was abundantly available throughout the country. One such company was the Southern California Gas Company (SoCal Gas), which, along with a number of other companies, embarked on a plan to develop and ship LNG from Alaska to Southern California by building liquefaction and loading facilities in Alaska and unloading and vaporization facilities in California.

D&M was chosen to prepare the EIRs for the project in 1973, and I managed the project as the "principal in charge." The LNG project would ultimately involve more than a decade of ongoing studies, including comprehensive in-situ seismic studies, the production of many reports and EIRs, and many local, state, and federal hearings in California and Washington DC.

LNG projects generally include three major components: first, a liquefaction terminal as well as transfer and loading facilities at the source; second, an unloading and vaporization plant at the end point; and third, special double-hulled ships to transport the LNG from the liquefaction terminal to the vaporization terminal.

At the liquefaction terminal, natural gas, which is predominantly methane, is squeezed to 1/600th of its original volume, condensed into liquid form by cooling it to -260°F, and then stored in cryogenic tanks for transfer. The LNG is then loaded into ships and transported to the vaporization plant, where it is converted back into its gaseous state and distributed through transmission pipelines.

The application for the project required identifying and selecting sites for the two terminals, and shipping lanes as well, that would result in minimal environmental impacts. In Alaska, the site selected for the liquefaction terminal and shipping facilities was Nikiski, on the east bank of Upper Cook Inlet. Three potential sites in Central and Southern California were considered for the vaporization terminal: Point Conception, about sixty miles north of Santa Barbara; Oxnard, about an hour north of Los Angeles; and the Los Angeles Harbor.

With Dr. Shirley Thomas in my office

D&M's studies for each of the three sites included investigators from ten major disciplines and eighty subdisciplines, including sciences, sociology, and economics. All of the investigators prepared reports that included the data they had obtained, the results of their investigations, and their conclusions. These reports were submitted to the managers in each discipline, who merged the investigators' findings into one report for each of the three sites.

These then came to me for review, after which I was to approve them for publication. However, the reports consisted of hundreds of pages of data, graphs, charts, tables, and other information presented in widely varied writing styles and formats that required heavy editing to be put into cohesive form. I hired my good friend, USC communications professor Dr. Shirley Thomas, to edit and check the grammatical accuracy of the final reports before they were printed and disseminated. Shirley was the author of several books including the eight-volume *Men of Space* series, which focused on men who had made significant contributions to the exploration of space.[1]

The project was so massive and our secretaries became so overwhelmed that, unknown to me, they contacted John Maloney, the manager of D&M's human resources department, for relief. When I learned that John had responded, "Jack got the job—let him take care of it," I remembered seeing a

1. Shirley Thomas, *Men of Space: Profiles of the Leaders in Space Research, Development, and Exploration* (Philadelphia PA and New York NY: Chilton Co. Book Division, 1960-1968).

notice in the lobby of our high-rise listing a vacancy on the eleventh floor just above our offices. I promptly called the building manager and leased all the space available on a month-to-month basis. Shirley knew several typists whom I hired. I then rented typewriters, desks, chairs, wastebaskets, ashtrays, and office supplies. Two days later, the new staff members were humming away on the eleventh floor.

Eventually, several hundred copies of each report were printed on recycled paper and distributed to the relevant local, state, and federal agencies.

The lead agencies then began rounds of public hearings during which the reports were scrutinized—and criticized. Because California was earthquake country, the issue of LNG safety in the event of a major earthquake was of great public concern, and all proceedings were made part of the record. During the hearings, some of which lasted late into the night, opponents of the project would make alarmist statements about the dangers of LNG and the potential inferno that could ensue.

Surrounded by stacks of unbound environmental impact reports,
Ian Macfarlane and I confer about the Point Conception project, which
generated more than 1 million sheets of paper and used 6 tons of paper.

AFTER THE LOCAL AND STATE HEARINGS, the federal administrative hearing on the project began in the summer of 1977 in Washington DC. As the "person most knowledgeable" ("PMK"), I had to attend every hearing, testify on every discipline covered by the reports, and respond to comments and criticisms. We were housed at the Watergate Hotel, and because this was just a few years after the Watergate scandal, to me the hotel did have an ominous atmosphere.

The US Federal Energy Regulatory Commission (FERC) judge, Samuel A. Gordon, was a tall, graying, bespectacled man. Because this was an administrative hearing, the courtroom was relatively empty, with only the judge, a court reporter, and the attorneys and witnesses on both sides in attendance.

The weather, typical for DC in the summer, was brutally hot and humid. In keeping with President Jimmy Carter's directives, the air-conditioning systems in government buildings had been turned off and replaced with electric fans. Judge Gordon's courtroom had two large oscillating pedestal fans buzzing in the back of the room in opposite corners. Every so often, the two fans would synchronize their movement and the buzzing would get louder.

The judge played tennis each day during the lunch break and would return for the afternoon session visibly tired and drained. After several days in his courtroom, I could tell to within a split second when he was about to doze off, to be awakened only when a loud "Objection!" would erupt during the testimony. He would first start blinking more and more slowly. Then he would lean back in his upholstered chair, tilt his head up, and stare with glazed eyes up at the ceiling as if trying to figure out the meaning of what the witness had just said. After some moments, he would return to his normal sitting position but place his right elbow on the top of his desk. Then his right thumb would edge over to his mouth, where he would rest it against his eyetooth to support the weight of his head. I would watch fascinated as his head drooped lower and the pressure of his tooth on the thumb increased until his eyes would eventually blink open as if he had been wide awake the whole time.

I have never forgotten the day I was testifying on earthquakes. Just before the lunch break, the opposing attorney asked me to explain the difference between the Mercalli intensity scale and Richter scale for measuring the scale of earthquakes using terms that laypeople could understand. Before I could finish, Judge Gordon adjourned for lunch.

After lunch, I returned to the witness chair and was reviewing my notes when the judge re-entered the courtroom, announced that the court was in session, and asked the examining attorney to continue. The attorney repeated his question about the Mercalli and Richter scales.

I asked the judge if I could approach the blackboard. He replied yes and rested his head against the back of his chair. Using different-colored chalks, I drew a palm tree with a brown trunk, green fronds, and brown coconuts hanging from it. I then drew a man standing five feet from the tree pulling and releasing a rope tied to it.

After completing my drawing, I noticed that the judge was resting his head in his "tooth position" with his eyes half open. The humidity, the buzzing of the fans in the quiet room, and the tropical image of the swaying palm tree apparently hypnotized the judge into a deep sleep. In slow motion, his tooth slipped off his supporting thumb and as his head nodded forward, his thumb dislodged the right earpiece of his glasses from his ear. His head then sank slowly onto his right arm and he fell sound asleep with his glasses dangling from his left ear.

I looked at the attorney, who with a shrug and a big smile shook his head and said, "Let's go ahead before I fall sleep, too."

I nodded and, moving my hand back and forth, said, "Imagine that this man is pulling and releasing the rope. This causes the tree to sway gently back and forth. Let us assume that as he shakes the tree, some of the coconuts fall. The number of fallen coconuts can be considered a parameter that measures the strength of the shaking, while the force that the man is using to pull on the rope would be another parameter. The Mercalli Scale is like counting the fallen coconuts—it is based on the observed damages to a structure following an earthquake. Measuring the strength that the man is using to pull on the rope is like the Richter Scale, which measures the magnitude of the shaking."

That afternoon, the only way that the judge would have known what had gone on in his courtroom would have been to read the transcript of my testimony.

In 1978, Point Conception received conditional federal approval as the site for the vaporization terminal, and SoCal Gas authorized D&M to carry out a comprehensive investigation of the site and to develop design parameters for the terminal.

Seismic Studies at Point Conception

By now, I was intimately familiar with the environmental setting of Point Conception. I knew that it was a significant part of California's coastal ecosystem as an area where the colder waters of the northern coast meet and merge with the warmer waters of the southern area. This creates unique ocean wave patterns that influence the ocean bottom and support a rare combination of marine life.

The coastal terrain features bluffs and marine terraces, created over millennia by the action of the ocean waves, that rise forty to eighty feet above the beach and are divided into vertical slices by narrow, poorly developed gullies called "arroyos" that drain the area. The local climate is windy and inhospitable. The frequent dense fog that rolls in from the ocean creates a cold, damp climate that could be bone-chilling even on summer days.

The LNG site was located in a complex geologic province known as the Transverse Range that had been formed by seismotectonic activities generated by the San Andreas and Santa Ynez faults, both of which trend northwest. The resulting deformations of the earth's crust had formed folds and faults throughout the area. The east-northeast trending faults exhibit high angle reverse components known as thrust faulting that are easily visible at rock outcroppings during low tide at the beach.

From the outset, I had been concerned about residual and ongoing crustal stresses in the area that could cause further ground displacements and therefore had to be taken into account in the design of the pads for the LNG storage tanks. With that in mind, and in the face of the project geologists' skepticism, I had ordered in-situ stress measurements performed at the site and had authorized Dr. Joel Sweet and Dr. Wolfgang Roth to create numerical models of the propagation of displacements throughout the overlying soil media where the tank pads were to be located.

One of our outside advisors was Dr. Richard Goodman, a professor of rock mechanics at UC Berkeley, who did not believe that the stresses measured were large enough to cause further deformations and thus were no cause for concern. However, his views changed after he visited an active open mining facility near the site where he observed the actual formation of a shallow faulting at the bottom of a pit while it was being excavated. This faulting occurred because the removal of the overburden pressure had altered the in-situ stress.

In the spring of 1978, toward the end of our geologic investigation, heavy rains washed away the loose bank-soils in an arroyo and exposed a geologic variation in the underlying bedrock that was similar to but somewhat larger than the high-angle vertical slips at the beach outcrops. In an area as large as the Point Conception site, the locations of such concealed geologic features are difficult to find unless and until the soil layers above them are removed.

That day, I and our geologists walked into the arroyo, the banks of which had been thoroughly mapped before the rain. The arroyo narrowed as we proceeded, and just as we reached its far end and saw the feature, a man appeared who turned out to be Donald Asquith, the geologist for the Hollister Ranch Homeowners Association, a planned community that lay north and west of the proposed LNG site and was a major opponent of the project.

"Hello there!" he shouted, grinning sarcastically as if he had caught us red-handed doing something wrong. He then informed us, with some elation, that he had actually discovered the eroded arroyo and the uncovered feature just before our geologists had. He promptly named it the "Arroyo Fault" and declared it to be a major active fault that was connected to other major active faults below the surface and was capable of triggering greater than 7.5 magnitude earthquakes during the lifetime of the proposed terminal. He also claimed that any such seismic event would result in disastrous ground displacements of more than ten feet at the site.

Although Asquith offered no probabilistic or deterministic data to support his claims, in the eyes of those opposed to the terminal, he did not need to substantiate his claims because his discovery of the feature was by itself proof of his credibility.

On May 2, 1978, SoCal Gas hurriedly issued a statement that included a quote from me stating that in my opinion the "feature" was a minor and benign geologic variation.

But the damage had been done. The opposition took full advantage of the "newly discovered fatal flaw" to try again to kill the project. They argued that the Arroyo Fault could cause the LNG tanks to rupture and spill their entire flammable contents into the ocean, which would cause an inferno forty miles in diameter. In fact, Edward Teller, the physicist known as the "Father of the Hydrogen Bomb" and a vocal critic of LNG generally, was brought in as an expert witness by the opposition. His presentations were very impressive, and no one dared to question or challenge the opinions that he expressed.

However, although he was only too happy to inveigh against the dangers posed by LNG, he never referred to the positive role that engineering design could play in minimizing potential hazards. And, of course, the general public did not want to be told that, just as the dangers of nuclear energy plants could be minimized and lowered to acceptable confidence levels by adequate engineering, the same could be accomplished when it came to LNG plants.

In any event, the burden of refuting these baseless allegations rested squarely on D&M—in other words, on me. We went into full damage-control

for MANAGEMENT of the PACIFIC LIGHTING COMPANIES

gas

Los Angeles
Special Issue
May 2, 1978

**PT. CONCEPTION LNG TERMINAL
FEASIBLE DESPITE 'FAULT'**
A variation in the geological structure near our proposed liquefied natural
gas terminal at Point Conception does not appear to affect the feasibilty of
building an LNG facility at the site, a consultant for our project said.

"The presence of such a variation is not unusual," said Jack Yaghoubian, a
partner with Dames & Moore, an engineering consulting firm for our
affiliate, Western LNG Terminal Associates. Such variations may influence
final design details but should not affect the basic design of the terminal,
he added.

Dames & Moore discovered the existence of a variation in geological
structure in studies already completed for us. As part of its
recommendation to us, the engineering firm assumed the occurrence of
an earthquake at the site.

Geologists from Dames & Moore are currently examining the variation to
determine its size and full significance.

Discovery of the variation was announced last Friday by George Allen,
attorney for Hollister Ranch Owners Assn., representing a large group of
land holders adjacent to our proposed site which is opposing the terminal.
The "potentially active fault" — as it is described by the geologist who
detected it — is located in the easterly portion of the site, on land that we
are planning to acquire in order to shift the terminal eastward to avoid
disturbing archeological sites.

"The important thing about a fault is how much energy is stored in it,"
Yaghoubian said. "This feature would have virtually no energy because it is
quite short."

According to Western LNG officials, the design of facilities is such that
they will withstand an earthquake greater than could be caused by the
variation which was reported last Friday.

SoCal Gas Company bulletin regarding the "Arroyo Fault"

mode and began gathering and providing physical evidence that the exposed
geologic "feature" was not a seismogenic structure capable of causing large
earthquakes.

This effort involved excavating several very deep stepped trenches in
strategic locations at the site. These resembled open mining pits and were
designed to intercept not only the "Arroyo Fault" but also to identify any

traces of ancient earthquakes that might have disturbed the proposed site within the last 11,000 years. The sides of the trenches were explored in minute detail and comprehensive geologic maps were prepared.

SHORTLY BEFORE DAWN ON A COOL February morning in 1980, I was awakened by an urgent call from one of my environmental engineers at the Point Conception site. He informed me that a group of Native Americans from the Chumash tribe had entered the site and set up camp. SoCal Gas wanted me at the site immediately, he said, adding that a helicopter was already waiting for me at the Santa Monica Airport. He could not tell me anything about why the tribe members had entered the site.

As I was getting ready to leave, I wondered what I was supposed to do about the situation. By this time, our comprehensive onshore and offshore ecological and environmental studies had been completed and our remaining studies related to the design of the facilities, including the seismic studies, were all but concluded. I sensed that the takeover was a hostile act intended to disrupt our investigations.

The night before, I had returned from a ten-day trip to the Middle East and Europe during which I had met with clients interested in LNG terminals in the Persian Gulf and Algeria. My body clock was running twelve hours ahead of West Coast time, but within thirty minutes I was driving

One of the "Arroyo Fault" investigation trenches at Point Conception

south on the deserted pre-dawn San Diego Freeway toward the airport.

As I cruised along, I remembered having met some members of the Navajo tribe in Arizona during negotiations regarding the construction of the coal-fired generating station near Page several years earlier. I recalled how excited I had been at the prospect of meeting real Native Americans for the first time. Having seen them only in movies, I had imagined the chief appearing over the crest of a hill on his white horse in full traditional attire, including a feathered headdress, and with the rest of his warriors riding behind him. I had been disappointed when the tribe's representatives had arrived in pickup trucks and wearing street clothes. Nor had there been any traditional dances or peace pipes during our discussions and negotiations.

LESS THAN AN HOUR AFTER HAVING received the engineer's call, I was on board the helicopter and we were taking off. As usual, we followed the coastline north, but the low early-morning fog made it hard to see the details of the land below. I glimpsed the headlights of early commuters along the Pacific Coast Highway fading in and out of the fog and spotted a few dedicated surfers out to catch whatever waves they could in the unusually calm waters. I had made this trip dozens of times, but usually around midday when the beaches were crowded with people. One of the main attractions of those flights was a small stretch of beach that had become a favorite spot for nude sunbathers. (The helicopter would usually descend to its lowest altitude when we reached that area.)

As we neared the site, I saw several tents and some blanket-draped figures walking around and gathered around a campfire. I could also see the earth-moving equipment and exploration drill rigs that we were using to carry out the excavations of the geologic trenches, which were clearly visible from the air.

I climbed out of the helicopter and saw a couple of poles with feathers secured to their tops near the campfire. This scene was a much closer match to what I envisioned as a gathering of Native Americans than what I had seen in Arizona.

Before the chopper's rotors had stopped turning, one of my geologists began briefing me about the situation. Apparently, the opponents of the LNG project had learned about the earth-moving activities and had assumed that construction had already begun. They had persuaded the elders of the Santa Barbara Chumash to join their cause and to stop the construction by occupying the plant site. There were even rumors that the star of the "Gunsmoke" television series, James Arness, who had a large house and a landing strip adjacent to the site, had taken part in organizing the protest.

As a group of blanket-draped tribe members slowly gathered around me, I asked who was in charge of the "illegal campers who had trespassed on private property." A heavyset man who claimed to be the chief replied that long before the white man had stepped on these lands, the Chumash had been the natives of Point Conception, where they had lived and hunted in the surrounding hills and fished in the ocean. He added that his people considered Point Conception to be the gateway to heaven through which the souls of the Chumash passed to begin their journey to the afterlife.

"In the western sky," he continued, "souls are cleansed and then return to live in this area." Pointing to rocks scattered throughout the site, he stated that they were used to grind corn and to make arrowheads. Finally, he said that the LNG terminal would desecrate the many unmarked tombs and burial grounds in the area and that the tribe would not allow the destruction to continue.

I assured him that construction had not begun and that we were carrying out environmental studies—and that these included detailed archeological explorations to survey, identify, and catalog any significant Indian artifacts that might exist at the site. I further explained that, if necessary, the terminal would be relocated to avoid disturbing any burial grounds or ancient dwelling sites that might be uncovered. I also promised that we would consult with the tribe should we uncover any sites that might be of interest to them.

Less than three hours later, the protesters vacated the site.

After they left, I took advantage of my unscheduled visit to check the final activities in the trenches. Dozens of geologists were busy scraping the sides of the trenches and using magnifying glasses to examine and mark different soil horizons in their search for nonconforming deposits that could have been caused by major seismic activities in the past. However, nothing was discovered to support the opposition's claim that the "Arroyo Fault" was a major active fault.

BASED ON OUR GEOLOGIC INVESTIGATION, Dr. Ron Scott supervised the physical modeling of the numerical model using Caltech's centrifuge. The main components of the centrifuge consisted of a rotating horizontal arm with a cube-shaped bucket, the bottom of which was modified to split and move along a 45-degree angle as the bucket turned. One end of the arm held a sample column of stratified soil that swiveled along a horizontal bar perpendicular to the arm. The split, which represented a thrust fault, caused the displacement in the soil to propagate through the sample. At the other end of the arm, a counterweight balanced the centrifugal forces.

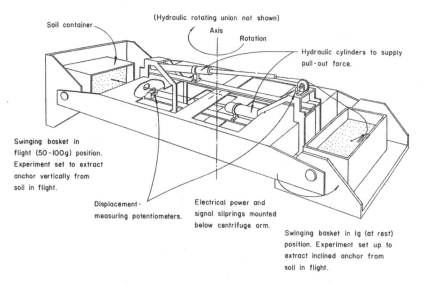

(Hydraulic rotating union not shown)

Soil container

Axis

Rotation

Hydraulic cylinders to supply pull-out force.

Swinging basket in flight (50-100g) position. Experiment set to extract anchor vertically from soil in flight.

Displacement - measuring potentiometers.

Electrical power and signal sliprings mounted below centrifuge arm.

Swinging basket in 1g (at rest) position. Experiment set up to extract inclined anchor from soil in flight.

Components of the Caltech centrifuge

Caltech centrifuge being readied for testing

As the horizontal arm rotated, it developed centrifugal forces at various "g" levels that pressed the sample against the bucket's bottom plate. Changes in "g" levels allowed us to scale the forces that needed to be exerted on the sample to duplicate the actual stress conditions at the site.

Both the pattern and the amount of the displacement were visible through the bucket's Plexiglas side, and a time-lapse camera recorded the entire process. There was a close correlation between the results of this physical modeling and the numerical model.

The results of our comprehensive field investigations and the engineering analysis of the SoCal Gas LNG terminal site filled eight volumes.

AT THIS POINT, SoCAL GAS began seeking internationally known academicians and scientists in earthquake engineering and geology as expert witnesses who could neutralize Teller's testimony. To meet that challenge, I retained a list of renowned expert witnesses that included Dr. Nathan Newmark of the University of Illinois, Dr. Richard Goodman of UC Berkeley, Dr. Charles Richter of Caltech, the inventor of the Richter Scale for measuring the magnitude of earthquakes; Dr. Ronald F. Scott, a professor of geotechnical engineering also at Caltech; and Dr. Richard Jahns, the dean of the geology department at Stanford University.

Richter, Scott, and Jahns were all partners of the Pasadena-based consulting firm of Lindvall, Richter and Associates (LRA), and LRA's president, geologist Eric Lindvall, was also on the team of expert witnesses. (Although I had no way of knowing it at the time, a few years later I would become one of their colleagues at LRA.)

In 1983, after a new round of hearings, the California Public Utilities Commission, in a unanimous vote, affirmed Judge Gordon's decision concerning the seismic safety issues at the Point Conception LNG site and denied the opposition's appeal.

By this time, however, the price of oil had once again begun to plummet. The LNG project became unfeasible economically, and Americans resumed their usual driving and energy consumption habits—until the next oil shortage.

Chapter 22

THE BEGINNING OF THE END WITH D&M

ALTHOUGH I WAS BUSY WITH PROJECTS and marketing activities throughout the late 1970s and early 1980s, certain trends and incidents during this period made me realize that I was increasingly at odds with the direction that the company was taking.

D&M's founders were nearing retirement and thinking about who would succeed them and what long-term strategies would guarantee the firm's success. However, I began hearing rumblings that uncertainty about the firm's future had taken the pleasure out of being a D&M partner.

In general, multidisciplinary projects produced more revenue than did smaller geosciences-focused services. Because of this, older partners who were content to practice geotechnical engineering were being coaxed to either leave the partnership, even though they were not yet of retirement age, or to learn how to market larger projects. Their higher salaries, and the higher fees charged for their services, began affecting D&M's position because these older partners were finding themselves facing more competition, especially in the field of geotechnical engineering.

This was a particular problem in the smaller offices in the Midwest, which were more centered on the narrower approach and faced with small, hungry start-up competitors who were willing to undercut D&M's pricing. The firm's offices on the two coasts and in major cities like Chicago, on the other hand, were bigger and more multidisciplinary, and thus able to maintain their competitive edge.

It was painful for me to watch older partners who had contributed immensely to the firm's growth and success gradually being assigned to lower-level jobs well beneath their abilities and experience. Some of these partners were even sent to smaller offices even though they had health problems and their assignments took them away from their homes and families. One case in point was the partner in charge of the Salt Lake City office. He was transferred to the Los Angeles office as a field engineer on one of my projects but ended up in the hospital due to a severe emphysema attack.

THE FATE OF D&M's SPECIAL MARKETS Management Team (SMMT) also fueled my discontent. In 1980, I was asked to organize a small group of partners with strong marketing records who would focus on forecasting future markets for D&M areas of interest that would allow the firm to expand, not just in engineering but also in environmental engineering.

In addition to myself, the SMMT's permanent members were Tidue Maini of the London office and Joseph Fischer from New York. The EO's Don Roberts was our liaison with upper management. We invited credible, well-known futurists, government economists, and representatives from think tanks to offer insights into future trends in businesses related to D&M's areas of expertise. Each session concluded with roundtable discussions and exchanges of opinions. Summaries and details about the meetings were included in formal reports submitted to the D&M management.

We SMMT members felt strongly that D&M's partnership structure, which apparently gave every partner veto power, limited its ability to join the ranks of major international firms, and we recommended strongly that the partnership be changed to a corporation because that would open up enormous opportunities globally. However, most D&M partners argued that the firm had done well as a partnership since its inception and that the SMMT was a waste of time and money.

It soon became apparent that D&M's top priority was not to simply identify new and future business markets, but to bring in large, pioneering projects. So, in 1981, when we saw no indication that the firm was interested in our recommendations, we decided to disband and turn our individual attention to projects that were fun to work on. At the same time, we hoped that over time we would be able to influence the company's thinking by osmosis.

AFTER THE SMMT DISBANDED, I STARTED looking around for other interesting projects to bring in and discovered a possibility right on our doorstep in Westwood. The 1978 Public Utilities Regulatory Policies Act (PURPA), another federally mandated energy-related bill, offered promising potential opportunities for D&M. This bill, targeted at developing sources of renewable domestic energy, especially encouraged cogeneration, or using steam generated in industrial plants to drive small turbines that would generate electricity.

When I learned that UCLA was planning to study building a cogeneration plant on its 400-acre campus, I arranged to meet with the facilities manager, John Palmer, who was to head up the study. Since D&M had never designed or constructed a power plant, I decided to emphasize the firm's experience and capabilities in a number of environmental fields and, if possible, its design and construction activities.

Because the campus included student dormitories and dining halls that generated large amounts of combustible waste, I suggested to John that rather than disposing of waste off campus, it could be used to fuel an on-campus cogeneration plant.

John was intrigued by this idea and asked about emissions because Los Angeles had banned the burning of waste throughout the city in the 1950s to decrease air pollution.

I found out about a small mobile incinerator located in northern California that could be used to test-burn UCLA waste so that the BTUs generated, as well as the composition of the particulate matter and any toxic emissions, could be measured. I then had to choose whether to have the mobile incinerator hauled to the UCLA campus or to ship a sample of the campus's waste to the incinerator.

Because of LA's ban on burning waste, it made more sense to ship the samples. The testing showed that both the BTU generated and the resulting emissions were within an acceptable range, and that the emissions could easily be controlled by small precipitators. John and I agreed that the option of burning campus waste on the campus should become the centerpiece of UCLA's application for state funding to build a campus-based cogeneration plant.

The application also included information about a proposed turbine generator that would be required. I visited a company in Boston that made turbines for small electric power plants, and the manufacturer agreed to become a joint venture partner for the project.

I then prepared a proposal to be submitted along with UCLA's funding application. After reviewing it, John called to tell me that he was pleased and that he wanted D&M to head up the project. However, the state review of the UCLA application was progressing at a snail's pace, I was becoming more impatient, and I had begun to contemplate leaving the firm.

The D&M Beirut Office Debacle

Throughout my career at D&M, I had a history of being at loggerheads with upper management regarding various issues, but I had continued to maintain my position in the firm because I was bringing in substantial amounts of business. Whenever I confronted management about my concerns, though, I was given excuses that things in the firm could not move as fast as I wanted them to.

For example, my concerns about the firm's decision-making in the Middle East dated back to the spring of 1971, when I learned that there were plans to open an office in Beirut. At the time, Palestinian guerrilla forces in Jordan, empowered by the Palestine Liberation Organization (PLO), were in the process of transferring their headquarters and military operations to Lebanon.

I sent a memorandum to management stating my misgivings, but the only response I received was a copy of a recent *Wall Street Journal* article describing Beirut as "the Switzerland of the Middle East" as a business hub. I was also informed that a partner had already been selected to manage the Beirut headquarters and that all signals were "go."

Because I knew how quickly the political situation in Lebanon was deteriorating, I then requested a meeting at which I asked to draw down my entire financial share in the partnership to avoid the losses that I knew were imminent and inevitable. My request was denied, whereupon I stopped my marketing of the firm's services. The management announced to the rest of the firm that Jack was "on strike," and some of my partners responded by urging the management to fire me immediately for my arrogance and insubordination.

Just weeks after the Beirut office opened, the armed struggle between the PLO and Lebanese forces exploded into full-blown war in the city's streets. The manager escaped with his family and later asked D&M to compensate him for the loss of his belongings, which he said had included expensive furniture as well as a number of antique Persian carpets that had been ransacked by the warring parties. In an effort to minimize my and the firm's losses, I asked my godchild, Vahe Gorjian, who was then living in Beirut, to verify the manager's purported losses. He told me that the manager's residence and furnishings had been untouched by the war.

In short, D&M lost its entire investment in Lebanon, but no one took responsibility for the fiasco.

My confidence in the firm was also shaken a few years later, when in the mid-1970s I began hearing from the clients and contacts I had known in Tehran that there were problems with the competence of both local and transferred D&M staff who had been assigned to proposed nuclear plants in Iran after our studies for the Bushehr plant had been completed. A major red flag went up when the Atomic Energy Organization of Iran (AEOI) stopped paying D&M's invoices after a competitor was brought in to review the firm's work and described it as "substandard."

GIVEN WHAT SEEMED TO BE GROWING problems within the firm, and the disrespect with which the older partners were being treated, I felt strongly that fundamental change was needed, and I wanted to be party to the change.

I saw no reason why our most experienced senior civil engineers could not continue to be productive members of the firm, given that it was continuing to offer civil engineering services as well as its other disciplines. That meant expanding not only geographically but also in other engineering disciplines, even if we had to acquire or merge with other engineering entities.

When, in August 1981, I received a letter from UCLA inviting D&M to be interviewed regarding the cogeneration facility project, this confirmed my belief that, if we put our minds to it and thought innovatively, we could join Fluor and the Ralph M. Parsons Corporation (RMPCO) at the pinnacle of the engineering industry worldwide.

And my excitement and enthusiasm only grew when, lo and behold, Frank Brennan of our London office informed me a short time later that RMPCO was interested in acquiring an established environmental entity!

Frank and I agreed that any association between RMPCO and D&M should be a merger rather than a direct acquisition because the D&M name itself would be an important asset for the joint company.

Frank obtained management approval to begin exploratory discussions with RMPCO regarding a merger. RMPCO's CEO, Bill Leonard, was seriously interested in the idea and arranged a three-day meeting with management from both firms at the La Costa Resort, near San Diego. I attended that meeting.

The meetings included presentations by both firms about the strengths and possibilities of the proposed merger. The discussions were all positive, and at the end of the second day RMPCO advised us that it was interested in pursuing the matter further. After thanking RMPCO for its hospitality and interest, William Moore stated that D&M's partnership agreement required that every partner had to consent before further discussions could proceed.

The next morning at breakfast, Bill told us that some partners were opposed to the proposed merger because they wanted to retain the title of "Partner" rather than "Vice President." This meant that it was therefore pointless to continue the merger discussions. My reaction was that if this news was supposed to be an opening joke, it was not funny to me. I decided then and there that I no longer wanted to be part of D&M.

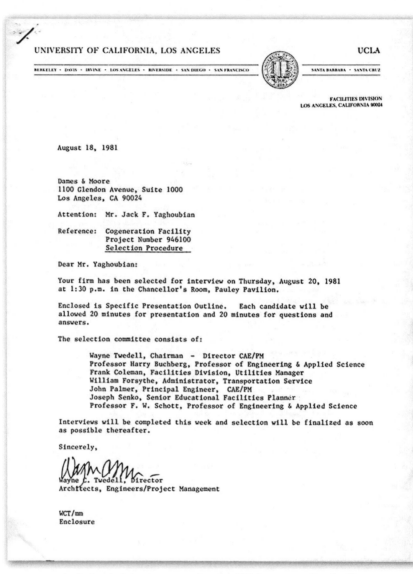

BERKELEY · DAVIS · IRVINE · LOS ANGELES · RIVERSIDE · SAN DIEGO · SAN FRANCISCO   SANTA BARBARA · SANTA CRUZ

FACILITIES DIVISION
LOS ANGELES, CALIFORNIA 90024

August 18, 1981

Dames & Moore
1100 Glendon Avenue, Suite 1000
Los Angeles, CA 90024

Attention: Mr. Jack F. Yaghoubian

Reference: Cogeneration Facility
            Project Number 946100
            Selection Procedure

Dear Mr. Yaghoubian:

Your firm has been selected for interview on Thursday, August 20, 1981
at 1:30 p.m. in the Chancellor's Room, Pauley Pavilion.

Enclosed is Specific Presentation Outline. Each candidate will be
allowed 20 minutes for presentation and 20 minutes for questions and
answers.

The selection committee consists of:

        Wayne Twedell, Chairman - Director CAE/PM
        Professor Harry Buchberg, Professor of Engineering & Applied Science
        Frank Coleman, Facilities Division, Utilities Manager
        William Forsythe, Administrator, Transportation Service
        John Palmer, Principal Engineer, CAE/PM
        Joseph Senko, Senior Educational Facilities Planner
        Professor F. W. Schott, Professor of Engineering & Applied Science

Interviews will be completed this week and selection will be finalized as soon
as possible thereafter.

Sincerely,

Wayne C. Twedell, Director
Architects, Engineers/Project Management

WCT/mm
Enclosure

Invitation to interview regarding the UCLA cogeneration facility

Even worse, a few months later a management memo went out stating that due to the adverse business environment, the firm would return to its core business of geotechnical engineering and soil mechanics and that all budgets for marketing non-core business were being canceled.

At that point, I began drafting my resignation letter.

Shortly before I submitted my resignation, Trent Dames, who knew that I was thinking of leaving, came to me and asked why I was resigning.

I replied, "I have to find out what makes me tick. Is it Dames & Moore, or Jack Yaghoubian?" He then graciously suggested that I take a six-month sabbatical to ponder my decision.

However, I was no longer interested. In August 1982, after eighteen years with D&M, I submitted my resignation and asked that someone else be assigned to the UCLA cogeneration plant project.

Quantech Systems

When I left D&M, we were living in a large house on Greenleaf Street in Sherman Oaks. Christina, who was then eighteen, was starting UCLA, and David, fourteen, was attending the private Buckley School in Sherman Oaks. He was on the school football team, the Griffins, and also played with the band during halftime.

Leaving D&M after almost two decades opened up many exciting opportunities and alternatives for me, including a number of offers from large and small geosciences firms. Also, after the 1979 Iranian revolution, many of my wealthy friends had moved to the US and settled in Southern California. They began actively recruiting me to take part in ventures related to agriculture, mining, the acquisition of established engineering and construction firms, indoor skiing facilities, housing developments, and other areas. In addition, I considered taking the California State Bar exam and practicing law. Still, embarking on and succeeding in establishing a new career two years short of my fiftieth birthday seemed like a long shot at times.

TEN YEARS EARLIER, IN 1972, I had established Quantech Systems Inc. (QS) as a California corporation and had stipulated a wide range of businesses in the articles of incorporation. After leaving D&M, I decided to offer all of my future business services through QS, so I set up my office in our den because leasing and furnishing a commercial office would have been premature.

I bought my first computer, a TeleVideo TS-802 equipped with two 5.25-inch floppy disk drives, for $3,500. The TS-802H, with a ten-megabyte hard drive, would have cost $5,000. With the addition of a printer, a computer desk, and file cabinets, my small workstation was complete. Before long, though, the noise from the nearby kitchen proved so distracting that I built a large separate home office in our backyard and remodeled our garage to include a workshop.

Our backyard's most impressive feature was a huge 400-year-old California live oak whose thick branches spread out more than thirty feet in every direction and provided umbrella-like shade. On warm summer days, I enjoyed working under it while the children and their friends splashed around in the pool under the ever-watchful eyes of our large German shepherd, Spark.

Meanwhile, my parents, who had immigrated to the US in 1970 and were living about five miles away in Glendale, would gather fruit from our "orchard" of plum, fig, orange, lemon, almond, pomegranate, and kumquat trees. My father would pick while my mother followed behind him with a basket. It was fun relaxing with them in the spa and listening to my dad telling different versions of his favorite stories.

My most touching memories of those days are of the conversations that my father and David used to have under our old oak tree. Even though my dad spoke only Armenian and David knew only English, they managed, each conversing in his native tongue, to communicate using hand gestures. Whenever David would smile to signal that he had understood what "Grandpa Hagob" was trying to convey, they would hug and move on to the next topic.

David loved his Grandpa Hagob more than anything. Years later, after obtaining his BA in history at UC Santa Barbara, his MA at UC Santa Cruz, and his PhD from Berkeley, David wrote and published articles about his grandfather's life and times as a truck driver in Iran. In 1992, he and his mentor, UC Santa Cruz professor Edmund Burke III, included a

In our spa with my parents

Grandpa Hagob and David, age eight

chapter on my father's story in *Struggle and Survival in the Modern Middle East*, a collection of personal accounts of life in the Middle East that was published by University of California Press.[1] The book appeared just weeks after my father passed away, and I was moved to tears at his funeral when I saw David slip a copy of the manuscript into his beloved grandfather's casket. The book became a must-read text in Middle Eastern studies at many American universities, with the chapter on Hagob Hagobian referenced most often.

I was content with my new life and in no hurry to get back to the hustle and bustle of the business world. Our financial resources afforded us a comfortable lifestyle despite the absence of regular paychecks. Accumulating wealth had never been one of my main objectives, anyway. While the family was gathered in the den in the evenings, I would busy myself assembling a Heathkit quadraphonic sound system that required the soldering of large numbers of solid-state electronic components.

AFTER LEAVING D&M, I HAD no further contact with the firm until 1983, when I was asked to assist with hearings at the World Court in The Hague related to D&M receivables from the AEOI and the National Iranian Steel Company.

1. Edmund Burke, III and David N. Yaghoubian (Eds.), *Struggle and Survival in the Modern Middle East*, 2nd ed. (Berkeley CA: University of California Press, 2006).

In the wake of the 1979 revolution and Iran's cancellation of all agreements with foreign nations and businesses, D&M attempted to recover about $4 million in receivables by attaching Iranian government assets in the United States. When that attempt failed, the firm was forced to write off the entire amount. The sum was also charged to the partners' capital interest, and as a partner I too lost money from my shares.

At The Hague, I met several Iranian colleagues with whom I had worked in Iran and who were now representing the Islamic Republic of Iran. During court recesses, I met with them privately, as friends and not as legal adversaries, and in our discussions I learned details that had not been included in the complaints but enhanced D&M's position.

The Iranian delegation spoke in Farsi, which interpreters then translated into English. However, because I understood Farsi, I did not have to wait for the translations but was able to offer prompt responses. The judges seemed to appreciate this contribution to the increased efficiency of the examinations and cross-examinations.

The World Court ultimately ruled in D&M's favor and awarded the firm $2 million. However, the partners who had left the firm before the ruling were never notified of the award. The entire amount recovered was distributed among the remaining D&M partners in proportion to their capital interest in the firm.

This action raised questions about whether D&M's action was fair to the former partners. I felt that D&M should be challenged legally for having acted in bad faith.

The partners who had left before the award designated me to initiate and head up litigation against D&M to recover our fair share. According to the partnership agreement, any disputes between partners had to be resolved through arbitration.

On behalf of our group, I filed a request for arbitration with the American Arbitration Association (AAA) in Los Angeles. A panel of three arbitrators heard all of us testify as complainants. Several days later, the panel ruled in our favor, and we received a percentage of the recovered funds. When I suggested that we all share equally in the award rather than devising proportional settlements, my former colleagues all agreed.

A week later, one of the AAA panel members called me and invited me to be a panel member on a construction defect case. I accepted, joined the AAA, and was appointed to its panel of arbitrators. Being an arbitrator was a wonderful experience that was tailor-made for me. Arbitration cases are judged based on the facts of the case and on the law. My background in both engineering and law was ideal, particularly for construction defect cases, and to this day I continue to both arbitrate and mediate cases.

Lindvall, Richter and Associates (LRA)

In September 1982, just weeks after I had left D&M, Eric Lindvall invited me to lunch. I knew him from the Point Conception terminal project when I had hired several of the distinguished academicians in his firm— Charles Richter, Richard Jahns, and Ron Scott, among others—as expert witnesses during hearings.

LRA had been founded after the 1971 San Fernando Earthquake by Eric's father, Fredric C. Lindvall, a former dean of engineering at Caltech. The firm's roster was so impressive that the firm's only marketing tool was a brochure which featured large photographs of the shareholders next to their resumes.

When we met, Eric asked me to consider joining LRA as a shareholder and as president. While at D&M, I had worked with all of the shareholders except Eric's father. Eric felt that with my marketing capabilities and my experience as a professional geotechnical engineer, I could bring in projects in the geosciences and in structural engineering, including earthquake engineering.

The prospect of working with prominent scientists like Richter was exciting, as was the challenge of making LRA grow. Also, the commute to Pasadena would be easy, so Lynn and I decided that I should give it a try. On October 1, 1982, Quantech Systems bought the shares offered by LRA, and I joined the firm as president and a director.

Richard Proctor, an experienced and capable geologist, and two equally qualified structural engineers, J. Brent Hoerner and Roy C. Van Orden, were working part-time in the LRA offices. A draftsman and a secretary were the only full-time salaried employees. LRA's limited cash flow made it impossible for the firm to hire full-time professional staff or to offer basic benefits to its employees. In addition, most of the LRA shareholders were not actively promoting or involved in LRA's business or day-to-day management. However, Dr. Richter's renown automatically guaranteed favorable consideration of any proposal that LRA submitted.

The Los Angeles Rapid Transit District (LA RTD) Metro Project

The first project I faced at LRA was a statement of qualification that the firm had submitted to the Los Angeles Rapid Transit District (LA RTD) regarding a proposed metropolitan rail project. Shortly after my arrival, the RTD, thanks to Richard Proctor's efforts, appointed several members of the firm to a "Board of Special Geotechnical Consultants for the Proposed LA Metro Project."

I immediately began initiating meetings with my former business contacts and informing them that I had joined LRA. Because I was so new to the firm, I lacked in-depth information about its past projects, so I focused on LRA's having been selected by the massive and prestigious LA Metro Rail project. This was, however, of great interest to many firms. Without exception, all the representatives of the Southern California companies I met with were eager to participate in the proposed undertaking and asked me if I could help them to get a "piece of the action."

Among my contacts was Eli Czerniak, a senior structural engineer and friend at Fluor Corporation. He told me that he had been asked to explore avenues for obtaining projects related to the Metro project. When he asked whether I could help, I immediately replied that one way would be for Fluor to acquire LRA as a subsidiary. When he asked whether LRA was for sale, I said, "Everything's for sale if the price is right."

The next day, Eli informed me that Fluor wanted to explore acquiring LRA as a vehicle to gain access to the LA Metro project and that Fluor project manager Al Sacer had been appointed to get the ball rolling. Two days later, Eric and I met with Eli and Al to discuss a possible merger. Although the merger ultimately did not happen, LRA and Fluor did collaborate on developing structural seismic design criteria for the underground Metro stations. And because of the potential of the project, LRA moved to the high-rise building next to Fluor's, east of Glendale in Eagle Rock, toward the end of 1982.

In addition to developing the seismic criteria for the Metro project, Ron Scott and I used Caltech's centrifuge (the bucket of which had been modified for the Point Conception project), to model potential displacements along the proposed subway route wherever it crossed active earthquake fault zones.

PART FIVE

RENAISSANCE
(1983–Present)

Chapter 23

NEW DIRECTIONS

Once the LA Metro project was proceeding on schedule, I began going through my files of contacts looking for other opportunities for LRA, and came across John McCabe's card.

One of my last client contacts as a D&M partner had been a lunch in late May 1982 with John, my old friend from Tidewater days who was at the Getty Oil building in Los Angeles. After reminiscing about our first meeting regarding the Tidewater drilling barge that I had warned him would sink in the Persian Gulf (and it had), we talked about what we had been doing since our last meeting in Iran and about our future plans. John told me stories about his long-standing friendship with J. Paul Getty, whom he referred to as "Mr. Getty."

I told John that on my helicopter flights to Point Conception for the LNG project, I had seen and always wondered why the Getty Museum was not fixing the landslide on Pacific Coast Highway in Malibu right under the museum building, and I asked him to introduce me to the management of the Getty Museum to help stabilize the slope.

In his customary drawl, John explained that the crumbling slope was actually under the Villa De Leon, an Italianate Revival palazzo dating back to the late 1920s that many people assumed was the Getty Museum. He went on to tell me that the museum was run by the J. Paul Getty Trust, independently of Getty Oil, and that I should contact the museum's director directly.

Seeing my interest in Mr. Getty's life, John sent me a copy of *As I See It: The Autobiography of J. Paul Getty*,[1] which mentions John several times, along with a short note dated June 1, 1982. The book contained interesting stories about the museum and his decision to build the new museum building

---

1. J. Paul Getty, *As I See It: The Autobiography of J. Paul Getty* (Englewood Cliffs, NJ: Prentice-Hall, 1976).

on his ten-acre property in Malibu to exhibit the art collections that he had formerly housed in his existing home there.

John and I later had lunch on several other occasions when we talked about his favorite subject, Mr. Getty. My response was always, "I have to visit the Getty Museum one of these days."

After Mr. Getty's passing in 1976, the Getty Oil Company was acquired and John retired. When I came across his card, it reminded me that I had intended to visit the Getty Museum in Malibu and meet its director. Perhaps the time had come to fulfill that intention.

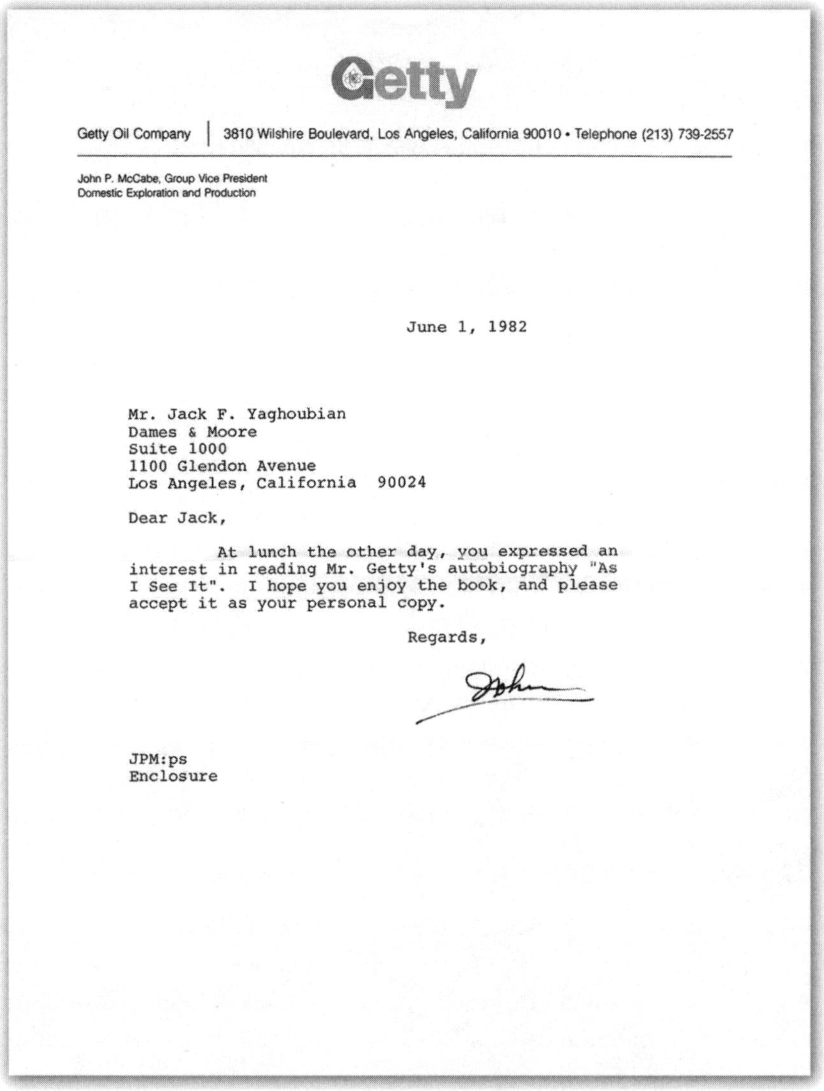

Getty

Getty Oil Company | 3810 Wilshire Boulevard, Los Angeles, California 90010 • Telephone (213) 739-2557

John P. McCabe, Group Vice President
Domestic Exploration and Production

June 1, 1982

Mr. Jack F. Yaghoubian
Dames & Moore
Suite 1000
1100 Glendon Avenue
Los Angeles, California 90024

Dear Jack,

At lunch the other day, you expressed an interest in reading Mr. Getty's autobiography "As I See It". I hope you enjoy the book, and please accept it as your personal copy.

Regards,

John

JPM:ps
Enclosure

John McCabe's letter

I had no idea that my initial visit to the Getty would lead to an unexpected next chapter in my professional career that would add museums and the world of art to the engineering settings in which I worked.

Discovering the J. Paul Getty Museum (JPGM) Villa

Just before noon on the morning of April 18, 1983, I turned into the J. Paul Getty Museum driveway from the Pacific Coast Highway. At the entrance gate, the female guard asked if I had reservations. I replied that I was visiting Los Angeles and had a few hours to kill before my scheduled flight, and that I wanted to take advantage of my free time to visit the museum that I had heard so much about.

The guard told me that visitors often showed up not knowing that reservations were required. "We make exceptions for out-of town visitors," she added. She gave me a pass and directed me to park in the visitors parking and go upstairs to the atrium. From there I could go to the galleries on the different floors. I thanked her and drove into the garage, which was practically empty except for cars parked under the "staff parking" sign.

The black-and-white photographs of the museum in Mr. Getty's book did not do justice to the indescribably beautiful complex. The view of the ocean and the long pool from the atrium level of the impeccable, secluded complex was breathtaking. In the entrance hall, large marble statues stood on ornate mosaic floors. Supported on a high pedestal in the center of the atrium was a large stone bust of a Roman soldier. Looking around and not seeing anyone, I gently bumped the pedestal a couple of times with my shoulder, which caused the pedestal and the bust to rock.

I took a picture of the bust and then went into galleries where magnificent grandfather clocks in different shapes and sizes and in working condition were exhibited. Some of the clocks were one piece of cabinetry, while others were in separate sections set on top of one another. The tall, narrow clocks looked vulnerable to earthquakes. Being the only visitor there, I peeked behind the clocks and saw that they were anchored to the walls with single metal brackets.

In another gallery, large pieces of pottery from the Molly and Walter Bareiss collection of ancient Greek vases, some of which had obviously been broken and glued back together, were housed in glass showcases. The vases, which were attached to the shelves of the showcases with small, inconspicuous metal clips at their bases, brought back memories of my watching the *chin-e band* repair broken china with thin wire clips. I thought that he would have appreciated having access to modern adhesives, but I did not think much of the way that the small bases of the antique vases were secured to the shelves.

There were marble heads supported on tall, slender stone columns. Attached to the bottoms of the columns were square metal plates to add stability, but the plates could not have prevented the assembly from rocking and falling during earthquakes.

I walked into galleries paneled with ornate antique wood and large matching chandeliers of varied shapes hanging from wood ceilings. An empty glass bowl resembling a fishbowl was attached to the bottom of one of the chandeliers. I thought that goldfish swimming in a bowl would have been a novel idea before the advent of television.

Another, rather darker room exhibited antique bedroom furniture. A massive chest of drawers held a tall, heavy, ornate, many-armed candelabra on its top. A closer look showed that lengths of fishing line were tied to the candelabra's arms at one end and fastened to the ceiling at the other. I could not believe what I was seeing. Also, the ceilings of rooms where paintings were exhibited had industrial dropped ceilings with acoustic tiles.

I was on a different planet from the rough-and-tumble world of construction sites filled with the crackling of welding steel, jackhammers busting concrete, and the constant beeping of construction equipment—not to mention workers in hardhats, steel-toed boots, and double-palmed cowhide gloves who strode around spitting out wads of chewing tobacco and uninterrupted profanities.

In stark contrast, the scattered, visibly bored uniformed guards, wearing black rubber-soled boots so as not to disturb the peace, walked quietly and aimlessly about the galleries in slow motion as they fought to stay awake.

The silence in the galleries was deafening. Figures that had been frozen in paintings and sculptures for centuries seemed to follow me with their eyes. Some looked as if they were begging to be freed from their agony. I thought about the stories that they would tell if only they could talk.

I approached one of the security guards and in a normal voice asked him how "the stuff" in the rooms was kept so clean and orderly. Seemingly happy to be asked a question other than "Where are the bathrooms?," he gestured for me to lower my voice and whispered that the museum had different departments such as curatorial, conservation, preparation, and facilities maintenance, that worked together to maintain the high quality of the art exhibits. His slow blinking made me yawn, and I asked myself what in the world I was doing there. I thanked him and left the heavy, somber environment. Outside, I felt revived by the fresh air, the splashing noise of the fountains, and the distant noise of the Pacific Ocean's waves breaking on the beach.

Remembering what John McCabe had told me, on my way out I asked the guard for the name of the museum's director. In a friendly and proud tone she answered, "Mr. John Walsh is the new director!" Taking advantage of her friendly manner and eagerness to chat, I asked what museum he had come from and learned that he was from the East Coast. The guard wished me a safe trip as I pulled away from the guardhouse.

DRIVING ALONG SUNSET BOULEVARD on my way back to Pasadena, I tried to envision what the museum would look like in the aftermath of a strong earthquake, and I could only liken it to the results of a wild bull having been let loose in a china shop.

I wondered if all those clips and base plates would keep the objects safe from earthquake hazards. The thought of the dropped ceilings breaking off from their supports during earthquake shaking and slashing priceless paintings sent shivers down my spine. "Pathetic!" was the only word I could think of to describe the way the large ornate candelabra on the top of the dresser was anchored to the ceiling with fish lines.

I could envision the glass showcases responding to earthquake-induced ground shaking by beginning to rock on their bases and eventually crashing on the hard marble floor, shattering the glass panes and the Greek vases into heaps of small fragments. I thought of the hazard that the Roman soldier's bust would pose for museum visitors during an earthquake.

But I soon shook off my thoughts of disastrous scenarios inside the museum and concentrated on the reason for my visit, which was mainly related to the response of the museum buildings to earthquake shaking. As the guard had told me, different departments (the titles of which I could not remember) kept "the stuff" there clean and orderly—but not safe from earthquakes. However, because substantially all of my time during prior years had been devoted to the study of seismic events along the west coast of the United States and to earthquake damage mitigation, I lowered the volume of my car radio and tried to concentrate on what I should write to the director that would be of sufficient interest that he would want to see me.

THE NEXT DAY I DRAFTED A LETTER TO John Walsh regarding the vulnerability of his museum to earthquakes. I felt an urge to include the subject of the museum contents also, but I decided to be vague and wrote, "We are uniquely qualified to assist you should you deem it necessary to evaluate the possible earthquake hazards to the existing J. Paul Getty Museum or its future expansions."

I showed the draft of my letter to Ron Scott and informed him that I was going to include a copy of *Earthquake Country*,[2] a Sunset Book by Robert Iacopi with a foreword by Dr. Charles Richter, and to direct Mr. Walsh's attention to page 103, which showed a photograph of a large statue of scientist Louis Agassiz at Stanford University that had fallen off its perch in the 1906 San Francisco Earthquake and plunged headfirst into the pavement.

I also showed Ron my photograph of the Roman soldier's bust and told him about its response to my bumping it. Ron thought that was a clever idea and asked to borrow the photograph. I finalized my letter and mailed the package to the museum.

Three weeks later, I was surprised to receive a letter signed by a Mr. Bruce Metro, the "head preparator," in which he stated that my letter to Mr. Walsh had been directed to him because his department was responsible for the museum's earthquake damage mitigation. He wrote that he would be happy to meet me and discuss the museum's ongoing program regarding the subject matter. I promptly called him and set up an appointment to meet him at the museum.

Ron was glad to hear the good news and asked to see me before the meeting. I went to his office at Caltech, where he showed me a small flipbook that he had made. It showed a crude movie of the Roman bust and how its pedestal would behave during an earthquake.

On the day of my appointment, I was greeted in the museum atrium by a big, rather stern-faced man in a blue smock who introduced himself as Bruce Metro, head preparator. He ushered me to his small office through a narrow passageway. His office was crowded with boxes and artifacts. A rolling stool and a large projector with different lenses and knobs stood in one corner. Square openings in the wall that looked out into the museum's main theater indicated that the office also served as a projection room. Bruce settled his large frame in his office chair and asked me to pull up the rolling stool and sit down.

With his hands behind his head, he nonchalantly and proudly informed me that since 1982, JPGM had had earthquake mitigation procedures in place that had been developed by the firm of Brandow and Johnston, the original structural engineers for the JPGM buildings; Melvyn Green of Melvyn Green & Associates, another structural engineer; and Dr. Nathan H. Shapira, a professor in the UCLA Department of Design in charge of industrial and interior design and the president of International Design and Management Consultants.

2. Robert Iacopi, *Earthquake Country* (foreword by Charles F. Richter), 3rd ed. (Menlo Park CA: Lane Books, A Sunset Book, 1971).

Statue of Louis Agassiz at Stanford after
the 1906 San Francisco Earthquake

Bruce continued, "Their recommended mitigation measures mainly consisted of anchoring art objects vulnerable to earthquakes to walls and floors, and attaching large metal plates to the bases of slim pedestals to prevent overturning. We are well into implementing the recommended earthquake mitigations."

Seemingly unmoved by my comment, "Art objects are not water heaters to be anchored to walls and floors," he jumped to his feet. "You might as well see our implemented mitigation measures, since you've taken the time to drive this far," he said, and began to lead the way. Although I had seen enough of his primitive and downright hazardous earthquake mitigation measures for protecting the collections during my first visit, I was there that day to focus on the JPGM buildings only!

On the way to the galleries, I asked Bruce what the responsibilities of his department were. His reply was that his department made mounts for the art objects and that, in addition to aesthetics, the mounts had to be earthquake-resistant also.

"How do you determine that the mounts you make are earthquake resistant?" I asked.

Annoyed by my seemingly incoherent question, he said, "As I mentioned, Professor Shapira of UCLA is one of our consultants, and he provides specific guidelines for making the mounts," and kept walking.

Our first stop was the gallery with the glass showcases that housed the Bareiss collection. Bruce said the showcases were very heavy and would not move during earthquakes and that the objects inside were fastened to the shelves for safety. He also informed me that newly ordered showcases made by Glasbau Hahn of Germany would replace the existing ones and opined that they would be equally heavy and strong, if not stronger than the existing ones.

I said sarcastically, "Earthquakes shake heavy and light objects the same." I noticed that Bruce was barely controlling his anger and agitation at my comments.

In the gallery where the grandfather clocks were exhibited, Bruce pointed to the brackets as an example of an "earthquake mitigation measure" and said the brackets would make the clocks "ride" with the walls and not tip over. I had already seen the metal brackets, and I responded that clocks resting on the floor would most likely pivot around the brackets during shaking and rattle as the partitions vibrated. This would cause heavy pendulums to swing, which would damage the clocks' mechanisms and splinter their antique wood and glass cabinetry. Bruce abruptly decided to go back to his office and began to walk ahead of me.

"This guy isn't very friendly," I thought as I followed him. Once again I wondered why he was so interested in talking about his primitive earthquake mitigations of objects and not the response of the museum buildings to earthquakes in general.

Back in the office, Bruce sat on his chair and, sounding very annoyed, said, "You criticized everything we've done, so let's hear your ideas!"

Figuring that I was not going to get any work out of the guy anyway, I said, "Look, you're unable to tell me the principles of your so-called 'earthquake mitigations.' What seismic event and corresponding building response do you use to determine that what you've done would protect the objects?"

Seeing his puzzled expression, I took the chance and went through a brief narrative about the importance of determining the response of buildings and their contents to earthquakes, on the basis of which a coherent protection system could be devised. I added that if the building collapses, then the manner in which objects are secured would not matter.

"No one in his right mind," I told him, "can recommend a mitigation measure without having some idea about the dynamic characteristics of the response of a building and its contents to a future design earthquake."

The meeting was awkward, to say the least. There I was with years of experience in earthquake engineering for critical facilities trying to avoid coming across as an arrogant and argumentative person while not knowing if Bruce understood what I was trying to tell him.

In somewhat more tactful terms, I explained that the JPMG buildings must have been designed in accordance with the building codes that had been in place prior to the 1971 San Fernando Earthquake but had since undergone major revisions. I strongly recommended that the existing structures be analyzed in light of the new building code and the site's seismic setting.

Seemingly disappointed by my not having anything positive to say about the JPGM buildings and the earthquake mitigation measures, or perhaps to just get rid of me, Bruce said, "Thank you for your time. I'll show you the way out."

I followed him to the atrium where, just as he was about to shake my hand, I said, "I almost forgot," and took the flipbook out of my pocket. I gave it to him while we were standing within a couple of feet of the Roman bust.

As he flipped the pages, his eyes opened wide and he kept repeating, "Oh, wow!" Then, pointing to the Roman bust, he said, "This is a loan from LACMA." I had no idea what Bruce was talking about as I had not heard of LACMA, but I later learned that he was referring to the Los Angeles County Museum of Art. After a short hesitation, Bruce said, "Why don't you send me a proposal?" and informed me that proposals would have to be reviewed and approved by the museum management and by the J. Paul Getty Trust.

BASED ON MY MEETING WITH BRUCE, I prepared and submitted a proposal dated May 8, 1983, which contained a detailed scope of work regarding my recommended site and structural studies. I was elated when a staff secretary at the museum informed me that Harold Williams, the president of the Getty Trust, had responded positively to my proposal.

I thought that this encouraging news was a good reason for LRA to set goals and objectives for growing the company, but Eric was adamantly against any management suggestions. Within two days after the positive news from JPGM, Eric was driving a brand-new Mercedes. In answer to my comment, "We need to think of the firm's business and marketing matters before new fancy cars," he replied, "You can go get one like mine, too."

The rift between our management styles being too deep, in June 1983 we decided to go our separate ways. Consequently, we signed an agreement which stipulated that I would manage and complete projects that I had initiated through QS—including the comprehensive studies at JPGM at Malibu.

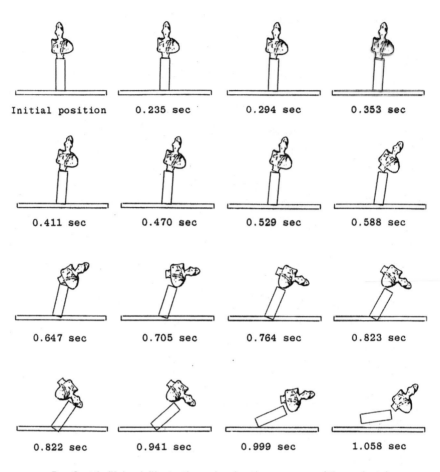

Initial position   0.235 sec   0.294 sec   0.353 sec

0.411 sec   0.470 sec   0.529 sec   0.588 sec

0.647 sec   0.705 sec   0.764 sec   0.823 sec

0.822 sec   0.941 sec   0.999 sec   1.058 sec

Ron Scott's flipbook illustrations showing the response of the pedestal
and mounted Roman bust subjected to earthquake shaking

The Blackhawk Development Project

Shortly after my resignation from LRA, I received the purchase order
from JPGM to commence the museum's site evaluation studies. I moved
out of the LRA offices and began working from my Sherman Oaks home
office. I organized a specialty team along discipline lines such as geosciences
and structural engineering to perform tasks outlined in the proposal, which
in scope was only a fraction of the LNG projects.

During the same period, Richard Proctor, who was still working part
time with LRA, told me that he had learned through one of his Northern
California colleagues that a rainstorm had caused numerous ground failures
which had damaged expensive homes in Blackhawk, a newly commenced

housing development in Danville, a community in the San Francisco East Bay. Billy Martin, the manager of the Oakland A's, owned one of the damaged houses, and a published photograph of his swimming pool filled with landslide debris had given prominence to the rainstorm and to Blackhawk. Richard asked me if we should approach the developers and propose our services in geosciences.

In July 1983, we contacted the Blackhawk Corporation (BC) and offered our joint services in geology and geotechnical engineering. Initially I was skeptical about our chances of getting onboard such a project since we were in Los Angeles and there were many large and prominent consulting firms like D&M and Woodward Clyde in the Bay Area that could do it at a more reasonable cost. Besides, neither QS nor Richard carried professional liability insurance. To my surprise, the president of BC, attorney Daniel Van Voorhis, was interested in talking with us. We flew to Blackhawk and drove through the area and saw the landslides before meeting with him.

At that time, wealthy property developers were buying up large parcels of rolling green hills used for grazing to develop upscale housing projects to meet the Bay Area's growing housing needs.

Kenneth Behring, a real-estate tycoon and vintage automobile collector who had owned a large car dealership in Florida, had acquired a vast ranch in Danville known as "Blackhawk," which was named after a horse there. Local architects, city planners, and engineers had prepared elaborate plans to subdivide Blackhawk properties into secluded unique communities connected with walking trails and attractively landscaped features. The initial phase of the land development plans included the construction of a lake and a plush clubhouse surrounded by championship golf courses. On weekends, golfers and families from neighboring areas visited the clubhouse to see the development and enjoy its luxurious environment. Meticulously maintained vintage autos parked near the clubhouse provided an ambience of past-era nostalgia that was very attractive to well-to-do prospective buyers.

BC, as the land developer, graded the hills, constructed roads, and installed utility lines that branched out inconspicuously through underground conduits to subdivided parcels. Homebuilders then bought the completed pads and constructed single and multi-unit dwellings. The recent heavy rains had damaged a few of the homes completed during phase one, and that had halted further development activities.

We met Dan Van Voorhis at BC headquarters in his opulently decorated large offices, staffed by beautiful young secretaries. After introductions, Dan said he had land development problems and hoped that we could help BC. I asked why he would not use one of the capable geotechnical firms like Woodward Clyde in Northern California and informed him that neither of us carried liability insurance.

"I don't care about insurance or that you're from Southern California" he said. "After the rains, we did talk to Woodward Clyde, and their advice was to put a chain-link fence around the entire Blackhawk area, lock the gate, and throw the key away. I'm looking for fresh ideas. Send me a proposal as soon as possible so we can get started." Dan also informed us that ENGEO, a local geotechnical firm, provided geologic and geotechnical services for mass grading and indicated that if we were so inclined, we could bring in another firm as long as everything was done under our supervision.

Richard and I decided that we could work with ENGEO in the capacity of BC's consulting representatives for the project. In that capacity, we reviewed ENGEO's work and made changes in the testing and analysis of subsurface formations at Blackhawk to assess the stability of the slopes more realistically. Firmly believing that, in addition to deterministic analysis, the stability of slopes should also be determined probabilistically, I retained Professor Armen Der Kiureghian of UC Berkeley, an expert in reliability analysis of structures, to develop the methodology for performing probabilistic analysis related to slopes to inform the homeowners of the landslide risks in their area.

IN CONNECTION WITH THE BC PROJECT, Richard Proctor provided critical information related to the geologic and seismic setting of Blackhawk, the most important of which was the geomorphology of subsurface stratification encountered at Blackhawk that was the root cause of land instability there.

The encountered geomorphology was caused by nearby Mount Diablo rising at the rate of two inches per year, which lifts the surrounding sedimentary formation, increasing crustal stresses resulting in slickenside beddings and shear interfaces and reducing the stability of the sloped terrains.

The Hayward Fault zone is known to be the most significant seismotectonic feature in the area. Based on the geologic information provided by Richard, I formulated parameters and construction criteria to stabilize the areas of interest for the design of structures.

The scientific question was whether the stress-strain in sedimentary deposits caused by Mount Diablo rising dissipated as it was being formed, or whether measurable residual in-situ stresses in the formation remained and maintained the natural terrain of the area in a state of static equilibrium. If the latter, then any natural or manmade action that altered the in-situ residual stresses would breach the static equilibrium, causing movements along subsurface stratifications.

Evidence of the unstable sloped terrain at Blackhawk

Two views of the 8-inch deep faulting around Canyon Lakes
that ruptured and eventually reached 100 feet in length

Source: Google Earth

A satellite image of Canyon Lakes, a subdivision of the Blackhawk development

To check the above proposition, I again contacted UC Berkeley's Richard Goodman, whose services I had retained for the LNG project at Point Conception and at JPGM. He suggested using equipment from his campus to measure the existence of such in-situ stresses if any.

While waiting for the equipment from Berkeley, I was asked to formulate the geometry of the proposed terraced earth embankment surrounding an existing artificial lake at Canyon Lakes, a Blackhawk subdivision on which houses with unobstructed views of the lake would be constructed. During my review of the construction of the terraced embankment, in a rare and exciting geologic moment I observed the slow formation of an approximately eight-inch vertical bedding-plane thrust faulting roughly 100 feet in length. Massive grading for the construction of the terraced embankment had breached the area's static state of equilibrium.

Based on the observed ground displacement, I calculated the thicknesses of the terraced embankment required to accommodate any ground displacements beneath the house pads so as to prevent structural damage.

The neighboring developers adopted the design and construction criteria that we developed for BC. The land instability caused by the heavy rains was under control, and the development of the 4,200-acre property to accommodate 2,400 dwellings and 2,000 acres of open space was back on schedule. The massive undertaking could continue without our involvement.

A recent satellite image of the Blackhawk museum
(in circle) and surrounding developments

The Blackhawk Museum Project

Throughout much of the time between 1983 and 1990 when I was involved with Blackhawk, I was also working concurrently with JPGM. However, when the Blackhawk project started, I had no idea that it would lead to another museum project—and to my involvement with museum-related work that is ongoing today.

It was not until Richard's and my final scheduled meeting with Dan Van Voorhis in 1989 that he showed us BC's plans for an elaborate multi-story museum to house Ken Behring's vintage auto collection. It would have a panoramic view of the entire Blackhawk development and the proposed large shopping plaza.

We were speechless. The situation became really stressful when Dan informed us that Mr. Behring was anxiously waiting for an answer regarding the constructability of the plans at the designated location.

The layout of the proposed museum showed the building extending into the side of a hill where a large excavation had to be made to accommodate the foundations. The plans also showed a "bench"—a long, wide flat area halfway up the slope—on which office buildings and access roads would be constructed. And at the top of the slope stood rows of multimillion-dollar-view homes.

Dan sat back on his chair, looked at us, and asked, "What do you guys think? Ken's waiting for your answer."

"Being a lawyer yourself," I said, "you realize that BC is facing a lawsuit by the residents on the top of the slope the minute they get a whiff of what you're planning to do. If we touch that slope, it will be destabilized and potentially drag down all those houses on the top."

Dan answered calmly, "That's why the plans were kept under wrap."

The houses on the top of the hill complicated the problem several-fold and caught me totally off guard. I looked at Richard, who appeared equally concerned. I sat back and said, "I need to think about it." To which Dan replied, "Well, you guys have all afternoon."

I said, "Do you know what this will cost, even if I knew what to do?"

Dan replied, "Don't worry about the cost. Just come up with a solution. I'm going to order some sandwiches for lunch."

We ate lunch in silence, and for the next hour or so I drew lines on tracing papers laid on the topographic map of the proposed museum location while talking to Richard about alternatives—only to lose my concentration due to Ken Behring knocking on the conference room door. Dan would go to the door, open it, tell him, "Not yet, Ken," and close it again. After the last knock, Dan said, "Ken's acting like an expectant father."

We had never been formally introduced to Mr. Behring, a rather heavyset, unassuming man who wore white short-sleeved shirts tucked into black polyester pants without belt loops. Seeing his unsmiling face when he kept showing up at the door made me really nervous. Eventually, I came up with a far-out idea that I was not sure I could explain without getting laughed at.

I broke the silence and said, "The only way I see it is to disrupt the hill's natural stratification which would destabilize the existing slope temporarily before it could be stabilized."

Richard said, "You want to pass that by me once more?"

The idea behind my suggestion was to excavate and backfill a zone of thick earthen fill in the area of the proposed project to temporarily support and prevent unraveling of the slickenside beddings during the excavations to accommodate the construction of the museum building's foundations.

Very patiently and in unusually calm voice, Dan asked, "And how are you going to do that?"

I replied, "The existing slope material would be excavated and placed back. The removal would temporarily jeopardize the stability of the cut slopes. However, the backfilled material would remold the bedding structure and hold back the cut slopes."

"Okay, go on!" Dan urged.

"The speed of the removal and replacement of the natural soils is the controlling factor during the entire operation," I said, and outlined the sequence of my suggested undertaking, stressing that a large number of high-capacity scrapers and other earth-moving machinery would be required to do the following: A train of empty scrapers using the surrounding open terrain would be driven to the designated point about halfway up the slope. From there, the scrapers would turn downhill and begin to excavate layers of undisturbed slickenside beddings, carving a vertical slot equal to the width of the scrapers to a recommended depth.

Loaded scrapers would return to the top of the slot and begin moving downhill while spreading their load in "lifts," or layers, to fill up the slot. The sequence of earthwork would continue by digging and filling slots next to each other until the designated area was replaced with temporary sloped fill extending fifty feet beyond the boundary of the proposed museum's footprint. I reasoned that the temporary fill soils compacted by the scrapers' rubber wheels would be more stable than the natural soil deposits because the continuity of the beddings in the replaced mass would be disrupted.

I emphasized that once the operation had begun, there could be no disruption whatsoever, including acts of God (a common clause included in construction contracts) throughout the entire earthwork, which should start and be finished within a single shift that would begin after nightfall and be completed the following morning before the neighbors could see what was going on.

After hearing me out to the end, Dan said, "I'm glad I'm not the engineer, and I hope you guys know what you're doing. Tell me exactly the logistics of what you need and I'll get it."

On a topographic map, I sketched out the area where the earthwork should take place and the depth of the excavation. Dan agreed to have BC's civil engineer of record calculate the earth-moving volume and the required number and types of equipment to complete the operation during the designated hours. After asking Dan to let us know when all the arrangements had been made, we left for LA.

Within a week, BC had signed contracts with several earth-moving entities in the area and had set the date for the project. We flew up on the morning of the scheduled earthwork day. The proposed plaza area resembled a construction equipment manufacturer's yard, full of yellow scrapers and other earthwork machinery.

Floodlights lit up the area like day at about 9 p.m. that evening. I stood on top of a large truck and began to observe and direct the operation. A couple of hours into the operation, David Knadle, a Blackhawk vice president, nervously approached me and pointed to a large mass of the undisturbed slope that had begun to move ever so slowly down the slope. When I calmly told him that he was witnessing geology in motion, he shook his head in disbelief. The ground was vibrating under the traffic of the scrapers and

The Blackhawk Museum today

crawling bulldozers. I had never witnessed such efficiency and cooperation between contractors.

By daybreak, the last of the scrapers and graders joined the rest of the idle equipment at the plaza level. I took a deep breath, elated that the re-constituted slope was stable and that the only visible evidence of what had happened that night was a large brown area void of the surface greenery that covered the undisturbed adjacent slopes.

The slope was ready for the construction of the proposed museum and the plaza—without the residents at the top of the slope having noticed what had gone on during that long night. This was our last major assign-ment at Blackhawk. Everyone was happy that our part of the project had been completed. Through 1990, we were occasionally asked to visit the development for consultation during the ongoing construction and to re-view data developed by instruments monitoring the long-term behavior of the constructed slopes.

In 2011, almost thirty years since that unforgettable night, I went back to Blackhawk. I did not recognize the area and had to ask for directions to the Blackhawk Museum. The plaza was full of people shopping and enjoying the outdoor fountains, cafes, and exclusive restaurants and shops. I walked to the museum and bought a ticket to get in. There were hundreds of an-tique vintage automobiles exhibited on two floors and also a bookstore. On the bookstore counter was a book with a smiling picture of Mr. Behring looking at the visitors. I was interested in how the building had performed during the years. The absence of cracks or signs of distress in the polished granite veneers that cover the entire interior of the complex brought me great joy and happy memories.

Getty and Blackhawk: Two Different Museum Legacies, Two Different Benefactors

Being involved in major museum projects at Blackhawk and JPGM concurrently exposed me to two different philosophies and objectives.

Blackhawk's "Money is time and time is money" ethos was infused with youthful vigor and modernity, while JPGM's principal objective was to preserve and protect millennia-old art objects for generations to come. And, in keeping with each entity's basic ethos, BC wanted to move at a lightning pace to maximize the return on its investment whereas the Getty, a tranquil and quiet institution committed to enjoying and studying the classic visual arts, was moving at a snail's pace.

The above was not the only difference. BC operated under the watchful eyes of regulators, lead agencies, and special interest groups advocating "no growth" in pristine areas of San Francisco Bay. JPGM, on the other hand, existed in the invisible bubble of the "art world," a fiercely competitive and secretive universe where words are whispered and smiles exchanged, but no one really knows what the other is thinking or up to.

In spite of the differences between the two entities, there were also some parallels. Mr. Getty, who loved the fine arts, bequeathed a substantial sum to build the museum to house his beloved art collections and gifted it to the public to enjoy. JPGM was built in Malibu, where he had a rambling ranch house in which his art collection had first been housed. Mr. Behring was also interested in building a museum to house his collection of vintage motorcars at Blackhawk and donating it to UC Berkeley, a public institution. Mr. Behring actively participated in the construction of his museum at Blackhawk, but Mr. Getty never saw his completed fine arts museum at Malibu.

Looking back, I feel fortunate to have been involved with both museums during much of the 1980s.

Chapter 24

THE GETTY VILLA MUSEUM PROJECTS

Seismic Studies at JPGM

In 1983-1984, while involved with Blackhawk, I also managed and supervised the entire JPGM seismic studies site evaluation project in association with Richard Proctor and structural engineer Brent Hoerner.

The details were presented in a written report, "Geologic and Seismic Safety Evaluation of the Main Museum Building, for The J. Paul Getty Museum Malibu, California," printed on LRA stationery. I signed the cover sheet as the project manager and as the civil/geotechnical engineer of record. Eric also signed the cover sheet as LRA president. Richard and Brent were the principal geologist and the structural engineer respectively for the project.

The studies, based on a literature search and probabilistic analysis of past seismic events in Southern California showed that the faults significant to the museum were the San Andreas Fault, located approximately forty-two miles from the museum, and the Malibu Coast-Santa Monica Fault, approximately 0.7 miles away.

As the report stated, JPGM's set acceptable risk level of seismic events occurring once every 225 years was postulated to a magnitude 8+ event on the San Andreas Fault and a magnitude 6.5 on the Malibu Coast-Santa Monica Fault capable of generating large free-field ground motion at the museum.

Parameters of ground motion such as duration of shaking, peak accelerations, and ground displacements at JPGM generated by each of the events were determined by scaling up and modifying existing recorded time histories of past large seismic events in Southern California such as El Centro (1941).

The response of the museum building to the ground shaking was determined by inputting the modified time histories into the numerical model of the main museum housing the art objects. The analysis produced both positive and disappointing results. The positive finding was that the rigid museum building would not undergo catastrophic collapse if subjected to the postulated time histories. On the negative side, the analysis showed that the ongoing earthquake mitigation measures undertaken by the preparation department since 1982 would be ineffective and would exacerbate the severity of damage to the museum collection.

Although numerical analysis indicated that the museum's structure was rigid, I wanted to verify the accuracy of the calculated results related to the rigidity of the building. For that, I initiated ambient measurements of the museum structure to determine its response to ambient vibrations. ANCO engineers provided the instrumentation for ambient measurements as a community service. The response to ambient vibrations confirmed the rigidity of the structure, indicating minimal change in fundamental periods at different floor levels. The measurements also revealed that the parking structure required stiffening to respond adequately to postulated earthquakes. In consultation with Brandow & Johnson, plans were prepared for the installation of shear walls between the columns of the parking structure.

Preserving the Past: The QS Base Isolation System for Protecting Antiquities (1983-1985)[1]

Based on JPGM's seismic setting and the particulars of the potential free-field earthquake-induced ground shaking there, my professional opinion was that new and unique approaches would have to be employed for the protection of its fragile art objects. I felt strongly that restraining art objects from falling during earthquakes would not be an adequate mitigation option, especially at JPGM, which was diligently trying to project an image of a unique institution where state-of-the-art and innovative advances in the conservation and protection of rare and fragile art objects were being made.

I strongly believed that vulnerable art objects should be exhibited in such a manner that earthquake-induced vibrations could not be transferred to the object itself in any form or shape. That was achievable only by effectively de-linking the objects from the floors. I discussed the above with Bruce Metro, who wisely advised me that convincing the curators and conservators

---

1. The heading of this section is a modification of an internationally televised documentary regarding a journey around the world and through time to preserve antiquities titled "The Future of the Past," an episode of "The Infinite Voyage" series produced by public television station WQED/ Pittsburgh in association with the National Academy of Sciences in 1990. Another PBS documentary, "Innovation: a New Perspective," produced by WNET/THIRTEEN in Newark, New Jersey, in 1989 featured engineering innovations in the conservation and protection of art objects. I was prominently featured in both documentaries, and this section of the book is a summary of my engineering solutions, which were presented in the above documentaries and televised worldwide.

about the application of unknown protection systems would be an uphill battle. He also warned me that the museum management would usually side with the curators.

In general, no known theories had yet been developed to successfully de-link large items from large earthquake forces and equally large displacements occurring simultaneously. Available literature regarding museums located in earthquake-prone regions was exclusively related to the response of museum buildings, not the items in collections.

The only viable alternative was to formulate a new concept and demonstrate its effectiveness with acceptable confidence levels to JPGM. Aside from the technical challenges of such an undertaking, I had to endure serious resistance from the nonengineer staff at the Getty, who argued that conservation departments are there to repair and fix damaged art and could not see or understand the need for engineering intervention.

The conservation of large stone sculptures dates back millennia and has been handed down from generation to generation. Modern conservators believe that they are disciples of the old masters and are ordained to preserve and protect centuries-old techniques using better mortar mixes, adhesives, and rust-resistant metals to repair damaged, fragile sculptures.

The riddle of "Which came first, the chicken or the egg?" applies to the history of sculpted art objects as well. Masters such as Michelangelo were also engineering geniuses and, well aware of the forces of nature that they had to contend with, they applied engineering principles to create magnificent art and monuments that have lasted for centuries—which invalidates the argument that engineering had no place in protecting and preserving art.

In that spirit, I envisioned the application of engineering principles to develop unique techniques to preserve and protect antiquities from the menace of earthquakes.

Had it not been for the support of visionaries like Harold Williams and John Walsh at the executive level, curators Gillian Wilson and Marion True, and preparator Bruce Metro—all of whom took a leap of faith in allowing me to implement my unconventional ideas to conserve and protect the JPGM's irreplaceable art collections—the concepts would have never materialized into useful inventions.

My experience in the field of machinery vibration problems intuitively directed my attention to energy-absorbing systems for the earthquake protection of fragile art objects. However, the measurable steady-state high-frequency and low-amplitude vibrations produced by machinery could be dissipated by devices such as spring and dashpot units and elastomeric media. In contrast, earthquake-induced ground shaking is chaotic and produces random vibrations with large accelerations and ground displacements that must be coped with.

To prevent the transfer of earthquake-induced shaking to a fragile art object without the potential for amplification, a single system had to be devised that would concurrently offset random large acceleration and displacements. During earthquakes, such a system would in effect make art objects behave as if they were suspended in the air, and they would therefore remain substantially unaffected by shaking. The creation of such a system was thought to be an impossibility at that time. However, I thought it would be a challenge to invent it.

A rigid object floating in the air can move in six degrees of freedom: linear motion along the X, Y, and Z axes, known as "translational modes," and rotation around the same three axes, known as "rotational modes." Anchoring fragile objects to floors and walls would lock them in place and transfer the entire spectrum of earthquake-generated forces to them. Only items specifically designed to resist such forces could survive strong earthquake shaking.

An object's response to earthquake shaking depends on its geometry, the engineering properties of the material from which it is made, and any intrinsic natural or physically induced weakness. While one object might be vulnerable to forces that cause translational response only, another object might be susceptible to a combination of translational and rotational loads. Because it is difficult to assess such vulnerabilities with confidence, de-linking unique art objects from all forces would be the prudent option.

In 1984, Bruce organized a meeting to introduce my thoughts regarding the earthquake protection of art objects to the JPGM management. Mathematical formulas and computerized animations not being a viable demonstration option for the attendees, I made a portable wooden shake table, the platform of which was supported on four hacksaw blades. The blades oscillated in a single degree of freedom in fundamental mode. Attached to it was a small variable-speed record player motor equipped with an eccentric weight that force-vibrated the platform with a peak-to-peak amplitude of about one inch. A dimmer switch controlled the frequency and amplitude of the platform's oscillation.

I took a variety of objects, including miniature toy statuettes and clocks, porcelain vases of different shapes and configurations, and furniture such as freestanding cabinets to the meeting. The grandfather clocks were modeled by pasting photographic cutouts of the clocks on thick wood backings. The clock models rested on an L-shaped stand that represented the museum's floor and walls. The clock models were anchored to the vertical

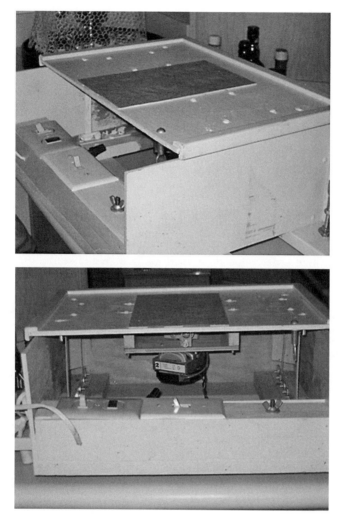

Two views of the model shake table. A 13-minute video, "The Genesis of Earthquake Isolation Systems for Protection of Art Objects," about the development of the base isolation system, can be seen at: http://www.quantechsystems.com/gallery/

"wall" section of the stand with a single bracket that was free to pivot around the Y axis while resting on the stand's horizontal "floor" component.

Another top-heavy model consisted of a metal statuette of an athlete attached to a slender cylindrical wood pedestal with a height-to-diameter ratio of approximately three, which could be supported on two interchangeable wood bases: one with a flat bottom and the other fitted with load-transfer bearings. To demonstrate the behavior of fragile art objects subjected to unknown past repairs anchored to floors and walls, I cut the pedestal into several pieces and reconnected the cut joints with coil springs that pressed the opposite cut faces, creating undetectable mechanical joints.

I arrived thirty minutes ahead of the scheduled presentation to set up the shake table. Besides Bruce, the other attendees were JPGM director John Walsh, his then deputy Stephen Roundtree, and Gillian Wilson and Marion True, the curators of decorative arts and antiquities respectively.

Bruce made a brief statement about the agenda, and I began my presentation. By placing the models on the vibrating shake table, I showed that an unanchored object will remain in a state of static equilibrium until external forces breach its equilibrium. Depending on the direction of the external forces acting on the object, it could move in translational, rotational, or a combination of modes such as sliding, rolling, bouncing, rocking, and twisting. I demonstrated that during its motion the object would be susceptible to being damaged by impact loads such as its falling or colliding with other objects.

I then demonstrated the behavior of anchored objects when subjected to shaking and showed that, depending on the magnitude of the applied forces and the objects' inherent strength, they would respond in one or a combination of modes. For example, they could stay in place and remain unharmed; or they could break at a vulnerable location; or their anchors could fail, causing the objects to move as if unanchored; or the applied forces would exceed the anchors' capacity, causing the objects to fall and be damaged.

To demonstrate the behavior of unprotected art objects when subjected to earthquake shaking, I placed small rectangular objects on the smooth and rough surfaces of the platform, which represented the showcases resting on different floor coverings. As the platform began to shake, the objects on the smooth surface slid back and forth, while the objects on the rough surface rocked and eventually tipped over.

To explain the behavior of large, heavy, and fragile objects anchored to floors and walls, I placed the grandfather clock model on the shake table and clamped its L-shaped stand to the platform. As the platform began to oscillate, the model clock started thrashing around as it dangled from the bracket to which it was fastened. Seeing the clock's behavior caused Gillian to cringe visibly. When I turned the shake table off, the participants were shaking their heads in disbelief imagining the fate of the actual clocks being subjected to large, real earthquakes.

Next, I attached the statuette of the athlete, and the pedestal that contained the mechanical joints representing unknown repairs, to an unanchored flat-bottomed base on the platform. Immediately after the platform began to shake, the model tipped over. After the same statuette and pedestal were fastened to the platform to represent anchoring, the shaking caused the mechanical joints to open and close. This showed the vulnerability of repaired joints to cyclical reverse loads transferred to the object and to its weaker joints as the platform shook. However, when I replaced the flat-bottomed base of the same model with a base supported on four ball transfers, the statuette was effectively de-linked from the shaking platform and remained motionless even when the platform shook to its full displacement capacity.

Basically, the ball transfers decoupled the shaking of the platform from being transferred to the object, which sharply reduced the friction between the model's base and the platform and prevented the models from rocking or tipping over.

After the demonstration, I summarized that unless the object to be protected could be evaluated and shown to be ductile—to behave linearly throughout the duration of ground shaking—it should be supported on a base isolation system.

What needed to be figured out was the design and manufacturing of a single mechanical system that would (a) minimize the transfer of ground motion to the object, (b) prevent random earthquake vibrations from being amplified by resonance, and (c) keep the object in its original position throughout the entire duration of shaking.

Simply, as long as the museum building responds linearly, a de-linking system would absorb any earthquake-induced shaking anywhere.

JPGM asked me to create a replica of a Hahn showcase as the first item to be supported on a base isolation system with the above characteristics. I was asked to outline the specifics of my recommended system in a preliminary report.

After several weeks of sleepless nights and endless calculations and experiments, I figured out the system and prepared a hand-drawn sketch of the device to meet the challenging criteria for the Hahn showcase.

In a QS report, "Seismic Stability Evaluation, Glass Showcase, Gallery 123, The J. Paul Getty Museum, Malibu, California, Dated, January 4, 1985," I presented an outline of my proposed system and the sketch of my device. JPGM then told me to proceed with making a model and testing it.

The inventiveness of the system was in the utilization of rolling friction and gravity respectively to absorb large accelerations and displacements without amplification. To minimize the potential for amplification, I configured the system to oscillate at periods of about three to four seconds.

To absorb design vertical accelerations under 1g and floor vibration,

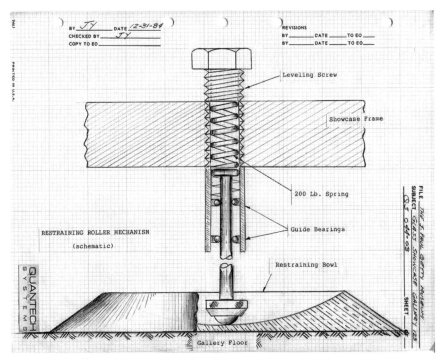

The original sketch of the damping and return mechanism

rubber or elastomeric spacers would be incorporated into the system. I also devised vertical dissipaters for vertical accelerations exceeding 1g.

The intense effort and sleepless nights caused health problems that required a short hospital stay, and my cardiologist recommended a curtailed workload for an indefinite period.

MY SYSTEM HAD TO BE TESTED to verify its calculated performance before it was placed in production. For that, a full-scale wooden replica of a Hahn showcase was constructed for testing on an industrial large triaxial shake table at the ANCO facilities in Los Angeles. Inside the case were two glass shelves, one of which held various objects such as plates and glasses. A large observation window cut out of one side of the showcase allowed monitoring of the behavior of the objects.

The test program, which was carried out in April 1985, consisted of shaking the replica without and with the isolators. The testing commenced by inputting a time history of small tremors into the remote control panel and then increasing the shaking levels to produce the time history of great historic seismic events. JPGM personnel observed and recorded the entire testing program.

Wooden replica of
Hahn showcase,
with glass shelving
and test artifacts,
on the ANCO
triaxial shake table

When the showcase replica was subjected to low levels of shaking without the isolator, it began to slide for few seconds and then to rock, causing the plates to fall off the glass shelf. With increased shaking, the model began to rock uncontrollably and was only held back from tipping over by the attached safety tethers. The test confirmed the showcase's vulnerability to earthquake-induced vibrations.

The next phase of testing consisted of shaking the replica supported on the decoupling system presented in the report. The sample pieces of china were reset on the glass shelves and the model was subjected to shaking. The wooden showcase remained in its original position while the shake table output of displacement and acceleration reached its maximum capacity, which exceeded the modified earthquake time history in the May 1984 geological and seismic safety evaluation by a factor of two. The duration of shaking did not influence the isolator's performance. The system I had devised performed beyond all expectations.

Instruments fixed on the model indicated that the isolator had consistently reduced the shake table output by 90 percent or better.

To show the energy dissipation properties of the isolation system visually to lay observers, two identical tall foam coffee cups filled with heavy nuts and bolts were placed, one on the shake table platform and the other on the top glass shelf of the model. Immediately following the table's first slow cycle, the cup on the table fell and spilled its contents. The cup on the model's glass shelf remained motionless throughout the shake table's maximum output.

For the fragile clocks and other art objects, I developed the less costly concept of isolating entire floors instead of individual objects. Color renderings

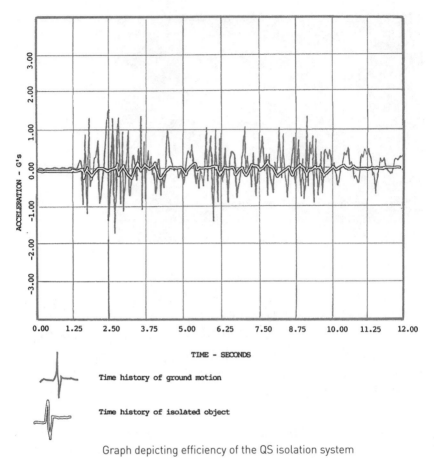

Graph depicting efficiency of the QS isolation system

of the floor isolation system were prepared by Massis Megerdoomian, who had obtained his doctorate degree in architecture and industrial design in Italy.

The success of the de-linking concept for art objects and the invention of the systems reverberated throughout JPGM and other museums worldwide. There was a tectonic shift at Getty that turned the established hierarchy there upside down. A new system to protect art objects from being damaged by earthquakes had come out of JPGM's lowly preparation department, known for packing and unpacking cargo and for mount making. The venerable and prestigious Getty Conservation Institute (GCI), where all new developments in conservation and protection of art were to originate, had been left in the dust.

In full damage-control mode, the GCI established a "Disaster Planning Steering Committee" and invited high officials from academia and institutions

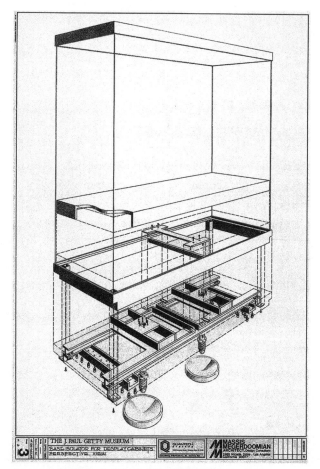

An exploded view of the QS isolation system
for Getty showcases

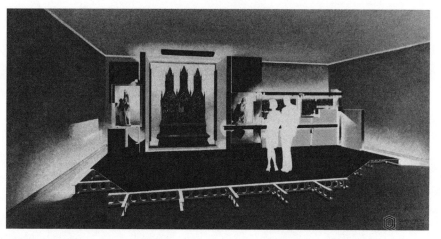

Rendering of the cross-section of an isolated floor

such as the National Science Foundation, the Smithsonian Institution, and the National Academy of Sciences. I was asked by the GCI to join the committee. The first meeting of the steering committee was held in March 1987 in Washington DC. No one from the museum at Malibu was invited to attend the meeting.

In an attempt to gain lost superiority and recognition in the field of earthquake protection of art objects, the GCI underwrote the publication of *Between Two Earthquakes: Cultural Property in Seismic Zones* by conservation architect Sir Bernard Feilden, which was published in late 1987. However, the GCI's reputation of "Innovations flow from GCI" was ignored, and different departments at JPGM began to look for opportunities to enhance their individual standings. Gradually Bruce's authority to coordinate the earthquake mitigation activities for JPGM through his preparation department was fading.

Chapter 25

ENGINEERING PRESERVATION
The Getty Kouros and Aphrodite

IN LATE 1984, ENCOURAGED BY the success of the new technologies in earthquake protection of art objects at JPGM, Bruce organized a symposium and invited engineers, curators, conservators, and members of academia to attend and present their ideas for protecting art objects. The theme of the conference was the protection of large sculptures in earthquake-prone areas. Attending the symposium were faculty members from Stanford University, USC, and UCLA.

Incredibly, the presenters failed to consider critical parameters such as geometry, the engineering properties of the material from which the sculptures were carved, and past conservation activities that would determine the response of sculptures to external loads. Different techniques to prevent statues from falling seemed to remain the participants' principal objective. In that regard, one of the structural engineers retained by JPGM since 1982 repeated the idea of using guy wires extending from statue's extremities to adjacent ceilings walls and floors. Another prominent professor in structural engineering promoted a system of air bladders (airbags) stowed in objects' pedestals that would pop out upon earthquake shaking and inflate and cushion the objects should they fall.

Other speakers promoted research related to the protection of art objects employed through the ages. The spokesperson for the USC group, an acquaintance of mine who had contacted JPGM soon after I had disclosed at a conference in San Francisco that my isolation system was being used at JPGM, recommended that the museum give USC a grant to evaluate different configurations of QS isolators and other earthquake-mitigation technologies for protecting art objects.

The lunch break could not come too soon for me. As I was impatiently playing with my car keys and my camera strap, ready to leave for the day, a young man approached me and informed me that Marion True had asked him to show me a new JPGM acquisition in the basement storage room to determine if it could be supported on the isolator system. This request was a welcome excuse for me to leave the conference before it was adjourned.

On the way to the basement storage, the young man introduced himself as Jerry Podany, an assistant technician at the JPGM conservation laboratory.

The Getty Kouros

On the floor of the basement storage room lay a long wooden crate that contained seven broken pieces of a large marble statue. The torso was the largest of the fragments. Jerry told me that the statue was known as "The Getty Kouros"—"kouros" being the term use to describe ancient Greek statues of young male nudes who were always shown standing and with one foot placed slightly forward. He said that this kouros was about seven feet tall, weighed about 1,000 pounds, and was believed to have been sculpted about 530 BC. I was also informed that the statue was undergoing "authentication."

I put on pair of white gloves as requested and proceeded to examine the different fragments. Matching the broken pieces at the fractures indicated that not much stone was missing at the broken joints.

"Did you say that Marion wanted to know if the statue should be supported on a base isolator?" I asked.

"Yes," Jerry replied.

I next asked if he knew how the broken pieces were going to be assembled and repaired to carry the weight of the torso. Jerry suggested that we visit the gallery where other large conserved statues were exhibited so he could show me the museum's conservation and earthquake mitigation methods.

In the gallery, several stone statues were supported by metal bars that connected them to massive pedestals. Jerry pointed to a statue labeled "Lansdowne Herakles" that was prominently exhibited in a stage-like setting as a comparable example for how the Kouros would be conserved and protected from earthquakes.

As we walked toward the statue, I noticed a metal object next to its right foot. Out of curiosity, I walked to the back of the statue to see what the metal object was. There I saw a contraption consisting of a pipe with a metal extension that was embedded in the statue's buttock at one end and extended into the pedestal on which the statue was standing at the other end.

"What is the purpose of the metal thing?" I asked the young man while taking pictures in the relatively tight area, which prevented me from getting the entire statue in my camera's viewfinder.

"That's to keep the statue from falling during earthquakes," he said,

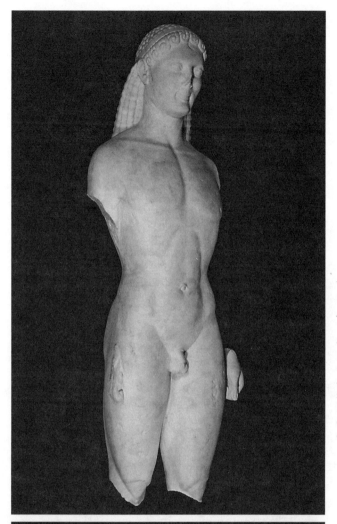

The largest of the
Kouros fragments.
A 7-minute video,
"The Getty Kouros,"
about the restoration
process and the
debate over its
authenticity, can be
seen at:
http://www.
quantechsystems.
com/gallery/

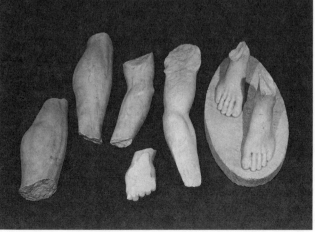

The remaining
Kouros fragments

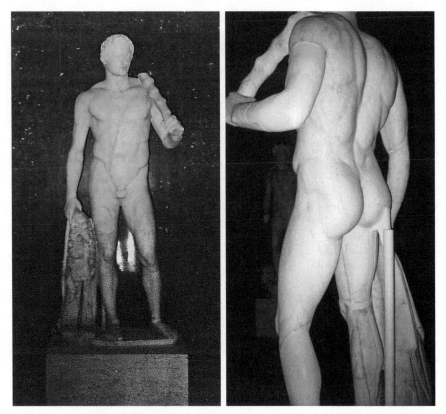

The Lansdowne
Herakles...

...and the Getty's
"earthquake protection system"

and continued, "The bar is anchored in the heavy pedestal that earthquakes cannot move."

I was speechless, and all I could utter was "That's abhorrent!" To which Jerry answered, "It isn't visible from the front."

As we walked back to the basement, I was shocked to see how primitive and downright dangerous JPGM's earthquake protection methods for antiquities really were.

Back in the basement, Jerry explained, "Inserting large-diameter stainless steel pins would connect the broken pieces, and because of the small plinth, an external support like the rods used for the Herakles would be utilized to anchor the statue to a massive base."

"If that's already been decided, then what is an isolator for?" I asked.

"Even with an isolator, external support would be necessary to keep the statue from falling," he replied.

Figuring it was a lost cause to argue with him regarding a subject about which he was clueless, I said, "I can think of better ways to assemble this statue and protect it from earthquakes," and headed toward the exit door.

As we were walking out of the basement, Jerry asked me, "What is the better way that you mentioned?"

I said, "Post tensioning." As we walked, I elaborated, "There would be no need for large-diameter drilling to insert pins. The broken pieces would be held together only by invisible thin wires."

He was puzzled and wanted to talk more about it, but there was no sense in my explaining further than I already had. He was not going to understand it.

Deep down I wished that I could put into practice what I had just told him. The daring thought of assembling the fragmented statue by post tensioning was exhilarating. But the prospect of convincing the museum to trust me with yet another "never done before" system to assemble the museum's $10-million-plus acquisition was a daunting task, to put it mildly.

FOR REASONS UNKNOWN TO ME, Bruce Metro was kept completely removed from matters related to the Getty Kouros, including the base isolation systems. As such, my only conduit to Marion True was through the young conservation assistant who seemed to have the curator's ear. Within a week of my seeing the Kouros fragments, Jerry informed me that she wanted to know more about what I had mentioned to him.

Once again I decided to make my point by means of a physical model so there would be no ambiguity as to the steps required to assemble the statue and isolate it from earthquake-induced ground shaking, not only in Malibu but anywhere else in the world where it might be exhibited.

To demonstrate the concept of post tensioning, I made a model that consisted of a two-foot-long log four inches in diameter that represented the original unbroken statue some 2,500 years ago. I drilled a two-foot-long, quarter-inch hole down through the center of the log, after which I cut it into several pieces with different orientations and geometry to represent the fragments of the Kouros. The cut pieces could not be loosely stacked on top of each other because the resisting shear forces on the corresponding cut faces were not sufficient to maintain the pieces in balance. To stabilize the log fragments and increase the resisting shear forces at the cut joints, I inserted a quarter-inch threaded rod through the center hole and tightened the rod from both ends by wing nuts that provided the necessary strength to resist the applied tensile and flexural forces.

I called Jerry and made an appointment to meet him at the museum's tea room, which at the time was located where the outdoor classical theater now stands. He came to the café with another conservation assistant named

Jerry Podany (left) and Dr. Michael King (right) taking measurements of the Getty Kouros with me and Dr. Richard Goodman observing (rear)

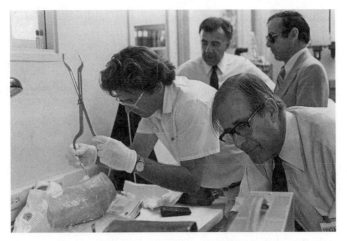

Fractured ankles and knees of the Kouros

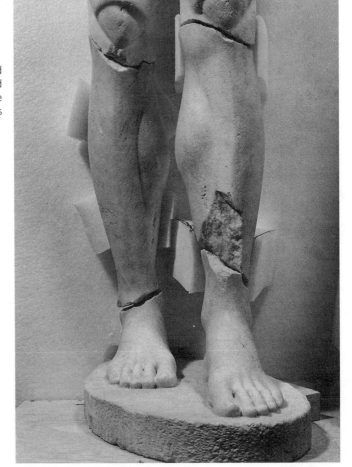

James Stahl. I showed them the model and how the threaded metal rod provided the necessary tensile strength to convert the fragmented log into a rigid composite system able to resist different load modes. Unlike Jerry, James readily grasped the applicability of this "mechanical joint" system to assembling the Getty Kouros. I asked them to take the model to Marion True and show her my proposed post-tensioning concept.

The following week, Jerry informed me that the museum had accepted the concept and decided to reimburse me for the cost of the mechanical joint model. They also requested a written report in which I would outline the exact steps I would recommend for reassembling the Kouros. I prepared a report, "Report, A Mechanical Joint System, for Kouros," dated January 21, 1985, in which I outlined the details of my recommended assembly system and referenced the wooden model.

The intricate undertaking was critical, and I required that all communications and decisions related to the conservation and protection of the Kouros be made through me. This made me responsible and liable for any mistakes causing harm to the statue. I had previously managed many critical projects. However, the assembly of a broken sculpture was different. There was zero margin of error! Everything had to proceed flawlessly during the course of the assembly. No mistake could be reversed without permanently disfiguring and damaging the statue. As such, I had to be absolutely satisfied that my system was going to work perfectly.

JPGM agreed to provide labor and materials as I deemed necessary. Jerry was Marion True's representative for the project. I was surprised to see how the Marion True and Jerry Podany duo worked together so closely in all levels of the antiquities department. At my request, it was stipulated that only museum personnel would physically handle the sculpture's fragments throughout all phases of the project. For the necessary hardware, I was to communicate with James Stahl.

The first order of studies was to evaluate the engineering properties of the stone fragments and take accurate measurements of each piece. There were two methods to determine physical properties of the stone: destructive and nondestructive testing. Destructive testing was not an option as it would defeat the purpose of the mechanical joint system, which was to minimize large-diameter coring for any purpose. Nondestructive testing was the only option. I called Richard Goodman at UC Berkeley, with whom I was already working on the Blackhawk development, to recommend a reliable organization to perform nondestructive tests on the Getty Kouros.

Goodman recommended retaining Dr. Michael King of the Lawrence Berkeley National Laboratories. The tests consisted of measuring wave velocities in the broken pieces utilizing ultrasound, acoustic emission, tomography, and other techniques. Getty personnel were to take physical measurements of the pieces as directed by Dr. King.

To confirm the validity of the range of values obtained by the nondestructive testing, a small-diameter short core was extracted from the center of one of the Kouros's fractures and the engineering properties of the stone were determined. The core test results were within the acceptable statistical range of Dr. King's nondestructive measurements.

I also contacted the Oakland-based firm of Hammon, Jensen, Wallen and Associates to prepare contour maps of the Kouros using photogrammetry for numerical modeling.

From large close-up photographs of the broken pieces, I mapped apparent discontinuities such as cracks, bedding planes, and solution cavities. Wave velocities measured by King indicated the existence of an outer zone of one to two centimeters of weathered rock. Weathered rocks have a diminished capacity to bear loads. The findings also confirmed that there was no chance that the Kouros's small ankles would have survived the drilling of large-diameter holes to accommodate the insertion of large-diameter metal pins.

The main question now boiled down to: Based on the test data, was the mechanical joint system viable for assembling the Kouros within acceptable confidence levels?

The computerized model of the mechanical joint system showed that the system was viable. However, confidence levels based on mathematical solutions could be misleading, and I wanted to validate the feasibility of the mathematical joint system by performing a series of physical tests also.

In my January 1985 report, I had detailed the process of stabilizing the broken joints to resist both compression and tension loads. The schematics showed that to stabilize the joints, interfaces or "seating material" would have to be used to conform the uneven fractures. The seating material had to be manufactured of isotropic material to withstand any static and dynamic loads transferred to the fractures. My schematic also showed that if the interface did not stabilize the joints fully, shear pins might have to be incorporated in the mechanical joint system.

The JPGM conservation department prepared full-size casts of the broken Kouros pieces below the knee fractures. The casts of the interface and broken fragments created a full-size replica of the statue below the torso. The replica, without the tension cable, was tested at the UC Berkeley Material Testing Laboratory to determine the stability of the fractures under gravity loads. Applied compressive loads well over the weight of the actual statue below the torso showed that the interface had stabilized the joints and that shear

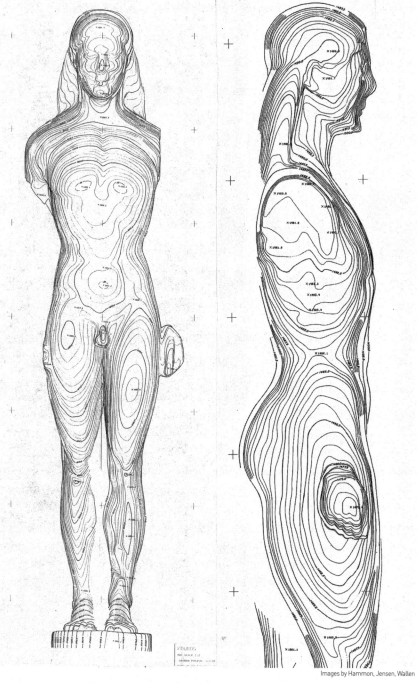

Images by Hammon, Jensen, Wallen

Photogrammetry "contour maps" of the Kouros

pins would not be necessary. I was satisfied that my mechanical joint system and the assembly of the Kouros could proceed with confidence.

As I had stated at the outset of the Kouros assembly project, the mechanical joint system was specifically devised to assemble the broken pieces to provide stability in a state of static equilibrium only. To protect the fragile statue from earthquake-induced ground motion, the assembled statue had to be supported on my isolation system. I prepared fabrication drawings and supervised the manufacturing of the isolator for the Getty Kouros so it would remain de-linked from any induced seismic disturbances, including floor bounce, anywhere.

Aircraft cables, rock anchors, flat washers to absorb excessive tension in the cables induced by potential external loads, and seating elements were made ready. James designed and manufactured the mechanism to pull the cables. The loose, broken pieces of the statue were put together and aligned in a horizontal position and secured in an aluminum cage, ready for the drilling of small-diameter holes to accommodate the tension cables.

A full-size horizontal drilling jig capable of drilling the entire length of the statue was set up in the Getty's conservation lab, and Jerry Podany began drilling the long small-diameter holes from the bottom of the plinth toward the middle of the upper thighs of the statue where the cables would be anchored. The slightest misalignment or heating of the drill bit could have caused the bit to break and get stuck or to break through the surface of the statue—either of which would have resulted in monumental tragedy.

Jerry accomplished the drilling flawlessly, and the cables were successfully anchored in the sculpture's thighs at one end and threaded into the load application and measurement devices fixed under the plinth at the other end. The aluminum cage was turned upright and placed on supports to keep the assembly high enough above the floor to accommodate the tightening of cables and the base isolator.

During the course of the assembly, I monitored the gradual stress increase in the mechanical joints through an oscilloscope on loan from UCLA. I checked the signals transmitted by strain gauges and geophones affixed to the statue near the mechanical joints. Any noise registered by the geophones would signal the crushing of stone crystals or slippage of the joints. Once the readings registered by the load cells were stabilized, indicating the stone's linear behavior, I signaled the crew to increase the cable's tension. The procedure was repeated until the specified cable tensions were achieved.

The Kouros, thus assembled, was fastened to the blue isolator, which carried the metal label "Quantech Systems, 044-06," and was ready to stand free of any support for the first time.

QS isolator components for the Getty Kouros

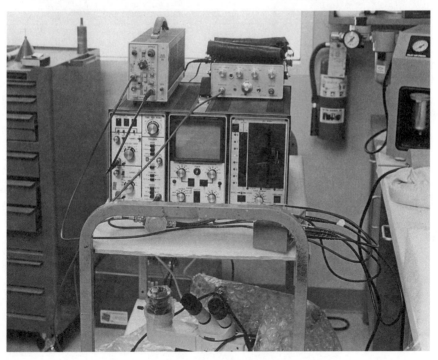

Monitoring equipment

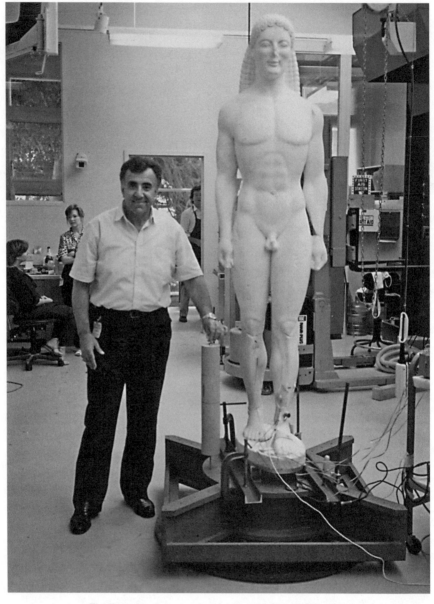

The Getty Kouros standing free again after 2,500 years

The bolts holding the aluminum cage's front panel were removed, and the front panel was moved away. The crew's body language, and their worried glances and nervous smiles at me, showed their extreme apprehension about what was going on and their uncertainty about how everything would end. With a swift hand gesture, I signaled for the remaining three panels to be removed and carried away.

Dramatically, there stood Getty Kouros free of any support. Loose wires hanging from the monitoring instrumentation attached to the statue and connected to the oscilloscope showed steady signals, indicating that all was well. The sight resembled a patient in an operating room hooked up to tubes and wires standing for the first time after surgery. Unlike the statue of Herakles, the Getty Kouros required no hideous external supports and could be seen and examined from all sides.

Jerry, looking at the freestanding sculpture on the isolator, pontificated, "The Kouros is now riding on roller skates," and went to call Marion True. In a low, disgusted voice, I repeated what he had just said—"Riding on roller skates"—and thought, "Will this guy ever understand what an earthquake isolation system is?"

While waiting for Marion to arrive, I asked James Stahl to take my picture for posterity holding the wood model of the mechanical joint, which was resting on the blue isolator that now supported the Kouros. The photograph depicts the complete cycle of my conservation and protection concepts that got the statue to where it stood without visible metal bars or external supports and without being anchored to floors, walls, and ceilings.

Soon Marion True walked into the lab and, in a state of wide-eyed disbelief and happiness, approached the Kouros and inspected it for the first time in its standing position. This must have been a triumphant moment for the JPGM curator and her staff, and one that elevated their standing among their peers throughout the world.

THE NEWS OF THE SERIES OF conservation and protection breakthroughs at the Getty spread quickly, aided predominantly by museum staff who were dispatched to all corners of the globe to make presentations about the breakthroughs without the necessary education or knowledge about the subject. Soon, the presentations became more about self-promotion than transferring technology to their colleagues in other museums.

The period that immediately followed the conservation of the Getty Kouros was confusing and marked by a sudden rash of spreading rumors, innuendos, less-than-honest behavior, and institutional jealousies, all of which were entirely foreign to me.

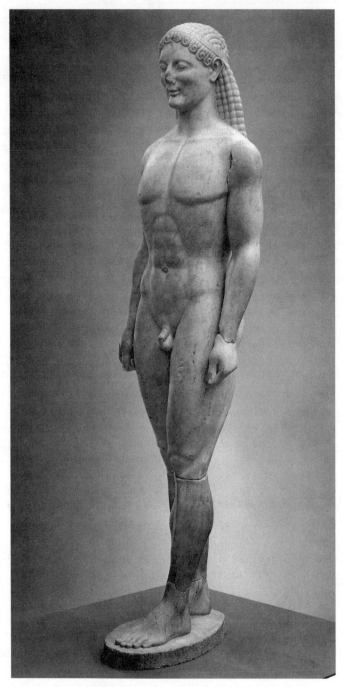

The Getty Kouros, ready for public viewing

I became aware of and came face to face with the darker side of the art world during one of my subsequent visits to the JPGM lab to make sure that the conservation of the Kouros was proceeding smoothly. That day, a tall man walked into the lab, suddenly froze in place, and, after gazing at the back of the Kouros for less than a minute, said audibly in a Germanic accent, "That statue is fake."

I asked the gentleman, who was later introduced to me as a conservator of antiquities at a museum in Bern, Switzerland, what made him think that the statue was a fake.

"Because the style of the curls does not match the style of other well-known and well-preserved Kouri," he replied. He then looked around and, seeing no one close by, whispered to me, "Most of the stuff in this museum is fake junk, including the Turkish Bronze."

I knew instantly that he was referring to the prized "Getty Bronze," the 300-100 BC "Victorious Youth," and implying that it had been made recently in Turkey. I thought that he couldn't be serious, coming to such a conclusion in just a few seconds.

"After all, Dr. True must be more knowledgeable about the stylistic features of Greek antiquities than a conservator," I thought.

In August 1986, however, *The Times* of London, the *New York Times*, and the *Los Angeles Times* published articles about the Getty Kouros that questioned its authenticity long before it was placed on exhibition.

As an engineer, it did not matter to me that the Getty Kouros could allegedly be a recent forgery. I would have followed the same procedure if the statue had been carved yesterday. But if it was indeed a recent forgery, it remained mysterious how the forger could have created the outer zone of 1 to 2 cm of weathered rock at the ankle areas as had been determined by Dr. Michael King. Rock weathering is a natural process caused by cyclical environmental factors over the course of centuries and extremely difficult, if not impossible, to create.

On November 10, 1986, before the Kouros was put on public display, I was invited by John Walsh to attend a small reception for those who had been involved with the statue. The gathering was a pleasant affair during which pictures were taken that included Walsh, Marion True, other staff, and me gathered around the Getty Kouros.

Unethical Behavior and False Claims at JPGM

Without my knowledge, museum personnel were out in full force bragging about their state-of-the-art and innovative techniques to conserve and

Getty team members around the Kouros the night before it went
on exhibit included Curator Marion True (center) and Jerry Podany
(to her right, with his hand on my shoulder)

protect the Getty Kouros to anyone who would listen to their nonsense.
And nonsense it was! Reporters were interviewing people who never understood or grasped the workings of the intricate systems undertaken for the
Kouros. The print media, eager to publish any news before their competitors
in general and news related to the J. Paul Getty Museum in particular,
rushed to publish their interviews promptly.

The first of such outright fabrications were published in the November
3, 1986, issue of the *Los Angeles Times* just a week before the reception with
the headline "Kouros to Go on View at Getty." It read as follows:

> One of the most remarkable aspects of the piece is its state of
> preservation. Arms, lower legs and feet had been broken off the
> sculpture hundreds of years ago, but only a few fragments were
> lost. The monumental young man now stands upright without
> visible means of support, benefiting from an innovative system
> devised by Jerry Podany, the museum's conservator of antiquities,
> and his staff.
>
> Instead of drilling large holes in the statue and inserting steel
> rods to join severed parts, Podany attached them with a flexi-
> ble-inch [sic] stainless steel cable. If the statue is subjected to
> an earthquake, its limbs are expected to open and close. As

another precaution against seismic stress, the base of the sculpture is mounted on ball bearings attached to a centering device.[1]

The above inaccuracies confirmed Jerry's ignorance of the intricacies of assembling the Kouros and the mechanism and workings of the seismic isolation system to protect the sculpture. The fact was that the isolator was designed and installed to prevent the transfer of any earthquake-induced ground motion to the Kouros whatsoever—so for Mr. Podany to refer to the "opening and closing of the mechanical joints" reflects a total misunderstanding of how the isolator worked. The mechanical joints were intended only to stabilize the statue, not to offer flexibility in case of an earthquake, so characterizing the isolator as "another" precaution against seismic stress was so preposterous that it deserved no comments to dignify it. Thanks to the First Amendment right of free speech, Mr. Podany was able to continue spreading these misrepresentations with impunity.

Not long after the *LA Times* article appeared, one afternoon while I was waiting for the elevator at the museum, a member of the conservation department staff hurried to join me. Once we were in the elevator, he informed me in confidence that just few hours earlier, a Japanese delegation visiting the museum was being ushered around by a senior JPGM employee. In the gallery where the Kouros was on exhibit, the senior employee had "demonstrated" the capability of the isolator to resist large earthquakes by repeatedly pushing and pulling the isolator to its maximum displacement limit.

The conservation lab staff member told me, "The violent jerking caused the mechanical joints to open up and created cracks in the surface coating on the statue. I was afraid that the whole statue was going to collapse and hurt someone."

I was furious and said, "These fucking idiots have never understood that the isolator is to prevent the statue from being subjected to earthquake-induced stress reversals while the floor shakes, and not a pair of 'roller skates' to push and pull it around!" In frustration, I wrote a letter to John Walsh and complained about the incident.

Soon after, I received a call from Jerry on behalf of Marion True, who asked me to inspect the Kuoros's damaged joints. Barely able to control my anger, in my return letter to Jerry, I outlined what I had been told about the incident and outlined procedures to evaluate and repair the damaged mechanical joints.

1. http://articles.latimes.com/1986-11-03/entertainment/ca-14823_1_getty-kouros

THE SITUATION AT JPGM WAS getting out of hand. The folks there were out aggressively advising other museums how to protect their collections from earthquakes without having any understanding of the matter. Their "monkey see, monkey do" behavior was becoming my greatest concern. The only way to put an end to the embarrassing situation was to patent my invention. I was well aware that patents provide only limited protection, but I hoped that this would deter further misrepresentations by imposters.

I summoned Bruce and Jerry for a meeting and informed them of my intention to file for a patent for my isolator. Bruce, who seemed to be fed up with Jerry's unprofessional conduct, said, "You started the whole thing and have every right to patent your isolator."

Jerry, who apparently had other ideas, asked, "Are you going to patent the mechanical joint system, too?"

I said, "I'm looking for protection of the concept of base isolation so people will not get the Getty and me in hot water. If the Getty would be willing, I would gladly file for a joint patent," to which he responded, "Getty is a nonprofit organization and could not be party to any patent."

I could not have cared less about how JPGM felt about my decision to file an application for a US patent and decided to proceed on my own.

JPGM retained a major Los Angeles law firm that specialized in patents and trademarks to stop me from filing for the patent. The Getty being a deep-pocket client, their legal counsel embarked on a thorough investigation of the matter to show cause why the US Patent Office should reject my patent application. However, the overwhelming evidentiary documentation in the Getty archives, consisting of my reports and fabrication drawings, proved that I was the sole inventor of the base isolation system for art objects. Their counsel's exhaustive search of patents for similar devices proved to be futile, and the US Patent Office accepted my application.

Despite intimidation and all sorts of unsubstantiated allegations by Getty counsel, the truth prevailed, and on February 23, 1988, the US Patent Office granted me Patent Number 4,726,161, defined as "Earthquake Isolating Support."[2]

As a professional courtesy and in good faith, I granted to the J. Paul Getty Trust an exclusive and royalty-free right to make and use my invention and isolation concept. JPGM was free to make and use the isolation concept without any constraints.

2. http://www.google.com/patents/US4726161; and https://docs.google.com/viewer?url=patentimages. storage.googleapis.com/pdfs/US4726161.pdf

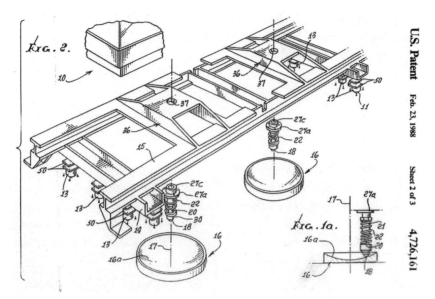

U.S. Patent   Feb. 23, 1988   Sheet 2 of 3   4,726,161

Page 3 of US Patent 4,726,161, "Earthquake Isolating Support"

Meanwhile, however, acting as if the patent was only a side issue, the Getty management continued to retain my services related to both JPGM and the new Getty Center, then in the planning stages near UCLA.

MEANWHILE, THE CHORUS OF DOUBT regarding the authenticity of the Getty Kouros was growing louder and more widespread in the art community worldwide. To blunt the criticism, JPGM decided to publish an elaborate pictorial album about the Kouros, the research into its authenticity, and its conservation and protection.

The book, which ultimately was never published, contained a foreword by John Walsh. I wrote the chapters on the statue's conservation and earthquake protection that were incorporated into the manuscript. Because the book was to be a scholarly publication, it contained detailed lists of published and unpublished references, including my reports regarding the "mechanical joint" and "isolation" systems.

I believe that the following excerpts from John Walsh's unpublished foreword provide a vivid and succinct snapshot of the circumstances and the museum's posture during the period when the Kouros was considered its prized acquisition. They also reflect his genuine desire to offer to other art institutions JPGM's advancements in preserving and protecting art objects:

No one who saw the Kouros when it first arrived in the basement of the Getty Museum in the autumn of 1983 will forget the sight. Lying in a packing case, broken at the ankles, knees, and shoulders, unable to stand upright, it was nevertheless taut with strength and radiant with life. Its reappearance after two millennia, complete and well preserved, seemed a miraculous gift for a relatively young collection of antiquities.

Our euphoria alternated with doubt. The statue had an unusual surface, different from that of most other archaic sculpture; a peculiar pale surface that looked severely cleaned. There were stylistic anomalies: parts of the body were anatomically accomplished, while others were strangely retardataire. Was it too good to be true? Could it be a shrewd modern pastiche?...

This book assembles the results of the most important work done on the kouros since 1983. Our hope is not only to cast light on a rediscovered masterpiece of Greek sculpture, but also to document the technical innovations used in its authentication and treatment, in order to make them available to sculpture conservators and conservation scientists...

Rejoining the broken statue by conventional methods would have required a drilling away of much original marble, thereby causing new weaknesses; instead, [Jerry] Podany devised a new system that lends greater strength and conserves more original material. Finally, the piece had to be ready to survive another earthquake (another, because one seems to have broken it in antiquity). The ingenious method devised by Jack Yaghoubian, president of Quantech Systems, for the statue's installation will not only keep the kouros on its feet during a seismic disturbance but should prove useful for the protection of work of art elsewhere.[3]

MEANWHILE THE FLOW OF MISINFORMATION from JPGM kept growing, and nothing was going to stop it. On November 29, 1987, the *LA Times Magazine* ran a cover story headlined: "The Bigger One: Scenes from

---

3. John Walsh, unpublished manuscript with handwritten notes

the Earthquake That Scientists Fear Most—a 7.5 Jolt on the Newport-Inglewood Fault."[4]

The article was a fictional account written as if "the bigger one" had occurred and correspondents were filing reports from various communities in the Los Angeles area. A "report" filed at 4:30:42 p.m. from the Getty Museum read:

> At the ersatz Roman villa housing the J. Paul Getty Museum, almost all is in ruin. A small irony: After 41 seconds, the replica is already in worse shape than some of the ancient buildings it was modeled on. The Greek vases from the 4th Century BC, Roman busts, French Impressionist paintings, all are torn from their moorings and covered in debris. But on the first floor of the museum, a miracle. Several of the Getty's most valuable sculptures stand on one of the most ingenious earth-quake-compensating mechanisms ever devised. As the shaking begins, the pedestals absorb the energy; during the worst of the quake, the statues move gently from side to side as though surrounded by shock absorbers. When the quake subsides, they stand like sentries amid the rubble.

The story was not only fake—it was misleading. The building's structural analysis had shown that such an earthquake would not have caused it to collapse. Further, the isolators would have ceased to function in an area covered with debris from the supposedly ruined buildings, exposing the protected statues to the same fate as those not supported on "earthquake compensating mechanisms," which is a poor description for earthquake isolators.

Such false accounts, repeated in technical presentations and widely circulated in print media, left the impression that utilizing isolators would protect objects even if the museum building were to undergo catastrophic failure—but nothing could have been further from the truth.

The Aphrodite—and the End of My Professional Services to JPGM

In October 1988, Jerry Podany contacted me to get my opinion related to another recent notable JPGM acquisition—a massive stone sculpture of the Greek goddess Aphrodite with the back half of its head missing. The

---

4. http://articles.latimes.com/1987-11-29/magazine/tm-25059_1_newport-inglewood-fault

imposing statue, which had been located by Marion True, was very different from the Kouros. Balanced and with no apparent weaknesses like the Kouros's small-diameter ankles, it was standing on its own and seemed perfectly stable and in equilibrium.

Jerry told me that he had already performed all of the necessary measurements and had located the center of gravity of each of the large pieces, and that the only thing he wanted to know was the tension required in the cables to connect the broken pieces and protect it from earthquakes.

I told him that the Aphrodite did not need a complex Kouros-type isolator because it was not vulnerable to torsion-induced seismic loads, and I recommended a simpler and less costly isolator system that I had developed for LACMA.

My QS Glider consisted of three horizontal plates separated by two sets of perpendicular camshafts and specially designed gravity and rolling friction return bearing tracks. Because the camshafts and bearing tracks functioned on two axes, the Glider was less costly to fabricate than the bowl-shaped base isolator system, which functioned on a 360-degree plane.

Jerry wanted to know how the QS Glider worked. Using books and round pencils, I demonstrated how the books moved on the rolling pencils along their X and Y axes. Still not understanding the Glider concept, Jerry said that Marion True wanted to use the Kouros-type isolator. By then, another conservation assistant named Wayne Haak was working for Jerry. He saw the Glider demonstration and later developed a version that he patented.[5]

After the meeting, Jerry forwarded me large, professional black-and-white photographs of all sides of the Aphrodite. Based on our conversations and on the photographs, I prepared a proposal dated November 2, 1988, that included details and my estimated time and costs for assembling and protecting the Aphrodite, and mailed it to the museum.

After mailing the proposal, I sensed a certain newly developed arrogance in the True-Podany duo that I had not observed before. Frequent, casual, friendly meetings to pick my brain for ideas were replaced with unprecedented formality.

In response to my proposal, I received a rather long letter dated November 14, 1988, with a handwritten footnote from Jerry that stated, "Jack, Let me know when you would like to meet about this more informally than this letter." Something foul was brewing by the duo that I could not put my finger on.

5. http://patents.justia.com/inventor/wayne-r-haak; see also: http://articles.latimes.com/
print/1989-10-26/entertainment/ca-960_1_getty-museum

The Getty Aphrodite. A 5-minute video, "Aphrodite & QS Glider," about the
Glider and its adoption by a number of museums, can be seen at:
www.quantechsystems.com/gallery/

During our meeting, instead of discussing the proposal, he asked me if I
could prepare a manual in which art objects could be categorized by their
geometry, weight, and most suitable earthquake mitigation method. He also
wanted to know the calculation for pre-stressing cables.

I responded sarcastically, "So you're looking for an earthquake conservation and protection cookbook for art objects?"

His answer was, "Yes!"

When I asked, "Are you serious?," he responded, "If you don't want to
do it, USC will."

I was not at all surprised by his bizarre request. He was waiting for my
answer, and I did not disappoint him. I said, "Let USC do it. I am really
tired of the stupidity that goes on in this organization," and I walked out.

My gut feeling was that, underneath the JPGM's urbane façade, something was festering at the core of the organization, and I decided to bring my consulting tenure there to an end. It was time for me to move on and end the chapter on JPGM.

OVER THE NEXT SEVERAL YEARS, my time at JPGM became a fading memory, but I continued to follow some of the news reports about activities there.

For example, to resolve the uncertainty regarding the authenticity of the Getty Kouros, the "Getty Kouros Colloquium" was held in Athens in 1992. The conference did not resolve the controversy because the opinions of the participants were divided equally. I was appalled reading papers by some JPGM personnel who unabashedly expressed their supposedly long-standing doubts about the statue based on their observations of some of the statue's stylistic anomalies. During the entire period of the statue's conservation, I had never heard any hints that it might be a recent forgery. Also, although there were discussions in Athens about its patina measured in microns, no consideration was given to the one to two centimeters of outer weathered rock that had been measured by the Lawrence Berkeley Laboratory. It would be interesting to see how forgers could possibly weather the surface of marble to depths of one to two centimeters. In any case, as of the publication of this book, the statue's label currently reads: "Unknown, Greek, about 530 BC, or modern forgery, marble."[6]

My memories of JPGM were also revived temporarily in July 1997 when I received an invitation to attend the closing of the museum for renovations. I saw and had a brief chat with Jerry Podany and Marion True that night. Both were upbeat and seemed to be on top of the world. Jerry wanted me to know that things were very different since I had left Getty. That night, several members of the conservation laboratory staff told me in confidence that things were not all well there. One senior conservator of antiquities made a point of letting me know that they were designing and manufacturing their own isolators but that these did not work properly, and he asked if I could talk to Jerry about it. This was not news to me. I had heard from others at different museums that the Getty isolators were not reliable. I had no desire to know about or interest in what was going on at JPGM.

MEANWHILE, I WAS BUSY WITH many projects when, on December 7, 1988, a magnitude 6.9 earthquake struck my fatherland Armenia. The quake was

6. http://www.getty.edu/art/gettyguide/artObjectDetails?artobj=12908

centered in Spitak near Gumri. The quake took more than 25,000 lives, many of them schoolchildren who perished in the rubble of their collapsed schools and kindergartens. The earthquake left many people homeless and without shelter in the severe winter. Housing became the survivors' most critical and urgent need, and the Armenian diaspora worldwide began organizing long-term aid for the affected population centers. Imported prefabricated houses and school buildings were a priority for helping the victims to reconstruct their shattered lives and families.

Many of the factories producing prefabricated housing were located in countries not prone to earthquakes and that lacked seismic codes for buildings. I traveled to some of the factories where prefab buildings were being made for Armenia and modified their specifications and structural systems to resist large seismic loads.

I also wrote a technical article, "Isolating Building Contents from Earthquake Induced Floor Motions," which provided both details and performance data about my isolation system and was published in 1991 in *Earthquake Spectra*,[7] the professional journal of the Earthquake Engineering Research Institute (EERI).

"Success Has Many Fathers…"

I also read and heard about the corruption gripping the Getty organization, such as illicit acquisitions of looted artifacts from Italy, including the Aphrodite, that had allegedly been arranged by Marion True.

The museum's conservation department replaced most of its staff with newcomers who all worked for Jerry Podany. They showered their boss with accolades and quoted his less-than-candid statements lavishly, for example in an April 23, 2003, *New York Times* article on Getty Museum mount makers and earthquake mitigation:

> The [earthquake mitigation] idea had its genesis with Jerry Podany, the head of antiquities conservation at the Getty. Mr. Podany, who has worked at the museum since 1978, said that

---

7. *Earthquake Spectra*, Feb. 1991, Vol. 7, No. 1, pp. 127-143. Abstract: A simple and effective system has been developed and is in use to isolate and substantially reduce both earthquake induced large accelerations and displacements simultaneously. The base isolation system protects building contents susceptible to damage by earthquake induced motions. The single isolation unit has been extensively tested during shake table test programs. The isolation system operates at about critical damping and can accommodate a large variety of random dynamic motions generated by earthquakes. The system is flexible and can be customized for different configurations and specific functional performances.

he began thinking seriously about seismic protection in the early 1980's. "We started looking at damage in other countries, and one day it was like, 'Oh, we have this serious problem,'" he said.[8]

Another *New York Times* article on March 12, 2008, stated:

> The other major protective device is the base isolator, the first of which was developed by Jack Yaghoubian, a local engineering consultant, *in collaboration with Mr. Podany.* It effectively disengages an object from the rocking, rolling and vibrating that can result from a quake.[9] (Emphasis added.)

These were continuations of total falsehoods that were spreading even before I ended my consulting services there. Claims of collaboration in developing anything at JPGM including my base isolation system are entirely false!

But then, Getty conservators are not the only ones who claim to have been collaborators of mine in developing the base isolation system. As the adage goes: "Success has many fathers, but failure is an orphan."

For example, although I did not discover this until I began doing archival research for this book, in 1986 the late UCLA professor Nathan Shapira had published a paper on earthquakes and art preservation while I was working with him and the Getty. In that paper, "Earthquakes and Art Preservation: A View from the San Andreas Fault,"[10] he recollects the state of J. Paul Getty's seismic safety studies as follows:

> The first Seismic Safety study for the J. Paul Getty Museum was completed in 1982 by the structural engineering office of Melvyn Green & Associates of El Segundo, California. It concentrated mainly on the display of sculptures, pottery and decorative arts. Its recommendations were to minimize earthquake hazards by simple systems of bracing, anchoring, and lowering the center of gravity of pedestals. (p. 406)

---

8. http://www.nytimes.com/2003/04/23/arts/behind-the-scenes-mount-maker-ready-for-an-earthquake.html; http://www.nytimes.com/2003/04/23/arts/behind-the-scenes-mount-maker-ready-for-an-earthquake.html?pagewanted=print&src=pm

9. "Protecting Treasures on a Shaky Planet," Carol Kino; http://www.nytimes.com/2008/03/12/arts/artsspecial/12seismic.html?pagewanted=print&_r=0

10. "Earthquakes and Art Preservation: A View from the San Andreas Fault," *Science of the Total Environment*, Vol. 56, Nov. 15, 1986, pp. 401-410; http://www.sciencedirect.com/science/article/pii/0048969786903438

In the same paper, Dr. Shapira also wrote:

> In our studies related to seismic controls we worked *in close collaboration with* Quantech Systems office of Sherman Oaks, California. Test of our proposals were [sic] carried out in Culver City at the facilities of ANCO Engineers. (p. 407, emphasis added.)

And on another page of the same paper, he wrote:

> This modular system of environmental modular components for museum and exhibition displays was designed by International Design and Management Consultants Inc. of Los Angeles *in collaboration with* Quantech System of Sherman Oaks (California). (p. 407, emphasis added.)

Because I did not learn about this article until after the good professor's passing in 2009, I never discussed it with him. I liked and respected Dr. Shapira. Sadly, however, I have to state categorically that he was not involved in developing the base isolation system for art objects with my company, Quantech Systems Inc., or me.

It pains me to close this JPGM chapter on a sour note because I have great memories of my association with many wonderful individuals there that I will cherish always. It is unfortunate that the insatiable greed of some there has stained the reputation of a great institution where I had some of my most gratifying experiences, including the early studies for the new Getty Center in Brentwood.

The Getty Center in Brentwood

In late 1983, shortly after I began working with JPGM, I was also retained by the Getty Trust to perform preliminary site reconnaissance studies for the newly announced Getty Center in Brentwood, near UCLA, so the Trust could obtain a conditional use permit prior to selecting the project architect.

At first, I reported directly to Nancy Englander, the Director of Programs for Planning and Analysis of the proposed Getty Center at the Getty Trust offices, and later to Stephen Roundtree, who moved from JPGM to the Trust's offices, then in Century City, to direct the new project. Timothy Whalen, who was working from the Trust's Santa Monica offices, was also heavily involved.

I prepared computerized drawings of the property that were utilized as a baseline to calculate and visualize various site grading configurations. The mathematical model was also utilized to evaluate the visual impact of the proposed development on the neighborhood and the seasonal sun-angles orientation for optimum landscaping designs.

I also performed a geosciences reconnaissance survey of the proposed site to determine its feasibility for the proposed project. The study showed that the site was suitable, with the caveat that the main geologic feature of the site, the Benedict Canyon Fault, which was classified as "inactive," could potentially influence the response of the site to earthquakes significant to the Getty Center. The fault zone that traverses the site is approximately 75 feet wide and consists of fractured rocks and gouge material.

IN 1984, AFTER RICHARD MEIER had been selected as the project architect, a meeting was held at the Getty Trust offices in Century City to review the results of my studies. On the day of the presentation, a white-haired man strode confidently into the room and was introduced by Steve Roundtree as Richard Meier. He glanced at the large sheets of computerized drawings and arrogantly announced, "I work with physical models only." His statement brought the presentation session to an abrupt end, and, having nothing else to talk about, he walked out with the same confident stride.

Steve, with his usual kind manner, looked at me and we both shrugged in puzzlement.

I said, "Well, that's that, Steve. Please let me know if there's anything else that I can do." To which Steve responded, "We'll see how it goes," and we agreed to keep in touch.

FINALLY, THE GETTY IMAGES LIBRARY collections were stored in relatively thin air-tight briefcase-shaped boxes on rows and rows of flat metal shelves and were thus vulnerable to sliding out by earthquake-induced shaking. I recommended a simple and inexpensive solution—tilting the back edges of the movable shelves and covering the shelves with antiskid material so the boxes would slide toward the back of the shelves rather than forward. It was gratifying to see the tilted shelves in the JPGM bookstore shortly after I had offered my recommendations.

One further note regarding the Getty Center: in response to the 1994 Northridge Earthquake, the welded joints of the steel frames under construction at the Getty Center developed stress cracks. No technical reports were produced by the Trust regarding specifics of the nonlinear behavior of the structures, which purportedly had been designed to respond adequately to a 7.5+ magnitude seismic event on the San Andreas Fault.

Although steel-frame structures in the San Fernando Valley also exhibited cracking at joints during the same seismic event, the cracks at the Getty Center were puzzling to me because, unlike the Valley structures, which were supported on thick alluvial soils susceptible to magnifying earthquake shaking, the Getty Center buildings are supported on relatively competent rock formations ideal for ductile structural systems. Until proven otherwise by geophysical studies at the site, it is plausible that the seventy-five-foot-wide fracture zone created by the Benedict Canyon Fault crossing the site adversely modified the propagating seismic waves generated by the Northridge Earthquake.

Chapter 26

PATHS TO THE PRESENT

THROUGHOUT THE 1980S, concurrently with the Blackhawk, JPGM, and Getty Center projects, I was also engaged in a number of projects for other museums and corporations, in addition to pursuing my interest in law and alternative dispute resolution.

The Los Angeles County Museum of Art (LACMA)

What became a series of ongoing studies for LACMA began after the magnitude 5.9 Whittier Narrows Earthquake of October 1, 1987, when I contacted other museums in California, including LACMA, to introduce the new earthquake protection systems that I had devised for Getty.

My initial contacts at LACMA were Dr. Pieter Meyers, the head of conservation, and Steve Colton, the head of the conservation laboratory, who was later replaced by John Hirx.

Because I had reviewed the soils and geologic reports for a proposed Los Angeles Metro station near the museum in 1983 while at LRA, I had first-hand information about the subsurface conditions underlying the site. The tar-soaked deposits there create a complex set of problems regarding the site response to earthquakes significant to the area.

Pieter and Steve agreed that the first order of earthquake protection for LACMA should be site characterization studies to establish design and evaluation parameters. I submitted a proposal for the site evaluation, and as mentioned earlier, later became engaged in earthquake protection of its collection. My work with LACMA is ongoing as of the publication of this book.

Compared to JPGM, LACMA is an island of tranquility. Located in the busy mid-Wilshire area, it is easily accessible and offers a casual and welcoming environment for Angelenos to visit the museum and enjoy its collections, which are housed in several buildings. The museum exhibits modern and classic art from many different cultures and countries. Special temporary exhibits, as varied as the region's ethnic population, are frequently featured there.

Although my association with LACMA started with earthquake mitigation measures, it has since expanded and includes a variety of systems that require engineering input to augment LACMA's in-house capabilities. I enjoy acting in the capacity of ad hoc LACMA resident engineer on call. Monetary matters are strictly secondary and are considered only after a problem has been identified and solved and is ready to be implemented. As such, an informal working relationship has been created where LACMA feels free to call me to discuss or evaluate a specific item or situation. It is a pleasure for me to go to LACMA and spend time with my friends there even if there are no specific matters that may need my input.

Of course, like other large organizations, LACMA also has its share of internal politics and interdepartmental idiosyncrasies that surface from time to time. However, these have never risen to the level of backstabbing and constant cunning that I had observed elsewhere.

A number of LACMA's sculptures are protected by the QS Glider isolators. None of the Gliders are anchored to the floors, and they are easily dismantled to accommodate storage or the rearranging of galleries.

The critical subject of studies to evaluate LACMA's seismic setting and the potential risk to the growing organization that I initiated some years ago is still an ongoing concern that needs to be addressed. LACMA's sprawling campus is located relatively close to the active Newport-Inglewood Fault and a trace of the Hollywood Fault. As mentioned earlier, the tar-soaked sands of the La Brea Tar Pits that underlie the area further complicate the situation. Trapped gas in the formation causes the tar to seep to the surface. This is visible in the nearby pond, which features replicas of prehistoric wildlife.

In addition to providing consulting services to art museums in California, predominantly in Southern California, I also consulted with museums in other states and in countries such as Armenia and Japan.

Activities in Engineering and Law

Engineering services to museums were only a fraction of QS's unique projects. Others were unrelated to art and required my travel to locations halfway around the world.

One such project, which overlapped with my development of the JPGM base isolation system, was in connection with the North Rankin "A"

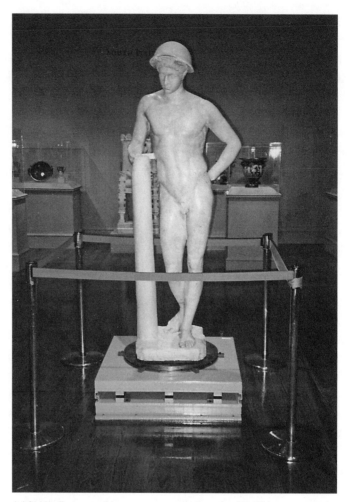

LACMA's Bateman Mercury, supported on the QS Glider, as seen in
the video, "Aphrodite & QS Glider," which can be viewed at:
http://www.quantechsystems.com/gallery/

offshore platform located northwest of Karratha on the Australian Conti-
nental Shelf and managed by Chevron USA.

Detailed site characterization studies for the installation of the platform
at sea with water depths in excess of 400 feet, performed earlier by an international geosciences firm, had overestimated the load-bearing capacity
of the natural formation to support the platform. During the installation
of the 300-foot-long piles, very little driving resistance was encountered in
the calcareous sands present at the site. Different pile configurations to compensate for the low friction resistance of calcarenite formation were recommended by members of academia from several universities in Australia and

Europe. However, the common thread in the earlier analysis was the lack of a clear understanding of the engineering properties and behavior of calcareous sands subjected to stresses beyond the normal loads considered in the field of geosciences. Within a low range of applied loads, calcareous sands look like and behave like silica or quartz sands. But extrapolating laboratory tests performed on calcareous samples to higher load levels provides misleading design values.

Chevron USA retained QS to evaluate the behavior of the material encountered at the site and to formulate design parameters for piles that would resist uplift forces during major storms there. Although I had encountered a similar situation on the Tidewater project in the Persian Gulf in the mid-1960s, little further research had been carried out beyond what I had known then regarding the behavior of calcarenites subjected to large stresses. Based on my QS physical model, Dr. Joel Sweet developed the numerical code to calculate the "crushup" parameters of calcareous sands and the accompanying volume changes as input for finite element analysis. The findings were presented to Chevron USA during a meeting in Holland.

Dr. Richard Goodman and Dr. Ron Scott, acting in a review capacity, were also team members. The details of the studies and recommendations were presented in a pioneering QS report of June 1984.

As MUCH AS I FOUND ENGINEERING ASSIGNMENTS challenging and invigorating, matters related to the resolution of disputes between opposing parties were equally fascinating to me. Generally, if opposing parties are unable to settle their dispute amicably, they submit their grievances to a third party to settle. Most common forums for resolving disputes related to engineering matters are courts of legal jurisdiction where parties file complaints known as "lawsuits" to be litigated either in a "bench trial" in front of a judge, or in a "jury trial," in which a judge presides and a jury arrives at the verdict.

A second option is alternative dispute resolution (ADR), in which the parties agree to have their dispute judged by a single neutral party or by a tribunal consisting of three neutrals.

I feel fortunate to have participated in both trials and ADR proceedings for many years. For ADR proceedings, I have acted as mediator, arbitrator, and umpire. I have also testified as an expert witness for both plaintiffs and defendants in many trials with substantial engineering components. Based on my experience and observations, I believe that in cases related to engineering and technical matters, our system of jurisprudence is somewhat flawed. Although not so stated in the US Constitution, it is generally held that "a jury of one's peers" decides cases in court proceedings. That view was further modified by reasoning that since all people are equal, therefore we are all peers of one another and that the only requirement is for the jurors to be impartial. That means that anyone who appears "impartial" can qualify for jury duty.

I believe that bench trials and ADR proceedings offer a greater chance of a fair resolution for the parties, especially in cases where technical issues are the critical evidentiary facts to be considered. It is more effective to present technical facts to a judge or to an arbitrator than to a jury of twelve who are usually not familiar with the charts and graphs presented by engineers in support of their testimony.

By mid-1993, I had mediated, arbitrated, and umpired several cases for the American Arbitration Association and for private referrals when my friend Ardashes's youngest son, Varouj (Var) Yerganian, got in touch with me. He had been working for an ADR organization called Judicate in New York and had been transferred to a new branch office opened by the CEO in Newport Beach, California. A few months later, the CEO was implicated in unpublicized alleged wrongdoings that led to his detention by local California authorities. The arrest caused the firm to cease its operations.

In a meeting with Var and his coworker, Alan Brutman, at the closed Judicate office, I recommended that they buy Judicate's tangible assets, mainly used office furniture, and any goodwill value that might have survived the debunked firm. They agreed, and I helped to draw up a contract for them to take over Judicate's operations in Orange County that was accepted by the accused CEO.

The new entity was renamed Judicate West, with Var owning 51 percent and Alan 49 percent of the new firm's shares. As a result of the new owners' hard work, within a short time Judicate West began to grow, and it established itself as an ADR firm to be reckoned with by its competitors in Southern California.

The 1994 Northridge Earthquake

At 4:31 a.m. on January 17, 1994, I was awakened by a strong jolt followed by seemingly eternal violent shaking that made all hell break loose in our vintage 1936 single-story Mediterranean-style house in Sherman Oaks. Although I had experienced many real earthquakes and had ridden on shake tables that simulated large earthquakes before, this shaking felt nothing like the garden-variety tremors often felt in many parts of California.

I had heard of but had never experienced the heightening of the human senses brought about by extreme shock and anxiety, which amplifies every little sound and exaggerates images of uncontrollable events happening all around. I jumped out of my bed but could hardly maintain my footing as the large, heavy mirrors and pictures hanging on our walls flew from their hooks and crashed on the floor with sharp, broken glass ricocheting every which way.

The moonlight entering through our wide-open and still swinging windows further dramatized the eerie scene. The cool, damp morning breeze entering the room made the curtains billow as if a long-neglected haunted mansion was being subjected to the rage of the resident ghosts. I heard the small, delicate, antique front doorknocker pounding chaotically, as if someone was trying to break down the door with a sledgehammer.

Then suddenly everything was quiet.

As I tiptoed through the shattered glass littering the floor, I felt a warm liquid running down the back of my leg. A large piece of flying glass had plunged into my right thigh. When I reached down to pull it out, the sharp edges cut my hand.

The quake had caused a power outage, and in the dark I could not see the damage that had produced the horrific noise. Lynn, wisely, had stayed in bed, and after the shaking stopped she was able to tend to my wound as I held a flashlight on it. I reached under the bed, pulled out the earthquake kit, and turned on the battery-powered radio. There were reports of large fires in the San Fernando Valley caused by ruptured underground gas lines and of gushing fire hydrants shooting water into the air. The Caltech Seismological Laboratory's initial estimate was a 6.8 magnitude earthquake on an unknown fault in the general area of the 1971 San Fernando Earthquake's epicenter. The shaking that had seemed to last for several minutes had actually gone on for less than sixty seconds.

The earthquake shook the San Fernando Valley and other random areas of Los Angeles County. Severe damage occurred in Northridge and Sherman Oaks. When dawn came, I saw the heavy damage that the earthquake had caused to our house. The brick chimney had collapsed entirely, the ceilings and the walls exhibited wide cracks, and the footings supporting the floors were dislocated. Fortunately, we were fine. The structural damage was reparable and the household items replaceable.

My resolution following the trauma was to develop base isolation systems for residences—not only to minimize earthquake damage to buildings but also to eliminate, to the greatest extent possible, the horrifying experience of major seismic events. For example, people can continue to suffer from "posttraumatic stress," and even sudden loud noises or slight vibrations, such as those caused by passing trucks, can make them panic-stricken.

ALTHOUGH NOT A GREAT SEISMIC EVENT, the Northridge Earthquake nevertheless was unique in terms of the pattern and extent of propagating waves never recorded before. It also damaged structures that had been designed in accordance with building codes developed after the 1971 San Fernando Earthquake. This debunked many forecasts and theories regarding the ground response to earthquakes and the earthquake design of structures that had been advanced with great fanfare twenty-three years earlier.

The observed damage caused by the Northridge Earthquake solidified my long-held belief regarding the incompatibility and inefficiency of low- to medium-strength reinforced concrete used in the construction of "life-lines" such as electrical power lines, gas and liquid fuels, telecommunications, transportation, waste disposal, and water supply lines. I believe that reinforced concrete elements constructed of high-strength concrete (a crushing strength of 20,000 psi and above) would substantially decrease the dimensions of the structural elements required and thus the overall dead load of massive structures—whose inertia alone accounts for the largest percentage of earthquake-induced stresses to be resisted.

The damage caused by the Northridge Earthquake was so vast that insurance companies transferred adjusters—most of them with no experience in evaluating and assessing earthquake losses—from other states. It seemed that adjusters were given only a "crash course" before being dispatched to assess the damages. The buzzwords most often used by imported adjusters to categorize observed apparent damages were "cosmetic" and "preexisting." The fact that most people file their policies without ever reading or understanding their loss coverage created a robust atmosphere for disputes between the parties as well as equally robust opportunities for lawyers to get involved.

The common dispute between parties came down to the insured wanting "the whole world" and the insurer trying to pay as little as possible by pointing to vague coverage language that seemed to cover a certain item on one page and exclude it altogether on another page of the same policy.

There was also a great deal of confusion regarding the safety of the damaged dwellings. The building and safety departments of the various municipalities all had ways of tagging buildings to classify them from "safe to occupy" to "condemn."

The adjuster assigned to my house was a young man from Kansas City who, after learning that I was an earthquake engineer, handed me all three categories of tags, told me, "You decide which tag you want to post," and estimated the loss at my policy limit.

I prepared a technical report and obtained the construction permit to repair our damaged dwelling. Lynn was in charge of architectural features while I supervised the construction. The remodeling of homes has always been a major factor in causing serious friction and rifts between couples, and during the two years that ours took, Lynn and I did not escape the curse of remodeling.

During that period, I also held ADR hearings for Judicate West and private referrals related to disputes between insurers and the insured. I also helped many of my friends and family members who had sustained varying degrees of earthquake damage. I prepared engineering reports that assessed the losses and made recommendations for appropriate fixes, of course at no charge. Substantially all of my reports submitted to insurers were accepted. Sincere gratitude for my help was all I needed as my compensation. It was very satisfying to see people's damaged residences repaired and retrofitted to withstand future quakes, and their lives return to normal.

Seeing the recipients of my help looking to the future with a brighter outlook provided me with instant gratification. There are instances when rewards are returned in the most mysterious and unexpected ways, and this gives a lot of credence to a poetic old Persian prophesy that translates as "Discard your good deeds in the river Nile, for someday God will return it all." Little did I know that this saying would come true for me unexpectedly and in a big way!

In 1996, Lynn and I returned to our repaired and remodeled house. By then my widowed mother was depending on me more and more. Christina was living in San Mateo and had given birth to my first grandson, Matthew, who was born with Down syndrome. David was completing his doctoral studies in Middle Eastern History at UC Berkeley. The adverse events had taken their toll on Lynn and me, but I did not think that in the long run the situation was unsalvageable.

My work schedule had left time for me to get back to my woodworking hobby, which I had stopped during the renovations of our house. While making decorative wood items for the garden and house, I was also thinking about earthquake isolation systems for residential buildings. My plans were to buy a vacant property on which to construct the first single-story house supported on a base isolator with a cut-off corner section that would allow the isolator and its components to be viewed for show-and-tell purposes.

Ominous Clouds on the Horizon

In late September 1996, related to business and respite, I made flight reservations to attend a meeting in New York regarding Japan's Miho Museum, designed by I. M. Pei, and from there to meet my friend, Ardashes, and his oldest son, Gary, also a civil engineer. We would then drive to Vermont to enjoy the annual fall foliage festival during the second week of October.

The night before my departure, I went to bed earlier than usual. I woke up the next morning and noticed that Lynn's side of the bed was untouched. Not thinking anything of it, I showered and went to the kitchen for breakfast. Afterward, when I still had not seen any sign of Lynn, I got concerned about her and looked through the other rooms and the garage. Her car was not there, and she was nowhere to be found. During my search, I found bizarre telltale signs that indicated that she had left the house in a state of panic and anxiety.

I called Christina, who said she was unaware of Lynn's whereabouts. Whatever the reason for her disappearance, it was absolutely uncharacteristic of her actions during our thirty-three-year marriage. I was clueless as to what could have caused her unexplained behavior. She had left no note about where she was going.

Her sudden disappearance that morning, although puzzling, did not seem serious enough for me to file a missing person report with Los Angeles Police Department. Having not much time left for my flight, I drove to LAX and flew to New York. During the five-hour flight, I could not think of any scenario that would explain her irrational action. What was baffling was that I had never threatened her or acted violently or in any way that would have led her to run away or be fearful of me.

Lynn was not a timid person by nature. When she was only twenty-two, she had taken a bold risk and traveled alone halfway around the world, from Chicago to Tehran, to marry me. She had taken that trip although she had no knowledge of the Middle East or of what the future might have for her in the strange land and culture when she married me.

Throughout our married life, we had an amicable marriage free of financial worries that had provided with her desired option of being a stay-at-home mom. We had two wonderful children with whom we spent summers on Catalina Island, at various beach camps, and in Hawaii. During winter school breaks, the family skied in Northern California. After the children left home to attend college, we took annual vacations in different parts of Europe, with Switzerland our favorite vacation destination.

(Left to right) Gary Yerganian, Christina, Lynn, and me
skiing at Northstar, Lake Tahoe

Like most married couples, we also had our share of disagreements and did not see eye to eye on every issue. After all, as John Gray titled his 1992 bestseller, *Men Are from Mars, Women Are from Venus*.[1]

Regardless of the troubles brewing at home, the Vermont visit with Ardashes could not have come at a better time. The fall foliage was truly magnificent. The hills looked as if they were covered with colorful Persian carpets, the shades and patterns of which were in constant flux from hour to hour and day after day. The visit to Vermont made the surreal events in Sherman Oaks feel like a bad dream that kept phasing in and out of my consciousness. Soon it was time for me to fly back home.

---

1. John Gray, *Men Are from Mars, Women Are from Venus: A Practical Guide for Improving Communication and Getting What You Want in Your Relationships* (New York, NY: HarperCollins, 1992).

With Ardashes, my childhood friend, in Vermont

I was apprehensive about what to expect once I returned to my house. When the taxi from LAX stopped out in front, I paid the driver and walked to the front door. The outside air was still and there were no lights on inside. I opened the front door and entered the dark, cold, and empty house where nothing had changed since I had left for New York. The scene was sad and depressing. The mail had spilled out of the mailbox and was scattered on the entry floor. The strong smell of fresh paint and floor varnish made the place feel strange and unwelcoming.

This was a far cry from the days when I would return home from business trips and be welcomed by my wife, the screaming children, and our big, excited German shepherd all vying for my attention. The dinner table would be set, and familiar smells would let me know that my favorite Armenian dishes were cooking in the kitchen. The children would wait anxiously for the souvenirs that I always brought back from my travels because of the old Persian custom of *soghatie*, which means "souvenir" and conveys to the loved ones left behind that they were never far from the traveler's mind.

As the days lingered on, my most agonizing chore became answering questions from friends about Lynn's whereabouts. My honest answer, "I don't know," did not seem to be a satisfactory explanation and was interpreted as my not wanting to talk about it. The fact was that I truly did not know.

IN THE FIRST WEEK OF JANUARY 1997, separation papers filed by Lynn were delivered to our residence. The document had two unchecked boxes, one for separation and the other for dissolution of marriage. Not interested in pursuing the matter any further, I marked the box asking for dissolution of our marriage. This set the stage for the legal proceeding regarding the distribution of assets. The court ordered that the Sherman Oaks house be sold and its proceeds and all other assets divided equally between us. The house was put on the market, and I moved to a small apartment nearby.

After the Northridge Earthquake, many homeowners had sold their drastically devalued homes and moved to other states. This caused the collapse of the Southern California housing market. After several months, our house sold at a fraction of its pre-earthquake valuation. To be forced to vacate a longtime home, every corner of which was filled with fond memories and items, was a very unpleasant task. Nothing seemed to matter any longer. Rows and rows of treasured reference books, periodicals, files, reports, and other materials that I had been keeping for posterity were carted to a large dumpster to be taken to the city dump.

For a moment, my father's escape from the Kurds who were killing my grandparents and burning their village, forcing him to abandon his home with only the shirt on his back, flashed before my eyes. I wondered, was history repeating itself half way around the world? "No, it is not," I concluded, and told myself, "Stop the self-pity and get on with the rest of your life!" That gave me a renewed determination to look forward to the future.

I set up my office furniture in the living room of the apartment and continued tending my business from there. I held many ADR hearings in my new place and continued consulting services to museums. While I kept myself occupied during business hours and days, the weekends were long and boring.

The only bright spot was my friend, Shahen, who had gone through his own divorce several years before. On weekends we would meet at Orange County malls, talk about past projects we had done together, and laugh at old, rehashed jokes. And although I looked forward to my friends' dinners and parties, I found these both enjoyable and awkward. For one thing, I was always reminded that I was no longer part of a couple—and I also sensed that my friends felt sorry for me and were trying to find some compatible female companions for me.

IN MAY 1997, I ATTENDED AN elaborate wedding where I sat at a table with my buddies and their spouses. There was loud Armenian music and energetic dancing that grew louder and louder as more liquor was consumed. The noise was making it impossible to carry on meaningful conversation with those at my table. Also, being a nondrinker, I was uninterested in the clapping and jumping up and down, and annoyed by being grabbed by my arm to join the giddy dancers, so I decided to walk away from the noise and give my overtaxed ears some relief.

In the lobby area, I saw Rubina Begoomian, one of my former Girl Scouts from Tehran, who had catered and organized the wedding. I said hello and after some small talk asked her, "How is the business?"

"Very busy," she said. "I'm booked every weekend for weddings until August. The last one is for Zareh, Lilit Marzbetuny's son whom you may know."

The name was not familiar to me, so I said, "I don't know her, but I'm glad that your business is thriving," and I wished her good luck.

Ignoring my good wishes, she asked, "You don't know Lilit Bassentzian?"

I said, "Of course I know Lilit Bassentzian. I didn't know that her married name is Marzbetuny. She's a very nice person, and I knew her parents. Please say hello to her for me." I then added, "Good to see you, Rubina," and decided to go home.

Driving home, I thought it was unbelievable that Lilit had a son old enough to get married. The last time I had seen her was in 1961 when she and Andre had taken me to LAX for my flight back to Tehran after I had finished my studies at U of I.

A Poetic Prophecy Comes True

One evening a couple of weeks after the wedding, I received a telephone call from a caller whose voice I recognized instantly. When the caller asked if I knew who was calling, I replied, "Of course I do. Nice to hear your voice, Lilit."

That phone conversation lasted four hours. During it, I learned that her parents had passed away in the early 1970s and that soon afterward her husband, Gevork Marzbetuny, had fallen ill in India while directing a movie and passed away upon returning to the United States. Their two sons, Vahe and Zareh, were about the same ages as Christina and David. She told me how proud she was of her little brother, Aram, who had graduated from UC Berkeley and was a successful architect in Orange County.

We talked and laughed a lot about the year that Andre and I had spent at Pepperdine University and about their engagement party and my being their best man. We had different recollections of the 1960 New Year's Eve in Chicago, but we both remembered our double date that evening vividly, and that Andre drove my 1953 Chevy with Lilit at his side and I had been in the back seat with Lynn. The whole conversation went on as if the three-decade gap had never happened.

It was 11 p.m. when Lilit said, "I called you to invite you to my younger son Zareh's wedding in August," and asked my address to mail me the invitation. I gave it to her and said, "If you're not in a relationship, perhaps we could have dinner and continue where we left off tonight." Lilit said she was not in any relationship and that it would be fun to get together. We set a date and she agreed to pick the restaurant for our dinner.

On the day of our date, which was only a couple of days after our long telephone conversation, I drove to her house in a gated area of Los Feliz adjacent to LA's Griffith Park. When I pulled up in front of her house, the front door opened and Lilit walked down the front stairs. I got out of my car, went toward her, and gave my long-lost friend a big hug and a kiss on her cheek. She had not changed at all and was as beautiful as ever.

As we drove through the gate and made a right turn on Los Feliz Boulevard, I had to stop at the first traffic light, which had turned red. I glanced over at her and without saying a word I decided there and then, "I will not let her go." During dinner, we continued our conversation where we had left off on the phone. The big difference was that I did not have to imagine what the person on the other end of the line looked like. There she was with all her grace and beauty unchanged. Also unchanged was her soft and kind manner, which I had always admired about her so long ago.

At the end of the night, while we were waiting for the valet to bring my car, I told her "We shouldn't wait for formal dinner dates. Whenever you feel like it, call me and we can grab a hamburger." We drove back to her house and I walked her to her door, where we said good-bye with her promise that she would call me when she felt like having hamburgers.

I knew her well, but not well enough to interpret her statement, "I will call you when I feel like having hamburgers." Her promise could have had different interpretations, including the possibility of my never seeing her again. But at least I was assured of seeing her one more time, and that was Zareh's wedding in August, just three short months away.

But my concerns about not seeing Lilit again melted away because we had hamburgers together less than twenty-four hours after our first formal dinner. From then on, we met every day, and not necessarily for hamburgers. The bond between the two of us grew ever stronger as we learned about our compatibility regarding our beliefs, our love of family, and all of the other characteristics that would let us live together forever. As one of our physicians said, we were truly "two peas in a pod."

I met Lilit's boys and had fun-filled dinners at her place where the older brother, Vahe, would make fun of Zareh for ending his freedom by proposing to his girlfriend, Armineh. At Zareh's wedding, I met the rest of Lilit's relatives and friends. In December, we attended David's wedding to his bride,

Jen, at Berkeley. My children grew so fond of Lilit that they constantly reminded me not to do anything foolish to derail our beautiful relationship.

On September 25, 1999, Lilit and I were married at her brother Aram's home. He was my best man, and his wife, Terez, was Lilit's matron of honor. Our only other guests were our children and their spouses.

During the wedding dinner, I stressed the virtues of kindness and helping people in need as expressed in the poetic Persian prophecy that had come true for me in such a big way.

ONE DAY ARAM POINTED OUT that under Lilit's pretty face was a sharp and capable businesswoman who by herself alone had provided the best of everything for her two sons. Through her two companies, she provides fire suppression services for thousands of clients in food businesses throughout the western United States.

Soon after Zareh's and Armineh's wedding, Vahe married the lovely Zaruhi. Since then, the two couples have blessed us with three grandchildren—Zareh and Armineh's son, Davite, and Vahe and Zaruhi's two daughters, Ava and Ella. Combined with Christina's three sons, Matthew, Grant, and Daniel, we have six grandchildren.

Lilit and I moved to a condominium in Toluca Lake a short distance from her office, which is also my base for continuing to provide consulting services. We are blessed to have a great circle of friends and family whom we see and visit regularly. Our grandchildren give us the joy of watching them grow and mature in their individual ways.

We enjoy traveling to Armenia as frequently as possible and we vacation in Europe. Lilit's one and only complaint is my 4:30 a.m. trips to the gym every other weekday morning. She joins me there a half-hour later for her own workout, after which she is glad that my routine provides her the necessary encouragement to work out regularly.

Breakfast is our favorite time of day, when we discuss various never-ending topics of interest with one constant reminder at the end: "We have to get on with making plans and reservations for our next trip."

Lilit's and my wedding photo: (seated, front row left to right) Terez Bassenian, Lilit, me, Aram Bassenian; (second row, seated on sofa arms) Tallenne Bassenian and Greg Bassenian; (standing, left to right) David and Jen Yaghoubian, Vahe and Zaruhi Marzbetuny, Christina and John Hillman, Armineh and Zareh Marzbetuny

POSTSCRIPT

ON "WE THE PEOPLE"
in Twenty-First Century America

ON "WE THE PEOPLE"
in Twenty-First Century America

WHEN I TOOK THE OATH to become a US citizen on September 26, 1969, the judge presiding over the ceremony quoted the opening words of the US Constitution, "We the people of the United States..," and also referred to President Dwight D. Eisenhower's farewell address about the importance of "an alert and knowledgeable citizenry." Those phrases stuck in my mind, and I promised myself that I would read the Constitution as soon as possible and learn about the beginnings of the American experiment.

Some time passed without my doing this, but learning about the Constitution became a necessity when I started my law studies. One afternoon, I decided to prepare for the intensive effort by clearing off an entire bookcase shelf to make room for the volumes that I thought contained it. I then went to the nearest bookstore and began searching the legal section looking for the many volumes of leather-bound books embossed with "The United States Constitution" in gold lettering on their spine.

When I could not find them, I marched over to the female clerk and asked whether they were sold out of copies of the Constitution.

"I don't believe so," she replied. "Did you look in the law section?"

"Well, I wasn't looking in the children's book section," I replied sarcastically.

I followed her back to the legal section, where she pulled out a thin hardcover volume, thrust it into my hands with obvious annoyance, and stalked off. At first, I thought she was paying me back for my sarcasm. Then I looked at the cover and read, *The Constitution of the United States of America*, with the Great Seal of the United States below it, both embossed in gold.

I could not believe my eyes. The book was only thirty pages long—scarcely more than a pamphlet! "Is this it?" I mumbled to myself as I grabbed ten copies and took them to the counter. The clerk eyed them, smiled, and said, "That will be twenty dollars including tax."

Walking home with the paper bag of booklets under my arm, I wondered whether the clerk had thought I was an idiot for not knowing what the US Constitution actually looked like. But I later realized that very few people, whether born in the US or having immigrated, have actually seen it, much less read it. Over the years, I used to give copies of it to my children and friends as Christmas presents.

Then, with my usual curiosity, I began to read it. The sentences being brief and sometimes ambiguous, I concluded that it must have been the product of an immense amount of discussion, deliberation, and argument among its framers, who had signed their names in Article VII as follows:

> The Ratification of the Conventions of nine States shall be sufficient for the Establishment of this Constitution between the States so ratifying the Same.

> Done in Convention by the Unanimous Consent of the States present the Seventeenth Day of September in the Year of our Lord one thousand seven hundred and Eighty seven and of the Independence of the United States of America the Twelfth.

> In Witness whereof We have hereunto subscribed our Names...[1]

Although I never doubted that the United States of America was a Christian nation, in my view Article VII substantiated that fact. I believed that the Constitution's framers were wise men and did not want to leave any ambiguity regarding the new country's religion.

These framers, with their immense worldly knowledge, were aware that different nations had created different calendars that had their beginnings in important past events and cultural concepts such as the births of prophets (in Christian and Arab societies), the crowning of kings (in Persia), the establishment of new dynasties (in modern Iran), and lunar and solar astrology (in China).

In light of the above, it is abundantly clear that, if the US Constitution's framers intended to establish a "state religion" for their new nation in which all religions and faiths would be equally relevant or irrelevant, they could have introduced a new calendar that began with the nation's first independence day as Year One, Day One.

---

1. http://www.archives.gov/exhibits/charters/constitution_zoom_1.html

Instead, they explicitly dated the document with "the Seventeenth Day of September in the Year of our Lord one thousand seven hundred and Eighty seven," followed by phrase "the Independence of the United States of America the Twelfth," thus systematically rejecting "universalism" and confirming that the United States of America was and shall remain true to the Christian faith and traditions.

In addition to my interest in America's national religion, I wanted to learn more and to feel the ambience and the mood that existed during the endless debates and arguments that must have taken place in the process of creating the US Constitution. Whenever I could take time away from my business responsibilities and legal studies, I read the articles and essays by Alexander Hamilton, James Madison, and John Jay in the *The Federalist Papers*, Thomas Paine's *Common Sense*, and other writings related to the principles of the US government, its powers, and interpretations of the Constitution. As a student of the law, I also studied David Barton's *Original Intent, the Courts, the Constitution, & Religion* among other works.[2]

The literature briefly pictured wealthy groups of colonists who owned large parcels of land and imported slaves to develop and cultivate their property. These colonists, along with the intellectuals of the period, eagerly promoted and formed a system of limited government with fresh and untested democratic ideals and with limited power to interfere in citizens' affairs. Thomas Jefferson, the nation's third president, although a keen intellectual, was also a rich man who had personally observed and experienced the possibilities that could be created by the combination of wealth and power, and he strongly believed that such a combination, driven by greed, could undermine the new nation's principles and future.

The more I read, the more I became disillusioned by the political sea changes and shifts in the America of the late twentieth and early twenty-first centuries. The original intent of the American experiment and the vision of the founders that had been brought into being in the eighteenth century were being ignored.

The America that has been my chosen country for the past forty-five years is the embodiment of Jefferson's fears—a land of burgeoning bureaucracies that have created opportunities for the rich to become richer while the poor increasingly lack the resources to lift themselves out of poverty. As I watched, America was fast becoming a country of two distinct and separate populations consisting of "haves" and "have-nots," with a rapidly disappearing middle class.

---

2. David Barton, *Original Intent, the Courts, the Constitution, & Religion* (Aledo, TX: WallBuilder Press, 2008).

Today, the policies and actions of our elected representatives are following the path of selfishness and getting reelected rather than doing what is good for America. The simple and innocent First Amendment clause that allows citizens to petition their government has turned into an ever-growing, uncontrollable, and destructive monster known as "lobbying" that sucks the oxygen out of the nation's ability to achieve freedom and pursuit of happiness envisioned by the founding fathers.

In my mind, nothing better illustrates the reckless disregard for our traditional American values and culture than the destructive lobbying of our Congress by local and foreign interests that began to take root in the late twentieth century.

In centuries past, three visionary American presidents—namely, George Washington, Abraham Lincoln, and Dwight Eisenhower—were victorious in major domestic and global conflicts that shaped the future not only of America but also of the entire world for the better. In their eternal wisdom, they issued caveats about protecting and preserving the independence of the republic.

On the eve of pending critical and major battles, all three of the above named presidents must have prayed hard that God would keep America forever safe and free of internal and external evil.

And if an opera were ever to be written about our presidents' private prayers on the nights before the battles that they had to lead at sunrise, their words would have most likely resembled the simple, elegant lyrics of Irving Berlin's "God Bless America" (which he gifted to the Boy Scouts and Girl Scouts of America).

Every president since the founding of the nation has, before leaving office or passing away, sternly warned future generations to avoid potential disasters that could irreparably harm the US and its system of government.

For example, in George Washington's farewell address, he cautioned against attachments with other nations, stating, "'Tis our true policy to steer clear of permanent Alliances, with any portion of the foreign world."[3]

However, in this twenty-first century, America is ignoring his warning and maintaining more than thirty alliances with foreign nations. The influence of foreign interests has neutralized American foreign policy and resulted in staggering losses of blood and treasure, to the point that our government is unable to maintain and improve existing infrastructure and crucial power, water distribution, gas, and other "lifelines" crucial to the nation.

3. http://www.pbs.org/georgewashington/milestones/farewell_address_read4.html

In the nineteenth century, Abraham Lincoln reiterated the words of the preamble to the Constitution in his Gettysburg Address by declaring that "... government of the people, by the people, for the people, shall not perish from the earth."[4]

And on January 7, 1961, President Eisenhower, commander of the Allied forces during World War II, said in his farewell address: "In the councils of government, we must guard against the acquisition of unwarranted influence, whether sought or unsought, by the military-industrial complex. The potential for the disastrous rise of misplaced power exists and will persist."[5]

Just a few years ago, however, the US Supreme Court, in *Citizens United v. Federal Election Commission*, unabashedly ruled that corporations and unions have the same political speech rights as individuals under the First Amendment.[6] In so doing, the Court undermined the bedrock of American democracy so eloquently declared by Lincoln, and in effect stopped whatever was left of our traditional system of government dead in its tracks as well as desecrating the memory of those who gave their lives in the Civil War.

Again, despite Eisenhower's stern warnings, the military-industrial complex has become an impregnable force capable of exerting enormous influence over the US Congress and absorbing huge portions of the federal budget—and there is no change visible for the foreseeable future.

Ignoring the warnings of our past presidents has resulted in increased poverty in America and the disenfranchisement of large segments of the population who are subjected 24/7 to the barrage of words and propaganda spewing from the mouths of both politicians and pundits.

Perhaps, in the eyes of people outside the US, America is the "shining city upon a hill" mentioned by President Ronald Reagan in his 1988 farewell address.[7] However, at the bottom ranges of this imaginary hill, millions of American children go to bed hungry each night and exist in a state of desperation with only dim prospects for their future.

This is not the America that used to feed the world and reached halfway around the globe to save and feed orphans like my parents. The gap between rich and poor is widening with frightening speed—all caused by excessive greed, selfishness, and the total disregard for the welfare of Americans. The middle class, the bedrock of the American family life since the turn of the nineteenth century, is fast disappearing and will not be reestab-

4. http://www.abrahamlincolnonline.org/lincoln/speeches/gettysburg.htm
5. http://www.ourdocuments.gov/doc.php?flash=true&doc=90
6. http://www.scotusblog.com/case-files/cases/citizens-united-v-federal-election-commission/
7. http://www.pbs.org/wgbh/americanexperience/features/primary-resources/reagan-farewell/

lished in the near future. Citizens have given up hope that the present situation will turn around soon, and they have lost faith in their elected representatives—a situation that severely undermines and unbalances our democratic institutions.

IT MAY APPEAR THAT AMERICANS NO LONGER have any mechanism by which "We the People" can be heard and can take part in shaping the affairs of the country—promises that were made by the founding fathers.

However, advances in electronic technologies may be the paths that will once again allow citizens to make their voices heard. The Internet and social media may finally allow Americans to turn the tables and express their views and opinions directly to vote-hungry representatives.

The emphasis throughout most of this book has been on my life and my professional career as an engineer. I made only brief mention of the political and social contexts that were the backdrop to my life in its various stages. One exception was Chapter 11, "Factionalism in the Streets," where I described how my growing up as a member of Iran's Christian minority made me keenly aware of political tensions. I did have limited political leanings that I expressed collectively as much as was allowed in a monarchy.

In the US, on the other hand, politics plays a part in almost all aspects of life, and this has been true for my own professional career. For example, the National Environmental Policy Act (NEPA), discussed in Chapter 20, created an intense political climate nationwide regarding how to meet the future energy demands of US industry. These situations sensitized me to the reality that public opinion was a tool that could make or break proposed major actions that required local, state, and federal approvals. These forms of public involvement included "public hearings" and other "public forums," such as letters written to major publications, that are considered "public opinion."

Public activism was not new to me, but since I had grown up in Iran, expressing my opinion in any public forum was a bit intimidating, to put it mildly. Nevertheless, over time I began responding to articles and editorials in the *Los Angeles Times* on topics ranging from the war in Iraq to earthquakes, world hunger, and the collapse of the Twin Towers in the 9/11 terrorist attacks. A letter about the Twin Towers was also published in 2005 in *Civil Engineering*, the journal of the American Society of Civil Engineers (ASCE).

Most of the letters I submitted were published, and some were actually quoted in subsequent letters written by other readers, thus allowing citizens to take part in a forum that they created rather than being lectured by politicians.

These letters are presented below, and it is truly rewarding to be involved in this kind of dialogue regarding subjects significant to "We the People" individually and collectively through print, electronic, and other available platforms.

My suggestion to readers is therefore: Stay connected and think of the endless possibilities open to you to help yourself advance and to extend a helping hand to those who are not as fortunate as you are. The ominous trends of the twenty-first century will require extraordinary solutions if America's democracy is to survive and thrive.

"We the People" are the best resource that America has to achieve and maintain the greatness of the United States of America!

Letters Published in the Los Angeles Times

My first opportunity to express my opinion took the form of a reply commenting on an August 13, 1999, *Los Angeles Times* editorial, "It's Time for a Fresh Look at Red Line Subway Plan: MTA brings in top soil and geology experts for reassessment."

My reply, which was published on August 25, 1995, read:

∷ Subway Study

Re "It's Time for a Fresh Look at Red Line Subway Plan," editorial, Aug. 13:

As a member of the Board of Special Geotechnical Consultants to the Southern California Rapid Transit District in 1983-84, I can assure you and Mayor Richard Riordan that Los Angeles-area conditions are not "inconsistent" with an underground subway route. The special board that included some of the most eminent geoscientists in the world was specifically organized by the district to address the soils and geologic conditions in the Los Angeles area related to the then-proposed Metro Rail Project.

The seismic and geologic setting of the Los Angeles area is one of the most studied and documented regions of the world. Your comments regarding lack of knowledge of potential strong ground shaking induced by hidden thrust faults before 1994 is grossly inaccurate. Further, this project is not the first underground construction in the Los Angeles area that is crisscrossed by fault zones.

In your editorial you wonder "why soil and geology experts weren't looking more closely at these issues much sooner." A review of the records dating back to the early 1980s would indicate that the problems related to the local soils and geology that were experienced during construction of the subway were indeed identified, studied and documented before even a shovel of soil was turned over or a construction contract awarded.[8]

That first letter to the *Times* was followed by a number of others on different subjects and events. Some of these are presented below, as is my 2005 letter to *Civil Engineering*.

⁜ Unearthing a Wrong Without New Evidence
[Re: The Mel Gibson film, "The Passion of the Christ"]
June 24, 2003

It is becoming quite annoying to be told by non-Christians with relentless zeal that Christians are a bunch of foolhardy and confused folks who do not know right from wrong about their own faith. Hollywood has made many movies that portray other religions in an offensive light to the followers of that faith. In such cases, Hollywood is quick to point out that movies are artistic expressions that are protected by the 1st Amendment and shrug off the criticism by suggesting that people who are offended should not pay to see the movie. People who are offended by Gibson's movie should follow that same advice.

Jack Yaghoubian
Toluca Lake[9]

⁜ Knight on Gay Marriage; S.F. Sues California
February 23, 2004

Re "S.F. Sues State Over Bans on Gay Marriages," Feb. 20: The law of the land is marriage between a man and a woman.

8. http://articles.latimes.com/print/1995-08-25/local/me-38756_1_los-angeles-area-angeles-area-geologic
9. http://articles.latimes.com/print/2003/jun/24/opinion/le-klein24.1

Moreover, there are no laws sanctioning same-sex marriages. By suing the state of California, are gays and lesbians seeking equal protection of the laws or protection from the law?

Jack Yaghoubian
Toluca Lake[10]

⁝⁝ The Battle with Starvation
August 13, 2005

Re "Season of Destruction Returns to Niger," Aug. 7

In my dream, the pro-life president of the US, during a press conference, announced that America, as the strongest and most blessed nation on Earth, is leading a coalition of the willing to occupy the nation of Niger. The president justified the occupation as "our moral obligation to humanity and life." He further stated, "We will not leave Niger until every child is fed and sheltered properly there."

Oh, how wonderful dreams can be!

Jack Yaghoubian
Toluca Lake[11]

⁝⁝ Where Are We Going in Iraq?
September 18, 2006

Your gut-wrenching Sept. 14 front-page image, and the headline "Death Toll Soars in Baghdad," made me wonder: Were those poor Iraqis really worse off before being liberated?

Jack Yaghoubian
Toluca Lake[12]

---

10. http://articles.latimes.com/print/2004/feb/23/opinion/le-kessler23.2
11. http://articles.latimes.com/print/2005/aug/13/opinion/le-saturday13.2
12. http://articles.latimes.com/print/2006/sep/18/opinion/le-monday18.4

⁑ Justices' Reversal of 9th Circuit Ruling
December 15, 2006

Re "Not so fast, 9th Circuit," editorial, Dec. 12

One can only hope that your characterization of the Supreme Court's overturning of the 9th Circuit finding in the San Jose case as "rebuff" and "wrist slapping" is not a factual assessment of how our system of jurisprudence works under any circumstances.

Jack Yaghoubian
Toluca Lake[13]

⁑ Pelosi's Syria Trip Gets Mixed Review
April 5, 2007

There is no sense for President Bush to fault Pelosi for her trip to the Middle East. She did what every mother would do instinctively when she feels the man falls short of meeting his home responsibilities—she took charge of the house!

Jack Yaghoubian
Toluca Lake[14]

⁑ Interesting Move
September 20, 2007

Because the only reaction to the Federal Reserve's rate cut was a soaring stock market, it is safe to say that Chairman Bernanke reacted with "irrational exuberance" to trumpet the dawn of the Bernanke era and to end that of his predecessor, who coined the phrase.

Jack Yaghoubian
Toluca Lake[15]

---

13. http://articles.latimes.com/print/2006/dec/15/opinion/le-friday15.5
14. http://articles.latimes.com/print/2007/apr/05/opinion/le-thursday5.1
15. http://articles.latimes.com/print/2007/sep/20/opinion/le-thuletters20.s3

:: Price of War
April 15, 2008

Re "Blood money," editorial, April 11

Your editorial's convoluted logic is off the mark. Let us face it: President Bush's adopted doctrine of "we are fighting there so that we don't have to fight here" has created the painful reality of "we spent a fortune there and now we don't have much to spend here." Meanwhile, everything else, including our vulnerability to terrorist attacks, remains unchanged.

Jack Yaghoubian
Toluca Lake[16]

:: In Thursday's Letters to the Editor
October 16, 2008

In Thursday's Letters to the Editor, the election conversation continues. Vince Buck, a professor emeritus at Cal State Fullerton, offers another reason opponents might dislike Proposition 11, the redisricting initiative discussed in this George Skelton column and in this news story:

> A more important reason for voting against this poorly-structured proposition is that the cure is worse than the disease.

> ...The process simply will not work, and apportionment will end up with the courts as it did in 1991. Why not just start there and save the state a lot of time and money?

Readers also take issue with Joel Stein's column suggesting that undecided Americans shouldn't vote. Writes Jack Yaghoubian, of Toluca Lake:

> Stein brands the 80 undecided voters seated at last week's town hall-style debate "idiots."

16. http://articles.latimes.com/print/2008/apr/15/opinion/le-tuesday15.S7

...He pontificates, "A high voter turnout doesn't make our democracy work better." In light of the fact that the bedrock of any democracy is the participation of its citizens in the affairs of the country, Stein's statement is what is idiotic.[17]

▪▪ Politics of the Bench
March 14, 2009

Re "We need judges, not partisan fights," Opinion, March 8

Dahlia Lithwick accurately portrays the sorry state of our federal courts. The judicial nomination process has deteriorated into ugly partisan discord unbecoming a civilized nation. Congress is an ideologue body with a pack mentality, unwilling to see matters in colors different from those of its own political interests.

One solution to this gridlock would be for the nominating committees to present a list of competent federal judges to the president, divided equally between the two parties, before sending it to Congress for consent.

This may not work for the Supreme Court justices, but it would go a long way toward helping appoint judges to the lower federal courts, where most of the nation's important legal matters are heard.

Jack Yaghoubian
Toluca Lake[18]

▪▪ Are Earthquake Alerts Worth It?
February 7, 2013

Re "Warning: It's a quake," Editorial, Feb. 3

One of the principal advocates for developing an early earthquake warning system, a geologist in California, once said:

17. http://opinion.latimes.com/opinionla/2008/10/proposition-11.html
18. http://articles.latimes.com/print/2009/mar/14/opinion/le-saturday14.S1

"Earthquakes don't kill people; buildings kill people." In light of that statement, it is disingenuous to ask for state funds to upgrade the existing California Integrated Seismic Network without addressing falling buildings.

Since the Sylmar earthquake in 1971, the state has installed large arrays of strong-motion seismic stations to study earthquake mechanisms and characteristics. But the fact is that the shorter the distance from an active fault, the shorter the arrival time of the seismic waves, and over the last few decades, large population centers have been formed close to major onshore active faults. As such, the proposed earthquake warning system would be mostly ineffective.

As an earthquake engineer, it is my professional opinion that funding such unproven systems would be a waste of scarce funds.

Jack Yaghoubian
Toluca Lake[19]

Predicting Landslides
March 30, 2014

Re "An area primed for disaster," March 28

Unlike earthquakes, landslides like the one in Washington state can be detected, preventing loss of life.

For decades, movements of large sloped land masses have been measured utilizing inclinometers that quantify the magnitude and geometry of soil movements at different depths. The measurements, combined with numerical modeling, produce a three-dimensional imagery of the subsurface soil mass and its directional movements.

To prevent future Hazel Slide disasters, government entities should mandate that developers install monitoring systems that transmit data to the U.S. Geological Survey and state and

19. http://articles.latimes.com/print/2013/feb/07/opinion/la-le-0207-thursday-earthquake-alert-20130207

local survey centers for analysis so any necessary alerts can be issued for evacuations.

Jack Yaghoubian
Toluca Lake

The writer is a licensed professional engineer[20]

∷ What the Getty Museum does for art
March 30, 2014

Re "Sorry, Italy, the 'Getty Bronze' belongs in L.A.," Editorial June 2

I do not mean this to condone the Getty Museum's acquisition practices of looted antiquities, but an important fact is nevertheless overlooked due to the sensational nature of the world's richest museum.

Most often the looted art objects such as "Aphrodite" and the "Getty Bronze" are discovered in the worst possible condition, damaged by centuries of exposure to environmental elements, including earthquakes.

The Getty Museum expends hundreds of thousands of dollars to conserve and protect every looted and damaged antiquity, utilizing state-of-the-art methodologies not available anywhere else.

Such Getty contributions remain as valuable gifts to the art world, regardless of where these pieces are exhibited.

Jack Yaghoubian
Toluca Lake[21]

---

20. http://www.latimes.com/opinion/la-le-0330-sunday-landslide-20140330,0,7030834,print.story
21. http://www.latimes.com/opinion/readersreact/la-le-0606-friday-getty-20140606-story.html

Letter Published in Civil Engineering

[Related to the collapse of Twin Towers on 9/11/2001]

∷ RE: The NIST Building and Fire Safety Recommendations
Civil Engineering, August 2005

> Laurie A. Shuster is right on target in categorizing the NIST recommendation to increase the structural integrity and resistance of tall buildings to progressive collapse as "most significant."

> Resistance of structural systems to catastrophic collapse is fundamentally governed by the integrity of joint systems that connect and distribute the imposed loads in the main frame. In a structural system where the structural members are connected with equally robust joints, total disintegration is improbable.

> Granted that fire played a major role in initiating structural failure in the impacted floors of the World Trade Center's Twin Towers. However, it is also noteworthy that the main frames of both buildings below the inferno disintegrated progressively while the temperature of the structural frames remained in ambient range with its fireproofing substantially intact.

> Jack Yaghoubian, PE
> Toluca Lake, California[22]

---

22. *Civil Engineering, A Magazine of the American Society of Civil Engineers*, Vol. 75, No. 11 (November 2005)

INDEX

INDEX

Civil engineer Jack Njdeh Yaghoubian lives and works in Los Angeles. His consulting firm, Quantech Systems Inc., specializes in earthquake engineering and earthquake protection systems.